HANDBOOK ON ADAPTIVE GOVERNANCE

ELGAR HANDBOOKS IN ENERGY, THE ENVIRONMENT AND CLIMATE CHANGE

This series provides a definitive overview of recent research in all matters relating to energy, the environment, and climate change in the social sciences, forming a comprehensive guide to the subject. Covering a broad range of research areas including energy policy, the global socio-political impacts of climate change, and environmental economics, this series aims to produce prestigious, high quality works of lasting significance. Each *Handbook* will consist of original contributions by leading authors, selected by an editor recognized as an international leader within the field. Taking an international approach, these *Handbooks* emphasize both the widening of the current debates within the field, and an indication of how research within the field will develop in the future.

Titles in the series include:

Research Handbook on Communicating Climate Change
Edited by David C. Holmes and Lucy M. Richardson

Handbook of Security and the Environment
Edited by Ashok Swain, Joakim Öjendal and Anders Jägerskog

Handbook of Sustainable Politics and Economics of Natural Resources
Edited by Stella Tsani and Indra Overland

Research Handbook on Energy and Society
Edited by Janette Webb, Faye Wade and Margaret Tingey

Handbook on Trade Policy and Climate Change
Edited by Michael Jakob

Handbook of Critical Environmental Politics
Edited by Luigi Pellizzoni, Emanuele Leonardi and Viviana Asara

Handbook on Climate Change and Disasters
Edited by Rajib Shaw

Handbook of Business and Climate Change
Edited by Anant K Sundaram and Robert G. Hansen

Handbook on Adaptive Governance
Edited by Sirkku Juhola

Handbook on Adaptive Governance

Edited by

Sirkku Juhola

Professor of Urban Environmental Policy, Faculty of Biological and Environmental Sciences, University of Helsinki, Finland

ELGAR HANDBOOKS IN ENERGY, THE ENVIRONMENT AND CLIMATE CHANGE

Edward Elgar
PUBLISHING

Cheltenham, UK • Northampton, MA, USA

Cover image: K8 on Unsplash.

Published by
Edward Elgar Publishing Limited
The Lypiatts
15 Lansdown Road
Cheltenham
Glos GL50 2JA
UK

Edward Elgar Publishing, Inc.
William Pratt House
9 Dewey Court
Northampton
Massachusetts 01060
USA

A catalogue record for this book
is available from the British Library

Library of Congress Control Number: 2022950339

This book is available electronically in the **Elgar**online
Political Science and Public Policy subject collection
http://dx.doi.org/10.4337/9781800888241

ISBN 978 1 80088 823 4 (cased)
ISBN 978 1 80088 824 1 (eBook)

Printed and bound by CPI Group (UK) Ltd, Croydon, CR0 4YY

Contents

List of figures vii
List of tables viii
List of boxes ix
List of contributors x
Acknowledgements xiii

1 Introduction to the *Handbook on Adaptive Governance* 1
  Sirkku Juhola

PART I THEORETICAL AND CONCEPTUAL DEVELOPMENTS

2 Operationalising adaptive governance: a research agenda 15
  Barbara Cosens, Holly Doremus, J. B. Ruhl, Niko Soininen and
  Lance Gunderson

3 Adaptive governance, law and regulation 35
  Niko Soininen, Barbara Cosens, J. B. Ruhl and Suvi-Tuuli Puharinen

4 Conceptualising the science–policy–practice interface of adaptive governance 54
  Carina Wyborn, Jasper Montana, Amber Datta and Elena Louder

PART II LATEST TRENDS IN METHODS

5 Futures-thinking: concepts, methods and capacities for adaptive governance 76
  Carla Alexandra, Carina Wyborn, Claudia Munera Roldan and Lorrae van
  Kerkhoff

6 Spatial data, methods, and mismatches for adaptive governance research 99
  Maija Nikkanen and Aleksi Räsänen

7 Serious games as an adaptive governance method 115
  Peter Edwards

PART III GOVERNANCE CONTEXTS AND CASE STUDIES

8 Adaptive governance in forest management 127
  Jesse Abrams and Marine Elbakidze

9 Adaptive governance for marine environments: methods, challenges,
  and lessons for ocean fisheries 143
  Barbara Quimby

10   Adaptive governance in open data ecosystems: experiences and insights
      on the role of sociotechnical arrangements   158
      Cancan Wang

11   Policy experimentation in the construction of ecological civilisation in China   176
      Ping Huang and Linda Westman

12   The role of adaptive governance in climate mitigation and adaptation:
      a local perspective   192
      Grete K. Hovelsrud and Hege Westskog

13   Adaptive and anticipatory governance in urban adaptation to climate change   207
      Alexandra Jurgilevich

14   Towards adaptive property: legal design for a climate-affected future   218
      Daniel Fitzpatrick

15   Adaptive governance for disaster risk reduction   233
      *R. Patrick Bixler, Sandeep Paul, Debasmita Bhakta, Tamar Farchy, Jessica
      Olson, Matthew Preisser and Paola Passalacqua*

16   The next decade of adaptive governance research: concluding remarks   252
      Sirkku Juhola

Index   260

Figures

2.1   Illustrates the increasing formality and state involvement needed as governance moves from a small self-organised community to adaptive, then transition, then formal governance: state-assisted adaptive governance is placed on this spectrum   22

2.2   Illustrating that state-assisted adaptive governance and transition management exist along with the traditional governmental tools of markets and regulation   23

3.1   The descriptive and normative perspectives to law in the context of adaptive governance   41

3.2   Substantive, procedural, and institutional roles of law steering, braking, and accelerating adaptive governance   43

4.1   Three conceptual models for thinking about the SPPI in environmental governance   57

11.1   The spatial distribution of the 498 designated "Ecological Civilisation Construction Demonstration Area"   185

11.2   Three phases of ecological demonstration in China   186

15.1   Phases of the hazard cycle from drivers to transformation   234

Tables

2.1   Governance terms   18

2.2   Guidelines for inquiry into the role of law in adaptive governance   26

2.3   Potential research methodologies for the role of law   28

4.1   Different ways in which science-push, policy-pull, and co-production
        models approach design considerations at the SPPI   62

5.1   Futures-thinking methods that support capacities for adapting and
        transforming   84

5.2   Scenario storylines   88

9.1   Challenges of adaptive marine governance   147

11.1   Experimental unit for the construction of National Ecological
        Demonstration Zone   182

11.2   Experiences gained from the construction of National Ecological
        Demonstration Zone   182

11.3   Designated demonstration zones for ecological civilisation construction   184

11.4   Key policies of ecological experimentation in China   186

12.1   A summary of the opportunities and weaknesses of adaptive governance
        emerging from reanalysing two case studies   201

Boxes

5.1   Futures literacy   80

5.2   Futures methods   81

5.3   Rethinking biodiversity conservation adaptation in times of change   86

5.4   Engaging communities with climate change futures in the Western
        United States   87

Contributors

Jesse Abrams is an Assistant Professor at the Warnell School of Forestry & Natural Resources and Savannah River Ecology Laboratory, University of Georgia, USA.

Carla Alexandra is a PhD Researcher at the Institute for Water Futures, Fenner School of Environment and Society, Australian National University, Canberra, Australia.

Debasmita Bhakta is a Researcher at the LBJ School of Public Affairs, the University of Texas at Austin, USA.

R. Patrick Bixler is an Assistant Professor at the LBJ School of Public Affairs, the University of Texas at Austin, USA.

Barbara Cosens is a University Distinguished Professor Emerita, University of Idaho College of Law, Moscow, ID, USA.

Amber Datta is a PhD Researcher at the W. A. Franke College of Forestry and Conservation, University of Montana, USA and the ARC Centre of Excellence for Coral Reef Studies, James Cook University, Australia.

Holly Doremus is a James H. House and Hiram H. Hurd Professor of Environmental Regulation, University of California, Berkeley, CA, USA.

Peter Edwards is a Senior Researcher at Manaaki Whenua Landcare Research, Wellington, New Zealand.

Marine Elbakidze is an Associate Professor at the Swedish University of Agricultural Sciences and Ivan Franko National University of Lviv, Ukraine.

Tamar Farchy is a Researcher at the LBJ School of Public Affairs, The University of Texas at Austin, USA.

Daniel Fitzpatrick is a Professor at the Faculty of Law, Monash University, Australia.

Lance Gunderson is a Professor of Environmental Sciences, Emory University, Atlanta, GA, USA.

Grete K. Hovelsrud is a Professor of Environmental Sociology at the Nordland Research Institute, Bodø, Norway.

Ping Huang is a Research Fellow at the Centre for Technology, Innovation and Sustainable Development (CTISD), The Institute for International Affairs, Qianhai (IIA), The Chinese University of Hong Kong, Shenzhen, China.

Sirkku Juhola is a Professor of Urban Environmental Policy at the Ecosystems and Environment Research Programme, University of Helsinki, Finland.

Alexandra Jurgilevich is a Postdoctoral Researcher at the Ecosystems and Environment Research Programme, University of Helsinki, Finland.

Elena Louder is a PhD Researcher at the School of Geography and Development, University of Arizona, USA.

Jasper Montana is a Junior Research Fellow, School of Geography and Environment, University of Oxford, United Kingdom.

Claudia Munera Roldan is a Researcher at the Fenner School of Environment and Society, Australian National University, Canberra, Australia.

Maija Nikkanen is a PhD Researcher at the Ecosystems and Environment Research Programme, University of Helsinki, Helsinki, Finland.

Jessica Olson is a Health and Human Services Advisor at Office of the Texas Lieutenant Governor, Texas, USA.

Paola Passalacqua is an Associate Professor and Leland Barclay Fellowship in Engineering, Civil, Architectural and Environmental Engineering, Cockrell School of Engineering, the University of Texas at Austin, USA.

Sandeep Paul is a PhD Researcher at the LBJ School of Public Affairs, the University of Texas at Austin, USA.

Matthew Preisser is a National Science Foundation Graduate Research Fellow and NASA Graduate Research Fellow, The University of Texas at Austin, USA.

Suvi-Tuuli Puharinen is a PhD Researcher, University of Eastern Finland Law School and Center for Climate, Energy and Environmental Law, Joensuu, Finland.

Barbara Quimby is an Assistant Professor of Marine Science and Policy in the Department of Natural Science at Hawai'i Pacific University, USA.

Aleksi Räsänen is a Research Fellow at the Natural Resources Institute Finland, Oulu, Finland.

J. B. Ruhl is a David Daniels Allen Distinguished Chair in Law, Director, Program on Law and Innovation, and Co-director, Energy, Environment and Land Use Program, Vanderbilt University Law School, Nashville, TN, USA.

Niko Soininen is a Professor of Environmental Law, University of Eastern Finland Law School and Center for Climate, Energy and Environmental Law, Joensuu, Finland.

Lorrae van Kerkhoff is a Professor at the Institute for Water Futures, Fenner School of Environment and Society, Australian National University, Canberra, Australia.

Cancan Wang is an Associate Professor at the Department of Business IT, IT University of Copenhagen, Denmark.

Linda Westman is a Research Associate at the Urban Institute, Interdisciplinary Centre of the Social Sciences (ICOSS), University of Sheffield, United Kingdom.

Hege Westskog is a Senior Researcher at the Centre for Development and the Environment, University of Oslo, Oslo, Norway.

Carina Wyborn is an Associate Professor at the Institute for Water Futures, Fenner School of Environment and Society, Australian National University, Canberra, Australia.

Acknowledgements

I am most grateful to all the authors who took part in this project and wanted to contribute, kept to the timetable, and provided excellent pieces of work to illustrate the state of play through their own work. This book would not have been possible without their interest in the approach and continued engagement with the research community.

I also want to thank Daniel Mather at Edward Elgar for a smooth process and support when needed, especially given the challenging conditions during the COVID-19 pandemic.

I also want to thank everyone at Urban Environmental Policy group at the University of Helsinki for either responding positively to the invitation to write, commenting on my ideas or patiently waiting with other work when I was completing the book. Finally, I want to thank my sister Marja for proofreading some chapters and patiently correcting my punctuation errors all these years.

Sirkku Juhola
Helsinki, 2022

1. Introduction to the *Handbook on Adaptive Governance*

Sirkku Juhola

OPENING REMARKS

Even though there has been much discussion of the interconnectedness and interdependence of societies globally, the COVID-19 pandemic has illustrated in a most revealing way how events in one part of the world cascade across the globe, leading to the need to act everywhere for not only governments but also for the private sector and individuals. The pandemic has illustrated the ways in which public and private decision-making differs across societies and how different policies to contain the pandemic led to non-linear and unpredictable outcomes themselves (Angeli and Montefusco 2020).

The pandemic, with rapid and severe consequences to societies, takes place in the backdrop of other global change processes, such as climate change and biodiversity loss, both of which equally threaten the ability to secure thriving societies but on longer time scales. Recent reports on the state of the global ecosystems and environment and climate both send a strong signal of the alarming rate and consequences of these developments (IPCC 2021, Pörtner et al. 2021). According to the Intergovernmental Panel on Climate Change, widespread and rapid changes in the atmosphere, ocean, cryosphere, and biosphere have occurred as a result of climate change, and many weather and climate extremes in every region of the globe are affected (IPCC 2021). As the climate is changing, it increasingly affects the distribution, functioning and interactions of organisms and ecosystems, which are already under pressure due to human influence (Pörtner et al. 2021).

Similarly, assessments of society and human welfare show institutional failures in terms of food, access to housing and levels of inequality, and overall wellbeing and sustainable development. A recent assessment shows that no country meets basic needs for its citizens at a globally sustainable level of resource use (O'Neill et al. 2018). According to the United Nations Development Programme's Special Report (2022), hunger is on the rise, with around 2.5 billion people suffering from food insecurity. In addition, the number of forcibly displaced people has doubled, resulting in over 100 million people being displaced in 2020 (UNHCR 2022). Many of these issues have been reinforced by the pandemic and may be further amplified by climate change and biodiversity loss.

These trends and increasing cascading and compound impacts of environmental and social phenomena mean that societies increasingly need to account for multiple sources of risk, demanding decision-making approaches that can anticipate and address complexity. There are increasing calls for large-scale societal transformations to move away from unsustainable development trajectories (Abson et al. 2017). While there is advancement in terms of conceptual development, it remains unclear to what extent large-scale changes are taking place (Scoones et al. 2020, Salomaa and Juhola 2020).

In the light of the above, the role of governance has become even more important in terms of driving these changes as well as addressing and identifying solutions and implementing them. Governance, a term used in several social scientific fields, and ubiquitously in policymaking, at its core denotes all manners governing processes by various actors, ideally covering both abstract analyses of who governs and how, and empirical debates about the changes in social and political life (Bevir 2013). In general, governance theory and theorists are interested in how governance arrangements come to be, how they are maintained and why they change, even though disciplinary diversity exists (Chhotray and Stoker 2009).

In the last two decades, several theories of governance with a prefix have emerged, denoting a specific type of a theoretical or normative approach to explain collective decision-making processes, often in relation to a specific issue of which governance is to be understood and improved. Many of these approaches to governance have emerged in those fields which address complex human–environment interactions with a focus on developing theory to manage those interactions. These approaches include, for example, reflexive governance (Vos and Bornemann 2011, Feindt and Weiland 2018), adaptive co-management (Plummer at al. 2012), collaborative governance (Ansell and Gash 2007), and anticipatory governance (Muiderman et al. 2022).

This is also true for adaptive governance, the focus of book. More specifically, the concept of adaptive governance emerged around the turn of the century to envision the way of governing that stresses the coupled nature of biophysical and social systems and their dynamics to ensure more desirable governance outcomes. First coined in 2003 (Dietz et al. 2003), adaptive governance has become a popular concept to examine the complexities of governing socio-ecological systems, and it has since been further developed and applied to analyse cases in a multitude of environmental and resource governance related fields. These cases have highlighted the dynamics and diversity of governance systems themselves across scales.

There are many things that unite governance approaches, but also differences are clearly visible. They can be identified when examining the aim of the theory, actors involved and the types of governing processes they are focused on. Reflexive governance places attention on the ways in which institutional frameworks and mechanisms can be transformed to address large-scale environmental degradation (Feindt and Weiland 2018), while adaptive co-management is focused on the governance of complex socio-ecological systems on a more regional and local scale with community resource management (Allen and Garmestani 2015). Anticipatory governance aims to use anticipation to guide decision-making, given the uncertainties related to sustainability and environmental challenges (Serrao-Neumann et al. 2013).

While collaborative governance does not specifically address what system is the objective of governance, it nevertheless recognises the role that multiple groups and individuals have in collective decision-making (Ansell and Gash 2007), similar to these other governance approaches discussed above. Depending on the system in question, the actors vary, but the starting point is that they go beyond the governmental actors towards including private sector, community groups and individuals.

In terms of the type of governing institutions and processes, all the approaches emphasise reflexivity or adaptability as a feature of institutions used for governance and inclusion of multiple actors in institution building and decision-making processes. The governance approaches here vary from descriptive, examining successful cases where certain types of institutional approaches have contributed towards sustainability to approaches that are prescriptive, using either empirical cases or theoretical tenets as starting points to discuss how certain types of institutions and mechanisms ought to or would lead to optimal outcomes, depending on the intended aims of the governance process.

Within this theoretical field, adaptive governance has cemented its position in this proliferation of approaches that seek to explain the processes of decision-making, as well as provide prescriptions on how to achieve better governing outcomes in real life governance situations. As adaptive governance will soon reach the end of its second decade as a theoretical approach and an analytical concept, this is an appropriate time to take stock of its emergence, as well as to chart future directions by scholars working within the field. In addition, it is pertinent to ask what the explanatory value of this theoretical strand has been, what issues related to governance continue to present challenges for adaptive governance, and why? The aim of this volume is to bring together the current state of the art in terms of adaptive governance. In doing this, the volume presents an exciting collection of contributions, ranging from theoretical and conceptual ones to presenting and demonstrating the richness of methodological approaches applied in the study of adaptive governance. This volume illustrates the variety of governance fields, from entirely new fields to more traditional ones in natural resource management.

ADAPTIVE GOVERNANCE: KEY FEATURES AND CONTRIBUTIONS

The concept of adaptive governance emerged around the turn of the century to envision the way of governing that stresses the coupled nature of biophysical and social systems and their dynamics to ensure more desirable governance outcomes. As an approach, it has predominantly been exploring natural resources and environmental issues (Olsson et al. 2006, Folke et al. 2005). The key feature has been the exploration of alternative ways to govern instead of a traditional top-down hierarchy presented by the state.

As with any conceptual approach, there is naturally an evolving discussion of the definition and key features, as well as the explanatory power of the concept to begin with. In one of the earliest definitions, Folke et al. (2005) argue that adaptive governance involves polycentric institutional arrangements, which consist of quasi-autonomous decision-making units, and can be found on and across multiple scales of decision-making. In their comprehensive review, Chaffin et al. (2013, p. 6) state that adaptive governance can be considered as "a range of interactions between actors, networks, organisations, and institutions emerging in pursuit of a desired state for social-ecological systems". There are also more recent definitions, including the one from Westskog et al., who define adaptive governance as a process of interaction in which societies are steered towards objectives that are negotiated collectively (Westskog et al. 2020, p. 555). This process ought to also allow for learning and readjustment of objectives as new knowledge emerges that may change the objectives, or the measures and policies used to reach them.

Much attention, particularly early on, was directed towards identifying a distinction between adaptive governance and adaptive co-management, due to the proximity of the concepts and scholars advancing the approaches (Hasselman 2017). In fact, adaptive governance was frequently used in conjunction with adaptive co-management (Plummer and Baird 2013). Adaptive co-management has been defined as an approach which strives for recognition of differential stakeholder needs, development of culturally embedded rules and norms, formation of networks to forge trust, use of variety of types of knowledge and enhanced capacity to deal with uncertainty (Armitage et al. 2009). Overall, the relationship between the two concepts has become to be seen as complementary in that adaptive governance provides the wider context, within which adaptive co-management is enabled (Folke et al. 2002), thus broadening the scope of analysis beyond day-to-day management decisions (Folke et al. 2007).

The key features of adaptive governance early on were considered to include systems in which resource use can be effectively monitored and verified with the support of those participating in the use of the resource, and in systems where rates of change are moderate, and communities are close-knit and well networked with an ability to exclude outsiders (Dietz et al. 2003). Since these early considerations and because of empirical work through adopting the adaptive governance lens, some of the key features have become reinforced while others have emerged as important.

Synthesising the developments of the first decade of adaptive governance research, Chaffin et al. (2013) consider three characteristics as crucial for adaptive governance. First, it is important to further clarify the reinforcing effects between adaptive governance and adaptive co-management. This means that adaptive co-management with its emphasis on learning within a broader adaptive governance setting is crucial, particularly since the learning processes enable the adjustment of management decisions, which are possible since the governance structures are adaptable (Huitema et al. 2009).

Second, while it is acknowledged that there needs to be a proper fit (Young 2002) between the governing system and the governed resources, it can be elusive since the issue of scale is not straightforward. The scale of governance ought to be adopted based on the social and ecological nature of the problem with sufficient flexibility (Cosens 2013). In fact, the issue of governance across scales, i.e., multilevel governance, has become an increasingly pertinent question as adaptive governance as a concept has been expanded to consider systems beyond local natural resources (Boyd and Folke, 2011).

Third, the inclusion of multiple scales of governance is partially driven by the acknowledgement that at least in theory, an adaptive governance system is based on nested institutions of diverse kinds at different levels, and these are connected by formal and informal social networks (Dietz et al. 2003). From this, key concepts of polycentricity, redundancy and diversity have become popular (Chaffin et al. 2013), which signify the mechanisms through which successful governance is carried out, even in the event of disturbances. As Chaffin et al. (2013) point out, there have been attempts to demonstrate the emergence of adaptive governance across scales empirically (Kallis et al. 2009, Elbakidze et al. 2010).

Since the concept has become more widely used, there has been a surge of empirical case work examining the potential of adaptive governance to emerge in various fields. Unsurprisingly, the natural resource fields have been well represented in this body work, ranging from marine resources (Cvitanovic et al. 2015, Österblom and Folke 2013) to forestry (Elbakidze et al. 2010) and ecosystem services (Schultz et al. 2015). More recently, there has been a flurry of work regarding climate change-related issues, predominantly adaptation (Munaretto et al. 2014, van Buuren et al. 2015), urban resilience (Boyd and Juhola 2015, Westskog et al. 2020) and food systems governance (Smith and Lawrence 2018). More recently, the approach has been picked up outside of the environmental and sustainability field, with applications in digital governance (Wang et al. 2018) and migration (Fitzpatrick and Monson 2020).

CRITIQUE OF ADAPTIVE GOVERNANCE

As studies concerning adaptive governance became more frequent, the concept also started to draw attention of the scholars wishing to explore the approach and its application more critically. These strands of criticism can be considered to emerge on two distinct but also connected lines of argumentation. First, scholars have paid attention to the advancement in the theory of adaptive governance, particularly those from more traditional political science fields. Second, the extent to which the tenets of adaptive governance hold in the real world has been questioned. And whether the theoretical underpinnings can indeed be validated through the extensive case work conducted across governance systems. These two will now be dealt with in turn.

The theoretical criticism directed at adaptive governance emerges from two different sources, which can be broadly categorised as internal and external. The internal criticism has been concerned with the theoretical and conceptual tenets of the approach, acknowledging that some underpinnings may be somewhat simplified. For example, Chaffin and Gunderson (2016) note that despite the growth in empirical studies, the conceptual basis of adaptive governance has remained largely under-theorised. Chaffin and Gunderson propose that a deeper engagement with the theory of panarchy may serve as a way to further explain the emergence and dynamics of institutions. Studies have also sought to advance particular aspects of adaptive governance theory, such as learning and functioning of the science–policy interface (Wyborn 2015). Wyborn suggests a conceptual re-framing of co-production that is designed to support adaptive governance practices.

Examples of advances in theorising societal dynamics and organisational behaviour within adaptive governance theory have included a Foucauldian analysis of natural resource management, an aspect of adaptive governance largely under-theorised. Van Assche et al. (2017) suggest that adaptive governance theory can benefit from this type of analysis in order to understand what the limits of adaptation in governance systems are to begin with. This can be done by analysing power/knowledge dynamics, which shows where resistant structures may be. Similarly, social systems theory based on Luhmann can also shed light on how organisations contribute to change in an adaptive governance system, and whether their contribution is fully understood (Van Assche et al. 2021).

The more external critique towards adaptive governance has been emanating from political ecology and more critical social and institutional theory orientations with the main critique that society and social systems in adaptive governance theory are often subjected to similar assumptions as ecological systems. This implies that social systems have underlying mechanisms which direct human behaviour, reducing human agency, and which can be discovered. This has resulted in simplistic explanations of governance situations that do not account for history, culture, power, and human agency (Davidson 2010, Cote and Nightingale 2012, Fabinyi et al. 2014). This lack of engagement with power and social dynamics and reluctance and unenthusiasm to engage with social theory has been pointed out as one of its greatest weaknesses (Cleaver and Whaley 2018). Cleaver and Whaley (2018) demonstrate in their critical institutional analysis how adaptive governance fails to fully explain why certain governance arrangements emerge, to provide a nuanced assessment of power between actors beyond triumphing champions of change, and to illustrate how meaning and values are crucial in the construction institutions for governing.

Adaptive governance has faced empirical critique in terms of its application in real world cases (Sharma-Wallace et al. 2018). Similarly, Wyborn (2015) notes that there needs to be further engagement beyond abstract design principles that are not empirically tested. To gauge the empirical literature, based on a systematic review of adaptive governance literature, Sharma-Wallace et al. (2018) assess the success and failure factors in 92 empirical cases of adaptive governance, and question what factors contribute to this over a longer timeframe. This review is particularly valuable as it captures the state of the art of adaptive governance cases and illustrates the state of the field (Sharma-Wallace et al. 2018). First, cases are predominantly based in Western institutions, and second, the contexts within which the cases are based, are overwhelmingly focused on water, coastal or fisheries management. Third, in almost half of the studies in the sample, there was a crisis context or a disaster event, in relation to which the emergence or success of adaptive governance was examined. Finally, in the case examples, around half were considered successful examples of adaptive governance, which may be a symptom of selection bias in the original studies themselves.

There are several important considerations that Sharma-Wallace et al. (2018) raise. While in most of the cases they examined there was a meaningful collaboration included in the analysis, and it was seen to contribute to adaptive governance, there was no critical reflection on who ought to be involved and in what capacity. Often "community" was treated as a homogenous entity and there was a discussion on the issues of equity. Lack of attention to scale and fit in the cases most often resulted in failure but could be overcome with networks and effective brokering. For successful cases, social capital and trust were considered crucial but these mainly developed incrementally, and this social capital had to be further supported by other types of capacity development, through training and organisational partnerships, for example. Finally, the cases also exemplify the role that scientific and other types of knowledge play, demonstrated by the fact that if there were no data collection efforts, then governance arrangements were ad hoc and often failed. Sharma-Wallace et al. (2018) have not been alone in calling for further elaborations of social dynamics, equity, and justice to be incorporated into adaptive governance. Karpouzoglou et al. (2016) also call for broadening of the theoretical concepts to increase the analytical rigour within adaptive governance research.

The most recent developments in the theorisation and empirical exploration of adaptive governance need to be examined in the context of increasing calls for transformations towards sustainability and the role of governance (Patterson et al. 2017, Linnér and Wibeck 2021) The main questions here are two-fold. The first question is whether, to what extent, and how adaptive governance can trigger or steer socio-ecological systems towards sustainability (Patterson et al. 2017, Visseren-Hamakers et al. 2021). This includes further redefining the aims of adaptive governance from a process towards a desired state to that desired state being entirely transformed from the previous one. This raises a number of questions, given that the desired state refers to both the social and the ecological side of the system. If the desired date is an entirely transformed one, what does this imply to both of those sub-systems as they are coupled? Second, the already existing questions regarding adaptive governance and its ability to contribute to successful governance remain relevant. What features of adaptive governance contribute to transformative change, if any, and what hinder these processes?

The second challenge emerging from the transformation discussion is to what extent adaptive governance as an approach or a practice has shown its ability to transform governance structures that facilitate larger system-wide transformations. This question is naturally built on the premise that existing institutional structures and arrangements are unable to trigger or facilitate this change, and therefore governance itself needs to be transformed (Patterson et al. 2017). In fact, Eshuis and Gerrits (2021) question the transformational effect of adaptive governance on the governance system and explore its effects. For a governance change to be transformative, Eshuis and Gerrits argue that it needs to involve deep changes, they have to be all-encompassing and also enduring. In their urban case of Rotterdam, the authors conclude that while adaptive governance features were introduced, the institutions did not change fundamentally or widely across the city, nor did the changes endure over time (Eshuis and Gerrits 2021).

The above raised points and critique continue to be relevant to those working with adaptive governance as an approach and are issues that are discussed in this volume. These are also other issues that are raised in the chapters of this book which need to be extensively discussed in order to push the field forward. If adaptive governance is to continue to contribute to the discussion on how different types of systems are to be governed, there is a need to engage with the wider theorisations on governance systems, its emerging questions and how they play out in real life situations.

CONTRIBUTION OF THIS VOLUME

This *Handbook on Adaptive Governance* brings together the current state of the art in adaptive governance. It consists of an exciting collection of contributions, ranging from theoretical and conceptual ones to demonstrating the richness of methodological approaches applied in the field. This volume also illustrates the variety of governance fields, from disaster risk management to urban planning and climate change governance to coastal zone management, within which adaptive governance is researched or implemented through co-design methodologies. This book is structured into three parts, presenting the state-of-the-art research in terms of theoretical and conceptual developments (Part I), latest trends in methods used in adaptive governance approaches (Part II) and different governance contexts and case studies (Part III).

Part I: Theoretical and Conceptual Developments

The first part of this book tackles the theoretical discussion related to adaptive governance. These include the fundamental question of any governance approach – what is the role of the state and other actors and what is legitimate governance. Questions in this part are also posed regarding the more formal governance instruments, i.e., law and how that could support adaptive governance approaches. At the heart of these questions of governance structures are also questions of science and different types of knowledge used in the governing process.

In Chapter 2, Cosens and colleagues begin with the starting point that adaptive governance as an approach promotes the emergence of self-organised management. However, the authors question to what extent this raises questions of legitimacy of governance and point towards open questions of when and how government should pursue this role, the degree of government involvement in relation to the type of problem, and the role of science in this more distributed governance. The authors present an interdisciplinary research agenda by unpacking these areas of inquiry and exploring the research methods in conjunction with these questions.

In Chapter 3, Soininen and colleagues further explore the role of government and specifically regulation and law in adaptive governance theory. The authors recognise that adaptive governance as a regulatory strategy and law may be seen as antithetical to each other but argue that in fact any adaptive governance approach is facilitated by law. This means that law maintains its significance in guiding society. As its main contribution, the authors present two legal perspectives to analyse adaptive governance, namely how existing legal systems regulate adaptive governance, and how the legal systems could ideally support adaptive governance. The authors argue that while connections can be made between adaptive governance criteria with various fields of law, legal systems will never fully facilitate adaptive governance. In conclusion, the authors present emerging research questions for legal adaptive governance research.

Knowledge, how it is produced and used in governance has been a central question in adaptive governance theory. The use of knowledge and information can be seen as one of the main sparks needed for the governance structures to adapt and actors to change their behaviour. In Chapter 4, Wyborn and colleagues conceptualise this as the science–policy–practice interface (SPPI). In any given case or context, these SPPIs are shaped by social, cultural, and political dynamics, which need to be identified and understood to mobilise change. This chapter presents a useful conceptual model, which can help to understand how problems are defined, what solutions are presented, and the dynamics involved.

Part II: Latest Trends in Methods

The second part of this book presents a number of interesting research methodologies and methods, which have been used in adaptive governance studies. These methods answer not only to the demand of engaging stakeholders in co-designing the research but also to visualising and capturing different types of knowledge these stakeholders have and use in their decision-making. While these presented methods naturally capture only a handful of possible methods used in the field, they highlight important issues that need to be considered when choosing and applying methods in adaptive governance research, and this may facilitate the emergence of adaptive governance and engage stakeholders on an equal footing.

The key focus in adaptive governance theory is a future oriented, adaptive approach to governance, given the uncertainties associated with socio-ecological systems. Futures oriented methods therefore have become of interest to scholars, given that they may be used to facilitate the change before irreversible changes occur. In Chapter 5, Alexandra and colleagues discuss futures-thinking and related futures methods, which can be used to actively engage stakeholders in facilitating that change and navigate choices in anticipation of socio-ecological change. The authors conclude that a futures-oriented methodology has the potential to help address future uncertainty and build support for transformative change.

The second chapter in this part focuses on different types of research methods in adaptive governance and takes note of the proliferation of spatially explicit methods and how they have been used in adaptive governance research. In Chapter 6, Nikkanen and Räsänen begin from the starting point of spatial mismatches, meaning that there is quite often a mismatch between the scale of the natural resource in question and the governance arrangement for its management. Mismatches may also occur due to conflicting priorities. While the issue of scale has been discussed for a long time among adaptive governance scholars, Nikkanen and Räsänen show that research that utilises geographic information systems (GIS) based methods has so far been scarce. In order to advance the field, the authors highlight the potential of these methods, mainly the possibility for spatio-temporal monitoring and projection of socio-ecological phe-nomena, as well as illustrating the spatial patterns of management.

Experimentation is a key feature of adaptive governance, and serious games have become an interesting tool of facilitation and decision-making, thus adding a new way to understand and illustrate the complexities related to natural resource management and decision-making. Edwards, in Chapter 7, brings together the theoretical discussion on adaptive governance and the ways in which serious games as a methodology can be used to engage communities, indi-viduals, and decision-makers in a safe innovation space for experimentation and learning. By examining elements of adaptive governance in turn, Edwards shows the potential of serious gaming in facilitating and enabling adaptive governance. The game situation, while often built on and relying on real world dilemmas, allows for participants to experience strategy making and the consequences of their actions without actual consequences in the real world.

Part III: Governance Contexts and Case Studies

The third part of this *Handbook* brings together chapters that show how adaptive governance thinking has been advanced and applied in numerous empirical fields of governance. While the more traditional fields – e.g., natural resource fields – dominate this part, some of the chapters also illustrate the interest towards and utility of adaptive governance beyond those fields.

Forest management has been undergoing a period of moving towards a more sus-tainability-oriented management, and adaptive governance and its role in this transition has been examined. Abrams and Elbakidze, in Chapter 8, examine the contributions of adaptive governance in the light of the emergence of new networked approaches to forest management, which incorporate polycentric design elements to co-exist with the existing hierarchical models. The authors review recent scholarship on adaptive governance in forest management and also show examples of what types of instruments, frameworks and initiatives have been successful in different forest contexts. In particular, Abrams and Elbakidze stress the need to account for institutional interplay across scales, as well as the power dynamics between actors.

Adaptive governance thinking can be said to emerge from the marine context, and this is perhaps the field in which the majority of the case studies continue to be conducted. Quimby, in Chapter 9, shows how formal institutional structures continue to be important for providing legitimacy and support for governance but that they can continue to lead to tech-nocratic approaches that fail to adequately incorporate the sociocultural and political context. Quimby, through a review of existing literature, illustrates the particular strengths of adaptive governance in marine settings, which include institutional design that can be configured for vast spaces, with cross-scale linkages that reflect and respond to organisational diversity and multiplicity at different levels. While there are clearly some cases where adaptive governance has been successfully implemented, Quimby points towards the need to incorporate the wider social context and discuss power sharing arrangements.

The governance of open data ecosystems is one of the new fields where adaptive govern-ance has been applied most recently. In Chapter 10, Wang begins to form the starting point that the development of data infrastructure across the world demonstrates similar complexities to those of socio-economic systems. Wang, through an open data ecosystem case in Shanghai, examines the usefulness of adaptive governance tenets in a system that involves citizens, communities, and policymakers. The case illustrates how there is continuous experimentation in the open data ecosystem and a mixing of different types of policy instruments. Overall, this paves the way of further utilising adaptive governance thinking beyond socio-ecological systems to include socio-technical systems and their combinations.

In Chapter 11 adaptive governance is examined in a national context, adding a new lens to adaptive governance studies beyond a single ecosystem focus. Huang and Westman explore China's approaches of policy experimentation in the construction of ecological civilisation through the lens of adaptive governance. According to Huang and Westman, an ecological civilisation entails many features which are central to adaptive governance, including policy experimentation, and bring an interesting historical analysis of its application in a country, which has largely been ignored by adaptive governance scholars to this date. The authors argue that three features of pragmatism, incrementalism, and verticality, can be clearly identified in the Chinese approach, illustrating how an adaptive governance approach may advance in an institutional and political setting mostly known for central planning.

The remainder of the chapters focus on global change drivers that necessitate local action, a concern outside of the local ecosystem. Addressing climate change requires both mitigation of greenhouse gas emissions and adaptation to the impacts as this continues to present a complex challenge at the local level of decision-making. Hovelsrud and Westskog discuss the potential weaknesses and opportunities of adaptive governance strategies to handle these climate change responses and discuss prerequisites for adaptive governance to work in a local level setting in Norway in Chapter 12. They demonstrate factors that need to be taken into account for adaptive governance to be successful in mitigation and adaptation at the local government level, namely sufficient time, including different forms of knowledge, alignment of policy goals and measures, sufficient human and financial resources, and attention to the power hierarchies in negotiation processes.

In Chapter 13, Jurgilevich deepens the focus on the impacts of climate change on cities and discusses adaptive governance in the context of urban climate change adaptation. To begin with, Jurgilevich outlines the challenge for urban planning to require a reduction in vulnerability, meaning decreasing people's enhanced exposure and improving people's adaptive capacity to deal with the impacts of climate change. The current frameworks and institutional structures are fragmented and compartmentalised, resulting in un-coordinated efforts and siloed planning. To address this, there is a need to consider institutional dynamics, learning processes and linking urban planning and adaptation to socio-economic development.

The consideration of steering mechanisms is also at the heart of Chapter 14, where Fitzpatrick considers the role of property law as part of the emergence of adaptive law. The acceleration of climate change is likely to worsen the already high numbers of displaced and landless people globally, meaning that there is increasingly a pressure to ask the question of when property law should allow for flexibility when it comes to land entitlements. Fitzpatrick, with the help of cases from the Philippines and Indonesia discusses to what extent there is a need to reconsider the formulation of property law away from its current focus on stability towards flexibility to account for the challenges of increasing displacement of people to come.

The final chapter of the governance fields relates to disaster risk reduction, of which importance is also underlined by the advances of climate change. Similar to the other chapters, the current governance arrangements and steering mechanisms are considered to be too rigid to account for the rapidly changing world. In Chapter 15, Bixler and colleagues begin by discussing the theoretical underpinning that unite disaster risk reduction and adaptive governance. Both incorporate a broad set of actors, often connected through networks, addressing multisectoral issues. However, these connections have not been exhaustively explored and the authors call for this by focusing on how polycentricity, collaboration, self-organisation, and learning can be advanced in what the authors call adaptive hazard governance. Bixler and colleagues use examples from the literature and a case of Houston, to discuss what challenges and opportunities may exist in fusing disaster risk reduction with adaptive governance features.

The book is concluded by a chapter that weaves together the insights from each of the parts in this *Handbook*, summarising the latest developments in terms of theory and concepts, methods used and fields of governance that have been examined. Chapter 16 also reflects the state of the field in relation to the first decade of adaptive governance (Chaffin et al. 2014) to see whether the questions laid out have been answered and reflected upon. The chapter concludes by pointing towards new areas of contention and inquiry for the next decade of adaptive governance research.

REFERENCES

Abson, D. J., Fischer, J., Leventon, J., Newig, J., Schomerus, T., Vilsmaier, U., von Werhden, H., Abernehty, P., Ives, C. D., Jager, N. W., and Lang, D. J. 2017. Leverage points for sustainability transformation. *Ambio*, 46, 1, 30–39.

Allen, C. R., A. S. Garmestani (eds.) 2015. *Adaptive Management of Social-Ecological Systems*, Springer Science+Business Media. https:doi.org/10.1007/978-94-017-9682-8_1.

Angeli, F., and Montefusco, A. 2020. Sensemaking and learning during the Covid-19 pandemic: a complex adaptive systems perspective on policy decision-making. *World Development*, 136, 105–106.

Ansell, C., and Gash, A. 2008. Collaborative governance in theory and practice. *Journal of Public Administration Research and Theory*, 18, 4, 543–571.

Armitage, D. R., Plummer, R., Berkes, F., Arthur, R. I., Charles, A. T., Davidson-Hunt, I. J., ... and Wollenberg, E. K. 2009. Adaptive co-management for social–ecological complexity. *Frontiers in Ecology and the Environment*, 7, 2, 95–102.

Bevir, M. 2013. *A Theory of Governance*. University of California Press, London.

Boyd, E., and Folke, C. (eds.). 2011. *Adapting Institutions: Governance, Complexity and Social-ecological Resilience*. Cambridge University Press, Cambridge.

Boyd, E., and Juhola, S. 2015. Adaptive climate change governance for urban resilience. *Urban Studies*, 52, 7, 1234–1264.

Chaffin, B. C., Garmestani, A. S., Gunderson, L. H., Benson, M. H., Angeler, D. G., Arnold, C. A.,

Chaffin, B. C., and Gunderson, L. H. 2016. Emergence, institutionalization and renewal: rhythms of adaptive governance in complex social-ecological systems. *Journal of Environmental Management*, 165, 81–87.

Chaffin, B. C., Gosnell, H., and Cosens, B. A. 2014. A decade of adaptive governance scholarship: synthesis and future directions. *Ecology and Society*, 19, 3.

Chhotray, V., and Stoker, G. 2009. Introduction: exploring Governance. In *Governance Theory and Practice* (pp. 1–15). Palgrave Macmillan, London.

Cleaver, F., and Whaley, L. 2018. Understanding process, power, and meaning in adaptive governance: a critical institutional reading. *Ecology and Society*, 23, 2, 49. https://doi.org/10.5751/ES-10212-230249.

Cosens, B. A. 2013. Legitimacy, adaptation, and resilience in ecosystem management. *Ecology and Society*, 18, 1, 3. http://dx. doi.org/10.5751/ES-05093-180103.

Cosens, B., Kundis Craig, R., Ruhl, J. B., and Allen, C. R. 2016. Transformative environmental governance. *Annual Review of Environment and Resources*, 41, 399–423.

Cote, M., and Nightingale, A. J. 2012. Resilience thinking meets social theory: situating social change in socio-ecological systems (SES) research. *Prog. Hum. Geogr.*, 36, 4.

Cvitanovic, C., Hobday, A. J., van Kerkhoff, L., Wilson, S. K., Dobbs, K., and Marshall, N. A. 2015. Improving knowledge exchange among scientists and decision-makers to facilitate the adaptive governance of marine resources: a review of knowledge and research needs. *Ocean & Coastal Management*, 112, 25–35.

Davidson, D. J. 2010. The applicability of the concept of resilience to social systems: some sources of optimism and nagging doubts. *Soc. Nat. Resour.*, 23, 1135–1149.

Elbakidze, M., Angelstam, P. K., Sandström, C., and Axelsson, R. 2010. Multi-stakeholder collaboration in Russian and Swedish model forest initiatives: adaptive governance toward sustainable forest management? *Ecology and Society*, 15, 2, 14. http://www.ecologyandsociety.org/vol15/iss2/art14/.

Eshuis, J., and Gerrits, L. 2021. The limited transformational power of adaptive governance: a study of institutionalization and materialization of adaptive governance. *Public Management Review*, 23, 2, 276–296.

Fabinyi, M., Evans, L., and Foale, S. J. 2014. Social-ecological systems, social diversity, and power: insights from anthropology and political ecology. *Ecol. Soc.*, 19, 4.

Fitzpatrick, D., and Monson, R. 2020. Property rights and climate migration: adaptive governance in the South Pacific. *Regulation & Governance*, https://doi.org/10.1111/rego.12365.

Folke, C., Carpenter, S., Elmqvist, T., Gunderson, L., Holling, C. S., and Walker, B. 2002. Resilience and sustainable development: building adaptive capacity in a world of transformations. *AMBIO: A Journal of the Human Environment*, 31, 5, 437–440.

Folke, C., Colding, J., Olsson, P., and Hahn, T. 2007. Interdependent social-ecological systems and adaptive governance for ecosystem services. *The Sage Handbook of Environment and Society*, 536–552.

Folke, C., Hahn, T., Olsson, P., and Norberg, J. 2005. Adaptive governance of social-ecological systems. *Annu. Rev. Environ. Resour.*, 30, 441–473.

Hasselman, L. 2017. Adaptive management; adaptive co-management; adaptive governance: what's the difference? *Australasian Journal of Environmental Management*, 24, 1, 31–46.

Huitema, D., Mostert, E., Egas, W., Moellenkamp, S., Pahl-Wostl, C., and Yalcin, R. 2009. Adaptive water governance: assessing the institutional prescriptions of adaptive (co-) management from a governance perspective and defining a research agenda. *Ecology and Society*, 14, 1, 26. http://www.ecologyandsociety.org/vol14/iss1/art26/.

IPCC, 2021: Summary for Policymakers. In: *Climate Change 2021: The Physical Science Basis. Contribution of Working Group I to the Sixth Assessment Report of the Intergovernmental Panel on Climate Change* [Masson-Delmotte, V., Zhai, P., Pirani, A., Connors, S. L., Péan, C., Berger, S., Caud, N., Chen, Y., Goldfarb, L., Gomis, M. I., Huang, M., Leitzell, K., Lonnoy, E., Matthews, J. B. R., Maycock, T. K., Waterfield, T., Yelekçi, O., Yu, R., and Zhou, B. (eds.)]. In Press.

Kallis, G., Kiparsky, M., and Norgaard, R. 2009. Collaborative governance and adaptive management: lessons from California's CALFED Water Program. *Environmental Science & Policy*, 12, 631–643. http://dx.doi.org/10.1016/j.envsci.2009.07.002.

Karpouzoglou, T., Dewulf, A. and Clark J. 2016. Advancing adaptive governance of social-ecological systems through theoretical multiplicity, *Environ. Sci. Pol.*, 57, 1–9. https://doi.org/10.1016/j.envsci.2015.11.011.

Linnér, B.-O., and Wibeck, V. 2021. Drivers of sustainability transformations: leverage points, contexts and conjunctures. *Sustainability Science*, 16, 3, 889–900.

Muiderman, K., Zurek, M., Vervoort, J., Gupta, A., Hasnain, S., and Driessen, P. 2022. The anticipatory governance of sustainability transformations: hybrid approaches and dominant perspectives. *Global Environmental Change*, 73, 102452.

Munaretto, S., Siciliano, G., and Turvani, M. E. 2014. Integrating adaptive governance and participatory multicriteria methods: a framework for climate adaptation governance. *Ecology and Society*, 19, 2.

O'Neill, D. W., Fanning, A. L., Lamb, W. F., and Steinberger, J. K. 2018. A good life for all within planetary boundaries. *Nature Sustainability*, 1, 2, 88–95.

Olsson, P., Gunderson, L. H., Carpenter, S. R., Ryan, P., Lebel, L., Folke, C., and Holling, C. S. 2006. Shooting the rapids: navigating transitions to adaptive governance of social-ecological systems. *Ecology and Society*, 11, 1.

Österblom, H., and Folke, C. 2013. Emergence of global adaptive governance for stewardship of regional marine resources. *Ecology and Society*, 18, 2.

Patterson, J., Schulz, K., Vervoort, J., Van Der Hel, S., Widerberg, O., Adler, C., Hulbert, M., Anderton, K., Sethi, M., Barau, A., and Barau, A. 2017. Exploring the governance and politics of transformations towards sustainability. *Environmental Innovation and Societal Transitions*, 24, 1–16.

Plummer, R., Crona, B., Armitage, D. R., Olsson, P., Tengö, M., and Yudina, O. 2012. Adaptive comanagement: a systematic review and analysis. *Ecology and Society*, 17, 3.

Pörtner, H. O., Scholes, R. J., Agard, J., Archer, E., Arneth, A., Bai, X., Barnes, D., Burrows, M., Chan, L., Cheung, W. L., Diamond, S., Donatti, C., Duarte, C., Eisenhauer, N., Foden, W., Gasalla, M. A., Handa, C., Hickler, T., Hoegh-Guldberg, O., Ichii, K., Jacob, U., Insarov, G., Kiessling, W., Leadley, P., Leemans, R., Levin, L., Lim, M., Maharaj, S., Managi, S., Marquet, P. A., McElwee, P., Midgley, G., Oberdorff, T., Obura, D., Osman, E., Pandit, R., Pascual, U., Pires, A. P. F., Popp, A., Reyes-Garcia, V., Sankaran, M., Settele, J., Shin, Y. J., Sintayehu, D. W., Smith, P., Steiner, N., Strassburg, B., Sukumar, R., Trisos, C., Val, A. L., Wu, J., Aldrian, E., Parmesan, C., Pichs-Madruga, R., Roberts, D. C., Rogers, A. D., Diaz, S., Fischer, M., Hashimoto, S., Lavorel, S., Wu, N., Ngo, H. T. 2021. Scientific outcome of the IPBES-IPCC co-sponsored workshop on biodiversity and climate change; IPBES secretariat, Bonn, Germany. https:DOI:10.5281/zenodo.4659158.

Salomaa, A., and Juhola, S. 2020. How to assess sustainability transformations: a review. *Global Sustainability*, 3.

Schultz, L., Folke, C., Österblom, H., and Olsson, P. 2015. Adaptive governance, ecosystem management, and natural capital. *Proceedings of the National Academy of Sciences*, 112, 24, 7369–7374.

Scoones, I., Stirling, A., Abrol, D., Atela, J., Charli-Joseph, L., Eakin, H., Ely, A. Olsson, P., Pereira, L., Priya, R., van Zwanenberg, Yang, L., and Yang, L. 2020. Transformations to sustainability: combining structural, systemic and enabling approaches. *Current Opinion in Environmental Sustainability*, 42, 65–75.

Serrao-Neumann, S., Harman, B. P., and Low Choy, D. 2013. The role of anticipatory governance in local climate adaptation: observations from Australia. *Planning Practice & Research*, 28, 4, 440–463.

Sharma-Wallace, L., Velarde, S. J., and Wreford, A. 2018. Adaptive governance good practice: show me the evidence! *Journal of Environmental Management*, 222, 174–184.

Smith, K., and Lawrence, G. 2018. From disaster management to adaptive governance? Governance challenges to achieving resilient food systems in Australia. *Journal of Environmental Policy & Planning*, 20, 3, 387–401.

UNDP 2022. SPECIAL REPORT New threats to human security in the Anthropocene Demanding greater solidarity. New York, United Nations Development Programme.

UNHCR. 2022. Ukraine, other conflicts push forcibly displaced total over 100 million for first time. Accessed 26 May 2022. https://www.unhcr.org/news/press/2022/5/628a389e4/unhcr-ukraine-other-conflicts-push-forcibly-displaced-total-100-million.html.

Van Assche, K., Beunen, R., Duineveld, M., and Gruezmacher, M. 2017. Power/knowledge and natural resource management: Foucaultian foundations in the analysis of adaptive governance. *Journal of Environmental Policy & Planning*, 19, 3, 308–322.

Van Assche, K., Valentinov, V., and Verschraegen, G. 2021. Adaptive governance: learning from what organizations do and managing the role they play. *Kybernetes*.

Van Buuren, A., Keessen, A. M., Van Leeuwen, C., Eshuis, J., and Ellen, G. J. 2015. Implementation arrangements for climate adaptation in the Netherlands: characteristics and underlying mechanisms of adaptive governance. *Ecology and Society*, 20, 4.

Visseren-Hamakers, I. J., Razzaque, J., McElwee, P., Turnhout, E., Kelemen, E., Rusch, G. M., … and Zaleski, D. 2021. Transformative governance of biodiversity: insights for sustainable development. *Current Opinion in Environmental Sustainability*, 53, 20–28.

Wang, C., Medaglia, R., and Zheng, L. 2018. Towards a typology of adaptive governance in the digital government context: the role of decision-making and accountability. *Government Information Quarterly*, 35, 2, 306–322.

Westskog, H., Amundsen, H., Christiansen, P., and Tønnesen, A. 2020. Urban contractual agreements as an adaptive governance strategy: under what conditions do they work in multi-level cooperation? *Journal of Environmental Policy & Planning*, 22, 4, 554–567.

Wyborn, C. 2015. Co-productive governance: a relational framework for adaptive governance. *Global Environ. Change*, 30, 56–67.

Young, O. R. 2002. *The Institutional Dimensions of Environmental Change: Fit, Interplay, and Scale*. Cambridge, MA: MIT Press.

PART I

THEORETICAL AND
CONCEPTUAL DEVELOPMENTS

2. Operationalising adaptive governance: a research agenda

Barbara Cosens, Holly Doremus, J. B. Ruhl, Niko Soininen and Lance Gunderson

INTRODUCTION

"Governance may be defined as organised efforts to manage the course of events in a social system" (Burris et al. 2008) and includes institutions ranging from very formal governmental institutions of the state (e.g., elected legislatures) to nongovernmental entities (e.g., neighbourhood watch groups; corporations) (Bevir 2012). The term has seen increasing use in the policy sciences as informal emergent networks and collaborative processes have emerged to fill gaps in governance that is heavily reliant on formal government (Pierre and Peters 2021, Cosens et al. 2020, Bevir 2012). Research to date has relied on empirical evidence to identify emergent governance and developed theories related to its emergence. Two areas of additional research are evident from this work and are necessary to understand adaptive governance within this area of literature.

First, a wide variety of theory and terminology has developed in an *ad hoc* fashion, often competing for attention as problems such as climate change are discussed. Each area, however, is based on empirical observation of similar societal responses to complexity. We hypothesise that this is a result of different disciplines focusing on different problems, sectors and scales, and that forms of emergent governance from "new" and "adaptive" to "transformative" and "transition" governance exist on a continuum representing increasing need for formal institutions through governmental involvement. Importantly, governance research may benefit from an interdisciplinary dialogue among those focused on these different aspects of emergent governance. In fact, this step is critical to any effort to operationalise adaptive governance. A research agenda to test this hypothesis, and in doing so, to identify the role of government in governance applicable to different types and scales of problems is explored in section 1 of the research agenda below.

Second, our recent work on adaptive governance has made the case that the emergence of these types of governance is too slow to address accelerating change in the Anthropocene. In addition, reliance on emergent, often informal, private forms of governance, does not necessarily facilitate governance in the public good. To address these issues, we have argued for a role for government in both facilitating emergence of adaptive governance and in managing legitimacy, equity, and justice, and for changes at the science/policy interface to inform governance in the face of change and uncertainty (Cosens et al. 2020, Cosens et al. 2021). While a framework for the role of government has been developed, the research remains to test and refine that framework by identifying and developing models for its operationalisation (Cosens et al. 2017). Section 2 of the research agenda will address this gap. Depending on the results of the proposed interdisciplinary dialogue in section 1, this research may also inform other areas of emergent governance.

Given the increasing pressure from global threats ranging from climate change to pandemics and the increased vulnerability of social-ecological-technological systems (SETS) to these threats, it is time to develop and pursue a comprehensive research agenda with the goal of providing a road map for operationalising adaptive (and potentially other forms of emergent) governance that hold promise for managing uncertainty and change.

SECTION 1: A RESEARCH AGENDA FOR INTERDISCIPLINARY LEARNING FROM EMERGENT GOVERNANCE SCHOLARSHIP

The recent increase in scholarship on governance and the empirical observation of an increasing role of informal actors coincide with the rise in collective problems that defy governmental boundaries and traditional mechanisms for problem resolution through regulation and market mechanisms. The result is a rich, but ad hoc, body of literature from different disciplines focused on a variety of problems in different sectors and at different scales. Nevertheless, each begins with empirical observation of emergent governance in response to increasing complexity coinciding with the intersection of globalisation, climate change, rapidly increasing population, and the digital revolution (Cosens et al. 2021). In reference to one area of scholarship – new governance – Karkkainen (2004) states:

> Finally, in its sheer novelty, the recent profusion of New Governance scholarship has not yet settled upon a common nomenclature, leaving even the most dedicated reader with the daunting task of sorting through and translating a bewildering babel of unfamiliar, competing, and possibly incompatible terminology, which may or may not describe similar phenomena in different terms, or different phenomena in similar terms. In this area of scholarship, as in many others, contestation over naming rights appears to be half the battle, but as a byproduct it tends to generate opacity and outright confusion [citations omitted].

Despite this negative connotation of the world of academic naming and claiming, the astute observation of Karkkainen also presents an opportunity. When disciplines studying systems ranging from globalising economies to SETS, and problems ranging from climate change adaptation to energy source transitions, to regulating global markets, are all observing similar emergent governance responses to change and complexity, something important is happening. This innovative multi-disciplinary discovery is often the first step in understanding an observed phenomenon. Each disciplinary focus involved from the political and policy sciences to economics, to ecology, to law brings a different world view to the observed behaviour and it is likely that none alone constitute a complete description (Eigenbrode et al. 2007). Thus, much like the fable of the blind men and the elephant where each touch and describe a very different aspect of the animal and arrive at their own conclusions, it requires integration of these views to understand the whole (Repko 2012). Our own experience with interdisciplinary dialogue[1] indicates that interdisciplinary dialogue combined with development of a common

[1]   The co-authors have participated in and led two pursuits at the US National Socio-Environmental Synthesis (SESYNC) Center in Annapolis, Maryland USA, on *Adaptive Water Governance Project, funded by the U.S. National Socio-Environmental Synthesis Center (SESYNC) under funding from the U.S. National Science Foundation, NSF DBI-1052875.*

database may lead to identification of common ground (Repko 2012) and form the basis for a richer understanding of, in this case, emergent governance.

This dialogue is also critical to an effort to operationalise any of these concepts of governance through a role for government. The "real" world of government does not reinvent itself in the face of every problem. Instead, it requires a range of tools for facilitating, steering, and promoting the legitimacy of emergent governance and guidance on when to apply them on a continuum of increasing formal intervention from adaptation to transformation.

The following paragraphs briefly summarise some of the terms applied by different disciplines to the growing presence of informal actors in governance and concludes with a research agenda to test the hypothesis that these types of governance are all descriptors for emergent governance responses to complexity and that they exist on a continuum reflecting an increasing role for formal government. This is followed by a discussion of the value of this work to identification of how government might use this information to identify the appropriate response to complex problems at a variety of scales.

The Multi-disciplinary Web of Emergent Governance Scholarship

The growing body of terminology to describe emergent forms of governance includes adaptive, new, transition, and transformative governance (the terms focused on in this chapter set forth in Table 2.1 for ease of comparison). The following paragraphs summarise the disciplinary source, problem focus, and governance tools of key literature associated with each term. In keeping with the limits of our own expertise, we treat adaptive governance in greater depth and provide only enough on other literature on emerging governance to support our argument that these various areas of scholarship can and should learn from each other.

Adaptive governance

The term *adaptive governance* was developed by those researching common pool resources and coupled social-ecological systems, and has generally focused at the bioregional scale (Chaffin et al. 2014). It was coined by Dietz, Ostrom, and Stern in a 2003 contribution in *Science* to a review of The Tragedy of the Commons (Diet et al. 2003). They described adaptive governance as the type of flexible governance institutions necessary to facilitate self-organisation shown to be successful in managing human interaction with local common pool resource systems,[2] while also managing external influence on local systems that can cause failure in purely self-organised governance (Dietz et al. 2003). They saw adaptive governance as a form of nested, polycentric governance that moves among self-regulatory, market, and collaborative mechanisms as warranted by the nature, evolution, and scale of the problem, with the capacity to scale up beyond the local scale dependant on the institutional framework (Dietz et al. 2003, Cosens et al. 2017). They identified the attributes of institutions that give rise to self-organisation as: access to good information about the resource, its use, and the values society holds with respect to the resource; mechanisms for resolving conflict; effective enforceable systems of compliance with rules; and capacity to adapt to change (Dietz et al. 2003). Dietz et al.'s focus was on both formal and informal institutions and did not call out

---

[2]   "Common pool resources (CPRs) are characterised as resources for which the exclusion of users is difficult (referred to as excludability), and the use of such a resource by one user decreases resource benefits for other users (referred to as subtractability)" (Heikkila and Carter 2017).

Table 2.1   Governance terms

Term	Definition as Used in this Chapter	Sources Relied on for Definition*
Adaptive Governance	Emergent, collaborative, self-organising governance, at the problem (often bioregional) scale with the capacity to adjust to change, and the formal and informal institutions necessary to allow self-organisation. Described in the context of social-ecological systems.	Dietz et al. (2003) Folke et al. (2005) Chaffin et al. (2014) Cosens et al. (2013) Cosens et al. (2020)
	To distinguish the self-organising aspects from the role of formal institutions in enabling self-organisation, this chapter specifically refers to the "role of government in adaptive governance."	
	Adaptive co-management and collaborative governance may exist within the umbrella of adaptive governance.	
	Tools: adaptive management; adaptive planning.	
New Governance	Networked and collaborative processes involving state and non-state actors and emerging in response to failures of the neoliberal economic reforms of the 1980s. Similar to adaptive governance, but described by different disciplines focused on different sectors. Karkkainen (2004) provides a bridge between the two areas of scholarship: adaptive governance and new governance.	Lee (2003) Karkkainen (2004) Burris et. al. (2008) Bevir (2012)
Transformative Governance	Formal and informal governance necessary to manage non-linear change (i.e., regime shift). Described in the context of social-ecological systems.	Chaffin et al. (2016) Schmitz and Scoones (2019)
	Tools: anticipatory governance.	
Transition Governance	Incremental, self-organising processes aimed at developing and scaling technological or social innovation for moving the larger socio-economic system into a new, typically more sustainable, system state.	Loorbach (2014)
	The term "transition management" is used to describe the government role in transition governance to provide steering.	

Note: * There are many additional articles that address these topics. Those listed here were specifically relied on in this chapter due to their foundational or synthetic nature.

specifically the role of formal governmental institutions (e.g., legislatures and administrative agencies) in their framework. Nevertheless, these attributes are all ones that could be served by government, as well as hindered by government if attention to their presence within a governmental framework is not fostered.

In their seminal article on adaptive governance, Folke et al. (2005) recognised the synergy between scholarship on adaptive governance and resilience theory. They asserted that the human institutions that govern natural resources were linked and tightly coupled to complex ecological systems and that both the human and ecological components change in dramatic and often unpredictable ways. They use resilience as a key descriptor of such non-linear system dynamics, stating:

> Emerging theories and approaches point to the importance of assessing and actively managing resilience, i.e., the extent to which a system can absorb recurrent natural and human perturbations and

continue to regenerate without slowly degrading or even unexpectedly flipping into less desirable states. Resilience in this context is defined as the capacity of a system to absorb disturbance and reorganise while undergoing change so as to still retain essentially the same function, structure, identity, and feedbacks [citations omitted]. (Folke et al. 2005, pp. 442–443)

Managing ecological resilience, they posited, requires a focus on supporting the processes that sustain the system as it adapts to change rather than seeking to maintain a static state of the system (Folke et al. 2005). Hence, governance itself must adapt to changing conditions of these coupled systems.

Folke et. al. (2005, p. 443) adopted the concept of adaptive governance from Dietz et al. (2003) and maintained the application to common pool resources with a focus on "local and regional governance of landscapes and seascapes" undergoing change. This focus continued an emphasis on the conditions necessary to facilitate emergence of self-organised private and public-private efforts to sustain common pool resources. It looked in particular at the support these collaborative processes may need in times of disturbance and change (Folke et al. 2005). The term "adaptive co-management" was used for these emergent, collaborative processes and considered a means to "operationalise adaptive governance" (Folke et al. 2005, p. 448). This article led to the uptake of "adaptive" governance as a means to manage resilience of complex social-ecological and social-ecological-technological systems (SES and SETS respectively) through fostering emergence of self-organising governance. Similar to Dietz et al. (2003), attention was not given to how government might also foster this emergence.[3] In addition to collaborative processes, the primary tool of adaptive governance within the resilience literature is adaptive management (Gunderson et al. 2006), but adaptive planning has also been called for in this literature (Arnold et al. 2010).

In an effort to synthesise the literature on emergent governance of SES, Chaffin et al. (2014) recognise the work on adaptive co-management and collaborative governance as falling within the umbrella of adaptive governance as described by Dietz et al. (2003) and Folke et al. (2005). This chapter follows that synthesis and considers these types of collaborative processes as "tools" to implement adaptive governance.

In proposing a research agenda, we consider the possibility that while adaptive governance shows promise in managing complex problems in SETS (Cosens et al. 2020), it also may be useful in application to problems beyond the landscape scale. Empirical work looking at the landscape scale Natural Resource Management effort in Australia, not only looks at the role of government, but provides additional evidence that adaptive governance may scale up within a nested system of government that provides local discretion and capacity building (Marshall 2008).

New governance
Coincident with the growth of scholarship on adaptive governance in the SES and SETS literature, political and policy scientists recognised the emergence of a greater role for private actors in traditional areas of government and in governance of socio-economic systems. They recognised its emergence at multiple scales and posited that it is triggered by a need to fill gaps left by the neoliberal economic reforms of the 1980s and 90s and the increasing globalisation of markets and social connectivity (Bevir 2012, Vandebergh et al. 2017). Much of the literature refers to this emerging private and public/private governance as "*new governance*"

---

3   For a synthetic review of this literature, *see* Chaffin et al. (2014) and Cosens et al. (2020).

and recognises the role of networks and collaboration in its emergence (Lee 2003, Bevir 2009, Burris et al. 2009, Karkkainen 2004). Similar to the facilitation or steering role for institutions envisioned by the definition of adaptive governance from Dietz et al. (2003), new governance scholars recognised that ad hoc, emergent private governance does not necessarily act in the public good (e.g., Al Qaida is a product of self-organisation), and is subject to corruption and inequities (Burris et al. 2009). Other than the emergent characteristic of new governance which tends to foster innovation by bringing together a diverse array of actors interested in the particular problem, the new governance literature is not focused on managing resilience in the face of disturbance and change, nor is it focused on managing in the face of uncertainty. This may be a real difference or a factor of the systems studied. It may also be considered part of the external environment that triggers emergence in this field of study.

Transformative and transition governance
Parallel to these efforts to develop concepts of governance for incrementally evolving systems, scholars are considering problems in which transformation to a new system state is either necessary or inevitable. This has led to use of the term "transformative" governance in the literature of SES and SETS to consider the governance necessary to manage regime shift as described in ecological resilience theory (Chaffin et al. 2016), and to consider the social transformation necessary in the sustainability literature (Schmitz and Scoones 2019). Similar to the work of Dietz et al. (2003), this literature does not distinguish between the role of government and other institutions in setting the stage for change.

Much more developed is the concept of "transition governance" used in the literature on systemic change within socio-economic systems. Transition governance refers to the observed emergent innovation that might, if scaled up, lead to a more sustainable path (Loorbach 2010).[4] The phrase "transition management" in this literature refers to the governmental role necessary for scaling up and steering transition governance. It echoes the call of adaptive and new governance literature for more formal institutions that can facilitate and steer society among various types of governance as external disturbance leads to failure in self-organisation and as governance problems increase in scale (Geels and Schot 2007, Loorbach 2010, Geels et al. 2019).

Transition management calls for a stronger role for government than envisioned by adaptive governance. Also, unlike adaptive governance with its roots in environmental management, transition management is not thought of in terms of a bioregional scale, but at multiple scales of existing government from the local to the national. Nevertheless, if we view the trigger for self-organisation as a particular problem, the focus of transition management on steering self-organised governance means it is similarly focused at the problem scale. Going beyond adaptive governance, transition management includes the role of government in "creative destruction" of unsustainable aspects of economies such as fossil fuel dependence by "destabilising and dismantling existing regimes and fairly compensating the losses involved" (Loorbach 2014). Loorbach envisions transition management as a balanced meeting of top-down (usually by government) and bottom-up (usually by informal and often self-organised institutions) initiatives. Similar to adaptive and new governance scholars, he finds this role of steering emergent innovative governance as necessary in governing complexity, stating:

---

   [4]   Transition management as presented in this article is a governance approach based on insights from governance and complex systems theory as much as upon practical experiment and experience.

Transition management then is theoretically a form of meta-governance: creating conditions under which the actions of autonomous agents somehow add up to contribute to a bigger whole. Transition management takes insights from transition concepts, governance, social sciences and complex systems theories as starting points for developing hypotheses on such conditions and experimenting in real-life settings with these. The original principles for transition governance (such as long-term thinking, a focus on experimentation and learning, selective participation and dealing with systemic uncertainties) are derived from the understanding of social change as systemic, non-linear and complex. (Loorbach 2014, p. 36)

In addition to creative destruction and steering, anticipatory governance may be a tool of use to transition management.

Understanding Emergent Governance through Interdisciplinary Dialogue: The Research Agenda for Section 1

Even this brief introduction to the literature illustrates not only the rich variety of disciplinary perspectives, but the existence of common ground. Both adaptive and new governance recognise the increasing role of private actors in emergent governance and its gap-filling aspects. The political science expertise associated with new governance literature brings disciplinary depth on the role of power to the study of emergent governance. In doing so it also brings depth and credibility to the somewhat muted call in the adaptive governance literature for a source of legitimacy as the role of private actors in governance increases (Cosens 2013). The transition governance literature appears to also have common ground with that of new governance in its focus on emergent behaviour in socio-economic systems and the recognition of the role of complexity in emergence. Whereas the new governance literature refers to emergent governance in the context of gap filling, the transition governance literature refers to the potential for emergent governance to lead to societal transformation. Thus, similar to adaptive and transformative governance as applied to SETS, new and transition governance may represent the adaptation and transformation spectrum in the socio-economic sector. The governance necessary may represent an increasing role for formal institutions from new to transition governance and from adaptive to transformative governance. The following sub-sections discuss the research necessary to develop a deeper understanding of emergent governance

The spectrum from new and adaptive governance to transition and transformation governance

We propose an interdisciplinary dialogue (Eigenbrode et al. 2007) focused on finding common ground and achieving a more holistic understanding of emergent governance of complex systems (Repko 2012, p. 98). This section 1 research effort would require contribution from the various disciplines researching different areas of emergent governance. An interdisciplinary effort would require integration across the strengths and viewpoints each of these disciplines brings to the problem of governance during rapid change.

The dialogue should be grounded in the same empirical observations that the various governance terms arose from. Thus, it should begin with development of a common database on observed examples of emergent governance regardless of the label attached. Database development could be initiated with an effort to mine the literature on new, adaptive, transition, and transformative governance (Table 2.1 above). The guiding questions to probe are: does emergent governance exist on a continuum of an increasing role for formal institutions including government (Figure 2.1), and does that lead to the conclusion that government might tailor its role in response to the circumstances?

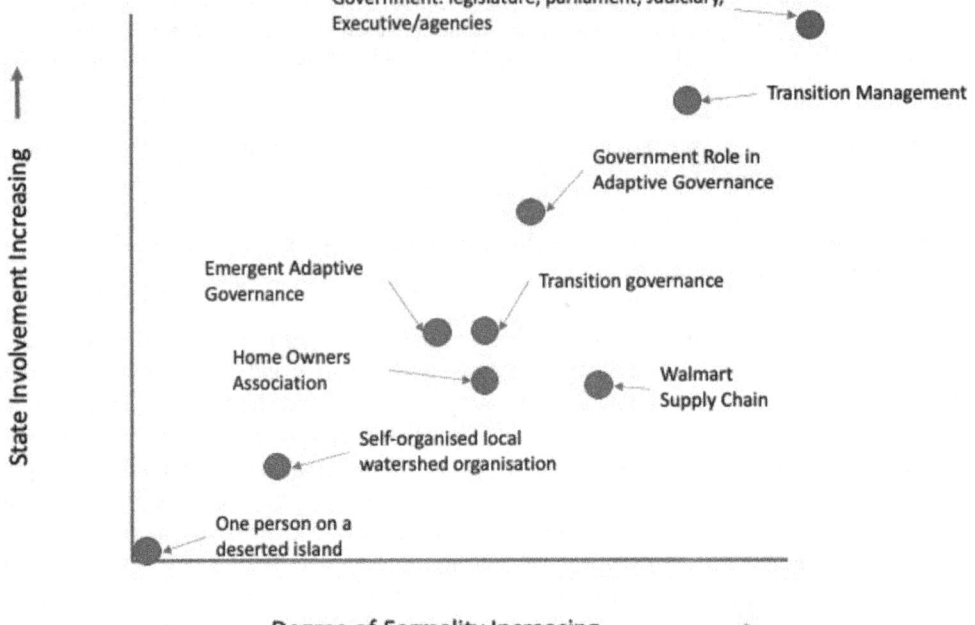

Figure 2.1   *Illustrates the increasing formality and state involvement needed as governance moves from a small self-organised community to adaptive, then transition, then formal governance: state-assisted adaptive governance is placed on this spectrum*

When is facilitation of emergent governance appropriate?

Our co-equal goal to developing a broader interdisciplinary understanding of emergent governance is to explore questions such as: what are the circumstances in which it is most appropriate for government to assist the emergent responses of society rather than employ the top-down imposition of regulation or rely on (relatively) hands-off market mechanisms; when is facilitation of the bottom-up process of self-organisation characteristic of adaptive governance appropriate and when is greater role of top-down steering and deconstruction of existing systems in transition necessary; is application limited by the type, scale, and complexity of the problem; and is the culture and system of government seeking to employ them relevant?

In probing the appropriate application of emergent governance, it is important to recognise that that self-organisation is shown to exist alongside and at times may even rely on traditional tools of markets and regulated markets at one end and top-down command and control regulation at the other (Figure 2.2). Current theory suggests that new forms of governance are suited to, and products of complexity characterised by problems resulting from the emergent behaviour of interacting systems, change, and uncertainty (Cosens et al. 2021, Cosens et al. 2020, Loorbach 2014). Empirical evidence indicates that they arise to fill gaps in governance that is heavily reliant on formal government (Lee 2003, Bevir 2009, Burris et al. 2008, Karkkainen 2004, Cosens et al. 2021, Cosens et al. 2020, Loorbach 2014) as accelerating change in society and the biosphere it relies on are outpacing current systems of law (Folke et al. 2021). Importantly, emergent governance appears to be more adaptive, innovative, and responsive to feedback in theses settings than regulation, while avoiding the secondary and unintended consequences common to complex systems, and that lead to market failure (Lee 2003, Bevir 2009, Karkkainen 2004, Cosens et al. 2021, Cosens et al. 2020, Loorbach 2014, Burris et al. 2008). The database would lay the foundation for much of the research proposed in section 2 of this chapter but would also be useful to test our assumptions about the context of various forms of emergent governance.

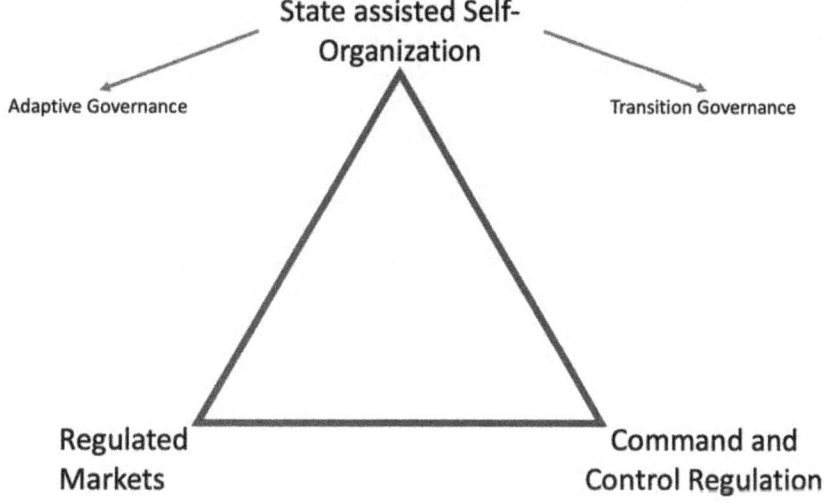

Figure 2.2   *Illustrating that state-assisted adaptive governance and transition management exist along with the traditional governmental tools of markets and regulation*

It may be useful to consider an example of what we hypothesise to be appropriate application of adaptive governance versus transition management in the context of two problems areas: climate adaptation (the efforts of society to adapt to the impacts of climate change whether in the form of drought, sea level rise, wildfire, or changing ecological function) and mitigation (the efforts of society to slow or reverse climate change whether in efforts to reduce emission of greenhouse gases or to sequester carbon).

At first glance, emergent governance appears to be a possible solution in each of our two settings: climate mitigation and adaptation. Both are complex problems with high uncertainty, evolving, and sometimes exhibiting surprising emergent manifestations. Both problems ignore state boundaries with the global reach of climate change driven by the physical nature of the atmosphere, and adaptation driven by the nature of the varying climate and landscape. But even in these admittedly complex settings, there is likely to be important nuance as they are unpacked.

Consider for example, that adaptation, while necessary globally, will be highly context specific in every geographic setting. In fact, the use of collaboration and local knowledge as society seeks to avoid unintended consequences as adaptation measures play out in integrated social-ecological settings may be critical. This is also a setting in which efforts to adapt may generate social disruption and the legitimacy of measures will therefore depend on participation. This might also be a setting in which state assistance in building capacity, promoting legitimacy, accountability, transparency, equity and justice will need to be focused at the local to landscape scale. Climate adaptation is thus an area to consider for adaptive governance.

In contrast, mitigation (with the exception of its focus on land use such as deforestation), is at first glance a problem of technology in which regulation on the one hand and market incentives on the other can play an important role. Innovation in the development of new energy sources and the scaling up of their application requires a top-down race-to-the-moon type effort, but also space for private actors and public private partnerships at multiple scales to experiment. This would seem to call for application of transition management. But mitigation also requires economic transition from a fossil fuel economy to something else. There may be inequity in this transition without state assistance. Governance that allows the participation of coal miners, pipeline workers, oil rig roughnecks, oil shipping contractors, etc. whether at the local or industry scale and considers culture in identification of energy alternatives sounds like adaptive governance.

It is also important to consider whether reliance on emergence of informal collective action is only likely at small scales. Adaptive governance scholarship focuses on the local to landscape scale, whereas new and transition governance models focus on multiple scales from local transition of public services to private providers, to respond to the failure of government reach as economic and climate issues globalise. Thus, arises our conjecture that adaptive governance is most relevant in the context of problems like climate adaptation where, despite the global application, specific measures must be tailored to specific geographic settings. In discussing a research agenda, however, it is important to avoid simply accepting the current state of scholarship as based on real limitations of the phenomena observed. The focus on the local to bioregional scale in the adaptive governance literature may be a result of disciplinary bias or researcher interest in certain problem scales.

To explore the issue of scale, let's return to the institutions that may facilitate the emergence of self-organising governance of Dietz et al. (2003), in the SES setting – i.e., access to good information about the resource; its use and the values society holds with respect to the resource; mechanisms for resolving conflict; effective enforceable systems of compliance with rules; and capacity to adapt to change. In 2003, the year of publication of Dietz et al., the possibility of these attributes at the local to landscape scale would have been clear. In 2022, a global internet and social media making possible global-scale networks, value alignment, and instantaneous information sharing that go beyond state boundaries, present new possibilities and inquiry should not be limited to the bioregional scale.

In addition to the type and scale of the complex problem to be addressed, it is important to consider the culture and system of government seeking to address it. A society with emphasis on individualism and local agency such as the United States, may be interested in legal reform that fosters self-organisation and emergence, whereas Finland may be comfortable with a more top-down approach, and China may require yet a third path. When we move to the research necessary to actually design legal mechanisms for a governmental role in adaptive governance below, therefore, it will be necessary to consider the research as specific to the legal system in question. It is at that point that the need for research on the political will within that system must be probed.

SECTION 2: OPERATIONALISING THE ROLE OF GOVERNMENT IN ADAPTIVE GOVERNANCE

With research to develop an interdisciplinary understanding of emergent governance and its appropriate application, we now focus our discussion on how to operationalise the role of government in emergent governance with specific attention to adaptive governance. Depending on the common ground found in the section 1 phase of the research agenda, this agenda may be equally applicable to new, transition, and transformative governance and may be expanded to capture any nuance. It is also important to point out that adaptive, new, and transformative governance, and transition management contemplate government that is nimble in moving among regulatory and market mechanisms when warranted, as well as steering and facilitating emergent self-organising government. Because modern governments have ample experience and models relevant to regulation and regulated markets, we focus our inquiry on the aspects of government intended to steer and facilitate emergent self-organising governance.

We contemplate a two-fold inquiry. First, how might government operationalise adaptive governance to speed adaptation and overcome the ad hoc nature of emergent processes while retaining their innovation and capacity to contextualise and innovate? How might government steer governance toward the public good and overcome the inertia or stability imposed by extant vested interests, while avoiding corruption or inequitable outcomes in a private, unguided process? Second, what role should science play in the value-laden policy space of governance in which the science has high levels of uncertainty, and the systems of technology, ecology, and society are evolving as integrated complex systems? How do we train scientists to play a positive role in this space? What ethical guidelines will secure the integrity of the science process while making effective use of expertise in decision making?

The Role of Government

An appropriate starting point to guide data collection on the role of government are the attributes of formal institutions identified by Dietz et al. (2003) – i.e., access to good information about the resource, its use and the values society holds with respect to the resource; mechanisms for resolving conflict; effective enforceable systems of compliance with rules; and capacity to adapt to change. Building on this work and its progeny and adding components to address concerns with legitimacy, accountability, transparency, equity, and justice in private self-governance, a framework for the role of law in adaptive governance was proposed in Cosens et al. (2013) and is reproduced from that work in Table 2.2 (Cosens et al. 2017).

While it would be premature to consider Table 2.2 the definitive framework, it provides a starting point for returning to the case studies in the database proposed above to extract the role of law and government in the structure, capacity, and process described in emergent adaptive governance. Since separating government and law from other institutions was likely not the goal of the prior research that will be compiled, it is also important that the research agenda include new case studies that specifically identify that role (Table 2.3 on research methodologies). In the final analysis, these categories of process may require development of

Table 2.2   *Guidelines for inquiry into the role of law in adaptive governance*

Structure	Polycentricity: multiple centres of authority. Law controls the locus of authority for governmental entities.
	Redundancy: common management and decision-making functions at multiple scales. Redundancy increases the likelihood that decisions can be made and implemented at the scale of a particular problem.
	Nesting: representation of decision-making and advisory bodies at lower levels in higher level entities. Nesting allows the formation of ad hoc networks in response to surprise and increases the potential for local innovation within stable governance at a larger scale.
	Complementarity: if one decision body fails to act or acts inappropriately than another body can step up.
	Subsidiarity: decision-making at the level closest to the resource as possible yet within the context of a government at multiple scales that fosters the conditions for implementation of management decisions. Subsidiarity increases the likelihood that local knowledge will be used, decisions will be tailored to specific problems, and innovation may occur at the local level supported by governance at larger scales.
	Integration: integration of water resources management across sectors that influence water allocation, quality, and land development, and of regulation of physically connected resources such as ground and surface water. Integration reduces the possibility of unintended consequences.
	Persistence: stability in representation and decision-making bodies to foster legitimacy and trust, potentially reducing response time to surprise.
Capacity	Adaptive: resources and legal authority to respond to change. Allows a system of governance to adjust during uncertainty and change.
	Participatory: those affected have the right and resources to have a role in decision making. For Indigenous communities, this equates to the capacity for self-determination. Participatory capacity reduces the likelihood of marginalisation of portions of society and increases the likelihood that all aspects of a system will be considered in decision making.

Process	Legitimacy: acceptance of authority because it is perceived to be exercised appropriately and because it is exercised appropriately. Legitimacy is necessary for public support of resource management, and includes requirements for science-based decision making, deliberation, accountability, transparency, consistency, stability, and review and recourse for those aggrieved by a governmental action.
	Procedural justice: transparency, the right to seek review, and engagement at the appropriate level. Procedural justice is necessary to identify unintended consequences, check corruption, and to avoid uneven application of the burden of adaptation. For indigenous communities, procedural justice requires processes allowing engagement at the governmental level.
	Problem solving approach: Authority and resources to use science and interest based collaborative processes. Allows for the possibility of solutions that are beneficial to all and contrasts with political and ideological approaches which are not subject to compromise.
	Reflection and learning: resources for monitoring and a process for feedback and consideration of new information. The opportunity for reflection and learning assures that response to change will not be rote, and that society will evolve with the approach to management.
	Balance stability and flexibility: adaptation timeframes that consider both the need for adjustment and the economic need for stability. Balance of stability and flexibility recognises that while adjustments must occur in the face of change, social systems and particularly economic systems require stability; both must be taken into account.
	Dispute resolution: process for resolving conflict and making final, binding decisions on trade-offs regarding scarce resources. Dispute resolution is essential as water scarcity in the face of climate change unfolds. There may come a point when consensus is not possible and unless a system for resolving issues is designed and agreed to beforehand, conflict is likely.

Source: Cosens, B. A., R. K. Craig, S. Hirsch, C. (Tony) Arnold, M. H. Benson, D. A. DeCaro, A. S. Garmestani, H. Gosnell, J. Ruhl and E. Schlager. 2017. The role of law in adaptive governance. Ecology and Society 22 (1): 30. [online] URL: http://www.ecologyandsociety.org/vol22/iss1/art30/ Used under the Creative Commons Attribution 4.0 International License.

Table 2.3   *Potential research methodologies for the role of law*

Aspect of Government	Attributes Sought	Research Methodologies
	State participation in emergent governance	• Database of case studies showing emergent adaptive and transition governance

Structure	Polycentricity:
	  Nesting
	  Complementarity
	  Subsidiarity
	  Integration
	
	  Persistence
		• Legal document assessment
		• Legal mapping
		• Network modeling

Capacity	Adaptive	• Resilience assessment
	Participatory	• Mixed methods of quantitative and qualitative social science research
Process	Legitimacy Procedural justice Problem solving approach Reflection and learning Balance stability and flexibility Dispute resolution	• Identification of legal models • Development of new legal models

new models and tools by legal scholars immersed in these questions in partnership with policymakers. These models may form a starting point for authorisation of the use of legal tools identified as appropriate for adaptation and transformation. It is also anticipated that as data is analysed on what has worked in specific case studies, the framework in Table 2.2 would be continually modified.

Table 2.3 shows the methodologies that may be useful in developing the information and are discussed in the context of each aspect of government below. The following paragraphs focus on the structure, capacity, and process of government identified in Cosens et al. (2017) as necessary to facilitate adaptive governance.

Structure of government

Research on the legal aspects of the role of government in adaptive governance begins with the *structure* of government as it relates to the attributes of formal institutions from Dietz et al. (2003) and added to by Folke et al. (2005) and others.[5] Document analysis is at the core of legal research. Analysis of the allocation of authority from constitutional and international frameworks to statutes, to administrative rules, to local ordinances, to practice is necessary to identify the structural framework, its interrelation, and the exercise of discretion within it. This type of analysis is also necessary to identify complementarity at various levels of government.

---

[5]   See also, Cosens et al. (2017) for discussion of the role of law in this nested, polycentric, multi-scalar setting.

Legal research also has much to learn from the methodologies of spatial and social analysis. A concept referred to as "legal mapping" (Stahl et al. 2020) uses geographic information systems to overlay governmental jurisdiction on the geographic problem space and scope of action by informal entities. This may also help in identifying the degree of subsidiarity. Due to its spatial nature, it may be particularly helpful in unpacking the role of government in the context of SES and SETS at the local to landscape scale.

In the complex setting of emergent governance in which interaction occurs among private and public actors, network modelling holds considerable promise (Kim 2020).[6] Network modelling of the interaction among government actors and private actors, among government actors across sectors, and among levels of government, followed by investigation of the legal authority for that interaction will help identify legal models as well as the role of discretion and the exercise of agency and power in government involvement. Unlike spatial data, network modelling is not limited to a geographically defined problem space and may be particularly useful in identifying the possibility of government facilitated adaptive governance at large, even global scales (e.g., Kim 2020).

Capacity to adapt and to participate

We consider two very important aspects of *capacity*: the capacity of the legal and governmental system to adapt and facilitate emergent adaptation, and the capacity of people to participate in self-organising governance, referred to as participatory capacity.

Assessing adaptive capacity, the first step in determining the role of government in capacity building, requires understanding the capacity for adaptation within the technological, ecological, and social aspects of a system both alone and as they interrelate, through data based on scientific methods as well as local and traditional knowledge – a process referred to in the SES setting as resilience assessment.[7] While there are numerous ways to undertake a resilience assessment, many past and current efforts do not specifically investigate the role of law and government.[8] Resilience assessment may be facilitated by using a tool like Wayfinder (Stockholm Resilience Centre 2018),[9] developed at the Stockholm Resilience Centre. "Wayfinder is a process guide for resilience assessment, planning and action in social-ecological systems," and is the culmination of many efforts to develop best practices in this process. Nevertheless, to unpack the role of government, we encourage the addition of assessment of the legal and governmental framework that focuses on the relevant aspects of structure, capacity, and process identified in this chapter. In addition, for problem scales that go beyond the local to landscape scale, other methodologies that can foster participation at larger scales must be developed.

Assessing participatory capacity could also occur within a resilience assessment process, but specifically requires qualitative and quantitative social science data developed through transdisciplinary research (see below) within marginalised communities within the problem

---

[6]   See for example Kim (2020) that looks at the use of network analysis to explore fragmentation, polycentricity, and complexity in global governance; Trebitz et al. (2021) applying social network analysis to the interaction among government and private actors at the watershed scale.

[7]   See, Resilience Alliance, Resilience Assessment website, URL: https://www.resalliance.org/resilience-assessment last visited November 18, 2021.

[8]   For an exception see e.g., Cosens and Gunderson (2018).

[9]   See https://wayfinder.earth.

space. Scholars often capture the concept of the degree of participatory capacity of a particular people as social capital (see e.g., Bodin and Crona 2008). At the community scale, this literature looks not only at access to financial and natural resources and infrastructure, but more difficult aspects to capture including trust, access to knowledge and political resources, degree of trust, and health (Emery and Flora 2006, Flora et al. 2006, Pigg et al. 2013).

Government process

Process is the area of research for the role of government in adaptive governance that is in its infancy. While administrative law generally provides means to promote legitimacy, transparency, and accountability, within state-imposed regulation, no model exists for fostering these attributes within private and public/private governance. Daniel Esty has explored the use of these tools developed at the scale of the state in international law (Esty 2006), and we have drawn on that work to consider similar approaches in adaptive governance (Cosens et al. 2017). Nevertheless, the starting point should be the search for those models within case studies in the database in which government is found to play a facilitative role. In the absence of models, legal scholars should explore the development of incentive-based tools to be used within a facilitative capacity to promote these important aspects of legitimacy in governance (Cosens et al. 2020).

Numerous management and planning tools have already been developed that promote problem solving, reflection, and learning including adaptive management (Holling 1978),[10] adaptive planning (Arnold 2010), anticipatory governance (Muiderman et al. 2020),[11] and scenario planning (Amer et al. 2013). The database of case studies should be mined for examples. How are these used within emergent governance and what is the role of government in their application and the legal authority for that role? What authorities are needed to enhance government facilitation in this area?

In government and law, we generally turn to the judicial branch to carry the role of procedural justice and dispute resolution. As pointed out by Dorf and Sabel (1998), judicial review of a process such as pre-project environmental assessment hinders efforts to manage in the face of uncertainty. They propose judicial review focused on progress toward goals at later stages in project implementation. Again, we know of no legal models for this approach, but the database should be consulted in development of new models (Pace and Cosens 2023).

In addition to the research shown in Table 2.3, research is needed to identify the specific legal authority that presented any barrier to emergent governance, legal authority that triggered emergence, and legal authority that allowed solutions developed in emergent processes to be institutionalised (Chaffin et al. 2018). These aspects could be revealed in each of the methodologies employed above, thus should be considered a thread running through the research agenda.

---

[10]   This concept of adaptive management has been translated into a legal model in: Craig et al. (2014).

[11]   While those who use the term "anticipatory governance" would likely dispute the characterisation of "anticipatory governance" as a tool, we use that characterisation here because while it overlaps with the literature on adaptive, transition, and transformative governance it adds an important planning and management tool. The important addition is to frame current governance decisions in the context of future scenarios. This differs from scenario planning, adaptive planning and resilience assessment, by its focus on choosing a certain path based on its potential future outcome in that it specifically focuses on the governance decisions to be made today.

The Role of Scientists at the Science–policy Interface in Adaptive Governance

Recently, along with others, we identified the need for a new type of scientist trained as an applied trandisciplinarian to work at the science–policy interface in situations of high uncertainty (Cosens et al. 2021). This would require training to understand the co-evolution of governance and the systems they govern. We proposed that this training occur within Long Term Social-Ecological-Technological Systems or LT-SETS to allow contextualisation and the study of change and transfer of knowledge through time. Key features of this training include the imbedding of students within the SETS they are researching, focus on the interactions and processes within the SETS, and the focus of research on system evolution through time. Thus, research focused on emergent behaviour due to the interaction of components within a complex system, while potentially transferrable to other settings, would be most valuable in their transference through time to inform the evolution of the very system studied (Cosens et al. 2021).

The research preformed within an LT-SETS would include the collection of data on governance and the role of law and government discussed above, as well as the science and social science relevant to the problem(s) faced by the specific SETS. What is new to discuss is: how to develop research questions with the society involved; how to develop research that allows for evolution not only of the system but of the research through time; what ethical guidelines are needed in situations in which research questions are developed with those who may also be research subjects; and what ethical guidelines are needed to ensure scientific integrity when the scientist is involved in the policy space?

Although beyond the scope of this chapter, considerable research on the development of transdisciplinary science is underway in this area and shows promise, see for example: Rigolot 2020, Clark and Harley 2020, Wyborn et al. 2019, Jahn et al. 2012, Klein et al. 2001. It is particularly encouraging to see the more recent focus on ethical issues that arise in imbedded research (Cockburn et al. 2018, Hall et al. 2016, Hall et al. 2014). We encourage bringing this research to development of an LT-SETS. The COVID-19 pandemic highlighted the need for ethical guidelines as much for protection of the scientists involved as for the science. It would be naïve to think that the traditional separation between science and policy is driven solely by a failure to realise the importance of integration. While there is reason to avoid doing science in settings where research questions and funding are driven by those with a political or profit related agenda, this is emphatically not the goal of co-creation of knowledge. It must, however, be acknowledged as one of the potential pitfalls and emphasises the need for clear ethical guidelines.

CONCLUSION

We have laid out an ambitious program of research aimed at helping government traditionally focused on top-down science-based decision making based on one-time review of best available science, develop a steering role that manages situations of complexity and uncertainty. Traditional tools of regulation and regulated markets remain important. It is the ability to move between governance approaches as the problem warrants, and to facilitate self-organisation in complex situations requiring contextualisation that requires new legal models.

It is critical to acknowledge that, in the face of accelerating change, the implementation of government assisted adaptive governance and transition management cannot wait on a multi-decade research programme. Thus, the research proposed should be adaptive itself by beginning with development of legal models that will allow application of the role of government in adaptive governance in the context of climate adaptation. These "pilot" efforts may be periodically modified and employed in other problem areas based on feedback from both implementation and the research proposed.

As our global transition to the digital age, the rise of global economies, and the worst effects of human impacts on the planet are felt, the ultimate question becomes: can social systems embrace complexity and tailor their institutions accordingly? This research agenda addresses how researchers might provide the information necessary for government to respond, but the question remains: will it do so? Will humankind have the foresight and political will to push its institutions to an appropriate response? We can only offer that the challenge to do so is ours, and the time to act is now.

REFERENCES

Amer, M., Daim, T. U., and Jetter, A. 2013. A review of scenario planning, *Futures*, 46, 23–40. https://doi.org/10.1016/j.futures.2012.10.003.

Arnold, C. A. 2010. Adaptive watershed planning and climate change, *Env't & Energy Law and Policy Journal*, 417, 5, 440–449.

Bevir, M. 2012. *Governance: A Very Short Introduction*. 3. Oxford, Oxford University Press.

Bevir, M. 2009. *Key Concepts in Governance*. 1–232. London, Sage Publications.

Bodin, Ö. and Crona, B. I. 2008. Management of natural resources at the community level: exploring the role of social capital and leadership in a rural fishing community, *World Development*, 2763–2779. doi:10.1016/j.worlddev.2007.12.002.

Burris, S., Kempa, M., and Shearing, C. 2008. Changes in governance: a cross-disciplinary review of current scholarship, *Akron L. Rev.*, 41, 1.

Chaffin, B., Gosnell, H., and Craig, R. K. 2018. The emergence of adaptive governance in the Klamath River Basin. In Cosens, B., and Gunderson, L. (eds) *Practical Panarchy for Adaptive Water Governance: Linking Law to Social-ecological Resilience*. Dordrecht, Springer Publications.

Chaffin, B. C., Garmestani, A. S., Gunderson, L. H., Benson, B. H., Angeler, D. G., Arnold, C. A, Cosens, B. A., Craig, R. K., Ruhl, J. B., and Allen, C. R. 2016. Transformative environmental governance, *Annual Review of Environment and Resources*, 41, 399–423. http://www.annualreviews.org/doi/abs/10.1146/annurev-environ-110615-085817.

Chaffin, B. C., Gosnell, H., and Cosens, B. A. 2014. A decade of adaptive governance scholarship: synthesis and future directions, *Ecology & Society*, 19, 3, 1–2. http://dx.doi.org/10.5751/ES-06824-190356 [https://perma.cc/X5EG-2FBB].

Clark, W. C. and Harley, A. G. 2020. Sustainability science: towards a synthesis. *Annual Reviews of Environment and Resources*, 45, 331–386.

Cockburn, J., and Cundill, G. 2018. Ethics in transdisciplinary research: reflections on the implications of 'science with society'. In Macleod, C., Marx, J., Mnyaka, P., and Treharne, G. (eds) *The Palgrave Handbook of Ethics in Critical Research*. Cham, Palgrave Macmillan. https://doi.org/10.1007/978-3-319-74721-7_6.

Cosens, B., Ruhl, J. B., Soininen, N., and Gunderson, L. 2020. Designing law to enable adaptive governance of modern wicked problems, *Vanderbilt Law Review*, 73, 6, 1687–1732.

Cosens, B., Ruhl, J. B., Soininen, N., Gunderson, L., Belinskij, A., Blenckner, T., Camacho, A. E., Chaffin, B. C., Craig, R. K., Doremus, H., Glicksman, R., Heiskanen A., Larson, R., and Similä, J. 2021. Governing complexity: integrating science, governance, and law to manage accelerating change in the globalized commons, *PNAS*, 118, 36. https://doi.org/10.1073/pnas.2102798118.

Cosens, B., and Gunderson, L. (eds). 2018. *Practical Panarchy for Adaptive Water Governance: Linking Law to Social-ecological Resilience*. Dordrecht, Springer Publications.

Cosens, B. A., Craig, R. K., Hirsch, S., Arnold, C., Benson, M. H., DeCaro, D. A., Garmestani, A. S., Gosnell, H., Ruhl, J., and Schlager, E. 2017. The role of law in adaptive governance. *Ecology and Society*, 30, 22, 1. http://www.ecologyandsociety.org/vol22/iss1/art30/.

Cosens, B. 2013. Legitimacy, adaptation, and resilience in ecosystem management, *Ecology and Society*, 3, 18, 1. http://www.ecologyandsociety.org/vol18/iss1/art3/.

Craig, R. K., and Ruhl, J. B. 2014. Designing administrative law for adaptive management, *Vanderbilt Law Review*, 67, 1, 45.

Dietz, T., Ostrom, E., and Stern, P. C. 2003. The struggle to govern the commons, *Science*, 302, 1907.

Dorf, M. C. and Sabel, C. F. 1998. A constitution of democratic experimentalism, *Columbia Law Review*, 98, 267.

Eigenbrode, S., O'Rourke, M., Wulfhorst, J. D., Althoff, D. M., Goldberg, C. S., Merrill, K., Morse, W., Nielsen-Pincus, M., Stephens, J., Winowiecki, L., Bosque-Pérez, N. A. 2007. Employing philosophical dialogue in collaborative science. *BioScience*, 57, 55–64. http://dx.doi.org/10.1641/b570109.

Emery, M., and Flora, C. 2006. Spiraling-up: mapping community transformation with community capitals framework, *Community Development*, 37, 1, 19–35.

Esty, D. C. 2006. Good governance at the supranational scale: globalizing administrative law. *Yale Law Journal*, 115, 1490–1562. http://dx.doi.org/10.2307/20455663.

Flora, C., Flora, J., and Fey, S. 2004. *Rural Communities: Legacy and Change* (2nd edn) Boulder, CO, Westview Press.

Folke, C., Polasky, S., Rockström, J., Galaz, V., Westley, F., Lamont, M., Scheffer, M., Österblom, H., Carpenter, S. R., Chapin III, F. S., Seto, K. C., Weber, E. U., Crona, B. I., Daily, G. C., Dasgupta, P., Gaffney, O., Gordon, L.J., Hoff, H., Levin, S. A., Lubchenco, Steffen, W., and Walker, B. H. 2021. Our future in the Anthropocene biosphere, *Ambio*, 50, 834–869. https://doi.org/10.1007/s13280-021-01544-8.

Folke, C., Hahn, T., Olsson, P., and Norberg, J. 2005. Adaptive governance of social-ecological systems, *Ann. Rev. Env't & Res.* 30, 441, 442–443.

Geels, F., Turnheim, B., Asquith, M., Kern, F., and Kivimaa, P. 2019. Sustainability transitions: policy and practice (EEA Report No. 9 /2019). Copenhagen, European Environment Agency.

Geels, F. W., and Schot, J. 2007. Typology of sociotechnical transition pathways, *Res. Policy*, 36, 399–417.

Gunderson, L., and Light, S. S. 2006. Adaptive management and adaptive governance in the Everglades ecosystem, *Policy Sciences*, 39, 323, 324.

Hall, T. E., Engebretson, J., O'Rourke, M., Piso, Z., Whyte, K., and Valles, S. 2016. The need for social ethics in interdisciplinary environmental science graduate programs: results from a nation-wide survey in the United States, *Science and Engineering Ethics*. http://dx.doi.org/10.1007/s11948-016-9775-0.

Hall, T. E., and O'Rourke, M., 2014. Responding to communication challenges in transdisciplinary sustainability science. In Huutoniemi, K. and Tapio, P. (eds) *Heuristics for Transdisciplinary Sustainability Studies: Solution-oriented Approaches to Complex Problems*. Oxford, Routledge. http://dx.doi.org/10.4324/9780203734834.

Heikklia, T., and Carter, D. P. 2017. Common pool resources, *Oxford Bibliographies*. https://www.oxfordbibliographies.com/view/document/obo-9780199363445/obo-9780199363445-0011.xml.

Holling C. S. (ed.). 1978. *Adaptive Environmental Assessment and Management*, Hoboken, NJ, John Wiley and Sons.

Jahn, T., Bergmann, M., and Keil, F. 2012. Transdisciplinarity: between mainstreaming and marginalization, *Ecological Economics*, 79, 1–10.

Karkkainen, B. C. 2004. "New governance" in legal thought and in the world: Some splitting as antidote to overzealous lumping, *Minn. L. Rev.*, 89, 471, 473.

Kim, R. E. 2020. Is global governance fragmented, polycentric, or complex? The state of the art of the network approach, *International Studies Review*, 22, 4, 903–931. https://doi.org/10.1093/isr/viz052.

Klein, J. T., Häberli, R., and Scholz, R. W., Grossenbacher-Mansuy, W., Bill, A., and Welti, M. (eds). 2001. *Transdisciplinarity: Joint Problem Solving Among Science, Technology and Society. An Effective Way for Managing Complexity*. Basel, Birkhäuser Verlag.

Lee, M. 2003. *Conceptualizing the New Governance: A New Institution of Social Coordination*, 4. http://citeseerx.ist.psu.edu/viewdoc/summary?doi=10.1.1.202.1474 [https://perma.cc/92VH-P378].

Loorbach, D. 2014. To transition! Governance panarchy in the new transformation, inaugural address, 62, Rotterdam, Erasmus University Rotterdam.

Loorbach, D. 2010. Transition management for sustainable development: a prescriptive, complexity-based governance framework, *Governance*, 23, 161–183, 163.

Marshall, G. R. 2008. Nesting, subsidiarity, and community-based environmental governance beyond the local level, *International Journal of the Commons*, 2(1), 75–97.

Muiderman, K., Gupta, A., Vervoort, J., and Biermann, F. 2020. Four approaches to anticipatory climate governance: different conceptions of the future and implications for the present. *WIREs Climate Change* 11, 673.

Pace, Bronson J. and Cosens, Barbara A. 2023. Environmental assessment in a time of rapid change and high uncertainty: the addition of resilience assessment to NEPA, *Environmental Law & Policy Review*, 47.

Pierre, J. and Peters, G. 2021. *Advanced Introduction to Governance*. Cheltenham, UK and Northampton, MA, USA, Edward Elgar Publishing.

Pigg, K., Gasteyer, Martin, S. K., Apaliya, G., Keating, K. 2013. The community capitals framework: an empirical examination of internal relationships, *Journal of the Community Development Society*, 44, 4, 492–502.

Repko, A. F. 2012. *Interdisciplinary Research*. London, Sage Publications.

Rigolot, C. 2020. Transdisciplinarity as a discipline and a way of being: complementarities and creative tensions. *Humanit Soc Sci Commun.*, 7, 100. https://doi.org/10.1057/s41599-020-00598-5.

Schmitz, H. and Scoones, I. 2019. Sustainability transformations in complex systems: A political economy perspective. In Galaz, V. (ed.) *Global Challenges, Governance, and Complexity*. Cheltenham, UK and Northampton, MA, USA, Edward Elgar Publishing.

Stahl, A. T., Fremier, A. K. and Cosens, B. A. 2020. Mapping legal authority for terrestrial conservation corridors along streams, *Conservation Biology*, 34, 4, 943–955.

Stockholm Resilience Centre. 2018. Wayfinder: resilience assessment tools. https://wayfinder.earth/.

Trebitz, K. I., and Shrestha, M. K. 2021. Suite of roles as a driver of core–periphery patterns in water resource governance networks. In Giordano, G., Restaino, M., and A. Slavini (eds) *Methods and Applications in Social Networks Analysis: Evidence from Collaborative, Governance, Historical and Mobility Network*. Milan, Computational Social Science Series.

Vandenbergh, M. P. and Gilligan, J. M. 2017. *Beyond Politics: The Private Governance Response to Climate Change* (pp. 8–16). Cambridge, Cambridge University Press.

Wyborn, C., Datta, A., Montana, J., Ryan, M., Leith, P., Chaffin, B., Miller, C. and van Kerkhoff, L. 2019. Co-producing sustainability: reordering the governance of science, policy, and practice, *Annu. Rev. Environ. Resour.*, 44, 1, 319–46.

3. Adaptive governance, law and regulation

Niko Soininen, Barbara Cosens, J. B. Ruhl and Suvi-Tuuli Puharinen

INTRODUCTION

In the contemporary era, humanity is both causing and experiencing several coupled social-ecological challenges, such as climate change, loss of biodiversity, and environmental degradation (Steffen et al. 2015). The human species is impacting the planet severely enough to merit the term 'Anthropocene', the age of humans (Steffen et al. 2007). The drivers and consequences of the Anthropocene are underpinned by complex dynamics in and between the biosphere and society (McPhearson et al. 2021). These social-ecological-technological (SET) systems are constantly changing as a consequence of interactions between agents and components of the systems (McPhearson et al. 2021). The operation of these coupled and complex systems cannot be entirely understood, nor can favourable systems states be designed or prescribed by any one actor, whether public (the United Nations, the United States, China, or the European Union) or private (Alphabet, Apple, or Tesla) (Ruhl 2007; Ruhl et al. 2017; Cosens et al. 2020).

Privatisation and markets as means of governing the complex SET systems have shown their limits, as have efforts to regulate the systems top down with legal instruments (designing and prescribing outcomes by law) (Dietz et al. 2003; Cosens et al. 2020; Cosens et al. 2021). Consequently, self-governing civil society initiatives and processes have emerged across the globe to respond to the accelerating change and the incapacity of markets and legal regulation adequately to promote the public good (Dietz et al. 2003; Folke et al. 2005; Pahl-Wostl et al. 2012; Cosens and Gunderson 2018). A typical feature of such initiatives is a civic group collaborating with other groups, companies, scientific communities, and public authorities to address a social-ecological-technological challenge that governments or markets have been unable to resolve (Cosens et al. 2020; Soininen et al. 2022). A good example are Water Vision processes in Finland in which private and public actors deliberate on how hydropower, fisheries, flood-protection, and recreation interests could be reconciled in a particular part of a river basin, for instance. In the United States, adaptive governance is recognised in numerous local collaborative processes including the settlement of major water allocation disputes among states, Native American Tribes and the United States federal government. These settlements have the characteristics of adaptation to local social-ecological conditions and values, use of local knowledge, collaboration, and are triggered by overarching legal requirements (Cosens and Chaffin 2016).

Initiatives and processes like these across the globe are typically labelled 'adaptive governance' (Dietz et al. 2003; Folke et al. 2005; Pahl-Wostl et al. 2012; Cosens and Gunderson 2018). In such thinking, 'governance' refers to an understanding of societal decision-making, which in addition to formal governmental decision-making covers also civil society decision-making and collaborations between public and private actors (Dietz et al. 2003). The collaboration is generally triggered by a problem or need, and the participants tend to self-select based on the relevance of the problem to themselves or the entity (public or private) they represent. Thus, adaptive governance is observed to be 'self-organising'. The word 'adaptive' refers to decision-making that can keep up with social-ecological-technological change and successfully manage the behaviour (i.e., resilience) of SET systems in the face of uncertainty, and at different scales ranging from local to global, depending on the specific challenge(s) at hand (Dietz et al. 2003; Folke et al. 2005; Cosens et al. 2020, p. 1715).

Three characteristics are key for adaptive governance: (1) it emerges as a result of public and/or private collaborative activity; (2) it seeks to manage a social-ecological-technological challenge in a specific spatial context which varies according to the challenge at hand; (3) it fits situations where the challenge cannot be effectively or efficiently managed by government design and decree, or by leaving it to the markets. Climate change, biodiversity loss, and environmental degradation are all complex challenges inviting adaptive governance responses, ranging from city networks to collaborative river-basin management processes. The spatial component of these adaptive governance initiatives differs considerably depending on the challenge at hand. The challenge of climate change mitigation is global in the sense that climate is a global common pool resource (IPCC 2021), whereas climate change adaptation (e.g., floods and droughts) and environmental degradation (e.g., pollution of a lake) are typically more regional or local in scale as challenges in the management of the respective common pool resources manifest at these scales (IPBES 2019; Nordgren et al. 2016). Loss of biodiversity (e.g., the decline of a certain genetic variant of a species) is somewhere in between with both global and local components.

In this chapter, we argue that although adaptive governance is often conceptualised as an alternative mode of governance to top-down legal regulation and markets, there are numerous connections between all three modes of governance (Ackerman and Stewart 1985; Elliot 1994; Holling and Meffe 1996). While accepting that legal instrumentation cannot be used in a command-and-control fashion to design and prescribe desired futures in responding to challenges produced by complex SET systems, we argue that adaptive governance initiatives are a thoroughly legal phenomenon in the sense that their operation is *surrounded* and *affected* by law. This means that law has important indirect roles to play in adaptive governance, and these roles are in some cases supportive of it and in some other cases impede it. This is something that is often missed in research focused on and propounded by economists, political scientists, and natural scientists focused on the self-organising aspects of adaptive governance. This was particularly true in the early phases of adaptive governance development before 2010, when legal scholars started to actively engage with adaptive governance (see Chapter 2). To help fill that gap, this chapter makes explicit the key legal perspectives to and roles of law in adaptive governance to facilitate a continued interdisciplinary discussion between adaptive governance scholars. The chapter also argues that due to legal systems' own complexity, law will always contain requirements that both impede and support adaptive governance. To make adaptive governance processes work will thus require legal expertise focused on innovating legal solutions for working around undesired but often deeply established substantive and procedural rules, and institutional arrangements.

For the purposes of this chapter, most of our examples in the different sections are from the water sector, but with close connections to both climate change adaptation and biodiversity loss mitigation. The reason for this choice of examples stems from the authors' recent projects that have had an aquatic focus. In the US, Professor Cosens was the PI of Adaptive Water

Governance (AWG) project. In the EU, Professor Soininen is the sub-project PI for BlueAdapt studying adaptive governance of Finnish river basins. Despite the examples being about water, we maintain that the observations made in the chapter about the role of law in adaptive governance of waters are generalisable to other sectors.

The structure of the chapter is as follows. In the second section we rehearse the original criteria for robust adaptive governance as developed by Dietz, Ostrom, and Stern. The third section then analyses the different legal perspectives to adaptive governance and the fourth section maps how law and the criteria for robust adaptive governance interact. The fifth section explains the argument concerning law's own complexity and its incapability of fully endorsing adaptive governance. Conclusions and future research pathways for legal adaptive governance research are provided in the final section.

CRITERIA FOR ROBUST ADAPTIVE GOVERNANCE

Adaptive governance is a theory of how to effectively govern and societally cope with complex and coupled SET-systemic challenges. A key argument of adaptive governance theory is that conventional command and control regulation, or privatisation and markets are not sufficiently effective policy instruments for governing complexity; rather, there is a need for governments and law to support self-organising collaborative and co-creative governance initiatives at the problem scale that are sufficiently nimble to take on the social and ecological nuances (Dietz et al. 2003). Similar arguments about how to effectively govern complex systems had been put forward earlier elsewhere under different banners, such as 'smart regulation' (Gunningham and Sinclair 2017).

The originators of the adaptive governance concept, Thomas Dietz, Elinor Ostrom, and Paul Stern, saw that robust (i.e., effective) governance of the complex social-ecological systems – that they dubbed adaptive governance – is contingent on the following criteria (see Chapter 2):

1. *Sufficient information:* the first criterion establishes that adaptive governance requires sufficient knowledge of the environment at the right decision-making scale, and rules that are congruent with ecological conditions. The information needs to be there to support decision-making at the right time and in a format that decision-makers can understand and include knowledge of uncertainties and values choices present in the production of that information to help manage trade-offs (Dietz et al. 2003, pp. 1908–1909).
2. *Dealing with conflict:* the second criterion requires the establishment of clearly defined boundaries for different user groups participating in adaptive governance, analytic deliberation about the rules, and conflict management mechanisms for resolving conflict about trade-offs. Collaborative processes with participation from central private and public interest groups can help build a shared knowledge-base and reduce potential conflict. When conflicts do arise, there need to be peaceful avenues for resolving them quickly and without excessive financial burden (Dietz et al. 2003, p. 1909).
3. *Inducing rule compliance:* the third criterion requires that the mutually agreed rules are generally followed. Here, increasing the severity of sanctions in time and gravity of the offence is a sound approach. The compliance mechanisms have been observed to rely on informal social enforcement at a local scale and in tightly knit groups, but at larger scales typically require formal legal sanctioning (criminal, civil, or administrative penalties).

A key challenge here is that it is hard to enforce formal rules on problems, such as diffuse pollution or protection of large conservation areas on which local communities may depend for their livelihood. Economic instruments (e.g., subsidies or other market incentives) may help but they typically suffer from not being able to account for factors that are not explicitly in the scope of the economic scheme or that spill over into other sectors or spaces. Voluntary information disclosure can be effective if there are sufficient incentives and transparency for the actors. The challenge with voluntary information disclosure is one of effective sanctioning (Dietz et al. 2003, p. 1909).

4. *Providing infrastructure:* the fourth criterion deals with the physical and technological infrastructure facilitating and setting limits on the degree to which commons can be exploited. Enforcement of access to a conservation site may be easily afforded with cellular monitoring, but prohibitively expensive otherwise. Also, communication infrastructure (e.g., social media platforms), physical infrastructure (e.g., roads, electricity networks, dams), and governance infrastructure (e.g., research and social capital) are significant here (Dietz et al. 2003, p. 1909).

5. *Preparedness for change:* The fifth criterion underscores the need to prepare governance institutions for change and uncertainty. If the rules are fixed, they tend to fail for placing too much confidence on the knowledge basis on which they are built. Moreover, authority should be allocated on various levels of governance in a nested manner, and with institutional variety to help prevent governance failures under changing circumstances (Dietz et al. 2003, pp. 1909–1910).

Adaptive governance and the listed criteria can be approached from several different legal perspectives (public v. private; descriptive v. normative; substantive, procedural, and institutional). We explain these legal perspectives first in the third section before continuing to discuss how law both facilitates and impedes the realisation of the adaptive governance criteria presented in this section.

LAW AS A STEERING WHEEL, BRAKE, AND AN ACCELERATOR FOR ADAPTIVE GOVERNANCE

The Role of Law in Society – Public v. Private Law

In a conventional text-book description of law's role in society, law is used as an instrument for prescribing planned and desired societal and market development top down: law prescribes the rules according to which societies and markets operate, and invokes enforcement mechanisms, such as administrative, civil, and criminal sanctions to deter unlawful activity (Hage 2017, pp. 2–4; Drahos and Krygier 2017, p. 12). The core idea of adaptive governance is antithetical to such a prescriptive starting point: due to the complexity of social-ecological-technological systems, these systems are not entirely, or even mostly, susceptible to conventional top-down legal regulation. Because of complexity, adaptive governance literature argues that governance solutions emerge rather than are planned and prescribed to respond to the practical mitigation and adaptation needs of the society (Ackerman and Stewart 1985; Elliot 1994; Holling and Meffe 1996). Hence, law can be seen as antithetical to adaptive governance.

In our view, understanding law as a mere top-down steering instrument is too narrow and does not do justice to law as a system. While we agree that law's top-down prescriptive roles, especially when considering public law regulating the relationship between the government and private actors (public law), can be seen as antithetical to adaptive governance, what is often overlooked is that private law regulating the relationships between private actors fits neatly with the idea of emerging and self-organising adaptive governance. People and companies are free to e.g., conclude contracts at will provided they operate within the limits of the law. Moreover, rather than seeing adaptive governance as a misfit to top-down regulation, it needs to be recognised that adaptive governance also operates in the context created by those laws. In other words, the forms of organisation, procedures, and substantive outcomes of adaptive governance are depended on and motivated – at least to some extent – by legal regulation.

Taking an example from environmental law, which is mostly public law regulating the relationship of governmental and private actors, law has conventionally (or rather, historically) been seen as a prescriptive, top-down instrument that attempts to lay down the environmental safeguards and operating norms, in line with the environmental law principles such as precautionary principle, best available technology, and best environmental practice (Fisher 2017, pp. 36–47). In line with such understanding, the legislator is seen as a single authority acting with the assumption that it has the capacity to lay down the exact rules, technological standards, and operative conditions for resolving environmental issues, such as industrial pollution, that other actors – administrative bodies, operators and citizens – need to comply with (Fisher 2017, pp. 34–47). Further, one of the key features of such conventional understanding of environmental law is that it is general, preventing the legislator from adopting entirely context- or situation-specific regulation.

However, stepping out of a narrow, conventional view of environmental law and looking at different fields of law that pertain to the human–environmental interface, we can see that perspective to law and law's role in society is more diverse. For example, in the field of property law regulating e.g., land and natural resources ownership, law is seen rather as a facilitator of private commercial, family, or institutional relationships than a commander and authority over their substance (Akkermans 2017, p. 82). In fact, market approaches to natural resource governance are also founded on law, where public law forms a stable societal context and private law supports market activities within that context (concept of property, contract, and so on). By looking at the law beyond its conventional public law steering role, we can see that law in general is not as antithetical to adaptive governance as it first seems.

In the next section, we discuss two foundational sets of legal perspectives: first, the separation between descriptive and normative perspective to law, and then law as substance, process, and institution. We rely on many of these categories later in the chapter when analysing how law interacts with the adaptive governance criteria established in the second section. The said distinctions are put forward especially for the benefit of an interdisciplinary audience not acquainted with the law.

Descriptive and Normative Perspectives to Law

Law in adaptive governance can be looked at both from descriptive and normative perspectives. *Descriptive perspectives* seek to describe how a particular legal system (e.g., Finnish, EU, or US law) bounds the process or the possible outcomes of adaptive governance. From a descriptive legal perspective, it may be that an adaptive governance process is geared toward a goal that will not be feasible in an existing legal setting, or that the outcome is subject to judicial review that may undermine the whole process. The key question asked in the descriptive context is: *how does* the law regulate the different aspects (e.g., the process and outcomes) of adaptive governance? The point of such a legal perspective is to make explicit how existing laws and legal institutions impede and promote adaptive governance.

Our first example is EU water law as a facilitator of adaptive governance. In 2015, the Court of Justice of the European Union (CJEU) issued the so-called *Weser*-judgment (C-461/13) concerning the water management objectives of the EU Water Framework Directive (WFD) (Rijswick and Backes 2015). In Finland, one of the key challenges of managing river basins toward multiple goals is that almost all the rivers had been dammed for hydropower during the 20th century. Despite major governmental and private effort to restore rivers and introduce fishways and other measures to mitigate the harm of hydropower dams to other interests, there had been slim results for reallocating river flows (Soininen et al. 2017). Arguably, a key reason for this has been the strongly legally protected status of hydropower operators and dams resulting in a situation, where the operators did not have sufficient incentives to participate in adaptive governance processes discussing the multiple uses of rivers (Söderasp and Petterson 2019, pp. 273–275). As the legal setting has come to emphasise the ecological status of waters alongside power generation through the WFD, and the legal protections of hydropower operators have partially shifted with the *Weser*-judgment, there has been a spur of adaptive governance initiatives in river basins across Finland with hydropower operators actively engaging and negotiating the reallocation of river flows. Moreover, the *Weser*-case opened discussion about entirely new instruments, such as ecological offsetting initiatives, to reconcile water use projects and with the need to preserving water status (Kyrönviita et al. 2021, pp. 262–264).

Our second example is law impeding adaptive governance in the US Everglades, which became highly degraded due to past water diversion projects and agricultural pollution. Federal and state legislation set up a collaborative process for employing adaptive management in a massive 30-year restoration effort known as the Comprehensive Everglades Restoration Plan (CERP) in 2000. The complexity of both the ecosystem and the restoration led to some interest groups being dissatisfied with CERP's progress, and other being dissatisfied by the planned outcomes. They turned to the courts, and a relentless proliferation of litigation under rigid, narrowly focused statutory schemes and provisions slowed progress and altered plans for comprehensive restoration. The statutes, which were not designed with restoration of the magnitude of the CERP in mind, imposed procedural impact assessment requirements and substantive standards the litigants used to pick away at details and bog down the agencies. The legislation authorising the CERP did not address how to manage the conditions regulated in the other laws and thus the courts did not have the discretion to apply them adaptively (Gunderson et al. 2019). A 2012 assessment by the National Academy of Sciences concluded that core restoration measures were far behind schedule and estimated that the project would take 50 years to complete.

The two examples dealt with situations in which the existing legal setting supported (reallocation of river flows in Finland) or impeded (US Everglades) adaptive governance without either being the explicit purpose of the law. These are descriptive examples of how law interacts with adaptive governance whether we like it or not (i.e., whether adaptive governance is designed to interact with law or not).

If, however, one is interested in intentional changes to the law to facilitate and speed up adaptive governance initiatives and processes, one takes a normative perspective to law. The key question asked in the normative context is: *what should* the law be like to facilitate and speed up adaptive governance? (Cosens et al. 2020, p. 1723). These normative legal questions started to emerge when legal scholars entered the adaptive governance discussion in 2010 (Cosens et al. 2020, p. 1718). In this context, legal research has established several criteria that law should meet in order to support adaptive governance better (Cosens et al. 2020). We will return to these in more detail later in the chapter.

The descriptive and normative perspectives to law and legal analysis can be summarised as shown in Figure 3.1.

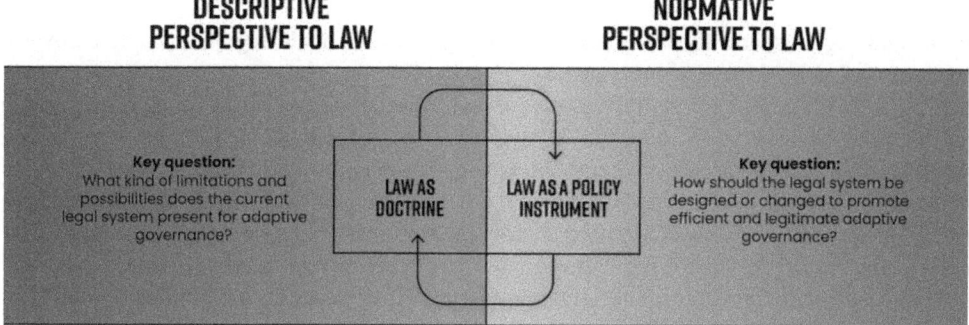

Figure 3.1   *The descriptive and normative perspectives to law in the context of adaptive governance*

Continuing further, both the descriptive and normative legal perspectives can vary in terms of which aspects of the law the analysis focuses on. Three key legal aspects are (1) substantive; (2) procedural; and (3) institutional. These are discussed in the next sub-sections.

Substantive Law

Substantive legal aspects focus on how the law regulates or should regulate the outcomes of adaptive governance, or other human uses and processes affecting it (Bosselmann 2013; Kotzé 2013), as well as striking the balance between the role of public and private actors. Generally, public law regulates many aspects of the human–environment relationship, providing substantive rules and goals for e.g., land-use and planning; emissions to air, water, and soil; equitable use of natural resources, such as mining minerals, water, wood, fish, and game and so on. Law also regulates production of goods, e.g., through chemicals regulation and technical standards. Moreover, law protects certain species, habitats, and areas, and considerably limits the use of land and natural resources in these areas. In contrast, private law facilitating market innovation usually does not prescribe substantive outcomes or specific rules, apart from minimum safeguards for values that are deemed to necessitate legal protection, such as consumer protection. The substantive aspects also contain property law and law of contracts, which affect the use of natural resources and their adaptive governance.

As noted in Chapter 1 of this *Handbook*, because there is no guarantee that adaptive governance led by private actors will act in the public good, it is essential to have a role for government in establishing goals and monitoring progress toward those goals (Chapter 2). In striking the balance between public and private roles, adaptive governance requires steering toward a public goal, but more room for innovation and self-organisation than allowed in the typical public law regulatory approach, and less free-wheeling than a market approach. The various public and private fields of law – and more – offer adaptive governance initiatives various recognised legal avenues for development. In the aggregate, such legal requirements form the legal-normative for basis and limits within which adaptive governance must take place unless the law is changed.

Procedural Law

Procedural legal aspects focus on how the law regulates or should regulate adaptive governance, and what kind of legal processes are connected to the adaptive governance process at hand. Typical questions are the factual basis on which the process is established, which actors are involved in the process, how the decision-making power is divided between the actors, who can challenge the process in court and when, how open must collaborative meetings and documents be to the general public, and what are the effects of decisions on the actors taking part in the process and to society more broadly (Waldron 2010; Cosens et al. 2020, p. 1730). Here again, typical public law regulation entails prescribed, formal processes, whereas private law often only provides loose, minimum requirements for enacting certain legal procedures (such as establishing a contractual relationship).

Adaptive governance favours a more facilitative role for government while ceding the choice of means to achieve the common goal to collaborative, or private actors. Some procedural aspects of adaptive governance can be freely agreed upon. An example is when a landowner willingly admits the use of her land for conservation or other purposes agreed on in the adaptive governance process. Some aspects of the process may, however, be limited by the law.

Institutional Law

Institutional legal aspects focus on how law divides or should divide substantive and procedural power between governmental actors, such as the legislative, executive, and judicial branches of government (Fuller 1969). Adaptive governance recognises the distribution of power among the three branches of government, as we note, but also the distribution between government and private institutions. One key question here is that when the outcome of an adaptive governance process would for instance require changes to existing environmental or natural resource permits, there are typically limitations on who can change the permits and how. In Finland, for instance, adaptive governance processes have no bearing on the permits granted by and belonging to the legally established mandate of the governmental permitting authorities. While this is arguably a challenge for adaptive governance, it would require a considerable change in the Finnish legal-institutional structures to grant formal decision-making powers to adaptive governance initiatives. Moreover, the institutional aspects also contain the law on associations, corporations, trusts, and other organisational forms, how actors can organise in forms that can make legal acts/transactions (e.g., enter a contract) and take on duties (e.g., permit holder position). These in turn may be key in facilitating adaptive governance.

Summary

The substantive, procedural, and institutional aspects of law can both support and impede adaptive governance while steering it. This is illustrated and summarised in Figure 3.2. This legal 'car' can be looked at from a descriptive perspective (i.e., what kind of a car do we currently have), or a normative perspective (i.e., what kind of a car we would like to have). The remainder of the chapter uses Figure 3.2 as an analytical lens to see the how law in *descriptive* terms surrounds adaptive governance.

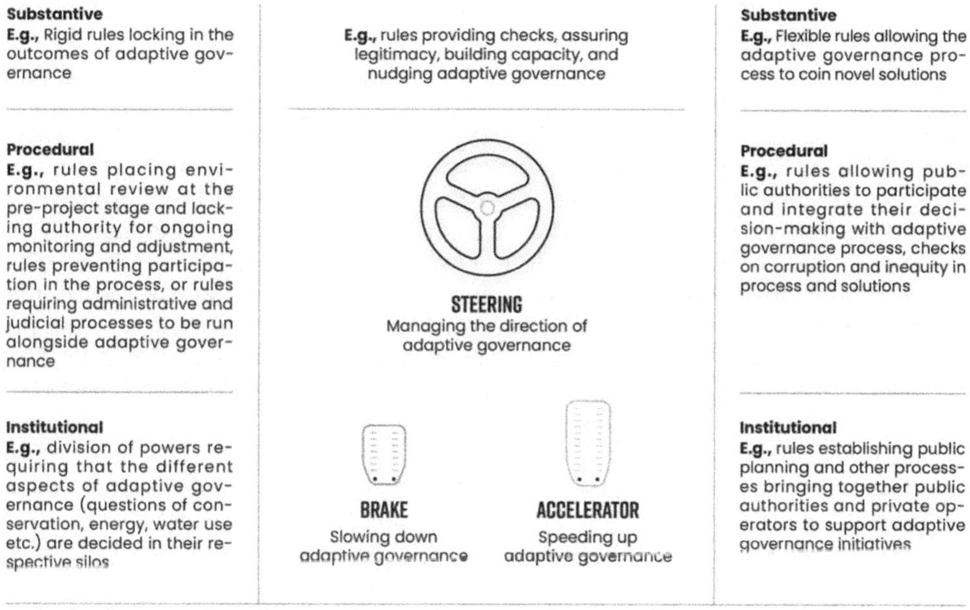

Substantive
E.g., Rigid rules locking in the outcomes of adaptive governance

E.g., rules providing checks, assuring legitimacy, building capacity, and nudging adaptive governance

Substantive
E.g., Flexible rules allowing the adaptive governance process to coin novel solutions

Procedural
E.g., rules placing environmental review at the pre-project stage and lacking authority for ongoing monitoring and adjustment, rules preventing participation in the process, or rules requiring administrative and judicial processes to be run alongside adaptive governance

STEERING
Managing the direction of adaptive governance

Procedural
E.g., rules allowing public authorities to participate and integrate their decision-making with adaptive governance process, checks on corruption and inequity in process and solutions

Institutional
E.g., division of powers requiring that the different aspects of adaptive governance (questions of conservation, energy, water use etc.) are decided in their respective silos

BRAKE
Slowing down adaptive governance

ACCELERATOR
Speeding up adaptive governance

Institutional
E.g., rules establishing public planning and other processes bringing together public authorities and private operators to support adaptive governance initiatives

Figure 3.2   *Substantive, procedural, and institutional roles of law steering, braking, and accelerating adaptive governance*

Now that we have clarified the descriptive and normative perspectives to law on the one hand, and the substantive, procedural, and institutional factors steering, supporting, and impeding adaptive governance on the other, the next section discusses how the different legal factors interact with the robust adaptive governance criteria developed by Dietz, Ostrom, and Stern.

INTERACTIONS BETWEEN LAW AND ADAPTIVE GOVERNANCE

Sufficient Information

The first criterion requires sufficient environmental information to ground the adaptive governance processes. As adaptive governance is particularly apt for managing complex problems with high uncertainty, there is a need for monitoring and ongoing assessment, and a movement of judicial review away from the pre-planning stage to the progress toward goal stage.

Law typically both promotes and impedes the accumulation of sufficient information for the adaptive governance process. Here, substantive aspects of law relate to in particular the public's and stakeholders' rights to (environmental) information and, contrarily, the confidentiality of information based on i.e., the protection of corporate immaterial rights and trade secrets. The procedural legal aspects regulate for instance the processes and responsibilities for producing information for administrative decision-making, as well as the extent of information and investigation required for administrative decisions. Further, the law may establish information generation infrastructures and dictate the extent to which they are integrated in the management processes.

EU

From the substantive point of view, the EU is a party to the Århus Convention (Convention on access to information, public participation in decision-making and access to justice in environmental matters, done at Aarhus, Denmark 26 June 1998) that contains substantive rights for the public to environmental information collected by the public authorities. For the implementation of the Convention, the EU has adopted the Environmental Information Directive (2003/4/EC) that aims to ensure that environmental information is systematically available and distributed to the public. On the procedural side, for instance, the Environmental Impact Assessments (EIA, 2014/52/EC and SEA, 2001/42/EC) connected to permitting are a good example of processes geared towards producing information on the environmental impacts of new developments and their relevant alternatives to support administrative decision-making. Although such EIA processes are typically one-time processes connected to plans and permits and are not as such the focus of adaptive governance, the information produced in EIAs may later be used also in adaptive governance processes. Institutionally, EU law puts forward several management frameworks on water and marine environment, the Water Framework Directive, the Marine Strategy Framework Directive (MSFD) and the Maritime Spatial Planning Directive, that require EU member states to establish processes for monitoring the status of waters, which are then integrated in the formulation of management policies and planning the future uses of the basins. Such information can also be highly beneficial for adaptive governance.

Similarly, the US National Environmental Policy Act (NEPA) requires federal agencies to provide an interdisciplinary scientific report to the public on the environmental impact of a proposed action and alternatives to the action. This is referred to as an Environmental Impact Statement (EIS). The outcome of the study does not require the federal agency to choose the most environmentally benign alternative or to mitigate impacts. It does, however, arm the public with information that can be used in the political process to seek changes to the project. The agency must allow a period of public comment and respond to those comments when it issues its final Record of Decision (ROD). Among the types of comments the public may provide are, inadequacy of the science and failure to use the best available science. Once the final ROD is released, citizens may sue, challenging the adequacy or process of the EIS. Unfortunately, NEPA does not require ongoing monitoring and adjustment once the federal action begins. Thus, no process for learning and adjustment occurs.

Dealing with Conflict

The second criterion requires the establishment of clearly defined boundaries for different user groups participating in adaptive governance, and procedures for the settlement of disputes. Key legal questions deal with how to ensure that the ad hoc participation of private actors in adaptive governance does not lead to corruption and unjust outcomes (Cosens et al. 2020, pp. 1729, 1731). Legal systems typically contain three main avenues for managing conflict. Administrative conflict resolution relates to a particular process, such as enforcing existing administrative legal requirements of a permit holder. Civil conflict resolution typically deals with compensation for damages, and criminal conflict resolution with the prosecution of crimes.

From the substantive law point of view this relates to striking a balance between competing uses of the environment and natural resources, as well as of technological, financial, and cultural resources in the substantive rules and standards provided in the law. Procedural aspects relevant to dealing with conflicts include e.g., rules dictating the grounds for initiating administrative or legal processes and consulting the parties during the process. Institutional aspects entail defining legal boundaries for the use of powers of the administration, establishing the judicial review systems, and determining conditions on the availability of these processes. The judicial system provides judicial review to secure that there is an independent body to decide entrenched conflicts that cannot be defused by other, voluntary, or collaborative means, or even at the first instance legal proceedings.

EU

The EU key directives establishing the frameworks for managing the water and marine resources contain flexibility in the substantive norms to reconcile conflicting interests related to these resources. The Water Framework Directive's objectives are ecology-oriented, but they are coupled with an exemption regime that allow integrating social, economic, and technological considerations in the objectives (Soininen and Platjouw 2018, p. 33). In turn, the Marine Strategy Framework Directive's objectives include also economic and social aspects together with ecological resilience, but the Directive also provides an exemption regime (MSFD Article 3(5) and 14). These Directives, however, leave considerable institutional and procedural discretion to the EU member states to decide the exact processes for implementation, which means that depending on the structure of national laws and the choices made in the implementation, conflicts arising in making management decisions can be dealt with through national administrative or civil processes, or even directly in adaptive governance processes. All the Directives also build on the idea that they are implemented in collaboration with regional and local actors, based on sufficient monitoring data and iterated and reviewed every six years.

US

The following example illustrates that conflict resolution mechanisms are useless if those involved do not have the capacity to use them and emphasises the role law can play in helping build that capacity. The stage was set for the recent efforts in the US to resolve disputes over the scope and use of Native American rights to water by a US Supreme Court case that recognised implied rights to water if water was necessary to fulfil the purposes of a Treaty (*Winters v. United States*, 207 US 564 (1908)). These water rights would be superior to those of settlers that were moving into ceded territory on shared watercourses. This ruling was made possible by the legal doctrine recognising the federal government as 'trustee' for the tribes. Without the aid of the trustee, it would have been years before most tribes had the capacity to pursue such a suit. The Court incorporated the legal concept that ambiguous language in a treaty memorialised in the language of one party will be interpreted in favour of the other party, into its canons of construction for Native American treaties by interpreting the treaty as the tribe would have understood it. In the latter half of the 20th century interest grew among states and water users in placing bounds on the scope and use of these superior water rights, and among tribes in obtaining funding to develop their water. In a number of states, processes were developed for a negotiated solution that would lead to 'wet' water for tribes (as opposed to a water right on paper as the result of litigation). Federal funding and participation again built tribal capacity to bring their own solutions to the table. In several cases, formal mediation facilitated dialogue between tribes and their neighbours. Federal, state, and tribal legislative processes institutionalised settlements. Federal and state contributions to settlement made water development possible.

Inducing Rule Compliance

The third criterion requires that the mutually agreed rules are generally followed. From a legal perspective, this may mean that the results of adaptive governance process are institutionalised in one way or another (Cosens et al. 2020, p. 1731). This means integrating adaptive governance in the legal institutions provided by law, including public planning and management processes, administrative decisions, or establishing contractual relationships between the participants of the adaptive governance process that are dictated with institutional aspects of law. Institutionalisation brings with it possibilities to coerce rule compliance by having legal avenues to enforce the agreed rules of adaptive governance. Substantive legal aspects related to this include the substantive norms applicable in the relevant legal institutions, such as substantive rules on permitting processes or contract law, or law on the accountability of actors such as corporate social and environmental sustainability criteria; in other words, substantive law provides what rules can be subject to coerced compliance. Procedurally, the law provides legal processes for coercing rule compliance depending on the legal institution where adaptive governance is integrated, such as administrative processes and sanctions, civil processes for enforcing contractual or tort obligations, and criminal processes that can relate to e.g., criminal liability for environmental damages.

EU

Substantive water law related to rules that adaptive governance participants need to comply with includes for instance the ecological criteria stemming from the Water Framework Directive and Finnish water law dealing with specific requirements for water quality and quantity. Further, the EU Environmental Liability Directive (2004/35/EC) provides a framework of substantive and procedural rules on when operators are to be held liable for water damages that member states are required to force them to prevent, mitigate, and remedy through administrative sanctions.

US

Implementation of the US Endangered Species Act, which prohibits causing injury to protected species except as authorised, uses a permitting regime that can be triggered by substantial modification of habitat. Land developers must prepare a Habitat Conservation Plan outlining steps to minimise and mitigate harm caused to the species and incorporating adaptive management processes for foreseeable changes in conditions. In practice, plan implementation standards and procedures are embodied in a contractual Implementation Agreement (16 U.S.C. 1539).

Providing Infrastructure

The fourth criterion deals with the physical and technological, or even governance infrastructure facilitating and setting limits to the degree at which commons are exploited. Substantive legal requirements can push for introducing new technical requirements to existing operations through re-evaluation of authorisations and permits or even wider infrastructural changes, which is the case for instance in the 'electrification' of societies due to climate change mitigation. Procedurally, the question of physical infrastructure may deal with e.g., whether and in what process it is possible to challenge existing natural resource allocations. In terms of the knowledge and monitoring infrastructure, the criterion is closely connected to the legal questions raised in the context of the first criterion, sufficient information. Institutional aspects of law include the governance infrastructure for monitoring and research.

EU

In the EU, a prominent example of a legal development explicitly facilitating adaptive governance and seeking to holistically govern questions of physical, technological, and governance infrastructure is the adoption of the Maritime Spatial Planning Directive (MSPD, 2014/89/EU) in 2014. The MSPD establishes a framework for spatial planning processes that are run and adapted to the circumstances of the different EU member states and the marine areas located in them (Preamble 22 of the MSFD). The core idea of the spatial planning framework is that regional public authorities invite public and private stakeholders from various sectors ranging from shipping to environmental protection to deliberate and establish the desired uses of marine spaces responding to the environmental, social, and economic challenges and needs in the area (Soininen 2015). The outcomes of these processes can vary with specific ecological, social, and economic needs and interests present in the area, and promoted by the participants. The MSPD processes also establish knowledge co-production between stakeholders to secure the shared knowledge-basis in the process.

US

Since the 1970s, a number of western states have spent considerable resources on adjudication of water rights to create comprehensive databases on who has a right to use water, for what, where, and when. In the state of Idaho, the coincident availability of Geographic Information Systems facilitated transparency in the process and created an interactive map-view database that anyone may access. The ready availability of this information along with its use for state and university modelling of the impact of groundwater pumping on surface water resources has been extremely useful in negotiated settlement of water disputes among irrigation districts in southern Idaho.

Preparedness for Change

The fifth criterion underscores the need to prepare governance institutions for change and uncertainty and is also closely connected to the sufficient information criterion discussed earlier as preparedness builds on past knowledge. Preparedness for change can relate to all the substantive, procedural, and institutional aspects of law from the perspective of how well the legal rules facilitate societal adaptation on the one hand, and on the other hand how the rules themselves can adapt to social-ecological-technological change.

Substantively, preparedness for change typically requires flexible legal standards allowing public managers to change past plans, permits, and other decisions to facilitate the outcomes of adaptive governance processes seeking to cope with changing circumstances (Cosens et al. 2020, pp. 1729–1730). Procedurally, there may be legal obligations for public authorities to participate in adaptive governance, or in some cases, limitations for such participation. Institutionally, public authority should be nested on various levels of governance and with institutional variety to help prevent governance failures under changing circumstances.

EU

In the EU, the core substantive legal provisions of the EU Water Framework Directive and the Marine Strategy Framework Directive are established in the form of environmental objectives that do not prescribe any detailed substantive rules but entail significant flexibility for the member states to decide on more specific rules on the implementation of the objectives in different water sectors. The objectives are thus quite flexible to facilitate adaption and the Directive's even contain mechanisms to adapt the objectives themselves in accordance with e.g., changes in environmental conditions induced by changing climate (Puharinen 2021). Procedurally, both Directives employ a programmatic approach mandating member states to take steps in formulating management approaches in a cyclical planning process geared towards adapting the knowledge-base and management choices during each cycle. However, it is a matter of national law if and how well the structures for taking management decisions facilitate adaptation; for instance, national permitting laws may enshrine strong permanence of permits and authorisations with only restricted possibilities of reviewing and adapting these decisions to change or new knowledge. Institutionally, in EU law, the nested approach is dubbed subsidiarity which means that authority to manage e.g., natural resources remain at the lowest spatial level possible.

US

In the United States, western water law is considered one of the most rigid legal systems with little room for flexibility as climate change leads to increasingly long and deep drought. Water is allocated to private interests in order of priority established by when the water was first put to use. During times of shortage, senior users have their full right satisfied, and junior users may receive nothing. The right is considered a property 'usufructry' right, thus altering this system of priority would invoke the Takings clause found in both the federal and state constitutions, requiring just compensation for governmental taking of private property. Nevertheless, this seemingly unchangeable system of water allocation has seen some increase in flexibility in recent years. The property right to water extends only to the amount of water use that is 'reasonable', and what is reasonable changes over time as technology, economics, supply, and demand change. This concept has always been an overlay on western water law but had not seen the full light of day until recent years of extended drought.

The reasonable use doctrine has seen its greatest use in recent years in Idaho to achieve greater equity between interconnected surface (generally older and thus senior) and ground-water (generally junior) rights. The Idaho courts have upheld agency enforcement of seniority that requires a senior water user to first provide evidence of reasonable use (*American Falls Reservoir v. Idaho Department of Water Resources*, 154 P.3d 433 (Idaho 2007); *Clear Springs Foods, Inc. v. Spackman*, 252 P.3d. 71 (Idaho 2011)) taking into account factors that include: (a) the amount of water available in the source from which the water right is diverted; (b) the effort or expense of the holder of the water right to divert water from the source; (c) whether the exercise of junior-priority ground water rights individually or collectively affects the quantity and timing of when water is available to, and the cost of exercising, a senior-priority surface or ground water right. This may include the seasonal as well as the multi-year and cumulative impacts of all ground water withdrawals from the area having a common ground water supply; (d) if for irrigation, the rate of diversion compared to the acreage of land served, the annual volume of water diverted, the system diversion and conveyance efficiency, and the method of irrigation water application; (e) the amount of water being diverted and used compared to the water rights; (f) the existence of water measuring and recording devices; (g) the extent to which the requirements of the holder of a senior-priority water right could be met with the user's existing facilities and water supplies by employing reasonable diversion and conveyance efficiency and conservation practices; provided, however, the holder of a surface water storage right shall be entitled to maintain a reasonable amount of carry-over storage to assure water supplies for future dry years. In determining a reasonable amount of carry-over storage water, the Director shall consider the average annual rate of fill of storage reservoirs and the average annual carry-over for prior comparable water conditions and the projected water supply for the system; (h) the extent to which the requirements of the senior-priority surface water right could be met using alternate reasonable means of diversion or alternate points of diversion, including the construction of wells or the use of existing wells to divert and use water from the area having a common ground water supply under the petitioner's surface water right priority (Idaho Administrative Code 37.03.11.42). The enforcement of these factors has led to increased efficiency as well as novel, self-organised solutions. It remains to be seen whether 'reasonable use' is sufficiently flexible for droughts to come.

Now that we have discussed how the substantive, procedural, and institutional aspects of law interact (steer, brake, and accelerate) with adaptive governance, the next section discusses legal systems' complexity as a key limitation for designing laws supporting adaptive governance with any impediments.

LAW AS A COMPLEX SYSTEM: REASON WHY LAW CANNOT BE DESIGNED TO PRESCRIBE ADAPTIVE GOVERNANCE

Normative legal research seeking to establish 'ideal' legal criteria for adaptive governance is bounded by the complexity of the legal system. A developed and still growing body of legal and policy scholarship is mapping key concepts of complexity science onto governance and legal systems (Ruhl and Katz 2015; Ruhl et al. 2017; Murray et al. 2019). The components of the legal system comprise a broad diversity of institutions – the organisations of people who make, interpret, and enforce laws – and of instruments – the laws, regulations, cases, and related legal content the institutions produce. These components are interconnected and interactive. Institutions are interconnected through structures and rules, such as hierarchies of courts and legislative creation and oversight of agencies, and they interact in forums such as judicial trials, legislative hearings and debates, and agency rulemakings. The instruments are also interconnected through mechanisms such as code structures, and they interact through cross-references and other devices. The highly interconnected architecture of such a system drives the way it behaves over time. An agency adopts a rule, which prompts another agency to enforce a different rule, which leads to litigation before a judge, who issues an opinion overruled by a higher court, which prompts a legislature to enact a new statute, and so on. The institutional agents follow procedural and substantive rules, but there is no central controller pulling all the strings. There are network hierarchies for various institutions (e.g., tiers of courts), and some governance systems are more centralised than others, yet there is no master agent governing the entirety of the legal system. This complex legal system is in turn interconnected with and influenced by other social systems (the economy; health care; etc.) and physical systems (water regimes; climate change) with which it co-evolves.

The complexity of legal systems means that a wholesale legal reform to cater for adaptive governance is unlikely, or altogether impossible (Dietz et al. 2003; Verbong and Loorbach 2012, p. 15; Ruhl et al. 2017; Garmestani et al. 2019; Patterson et al. 2021; Soininen et al. 2021). Governance emerges from the inputs of these institutional actors, rather than being designed to prescribe a certain future state of societal affairs. A global, regional, or national legislature, for instance, even if endowed with sufficient political will to facilitate adaptive governance to the fullest, is typically faced with various legal boundaries limiting their mandate and policy choices. These boundaries include, among others, constitutional requirements such as the separation of powers between the different branches and levels of government (Fuller 1969; Raz 1979; Waldron 2010, pp. 5–6); demanding due process and administrative requirements in implementing transformative legal initiatives (Fuller 1969; Raz 1979; Waldron 2010, pp. 5–6); and substantive rights, such as protection of property and protection of legitimate expectations concerning once granted authorisations to use natural resources (Kotzé 2013, p. 135; Bosselmann 2013, p. 42). These are all tried elements of the rule of law which is a key feature of modern legal systems. The archetypical legal instrumentation discussed here (international agreements, laws, and regulations) does not have the power to quickly change the deeper, cultural elements of legal systems.

The above listed cultural elements of modern legal systems evolve much more slowly than the surface level of legal instruments that are currently being used to facilitate adaptive governance (Tuori 2016). The rule of law establishes legitimate hurdles to adaptive governance that cannot be overcome by any flick-of-the-switch legal reform. Indeed, such attempts to intervene with perceived silver bullet solutions can backfire with unintended consequences. In fact, the whole concept of adaptive governance is that law and government alone are not up to the challenge of complexity in SET systems undergoing rapid change. The feasibility of law fully providing or supporting adaptive governance is both questionable and, by definition, the antithesis of adaptive governance. Managing change in complex SET systems is the responsibility of both society and government.

Even though legal systems cannot be fully designed to facilitate adaptive governance, there are multiple low-hanging fruits that the legislative and executive branches can pick to facilitate adaptive governance. Legal research on adaptive governance has established that law has important roles to play in catalysing, facilitating, steering, and providing oversight for adaptive governance (Cosens et al. 2020, pp. 1727–1731). In other words, law provides a – hopefully legitimate – setting within which adaptive governance can run its course in seeking to govern complex systems.

DISCUSSION AND CONCLUSIONS

Adaptive governance is surrounded by law, and law is a key component in its success (either in the positive opening a window of opportunity for it, helping scale, and institutionalise it, or otherwise supporting it), and at other times law may be the single biggest obstacle for adaptive governance's success. Against this background, law's roles can be understood as the substantive, procedural, and institutional legal requirements steering, braking, and accelerating adaptive governance as suggested in Figure 3.2. These different aspects can be studied from descriptive (existing law, *de lege lata*) and normative (ideal law, *de lege ferenda*) legal perspectives. Due to law's complexity, however, modern complex legal systems will always contain rules that both impede and support adaptive governance. In other words, legal systems cannot be designed to dictate and prescribe adaptive governance, they can only be designed to facilitate the emergence of adaptive governance.

The last decade of adaptive governance and legal scholarship has sought to reimagine law in a way that would be supportive of adaptive governance like Dietz, Ostrom, and Stern imagined. The different roles of law have also started to attract considerable empirical research (Cosens and Gunderson 2018). One important avenue for future legal research on adaptive governance is to provide a fuller account of how legal systems interact with adaptive governance beyond the environmental and natural resources law, to capture the full scope of adaptive governance in SET systems. Adaptive governance discussions have conventionally attracted environmental and natural resource law scholars with a public law background, but in the future, there is a need to bring in legal scholars with expertise on various fields of law, including different branches of private law, such as contract law, property law, tort law, and corporate law into the scene.

REFERENCES

Ackerman, B. 2017. Property law. In Hage, J., Waltermann, A., and Akkermans, B. (eds) *Introduction to Law*, Dordrecht, Springer, pp. 79–108.
Ackerman, B. and Stewart, R. B. 1985. Reforming environmental law, *Stanford Law Review*, 37, 41333.
Bosselmann, K. 2013. Grounding the rule of law. In Voigt, C. (ed.) *Rule of Law for Nature. New Dimensions and Ideas in Environmental Law*, Cambridge, Cambridge University Press, pp. 75–93.
Cosens, B. and Chaffin, C. 2016. Adaptive governance of water resources shared with indigenous peoples: the role of law. Special Issue: 'Water governance, stakeholder engagement, and sustainable water resources management', *Water*, 8, 3, 97. http://www.mdpi.com/2073-4441/8/3/97/html.
Cosens, B. and Gunderson, L. (eds) 2018. *Practical Panarchy for Adaptive Water Governance: Linking Law to Social-ecological Resilience*, Dordrecht, Springer.
Cosens, B., Ruhl, J. B., Soininen, N., and Gunderson, L. 2020. Designing law to enable adaptive governance of modern wicked problems, *Vanderbilt Law Review*, 73, 6, 1687–1732.
Cosens, B., Ruhl, J. B., Soininen, N., Gunderson, L., Belinskij, A., Blenckner, T., Camacho, A. E., Chaffin, B. C., Kundis, C. R., Doremus, H., Glicksman, R., Heiskanen, A.-S., Larson, R., and Similä,

J. 2021. Governing complexity: integrating science, governance, and law to manage accelerating change in the globalized commons, *PNAS*, 118, 36.

Dietz, T., Ostrom, E., and Stern, P. C. 2003. The struggle to govern the commons. *Science*, 302, 1907–1912.

Drahos, P. and Krygier M. 2017. Regulation, institutions and networks. In Drahos, P. (ed.) *Regulatory Theory: Foundations and Applications*, Canberra, ANU, pp. 1–23.

Elliot, E. 1994. Environmental TQM: anatomy of a pollution control program that works! *Michigan Law Review*, 92, 1840–1849.

Fisher, E. 2017. *Environmental Law: A Very Short Introduction*, Oxford, Oxford University Press.

Folke, C., Hahn, T., Olsson, P., and Norberg, J. 2005. Adaptive governance of social-ecological systems, *Annual Review of Environment and Resources*, 30, 441–473.

Fuller, L. L. 1969. *The Morality of Law*. Revised edn, New Haven, Yale University Press.

Garmestani, A., Ruhl, J. B, Chaffin, B. C., Craig, R. K., van Rijswick, H. F. M. W, Angeler, D. G., Folke, C., Gunderson, L., Twidwell, D. and Allen, C. R. 2019. Untapped capacity for resilience in environmental law. *Proceedings of the National Academy of Sciences of the United States of America*, 116, 40, 19899–19904.

Gunderson, L. H., Garmestani, A., Rizzardi, K. W., Ruhl, J. B., and Light, A., 2019. Escaping a rigidity trap: governance and adaptive capacity to climate change in the Everglades Social ecological system, *Idaho L. Rev.*, 51, 127. https://digitalcommons.law.uidaho.edu/idaho-law-review/vol51/iss1/4.

Gunningham, N. and Sinclair, D. 2017. Smart regulation. In Drahos, P. (ed.) *Regulatory Theory: Foundations and Applications*, Canberra, ANU Press, p. 133–48.

Hage, J. 2017. Sources of law. In Hage, J., Waltermann, A., and Akkermans, B. (eds) *Introduction to Law*, Dordrecht, Springer, pp. 1–20.

Holling, C. S. and Meffe, G. K. 1996. Command and control and the pathology of natural resource management, *Conservation Biology*, 10, 2, 328–337.

IPBES. 2019. Summary for policymakers of the global assessment report on biodiversity and ecosystem services of the Intergovernmental Science-Policy Platform on Biodiversity and Ecosystem Services. https://doi.org/10.5281/zenodo.3553579.

IPCC. 2021. Summary for policymakers. In *Climate Change 2021: The Physical Science Basis*. https://www.ipcc.ch/report/ar6/wg1/downloads/report/IPCC_AR6_WGI_SPM.pdf.

Kotzé, L. 2013. Sustainable development and rule of law for nature. In Voigt, C. (ed) *Rule of Law for Nature. New Dimensions and Ideas in Environmental Law*, Cambridge, Cambridge University Press, pp. 130–145.

Kyrönviita, J., Langlet, D., Soininen, N., Belinskij, A., Kymenvaara, S., and Margrethe Basse, E. 2021. Achieving blue growth post-Weser: a study of aquaculture regulation in the Nordic region, *Journal for European Environmental & Planning Law*, 18, 256–274.

Murray, J., Webb, T., and Wheatly, S. 2019. *Complexity Theory and Law. Mapping an Emergent Jurisprudence*, Abingdon, Routledge.

Nordgren, J., Stults, M., and Meerow, S. 2016. Supporting local climate change adaptation: where we are and where we need to go, *Environmental Science & Policy*, 66, 344–352.

Pahl-Wostl, C., Lebel, L., Knieper, C., and Nikitina, E. 2012. From applying panaceas to mastering complexity: toward adaptive water governance in river basins, *Environmental Science & Policy*, 23, 24–34.

Patterson, J., Soininen, N., Collier, M., and Raymond, C. 2021. Finding feasible action towards urban transformations. *NPJ Urban Sustainability*, 1, 28, https://doi.org/10.1038/s42949-021-00029-7.

McPhearson, T., Raymond, C. M., Gulsrud, N., Albert, C., Coles, N., Fagerholm, N., Nagatsu, M., Olafsson, A. S., Soininen, N., and Vierikko, K. 2021. Radical changes are needed for transformations to a good Anthropocene, *NPJ Urban* Sustainability, 1, 5, https://doi.org/10.1038/s42949-021-00017-x.

Puharinen, S.-T. 2021.Good status in the changing climate? Climate proofing law on water management in the EU, *Sustainability*, 13, 517.

Raz, J. 1979. *The Authority of Law: Essays on Law and Morality*. Oxford, Oxford University Press.

van Rijswick, H. F. M. W. and Backes, C. W. 2015. Ground breaking landmark case on environmental quality standards? *Journal for European Environmental & Planning Law*, 12.

Ruhl, J. B. 2007. Law's complexity: a primer. *Georgia State University Law Review*, 24, 885.

Ruhl, J. B. and Katz, D. M. 2015. Measuring, monitoring, and managing legal complexity, *Iowa Law Review*, 101, 191.

Ruhl, J. B., Katz, D. M., and Bommarito II, M. J. 2017. Harnessing legal complexity. *Science*, 355, 6332, 1377–1378.

Söderasp, J. and Petterson, M. 2019. Before and after the Weser case: legal application of the water framework directive environmental objectives in Sweden, *Journal of Environmental Law*, 31, 265–290.

Soininen, N. 2015. Marine spatial planning in the European Union. In Hassan, D., Kuokkanen, T., and Soininen, N. (eds) *Transboundary Marine Spatial Planning and International Law*, Abingdon, Routledge, pp. 189–201.

Soininen, N., Belinskij, A., Vainikka, A. and Huuskonen, H. 2017. Bringing back ecological flows: migratory fish, hydropower and legal maladaptivity in the governance of Finnish rivers. *Water International*, 44, 3, 321–336.

Soininen, N. and Platjouw, F. M. 2018. Resilience and adaptive capacity of aquatic environmental law in the EU: an evaluation and comparison of the WFD, MSFD, and MSPD. In Langlet, D. and Rayfuse, R. (eds) *The Ecosystem Approach in Ocean Planning and Governance Perspectives from Europe and Beyond*, Leiden, Brill, pp. 17–79.

Soininen, N., Romppanen, S., Huhta, K., and Belinskij, A. 2021. A brake or an accelerator? The role of law in Sustainability Transitions, *Environmental Innovation and Societal Transitions*, 41, 71–73.

Soininen, N., Raymond, C. M., Tuomisto, H., Ruotsalainen, L., Thorén, H., Horcea-Milcu. A.-I., Stojanovic, M., Lehtinen, S., Mazac, R., Lamuela, C., Korpelainen, N., Vainio, A., Toivanen, R., McPhearson, T. and Nagatsu, M. 2022. Bridge over troubled water: managing compatibility and conflict among thought collectives in sustainability science, *Sustainability Science*, 17, 27–44.

Steffen, W., Crutzen, P. J. and McNeill, J. R. 2007. The Anthropocene: are humans now overwhelming the great forces of nature? *Ambio*, 36, 614.

Steffen, W., Richardson, K., Rockström, J., Cornell, S. E., Fetzer, I., Bennett, B. R., Carpenter, St. R., de Vries, W., de Wit, C. A., Folke, G., Heinke, J., Mace, G. M., Persson, L. M., Ramanathan, V., Reyers, B. and Sörlin, S. 2015. Planetary boundaries: guiding human development on a changing planet, *Science*, 347, 6223, 736.

Tuori, K. 2016. *Critical Legal Positivism*, Abingdon, Routledge.

Verbong, G. and Loorbach, D. 2012. Introduction. In Verbong, G. and Loorbach, D. (eds), *Governing the Energy Transition: Reality, Illusion or Necessity?* Abingdon, Taylor & Francis Group.

Waldron, J. 2010. The rule of law and the importance of procedure. In Fleming, J. E. (ed.) *Getting to the Rule of Law*, Nomos L, Yearbook of the American Society for Political and Legal Philosophy, pp. 3–31.

4. Conceptualising the science–policy–practice interface of adaptive governance

Carina Wyborn, Jasper Montana, Amber Datta and Elena Louder

INTRODUCTION

From the outset, the creation and provision of information has been deemed to be a core function of adaptive management and governance in complex systems (Dietz et al. 2003, Folke et al. 2005). This includes information about the resource systems being managed and the human–environment interactions surrounding those resources. The importance of local, practical, and traditional knowledge has long been recognised within adaptive governance scholarship, and is assumed to sit alongside scientific information to support governance that is more responsive, effective, and equitable (Dietz et al, 2003, Folke et al. 2005, Berkes 2000, Berkes and Berkes 2009).

Adaptive governance emerges from the self-organisation of stakeholders and decision-makers as they pursue creative, flexible ways of navigating change towards desired outcomes (Folke et al. 2005, Chaffin et al. 2014). Key processes that support adaptive governance include adaptive management, inclusive participation, nested and scale appropriate approaches to address problems (e.g. local site to entire bioregion), and integrating multiple types of knowledge (Folke et al. 2005). Many scholars suggest that these processes can be facilitated by a polycentric structure, in which there are multiple, overlapping centres of decision-making at nested levels (Folke et al. 2005).

Instrumentally, adaptive governance scholars take the view that diverse forms of knowledge are required to provide holistic understandings of complex, uncertain problems, and that the participation of diverse actors will foster governance that is more responsive and effective. Normatively, the proposition rests on the rights of all knowledge- and stake-holders to be included in deliberations about facts and values concerning governance decisions that impact their lives and livelihoods. As Dietz et al. (2003) propose:

> Effective governance requires not only factual information about the state of the environment and human actions but also information about uncertainty and values. Scientific understanding of coupled human-biophysical systems will always be uncertain because of inherent unpredictability in the systems and because the science is never complete.

The role of science in adaptive governance scholarship, however, is not straightforward. Some early scholarship implicitly privileges scientific expertise in identifying environmental problems, setting ecosystem management goals, and supporting adaptive management (e.g. Gunderson and Light 2006, Olsson et al. 2008). In other areas, scholars suggested that natural resource conflicts often emerged from scientific management that was driven by central scientific authorities that sought to rise above politics in the delivery of efficient command-and-control interventions (Brunner and Steelman 2005). Accordingly, centralised and bureaucratic forms of expertise were seen as antithetical to adaptive governance, while the integration of other types of knowledge alongside science into governance were seen to advance a more common interest and open decision-making approach (Brunner and Steelman 2005, Berkes et al. 2000). Others have emphasised a shift from detached scientific experts delivering knowledge to an approach that sees scientific actors as one of many engaging in developing knowledge for governance (Folke et al. 2005). Such a perspective recognises the importance of knowledge held by those whose daily lives and lived histories provide authoritative knowledge of ecosystem dynamics. This perspective built on the work of anthropologist Fikret Berkes and colleagues who illustrated the inherent value of indigenous and local knowledge (ILK) to adaptive management (Berkes et al. 2000, Berkes and Berkes 2009). They argue that the adaptive, integrative, and holistic nature of ILK provides a strong foundation for adaptive governance because it acknowledges changing environmental conditions and the complex relationships between human and non-human worlds. The way in which diverse forms of knowledge are developed, organised, and shared is therefore critical to adaptive governance (Folke et al. 2005).

The academic field of science and technology studies (STS) examines the various ways in which science and society interact, thus generating useful insights for scholars and practitioners of adaptive governance. In a review of studies that considered how interactions between science and governance vary across cultural contexts, Miller (2008) identifies three foundational assumptions that provide a starting point for considerations of the interactions between knowledge and governance[1] in this chapter. First, knowledge is comprised of complex judgements about evidence, credibility and interpretation, values and problem framings. Knowledge is not, therefore, a simple statement of truth or fact. Second, the complex judgements central to producing knowledge are inherently social processes, where competing knowledge claims are put forward, debated, negotiated, and either accepted or rejected. Third, knowledge and social processes are co-constituted in ways that give rise to particular epistemic frameworks, social, and political arrangements. Following from these propositions, Miller argues that it is not possible to separate ways of knowing and reasoning about policy problems from ways of organising politics, policy, and governance. In essence, this work highlights that how society comes to know and govern policy problems is culturally and socially situated. These ways of knowing and governing are both relatively stable in that they are embedded within existing institutions and practices, while at the same time being dynamic, shaped over time by interactions between epistemic, social, and political practices (Miller 2008).

In this chapter, we discuss the concept of science–policy–practice interfaces (SPPIs). The concept of SPPIs is a catch all term to describe 'the processes and settings in which decision-makers in government, civil society, and business use, misuse, or reject scientific research in forming their thinking, analysis, or decision-making' (van den Hove 2007). SPPIs can take a variety of forms. They may be: mechanisms to facilitate knowledge brokering; organisations that are explicitly established to mediate between science and policy/practice; global environmental assessments such as the Intergovernmental Panel on Climate Change (IPCC); or collaborative processes where people from diverse sectors come together to

---

[1]   Throughout this chapter, we use the term 'governance' to refer to decision-making processes that take place at various levels of policy, management, and practice, and 'science' to encompass academic modes of knowledge production that is inclusive of social and biophysical sciences and the humanities.

generate knowledge and make change. The precise characteristics of an SPPI for adaptive governance will depend on the social, cultural, and institutional context, the actors involved, and the nature of the problem at hand.

Thinking about SPPIs as a concept, rather than just a method is important for adaptive governance, because SPPIs are implicit in key processes such as participation of diverse stakeholders, addressing cross-scale challenges, and learning from adaptive management. Explicitly recognising SPPIs embedded in these processes makes it possible to examine the ways in which this interface may be hindering or enabling processes to support stakeholders and decision-makers as they navigate change. Attention to SPPIs elevates the general call for integrating knowledge types within adaptive governance to a more actionable discussion of exactly whose knowledge is needed where, and how it is incorporated (or not). Careful evaluation of SPPIs can elucidate and potentially improve upon participatory and polycentric processes to support the ability of actors to address issues that cut across scales, and tailor their actions to particular local contexts. Enabling adaptive governance thus inherently requires SPPIs that allow for the effective and rapid creation, transfer, and use of relevant knowledge, but to date attention to these processes has been muted (but see Wyborn 2015).

Insights from previous research suggest that enabling governance that effectively integrates knowledge of rapidly changing social, political, or ecological contexts is unlikely to be simple. Rather, in many adaptive governance contexts, the interface between science and governance will be beset with differing perspectives, values, and knowledges of actors who are unlikely to always agree on the nature of a problem, and how it should be governed. Thus, a more nuanced understanding of SPPIs can be helpful when analysing and intervening in the processes by which knowledge is accepted or rejected by those who have the agency to make changes in the governance context.

This chapter begins by setting out three conceptual models that commonly shape how SPPIs are understood and organised and can provide a basis for asking questions about the politics of operating at the interface of science and governance. We then move on to focus on the politics of SPPIs, pointing to the political nature of design choices that shape how SPPIs are organised and understood, and how that in turn shapes adaptive governance interventions. Our framework centres on a set of questions that are intended to guide scholars and practitioners to think through the political dimensions of SPPIs, by asking:

- How is a problem framed?
- Who is included in SPPIs?
- Who sets the agenda of SPPIs?
- How are interactions of actors facilitated by SPPIs?
- How are SPPI processes and outcomes justified?

This approach recognises and responds to critiques that the political dimensions of adaptive governance remain undertheorised (Karpouzoglu et al. 2016). We explicitly focus on the politics of interactions between science and governance to emphasise the need to move beyond ideas that diverse forms of knowledge can simply come together to catalyse changes in governance. Rather, we argue that intentional engagement with the political aspects of SPPIs has the potential to open pathways to more just, equitable, and adaptive modes of governance.

MODELS OF SCIENCE–POLICY–PRACTICE INTERFACE

There are innumerable conceptualisations and modes of organising SPPIs for the governance of sustainability challenges. Each iteration will no doubt depend upon the mental models held by those involved relating to the nature of science, policy, and practice, and how they interact. As a heuristic to understand this multiplicity, conceptualisations of SPPIs can be thought to follow generalised assumptions about the relationship between science and governance. These typically relate to the extent to which science is seen as discrete from governance and decision-making processes, or whether the two are tightly intertwined, co-informing one another, either through intentional mechanisms of co-production, or implicitly as an emergent outcome of knowledge production in contemporary society.

Here, we outline three broad conceptual models that are commonly applied for thinking about SPPIs in environmental governance (Figure 4.1). Drawing on the analysis in Dunn et al. 2018 on urban water governance in Australia, these can be understood as the *science-push model*, where science aims to drive decision-making; *the policy-pull model*, characterised by science being requested and defined by governance actors; and *the co-production model*, where science and governance are infused to intentionally or unintentionally co-produce knowledge and action at the same time. Recognising that many other conceptualisations of SPPIs are plausible (see Pregernig 2014, Wyborn et al. 2017, van Kerkhoff and Lebel 2006), these three models offer a useful illustration of the distinct ways in which the relationship between science and governance can be imagined, and thereby they can help inform considerations of what type of SPPI is appropriate for a given adaptive governance context.

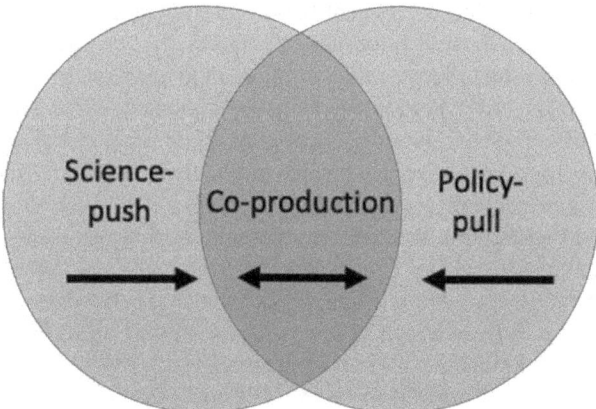

Source: Adapted from Dunn et al. (2018).

Figure 4.1   *Three conceptual models for thinking about the SPPI in environmental governance*

The Science-push Model

The science-push model conceptualises science and governance as operating in distinct worlds, where scientific knowledge is depicted as distinct from values-based deliberations that are characteristic of policy and politics and therefore able to 'speak truth to power' through the provision of impartial evidence to inform decision-making (Jasanoff and Wynne 1998). Sometimes termed 'the linear model', proponents of the science-push model argue that decision-makers must be provided with rigorous, objective scientific evidence from which to base decisions (Cook et al. 2013). An underlying assumption is that 'science compels action' (Beck 2011) and therefore the task of the scientist is to not only identify matters of fact, but to convey them in the right form at the right time so that action can be taken.

In practice, the science-push model might be seen to play out in part in relation to calls for evidence-based policy. Evidence-based policy relates to a diverse array of practices both in the collection and collation of evidence, as well as its use in decision-making (Nutley et al. 2003), and often places emphasis on the rigour of methods such as quantitative models, assessment reports, research synthesis, and decision-support tools. The aspirations of evidence-based policy are that policies should be driven by the best available science, including evidence on 'what works' in terms of interventions.

Critics point out that this model takes a naïve view of the policy process; it suggests a rational and linear system and neglects the normative, messy, and power-laden nature of politics (Adams and Sandbrook 2013, Head 2016, Juntti et al. 2009). Importantly, it assumes that poor decisions are made because of a lack of good information, and not other confounding factors (Adams and Sandbrook 2013). Adams and Sandbrook (2013) argue that generally, the information that counts as evidence is quantitative and limited to formal, published research. This excludes important sources of information, such as local or traditional knowledge, and Indigenous knowledges, which are potentially important in addressing sustainability problems (ibid., Berkes and Berkes 2009). Although adaptive governance scholars have long advocated for the integration of knowledge types (Berkes et al. 2000, Folke et al. 2005), much of the early examples of emerging adaptive governance implicitly drew on the 'science-push' model – namely by scientists advocating for the incorporation of science-based adaptive management (e.g. Gunderson and Light 2006). Recognising that this SPPI model is embedded in adaptive governance scholarship takes a first step towards intentionally deliberating the role of this model versus other SPPIs in enabling adaptive governance. Such a discussion allows for differentiating the role of *science* in adaptive governance from the politics-laden role of *scientists* (versus other knowledge holders) in adaptive governance.

The Policy-pull Model

The policy-pull model is similar to the science-push model in that it maintains a clear distinction between science and governance as domains of action, however in the policy-pull model, decision makers determine the scope of science that is brought into decision making. This model emphasises the need for an exchange between experts and decision-makers by which decision makers ask scientists for the provision of an evidence base or an expert opinion on issues.

The policy-pull model can take a myriad of forms. Commonly the model plays out in science advisory processes where expert advice or opinions are requested by decision makers through formal and informal processes. At the national level, national academies or expert committees often engage in solicited science advice on specific issues, from flood management to the ethics of emerging technologies. It is increasingly common for individual scientists to be appointed into roles, such as Chief Scientist or Chief Medical Officer (as in the recent context of the COVID-19 pandemic), mediating between the scientific research community and political leaders, but also supporting governance through strengthening the public understanding of science amongst the media-consuming public. At the international level, global environmental assessments, such as the IPCC and Intergovernmental Science-Policy Platform on Biodiversity and Ecosystem Services (IPBES) generate expert opinions in response to questions that are decided by an intergovernmental process. Locally, policy-push approaches could take the form of expert advisors supporting local government or community planning processes, for example in the development of climate adaptation plans. While formal procedures guiding these modes of science advice are now common, it can also take place through more ad hoc personal interactions and relationships between researchers and decision-makers.

Critics of the policy-pull model would say that in practice, these approaches overly emphasise formal knowledge as valid evidence for decision-making, and can exclude both publics and diverse forms of knowledge from decision-making. For example, some analysts have suggested that the prominence of experts in contemporary democracies leads to a democratic deficit where issues are 'depoliticised' and therefore made unamenable to public debate (Swyngedouw 2011). Others argue that the reliance on independent expert advice maintains an apolitical view of science in decision making, rather than explicitly emphasising the inherently political choices in sustainability governance (Stirling 2008). If the policy-pull model is embedded in emergent adaptive governance processes, it may unwittingly lead to reinforcing unequal power between different knowledge holders. This would conflict with the pursuit of democratic participation to uphold adaptive governance, underscoring the importance of identifying SPPIs within adaptive governance processes early on.

The Co-production Model

In contrast to the science-push and policy-pull models, the co-production model suggests SPPIs can be conceived as breaking down the boundaries between science and governance in order to collectively produce both knowledge and action. Theoretically, co-production has developed as an analytical lens within science and technology studies to understand the complex and co-evolutionary processes through which science and society shape and inform one another. In practice, the co-production model largely plays out as a methodology in fields such as sustainability science and public administration, in which actors from across the SPPI come together to produce knowledge or public services in the service of policy goals or sustainability interventions (see Wyborn et al. 2019 for more details). Both ways of thinking about co-production are central to the idea in adaptive governance that diverse actors could come together to change governance practices or management decisions through collaborative processes that enable social learning to respond to existing or emerging challenges.

Sustainability sciences and public administration scholarship have focused substantial attention on the stages, characteristics, and principles of 'successful' co-production processes. Norström et al (2020) for example, posit that co-production processes should be *context-based*, situated within a particular context, place, or issue; *pluralistic*, explicitly recognising multiple ways of knowing and doing; *goal-oriented*, working towards defined, shared, and meaningful goals; and *interactive*, allowing for ongoing learning and engagement through frequent interactions. In a global analysis of 32 cases from six continents, Chambers et al. (2021) identified six distinct 'modes' of co-production, each with their own unique opportunities to realise certain outcomes, and potential risks to the process and its success. This suggests that there is no one 'right way' to implement co-production processes, rather they need to be tailored to a given context.

Co-production processes are time and resource intensive, and often rely on the unpaid time of citizens and community members while academics and government professionals participate as part of their 'day job'. Moreover, conflict is common within co-production processes, as they face challenges navigating diverse values, perspectives, ways of knowing, and senses of reality (Oliver et al. 2019). Others have questioned the assumption that co-production processes will lead to 'better' outcomes (Sutherland et al. 2017), a critique that is often backed up by the scant evidence supporting claims of outcomes and impact. Perhaps more profoundly, co-production processes and scholarship have been critiqued for failing to adequately address power dynamics that are inherent to collaborative processes (Turnhout et al. 2020). These challenges are shared with efforts to enable adaptive governance, given that at their core, they stem from issues of participation and representation in decision-making processes concerning complex, uncertain, and multi-scaled challenges. As we discuss further below, the political dimensions of SPPIs and adaptive governance require attention to design choices that shape how these efforts are organised and understood.

The three models above – science-push, policy-pull, and co-production – represent different constructs that describe and legitimise different ways of organising SPPIs. They are based on foundationally different understandings of the relationship between science and governance, and the ways in which they can productively inform and shape one another. The preference for one SPPI framework over another likely depends upon the disciplinary training of individuals and their professional experience operating within SPPIs (i.e., Montana and Wilsdon 2021). However, it is important to note that they are not intended to be accurate representations or 'ideal type' SPPIs. Rather, they are heuristics that draw attention to the underlying assumptions about how SPPIs should be governed and organised. As we go on to explain, adherence to the principles of adaptive governance would suggest that SPPIs themselves can and should be adapted and iteratively improved in response to changing needs and decisions. We argue that embracing a pluralistic understanding of SPPIs is helpful for recognising their inherently constructed and flexible nature, which can be strategically arranged to suit different governance contexts.

In the next section of this chapter, we expand on these models of the SPPI by setting out a framework of questions that can guide scholars and practitioners to think through the political dynamics of SPPIs for adaptive governance. Adopting a pluralistic understanding of SPPIs within adaptive governance means not only recognising that there are multiple ways in which to conceptualise a given SPPI, but also that there is a politics associated with how those conceptualisations of the SPPI are organised in practice. In highlighting these politics, we seek to show that the organisation of SPPIs not only shapes how an issue is understood, but also serves some interests over others.

POLITICS OF OPERATING AT THE INTERFACE

Thinking about the political dynamics of SPPIs for adaptive governance can be aided by working through a set of questions focused on how SPPIs are being conceptualised and organised in particular cases. These questions include: How is a problem framed? Who is included in SPPIs? Who sets the agenda of SPPIs? How are interactions facilitated by SPPIs? And, how are SPPI processes and outcomes justified? The answers to all these questions will be subjective, and in practice will be the result of negotiation. However, they are important, because the decisions made in answering these questions will shape which voices are heard, and which are silenced, and thus can be a contested site of politics and trade-offs that is too little acknowledged in adaptive governance. Dialogue and reflection on these questions at the outset, and throughout the design and implementation interventions, will help with the development of efforts that are 'fit for purpose', and critically reflexive about the politics that underpins them.

Table 4.1 reflects on these questions for the three conceptual models of SPPIs (science-push, policy-pull, and co-production) identified above to provide practical examples of how these questions might shape different ways of operating within, and organising SPPIs for adaptive governance. In the text that follows, we elaborate on the questions and point towards potentially useful concepts from critical perspectives to inform practice in adaptive governance.

How is a Problem Framed?

Sustainability 'problems' that need to be 'solved' are not pregiven, while they clearly have some basis in material reality – climate change is a real phenomenon with significant consequences – how we understand and experience climate change, and which aspect of the climate problem should be the focus of interventions at the SPPI is subjective. When framed as a technical problem, by technical experts, climate interventions focus on, for example, emissions reductions technologies or carbon accounting. Economic problem frames tend to market solutions or critiques of capitalism, while justice-based frames highlight the unequal distribution of climate impacts, often leading to efforts to empower marginalised communities. Within a science-push model, academic expertise is prioritised in the identification of problems and their framing for policy, whereas the policy-pull model, the problem frame emerges from the policy domain and shapes which type of research is called upon to address it. In contrast, within a co-production model, problem framing is an iterative and emergent process, where diverse knowledge-holders come together to develop a shared understanding of the problem, or at least the different views of that problem.

In practice, governance decisions are shaped by many more factors than research evidence, which must also take into consideration for example social and cultural acceptability, and economic impact. Perhaps more profoundly, different sources of evidence can point to different recommendations for action (Sarewitz 2004), for example, an engineer and a fish biologist will likely provide quite different recommendations with respect to environmental flows on rivers. Further, research itself is not a value-neutral pursuit, as the questions scientists pursue, or the funding bodies that support research, are shaped by social and political values. How problems are framed, and by who, shapes what kind of interventions are developed, what kinds of expertise are viewed as relevant, and which 'stakeholders' or 'knowledge holders' should be engaged in an intervention, and how.

Table 4.1   *Different ways in which science-push, policy-pull, and co-production models approach design considerations at the SPPI**

	Science-push	Policy-pull	Co-production
How is a problem framed?	By academic experts	By policy elites	By diverse stakeholders and knowledge holders
Who is included in SPPIs?	Academic experts	Policy elites and academic experts	Potentially any stakeholders and knowledge holders
Who sets the agenda of SPPIs?	Academic experts	Policy elites	Theoretically, set through collaborative process; however, in practice, elites – academic or policy – tend to maintain power
How are interactions of actors facilitated by SPPIs?	Actors are kept separate; the boundary between facts and values maintained; science is delivered to governance	Some interaction between actors; boundary between facts and values maintained; governance requests science products	Regular interaction between actors, boundary between facts and values blurred, knowledge production and action co-constructed
How are SPPI processes and outcomes justified?	*Credibility* – academic expertise; *Relevance* – research agenda determined by scientists; *Legitimacy* – through separation of facts and values	*Credibility* – established trust in experts; *Relevance* – research agenda set by governance context; *Legitimacy* – careful curation of separation of facts and values	*Credibility* – diverse knowledge holders with experience related to the problem; *Relevance* – research agenda set by governance context; *Legitimacy* – through inclusive, transparent participatory process

Note: * These are necessarily simplifications of a more complex reality that unfolds in practice.

Who is Included in SPPIs?

Perhaps one of the most central questions to an SPPI is who is included? Here, inclusion not only includes possible experts and stakeholders, but also the knowledge that they bring to efforts to bridge science and governance. Indeed, when it comes to questions of who should participate in an SPPI intervention, much of this thinking aligns with longstanding considerations about participation in adaptive governance processes. As Biermann suggests:

> stable, credible and adaptive governance mechanisms require maximum inclusion and participation. Otherwise, excluded actors could later reject agreements, destabilise them, threaten the credibility of commitments over time, or resist co-operation if changing circumstances makes the participation of excluded stakeholders suddenly more relevant (Biermann 2016: 15).

Thus, SPPI interventions extend existing considerations of inclusion and exclusion to consider whether a representative group of knowledge holders are engaged appropriately through a project or process. What is 'representative' and who is representing whom, should also be questioned, as representation requires agreed mechanisms to ensure that those speaking on behalf of a group, or of a particular expertise have the legitimacy to do so (Montana 2019). Representatives hold power within participatory processes to shape how an issue is framed, what is conceded, or agreed to within deliberation – making representation a critical site for the framing and implementation of policy agendas at the SPPI (Jasanoff 2005).

Increasing recognition of the role of diverse expertise in addressing sustainability problems has reduced the differentiation across the different models of the SPPI with respect to questions of who sets the agenda. While the science-push model tends to be essentialised as centralised and bureaucratic, arguably it does not need to be as such, and there is increasing experimentation in the ways in which expertise is understood, leading to more processes that are more inclusive of alternative understandings and lay expertise (i.e. competency groups (Landström et al. 2011). In the policy-pull model, increasingly both expert panels and individuals are responding to a recognised need for diversity, for substantive, instrumental, and normative reasons, seeking to also consider input knowledge from social sciences, humanities, and Indigenous knowledges (Tengö et al. 2017). Perhaps what differentiates the co-production model here is the strong emphasis on pluralism, a greater recognition of the need for public engagement in the SPPI and an intentional effort to blur boundaries between the 'producers and users' of knowledge to suggest that all participants are learning and acting together (Chambers et al. 2022).

Who Sets the Agenda of SPPIs?

Closely related to the question of how a problem is framed, the question of who sets the agenda gets at how power is distributed within SPPIs and the role of experts within SPPI processes. Chambers et al. (2022) identified four archetypal roles for experts within SPPI interventions: the hero, the host, the genie, and the woodpecker, which play distinct roles in navigating the tensions inherent to working at the SPPI. The hero sees their role as solving predefined problems to realise desired impacts, while also maintaining control over which strategies and actors are relevant to achieve them. The genie sees their role as mobilising diverse expertise to help further others' agendas, explicitly choosing to release control to others, for example policy-makers or communities to set research agendas. Like the hero, the woodpecker seeks to maintain control over the process, but focuses efforts on critiquing dominant problem and solution frames. The host also focuses on reframing problems however, they relinquish control to participants in the process, actively seeking to create spaces where participants can reflect on what matters. In their analysis, Chambers and colleagues found that effectively navigating tensions that are inherent to working at the SPPI required 'agility' among these roles, to weave together approaches that were both critical and solution oriented, while delicately balancing and sharing power among actors.

Returning to the SPPI models identified above, the science-push model primarily engages the expertise of academic experts, whose role is simply to produce knowledge and would play a negligible part within SPPI interventions. Beyond traditional academic publications, this could include efforts like the 'scientists warning of a climate emergency', where a group of academics came together to make an open declaration that is not pointed towards a particular decision-context but is a statement of the 'problem' and strategies identified by this expert group that could be mobilised to address it (Ripple 2020). In the policy-pull model, the emphasis still largely remains with academic experts, however there is more interplay between the two where the policy context dictates the agenda, and research is conducted accordingly. The US National Climate Assessment is a good example of this model, the assessment is mandated under the Global Change Research Act to report to Congress and the President on the state of climate knowledge and impacts in the US every four years. In the co-production model, a more diverse range of actors are viewed as knowledge holders, and processes are geared towards facilitating knowledge exchange among equals to generate situated actions and strategies. For example, bringing together a diverse group of experts to develop climate adaptation strategies for protected areas (see van Kerkhoff et al. 2018).

How are Interactions of Different Actors Facilitated by SPPIs?

The interactions of different actors within SPPIs (such as scientists and policymakers) will be determined by where the boundaries are drawn between science and governance, and the extent to which those boundaries are strongly maintained or deliberately navigated. Here, the concept of 'boundary work' usefully describes the strategic work of those representing SPPIs that demarcates the 'boundaries' between science and non-science (Gieryn 1983). Early studies of boundary work showed that credibility was not an inherent property of scientific knowledge, rather, credibility was constructed through the actions undertaken by scientists to justify which knowledge claims should be acted upon and which should not (Gieryn 1988). The different SPPIs models identified above would delineate boundaries between science and governance in different ways guided by assumptions about the need to separate (science-push, policy-pull) or conflate (co-production) facts and values in SPPIs and the degree to which the SPPI is constructed to privilege a hierarchy (science-push, policy-pull) or plurality (co-production) of knowledges in framing and addressing problems.

Practically, boundary work scholarship and practice focus on the ways in which objects, intermediaries, or organisations can actively facilitate exchange among actors across SPPIs. This scholarship has highlighted just how much work goes into enabling these interactions to bridge disparities of power and knowledge (Guston 1999, Bednarek et al. 2015, Bednarek et al. 2018). Boundary 'spanners' are individuals (often but not always with scientific training) who operate in various ways to support engagement across SPPIs (Bednarek et al. 2018) while boundary objects are artefacts, objects, or concepts that enable collaboration through interpretive flexibility that enables actors to view the object through a different lens, yet have enough commonality in their interpretation to provide a shared focal point for dialogue (Star and Griesemer, 1998). For example, Fuller (2009) describes how boundary objects were used in the California Bay Delta Program where the steering committee successfully used spreadsheets, PowerPoint presentations, conceptual diagrams and other material artefacts to create a shared representation of the river system and its ecosystems that provided a starting point for dialogue among actors who had previously been engaged in contentious conflict over agricultural water use.

Boundary organisations work at the interface of science and governance, with an explicit intention to foster connections and exchange between the two. These organisations operate in a range of ways, underpinned by the different models of SPPIs. In a science-push model, boundary work focuses on maintaining a separation between science and values. Boundary organisations, for example the Cochrane Collaboration in public health, or the Centre for Evidence Based Conservation synthesise and communicate systematic reviews of evidence for policy and practice, thus following a model and understanding of expertise that privileges scientific knowledge in understanding policy problems and how to address them. In a policy-pull model, boundary work focuses on the interlopers – be they individuals, organisations, or objects who work across the boundary. In the Lenfest Ocean Programme at the Pew Charitable Trusts program staff identify what kinds of questions are amenable to being addressed with scientific advances, or where the frontiers of science could be applied in policy or practice. They commission collaborative projects, task forces, or research synthesis to be mobilised for policy and practice, however the knowledge production in these projects remains largely separated from the decision-contexts it seeks to inform. In the co-produced model, boundary work focuses on dissolving the boundary or to operate in a manner that accepts that it never existed in the first place. The Luc Hoffmann Institute is an example of this model, seeking to enable actors from across science and governance with different expertise and experience to come together to innovate solutions directly connected to pathways of action. Across these three models, different rules will shape engagements at the SPPI which will reflect the assumed proximity of science from governance, and the degree to which facts and values should be separated or intertwined.

How are SPPI Processes and Outcomes Justified?

Such a focus moves beyond the specifics of an individual intervention to ask broader questions about the governance context that will define how the SPPI is structured, and how interventions operate to realise the goals of adaptive governance. Most notably, the notion of 'usable knowledge' suggests that knowledges (and the SPPIs that bring it into governance systems) are more likely to have impact and influence if they are recognised to have three attributes: first, they need to be seen as *credible*, a measure that relates to the perceived quality, validity, and adequacy of the knowledge; second, they need to be seen as *relevant*, in that the knowledge is tailored to the context of use; and third, they need to be seen as developed through *legitimate* process marked by balanced participation and fair treatment of different values and interests (Cash et al. 2003, Sarkki et al. 2015). These attributes, which have come to be known as the 'CRELE' criteria (made up of first two letters of each attribute), provide guideposts for considering what type of knowledge might be useful in a given governance context, however they are agnostic to different SPPI arrangements. Given the different cultures, structures, and incentives shaping the practices of science and governance, boundary work involving communication across actors, mediation among perspectives, and translation of jargon is required to develop usable knowledge (Cash et al. 2006) with some specifically identifying the need for such dialogue to be iterative (Sarkki et al. 2015, Dilling and Lemos 2011).

Each SPPI models leads to different ways of thinking about CRELE. In the science-push model, for example, credibility relies upon traditional academic credentials, and the legitimacy of the research requires experts are kept out of debates about values to maintain the purity and validity of the research through its separation from politics. In this model, relevance is not a driving factor shaping the production of research, as researchers set the research agenda, do independent research, and then transfer the results to 'end-users' who then apply that knowledge in decision-making. The science-push model sees academic expertise as providing evidence to compel action within a technocratic style of decision-making where expert knowledge is privileged over societal values.

For the policy-pull model, CRELE is more likely to depend upon the maintenance of trust and authority of expert advisors and committees as sources of reliable knowledge for decision making (Gluckman 2014). Here, notions of credibility rely on ensuring that trust is established and maintained through careful choice of experts and deliberate planning of how expert knowledge is developed and delivered. Relevance is generated through the dialogue between experts and decision-makers in developing problem frames and identifying issues in need of scientific expertise. Legitimacy is maintained through the careful curation of a separation of experts and decision-makers, assuming that experts are the producers of knowledge, while decision-makers make judgements on policy decisions. In a policy-pull model, societal values may inform the framing of policy problems, but expert knowledge is still largely privileged and kept separate from decision-making.

Finally, in the co-production model, credibility is about the potential contribution that a knowledge holder may make to the topic domain, and does not necessarily require academic expertise, rather it can be the provision of practical, experiential, local, contextual, or traditional knowledge. The co-production process is thus used to identify what kinds of knowledge, and what kinds of research might be relevant through iterative dialogue, and it is the inclusion of diverse knowledges through fair and equitable processes that attend to power disparities that affords legitimacy to the process, as well as the knowledges and changes it produces. Within the co-produced model decision-making and action are not separated, and diverse expertise and styles of reasoning are deployed to justify action.

It is important to recognise that what are considered to be credible, relevant, and legitimate processes and outputs will depend on the context, as illustrated by these three examples. Critically, what is perceived to be an optimal arrangement for an SPPI will be contingent on the social and political context. Different nation states, for example, have different cultures by which appropriate knowledge is defined and its use in decisions is justified (i.e. civic epistemologies, Jasanoff 2005).

TOWARDS A POLITICALLY AWARE SPPI FOR ADAPTIVE GOVERNANCE

Effective engagement between science and governance is critical to realise the aspirations of adaptive governance to be responsive to changes in context, and the knowledge of that context.

However, interactions between science and governance are rarely simple, due in part to the complex, uncertain, and often contested knowledge that is drawn on to inform choices that inevitably will prioritise some values or social groups over others. We argue that these challenges are not unique to the SPPI for adaptive governance, but rather resonate with broader considerations in adaptive governance efforts to support adaptive management, inclusive participation, and identify appropriate representation in nested or polycentric governance structures. In the previous section, we highlighted some important questions that can help scholars and practitioners of adaptive governance understand the design choices and considerations that shape engagements at the SPPI. In this final section, we draw attention to 'civic epistemologies' – the deep-seated patterns of social, political, and cultural practice that shape relationships between science and governance (Jasanoff 2005). These patterns of practice will influence how the politics of an SPPI play out, and shape the ways in which responses to the design choices identified in the previous section will be viewed as credible and legitimate.

Civic epistemologies are cultures of knowledge production and decision making that underpin both formal structures – expert bodies, review committees, regulatory mechanisms – and informal processes of deliberation and negotiation between citizens. Critically, these are not uniform, they vary across socio-cultural contexts, and have implications for the legitimacy and acceptance of knowledge claims and actions developed to address physical, political, or moral risks (Jasanoff 2012). While it is not easy to directly and intentionally change such systems when designing adaptive governance or SPPI interventions, having an awareness of these 'deep seated patterns' of social, political, and cultural practice offer insights into how judgements about knowledge reflect, reinforce, and shape social rules and practices (van Kerkhoff and Pilbeam 2017). Civic epistemologies are the reason *why* a given group identifies knowledge as credible, relevant, or legitimate, providing important insights into the rules, norms, and practices through which legitimacy for action is built. To ground this practically, we briefly highlight three aspects where an awareness of civic epistemologies can contribute to adaptive governance.

First, adaptive governance has long maintained a focus on the role of ILK within adaptive governance and management with attention drawn to the importance of these knowledge holders in both understanding problems as well as their right to be central to deliberations over the governance of their resources. ILK cannot, however, be simply plucked from its embodied context and inserted into knowledge production and governance processes that are shaped by fundamentally Western norms. For example, in a study of conservation governance in the Pacific Island nation of Palau, van Kerkhoff and Pilbeam (2017) highlight the differences between Western and customary ways of validating and building trust in knowledge, the foundations for expertise, and mechanisms to resolve and navigate conflicts over knowledge that need to be considered when designing interventions or engaging at the SPPI interface for adaptive governance. It is important to recognise that there are rules and cultures about who can hold and share knowledge within Indigenous cultures, whereas in the Western context there is an assumption that anyone who has the training can hold/share knowledge. Interventions designed based on this Western assumption will clash with a culture based on other assumptions.

Second, adaptive governance has foundationally assumed that dialogue between stakeholders and knowledge holders will enable the development of strategies that emerge from the collective insights of their different perspectives, and the resolution of conflicts over resources. This assumes deliberative consensus-oriented approaches can resolve tension through dialogue, yet agonistic approaches hold value-conflicts as given, seeking instead to work through tensions in ways that build processes for the ongoing navigation of difference (Mouffe 2013). In the context of synthetic biology, Scott (2022) argues that grounding SPPI interventions in agonistic styles of reasoning would require approaches that *transform power relations* by exploring and exposing who benefits, who stands to harm, and whose voices are heard; *seek out dissent* to identify and empower potentially conflicting perspectives to enable difference to be negotiated on political terms; and *make room for the political* by acknowledging the differing visions of society that underpin conflicts over emerging sciences and technologies.

Finally, uncertainty is an ever-present, and long recognised feature of adaptive governance, focusing on learning, experimentation, precaution, and monitoring as means of developing adaptive responses to uncertainty (Cooney and Lang 2007). While this moves adaptive governance discourse beyond styles of public reasoning predicated on certainty, it can be helpful to further unpack how uncertain knowledge interfaces with governance, and how decision-making cultures respond to it. For example, in the regulation of uncertain risks, the precautionary principle features far more prominently in European public policy than in the United States where there is a greater need for evidence of harm prior to regulation (Weiner and Rodgers 2002). Treatment of uncertainty is thus a product of the civic epistemologies in a given context and the underlying political dimensions of a problem (Jasanoff 1999). This recognises that uncertainties are not simply an absence of knowledge, but have lived, embodied, and socially constructed dimensions: they are not experienced uniformly, and are reflected in imaginaries of good and desirable futures (Scoones and Stirling 2020). Indeed, according to Sarewitz (2004) uncertainty is not only an indication of the complexity of a problem, but also of multiple competing values that need to be explicitly attended to by the deliberation of value positions outside of a scientific context.

These brief examples show that civic epistemologies vary across cultures and issues, requiring approaches to adaptive governance that are cognisant of how deep seated cultural and social practices of a given context will influence deliberations over the nature of a problem and how it should be governed.

Two Case Examples

In this final section, we set out two examples of SPPIs that illustrate efforts at adaptive governance. The first example is a global environmental assessment, the IPBES, and the second example is the case of fisheries in the Solomon Islands. As these two examples show, it is not possible to realise the aspirations of adaptive governance without considering the intersection between science and governance (Wyborn 2015). SPPIs are not linear and mechanistic aspects of adaptive governance, where knowledge of a problem or resource is simply drawn on to inform changes in governance. Instead, they are shaped by social, cultural, and political dynamics that determine who should be included, how the SPPI should operate, and how its outcomes are justified. Moreover, understanding the social, cultural, and political patterns of behaviour that shape how problems are known and governed in a given context, is important to the development of more culturally appropriate, ethical, and effective modes of adaptive governance.

Example 1: The Intergovernmental Science-Policy Platform on Biodiversity and Ecosystem Services (IPBES)

IPBES is a science advice mechanism that has adopted an intergovernmental structure, akin to the Intergovernmental Panel on Climate Change (IPCC). This means that member-state governments are responsible for overseeing the Platform's operations, directing its programme of work, and approving its outputs. Since its establishment in 2012, the involvement of governments in IPBES has been seen as a means of strengthening the credibility, legitimacy, and relevance of the Platform to serve decision makers in multilateral environmental agreements (Koetz et al. 2012).

This SPPI has a mandate 'to strengthen the science–policy interface for biodiversity and ecosystem services' (IPBES 2012). The aim of the Platform is to both build stronger relationships between science and governance, and generate usable knowledge that can be applied in diverse governance contexts. Global environmental assessments are therefore a type of intervention directed specifically towards the production of knowledge to enable action and change towards sustainability goals (Clark et al. 2016; Chambers et al. 2021). Thus, understanding the governance that shapes how those interventions unfold, and the governance context in which they are seeking to make change is critical to their success.

For many analysts, IPBES is regarded to have emerged into a different social and political context than the IPCC, which came before it (Brooks et al. 2014). In recent decades, there have been important developments in recognising equity within UN processes, foregrounding the voices of Indigenous peoples and local communities and ensuring effective representation of actors from the Global South (Turnhout et al. 2012). Arguably too, biodiversity is a different environmental context than climate change (Zaccai and Adams 2012), in that it is differentially understood, experienced, and valued in different parts of the world, and therefore necessitates more pluralistic inputs of knowledge (Pascual et al. 2021). As a result, IPBES has innovated with regards to also being a more inclusive expert body (Díaz-Reveriego et al. 2019). This has not been a straightforward development, as IPBES has had to navigate its pursuit of authority as a consensus-based intergovernmental Platform and an organisation engaged in exploratory sense-making about a pluralistic natural environment (Montana 2020).

IPBES is an example of the ways in which SPPIs themselves can be adaptive components of governance systems. The establishment of IPBES as a new expert organisation provided a reasonable amount of room for new developments in response to changed understandings of the political and social context. However, scholars of SPPIs have called on IPBES to remain reflexive even as it continues to operate (Beck et al. 2014). Doing so suggests that IPBES needs to remain sufficiently flexible in its institutional structures and processes that it is amenable to transformative learning, while remaining open to critical scrutiny from internal and external review processes (Borie et al. 2020). Areas in which learning is still to take place, for example, include the continued broadening of the base of expertise that is accommodated within the Platform, such as the social sciences and humanities, and the potential for the organisation to recognise itself as a space of debate and deliberation across different value systems, and not just focused on forging consensus around environmental truths (Díaz-Reveriego et al. 2019).

Example 2: Fisheries management in the Solomon Islands

The organisation of SPPIs for fisheries in Solomon Islands is determined less by centralised expertise, and more by longstanding traditions and recent legislative changes. This case shows that for governance to be adaptive, SPPIs need to facilitate continuing and multimodal inputs of knowledge – be that scientific, local, Indigenous, experiential, or practical – in order to adapt responses over time as changes in the social, ecological, or political context in which it operates are detected. An interface that does not facilitate knowledge exchange, critical analysis of diverse perspectives, and provide equitable voice to different knowledge holders, is unlikely to enable governance that is adaptive to new knowledge or understandings of existing or emerging challenges.

Solomon Islands is a legal pluralist South Pacific nation where fisheries are governed through a complex overlap of customary marine tenure and a parliamentary democracy that follows English common law (Rohe et al. 2019). The Ministry of Fisheries and Marine Resources is tasked with managing inshore fisheries, but primary authority over inshore fisheries belongs to customary rights holders. The 2015 Solomon Islands National Fisheries Management Act (FMA) is the first legislation to attempt to legally link customary and common law to manage inshore fisheries. The FMA creates an option for communities to utilise the national police and court system to augment enforcement of customary fishing rules (Schwarz et al. 2020). To harness this enforcement power, which follows common law, communities must design, register, and regularly review community fisheries management plans that must recognise customary rights, provide clear geographic boundaries, identify monitoring indicators, and make provisions for revision (see FMA 2015, Section 18 and Schedule 2). The plans must be approved by the customary rights holders and government (national and provincial).

The FMA (2015) exists at the intersection of differing cultural logics and capacities regarding what and how knowledge is incorporated into decisions. The provision that plans must include monitoring provides one example where these logics may clash. Though the FMA (2015) does not specify a definition for 'monitoring' or 'indicators', the fact that these are required in plans introduces a scientific style of adaptive management more typical of resource management in the Global North (e.g. Gunderson and Light 2006), such as relying on fishing areas with distinct boundaries and relatively stable access rules nominally based on best available scientific data (Datta and Chaffin 2022). In Solomon Islands, customary management of natural resources is underpinned by adaptable rules based on fishers' knowledge, local leaders' concerns for community needs, and deliberations amongst customary rights' holders (Aswani et al. 2007, Foale et al. 2011). The communities have extremely limited capacity to conduct full-fledged scientific monitoring, with most drawing on practice-based knowledge (Foale et al. 2011).

The changing legislative landscape for fisheries management in Solomon Islands thus impacts the evolving organisation of SPPIs in the adaptive governance of fisheries. The extent to which fishing communities will choose to engage in the SPPI created by the standards for plans in the new FMA legislation will hinge in part on how government decision-makers and the national court interpret the requirement for 'monitoring', and whether they accept local and practice-based knowledge, especially when scientific data is not available. These decision-makers will thus serve as arbiters of whose knowledge counts, ultimately affecting how this policy will reshape the SPPI for fisheries governance in Solomon Islands. See Schwarz et al. 2020 and Datta and Chaffin 2022 for more details.

CONCLUSION

We have intentionally not identified a single approach to thinking about SPPIs for adaptive governance, as we advocate for a plurality of approaches to be valued and considered in the context in which they might be deployed. Instead, we have offered a set of concepts – the science-push, policy-pull, and co-production – that shape how SPPIs can be conceptualised and organised. We further highlighted the political considerations that manifest at the SPPI, through the design choices that shape how a problem is framed; who is included in an SPPI intervention; who sets the agenda; how relationships between actors are maintained; and how SPPI practices and outcomes are justified. These concepts and political considerations are relevant across instrumental efforts that deliberately intervene to enhance relationships between science and governance (e.g. IPBES), as well as interventions that are focused on the governance of sustainability problems which inherently require awareness of the range of ways in which that problem is known (e.g. Solomon Islands FMA).

Irrespective of the context, we stress that it is important to recognise that SPPIs are not pregiven, but rather constructed through either intentionally designed processes or emergent relationships between science and governance that are shaped by the social, political, and cultural context in which they occur. This also means that SPPIs are dynamic and should in themselves, embody the *adaptive* element of adaptive governance, to respond to changes in a context, or in knowledge of that context. Ultimately, within the scope of adaptive governance, SPPIs themselves are sites in which adaptive responses to changes in context can also occur. Rather than SPPIs being seen as the simple conduit for knowledge about the context that then informs how the governance system evolves, SPPIs that are adaptive are also necessary. As the case of IPBES shows, fostering reflexivity within the SPPI itself is critical here. So, knowledge of the functioning of the SPPI and a clear understanding of the goals that it seeks to achieve is also crucial for critical analysis and adaptation within an adaptive governance system.

We have also stressed the inherently political nature of SPPIs. Relationships between science and governance, whether intentional or emergent, will privilege particular issues, actors, and modes of governing. There is therefore a need to take seriously the politics of who benefits and who decides in designing SPPIs for adaptive governance, and ask whose knowledge, and which modes of governing are being marginalised as a consequence of the design choices being made (consider the Solomon Islands case study). Advances in knowledge cannot simply be inserted into a governance process with the expectation that the knowledge will not be questioned, and proposed strategies unproblematically accepted. Conflicting values or epistemologies cannot be done away with. Engaging with technical expertise, science, and other knowledges requires adaptive governance processes that are equipped to deal with conflicts without reverting to simplistic or naïve assumptions about their resolution. Thus, we argue that SPPIs for adaptive governance ultimately need to be reflexive about the role of knowledge in making change, the processes being used to enhance relationships between science and governance, and the politics underpinning how sustainability challenges are understood and governed.

REFERENCES

Adams, W. M. and Sandbrook, C. 2013. Conservation, evidence and policy, *Oryx*, 4703, 329–335.

Aswani, S., Albert, S., Sabetian, A., and Furusawa, T. 2007. Customary management as precautionary and adaptive principles for protecting coral reefs in Oceania, *Coral Reefs*, 264, 1009–1021.

Beck, S. 2011. Moving beyond the linear model of expertise? IPCC and the test of adaptation, *Regional Environmental Change*, 112, 297–306.

Beck, S. et al. 2014. Towards a reflexive turn in the governance of global environmental expertise, *Gaia*, 232, 80–87.

Bednarek, A. T., Shouse, B. and Hudson, C. G. 2015. Science – policy intermediaries from a practitioners perspective: the Lenfest Ocean Program experience, *Science and Public Policy*, 432, 291–300.

Bednarek, A. T. et al. 2018. Boundary spanning at the science–policy interface: the practitioners perspectives, *Sustainability Science*, 13, 1175–1183.

Berkes, F., Colding, J., and Folke, C. 2000. Rediscovery of traditional ecological knowledge as adaptive management, *Ecological Applications*, 105, 1251–1262.

Berkes, F. and Berkes, M. K. 2009. Ecological complexity, fuzzy logic, and holism in indigenous knowledge, *Futures*, 411, 6–12.

Biermann. F. 2006. Earth system governance: the challenge for social science. Global Governance Working Paper No 19. *Amsterdam et al.: The Global Governance Project*. Available at www.glogov.org.

Borie, M. et al. 2020. Institutionalising reflexivity? Transformative learning and the Intergovernmental science-policy Platform on Biodiversity and Ecosystem Services IPBES, *Environmental Science and Policy*, 110, May, 71–76.

Brooks, T. M., Lamoreux, J. F., Soberon, J. 2014. IPBES not equal IPCC, *Trends in Ecology and Evolution* 29, 543–545.

Brunner, R. and Steelman, T. 2005. Beyond scientific management. In Brunner, R. D., Steelman, T. A., Coe-Juell, L., Cromley, C. M., Edwards, C. M., Tucker, D. W. (eds) *Adaptive Governance: Integrating Science, Policy and Decision Making*, Columbia University Press, pp. 1–46.

Cash, D., Clark, W., Alcock, F., Dickson, N., Eckley, N., Guston, D., Jager, J., and Mitchell, R. 2003. Knowledge systems for sustainable development, *PNAS*, 10014, 8086–8091.

Cash, D. W., Borck, J. C., and Patt, A. G. 2006. Countering the loading-dock approach to linking science and decision making: comparative analysis of El Nino/Southern Oscillation ENSO. Forecasting Systems. *Science, Technology & Human Values*, 314, 465–494.

Chaffin, B. C., Gosnell, H., and Cosens, B. A. 2014. A decade of adaptive governance scholarship: synthesis and future directions, *Ecology and Society*, 193. https://www.jstor.org/stable/26269646?seq=1.

Chambers, J. M. et al. 2021. Six modes of co-production for sustainability, *Nature Sustainability*, 411, 983–996.

Chambers, J. M. et al. 2022. Co-productive agility and four collaborative pathways to sustainability transformations, *Global Environmental Change*, 72, 102422. doi: 10.1016/j.gloenvcha.2021.102422.

Clark, W. C. et al. 2016. Crafting useable knowledge for sustainable development, *PNAS*, 1137, 4570–4578.

Cooney, R. and Lang, A. T. F. 2007. Taking uncertainty seriously: adaptive governance and international trade, *European Journal of International Law*, 183, 523–551.

Datta, A. and Chaffin. B. 2022. Evolving adaptive governance: challenging assumptions through an examination of fisheries law in Solomon Islands, *Ecology and Society*, forthcoming.

Díaz-Reveriego, I., Turnhout, E., and Beck, S. 2019. Participation and inclusiveness in the Intergovernmental Science–Policy Platform on Biodiversity and Ecosystem Services, *Nature Sustainability*, 2, 457–464.

Dietz, T., Ostrom, E., and Stern, P. C. 2003. The struggle to govern the commons, *Science*, 3025652, 1907–12.

Dilling, L. and Lemos, M. C. 2011. Creating usable science: opportunities and constraints for climate knowledge use and their implications for science policy, *Global Environmental Change*, 21, 680–689.

Dunn, G., Bos, J. J., and Brown, R. R. 2018. Mediating the science-policy interface: insights from the urban water sector in Melbourne, Australia, *Environmental Science and Policy*, 82, 143–150.

Foale, S., Cohen, P., Januchowski-Hartley, S., Wegner, A., and Macintyre, M. 2011. Tenure and taboos: origins and implications for fisheries in the Pacific, *Fish and Fisheries*, 12, 357–369.

Folke, C. et al. 2005. Adaptive governance of social-ecological systems, *Annual Review of Environment and Resources*, 30, 441–73.

Fuller, B. W. 2009. Surprising cooperation despite apparently irreconcilable differences: agricultural water use efficiency and CALFED, *Environmental Science & Policy*, 126, 663–673.

Gieryn, T. F. 1983. Boundary-work and the demarcation of science from non-science: strains and interests in professional ideologies of scientists, *American Sociological Review*, 486, 781–795.

Gieryn, T. F. 1998. *Cultural Boundaries of Science: Credibility on the Line*. University of Chicago Press.

Gluckman, P. 2014. Policy: the art of science advice to government, *Nature*, 507, 163–165.

Gunderson, L. and Light, S. S. 2006. Adaptive management and adaptive governance in the everglades ecosystem, *Policy Sciences*, 39, 323–334

Guston, D. H. 1999. Stabilizing the boundary between US politics and science: the role of the Office of Technology Transfer as a boundary organisation, *Social Studies of Science*, 291, 87–111.

Head, B. W. 2016. Toward more 'evidence-informed' policy making?, *Public Administration Review*, 763, 472–484.

Jasanoff, S. and Wynne, B. 1998. Science and decision making. In Rayner, S. and Malone, E. (eds) *Human Choice and Climate Change*. Volume One. Columbus, Ohio, pp. 1–87.

Jasanoff, S. 2005. *Designs on Nature*. Princeton University Press.

Jasanoff, S. 2012. *Reason in Practice: In Science and Public Reason*, Taylor & Francis, pp. 1–22.

Juntti, M., Russel, D. and Turnpenny, J. 2009. Evidence, politics and power in public policy for the environment, *Environmental Science and Policy*, 123, 207–215.

Karpouzoglou, T., Dewulf, A. and Clark, J. 2016. Advancing adaptive governance of social-ecological systems through theoretical multiplicity, *Environmental Science & Policy*, 57, 1–9.

Koetz, T., Farrell, K. N., and Bridgewater, P. 2012. Building better science-policy interfaces for international environmental governance: assessing potential within the Intergovernmental Platform for Biodiversity and Ecosystem Services, *International Environmental Agreements*, 12, 1–21.

Landström, C., Whatmore, S. J., Lane, S. N., Odoni, N. A., Ward, N., and Bradley, S. 2011. Coproducing flood risk knowledge: redistributing expertise in critical participatory modelling, *Environment and Planning A: Economy and Space*, 43, 1617–1633.

Miller, C. A. 2008. Civic epistemologies: constituting knowledge and order in political communities, *Sociology Compass*, 26, 1896–1919.

Montana, J. 2019. Co-production in action: perceiving power in the organisational dimensions of a global biodiversity expert process, *Sustainability Science*, 14, 1581–1591.

Montana, J. 2020. Balancing authority and meaning in global environmental assessment: an analysis of organisational logics and modes in IPBES, *Environmental Science & Policy*, 112, 245–253.

Montana, J. and Wilsdon, J. 2021. Analysts, advocates and applicators: three discourse coalitions of UK evidence and policy. *Evidence & Policy: A Journal of Research, Debate and Practice*, 1–14. doi.org/10.1332/174426421X16112601473449.

Mouffe 2013. *Agonistics: Thinking the World Politically*. Verso.

Norström, A. et al. 2020. Principles for knowledge co-production in sustainability research, *Nature Sustainability*, 3, 182. doi: 10.1038/s41893-019-0448-2.

Nutley, S. 2003. Increasing research impact: early reflections from the ESRC Evidence Network No. Working Paper 16. Retrieved from http://www.kcl.ac.uk/sspp/departments/politicaleconomy/research/cep/pubs/papers/paper-16.aspx.

Oliver, K., Kothari, A., and Mays, N. 2019. The dark side of coproduction: do the costs outweigh the benefits for health research? *Implementation Science*, 3, 1–10.

Olsson, P., Folke, C., and Hughes, T. P. 2008. Navigating the transition to ecosystem-based management of the Great Barrier Reef, *Australia Proceedings of the National Academy of Sciences*, 10528, 9489–9494.

Pascual, U. et al. 2021. Biodiversity and the challenge of pluralism, *Nature Sustainability*, 47, 567–572.

Pregernig, M. 2014. Framings of science-policy interactions and their discursive and institutional effects: examples from conservation and environmental policy, *Biodiversity and Conservation*, 2314, 3615–3639.

Ripple, W. J. et al. 2020. World scientists warning of a climate emergency, *BioScience*, 701, 8–12.

Rohe, J. R., Govan, H., Schlüter, A., and Ferse, S. C. A. 2019. A legal pluralism perspective on coastal fisheries governance in two Pacific Island countries, *Marine Policy*, 100, 90–97.

Sarewitz, D. 2004. How science makes environmental controversies worse, *Environmental Science & Policy*, 75, 385–403.

Sarkki, S. et al. 2015. Adding 'iterativity' to the credibility, relevance, legitimacy: a novel scheme to highlight dynamic aspects of science–policy interfaces, *Environmental Science and Policy*, 54, 505–512.

Schwarz, A. M., Gordon, J., and Ramofafia, C. 2020. Nudging statutory law to make space for customary processes and community-based fisheries management in Solomon Islands, *Maritime Studies*, 19, 475–487.

Scoones, I. and Stirling, A. (eds) 2020. *The Politics of Uncertainty: Challenges of Transformation*, Routledge.

Scott, D. 2021. Diversifying the deliberative turn: toward an agonistic RRI, *Science, Technology, & Human Values*, https://doi.org/10.1177/01622439211067268.

Star, S. L. and Griesemer, J. R. 1989. Institutional ecology, translations and boundary objects: amateurs and professionals in Berkeley's Museum of Vertebrate Zoology, 1907–39, *Social Studies of Science*, 193, 387–420.

Stirling, A. 2008. 'opening up' and 'closing down': power, participation, and pluralism in the social appraisal of technology, *Science, Technology, & Human Values*, 332, 262–294.

Sutherland, W. J., Shackelford, G. and Rose, D. C. 2017. Collaborating with communities: co-production or co-assessment?, *Oryx*, 5104, 569–570. doi: 10.1017/S0030605317001296.

Swyngedouw, E. 2011. Depoliticized environments: the end of nature, climate change and the post-political condition, *Royal Institute of Philosophy Supplement*, 69, 253–274.

Tengö, M. et al. 2017. Weaving knowledge systems in IPBES, CBD and beyond: lessons learned for sustainability, *Current Opinion in Environmental Sustainability*, 26–27, 17–25.

Turnhout, E., Bloomfield, B., Hulme, M., Vogel, J., and Wynne, B. 2012. Conservation policy: listen to the voices of experience, *Nature*, 488, 454–455.

Van den Hove, S. 2007. A rationale for science–policy interfaces, *Futures*, 39, 807–826.

Van Kerkhoff, L. and Lebel, L. 2006. Linking knowledge and action for sustainable development, *Annual Review of Environment and Resources*, 311, 445–477.

Van Kerkhoff, L. and Pilbeam, V. 2017. Understanding socio-cultural dimensions of environmental decision-making: a knowledge governance approach, *Environmental Science and Policy*, 73, September 2016, 29–37.

Van Kerkhoff, L. V. et al. 2018. Towards future-oriented conservation: managing protected areas in an era of climate change, *Ambio*, 48, 699–731.

Westcott, D. A., Fletcher, C. S., Babcock, R. C., and Plaganyi-Lloyd, E. 2016. A strategy to link research and management of crown-of-thorns starfish on the Great Barrier Reef: an integrated pest management approach. *Report to the National Environmental Science Programme*, 77. Reef and Rainforest Research Centre Limited, Cairns.

Westcott, D. A., Fletcher, C. S., Kroon, F. J., Babcock, R. C., Plagányi, E. E., Pratchett, M. S., and Bonin, M. C. 2020. Relative efficacy of three approaches to mitigate Crown-of-Thorns Starfish outbreaks on Australia's Great Barrier Reef, *Scientific reports*, 101, 1–12.

Wiener, J. B. and Rogers, M. D. 2002. Comparing precaution in the United States and Europe, *Journal of Risk Research*, 54, 317–349.

Wyborn, C. 2015. Co-productive governance: a relational framework for adaptive governance, *Global Environmental Change*, 30, 56–67.

Wyborn, C., Leith, P., Hutton, J., Ryan, M., Montana, J., and Gallagher, L. 2017. The science, policy practice interface. Luc Hoffmann Institute Synthesis Paper. Gland, Switzerland: Luc Hoffmann Institute. doi: 10.13140/RG.2.2.10454.96322.

Wyborn, C. et al. 2019. Co-producing sustainability: reordering the governance of science, policy, and practice, *Annual Review of Environment and Resources*, 441, 319–346. doi: 10.1146/annurev-environ-101718-033103.

Zaccai, E. and Adams, W. M. 2012. How far are biodiversity loss and climate change similar as policy issues? *Environment, Development and Sustainability*, 14, 4, 557–571.

PART II

LATEST TRENDS IN METHODS

5. Futures-thinking: concepts, methods and capacities for adaptive governance

Carla Alexandra, Carina Wyborn, Claudia Munera Roldan and Lorrae van Kerkhoff

INTRODUCTION

Accelerated impacts of climate change and other global drivers pose significant challenges for governance, not least because of the increased uncertainty they add to futures that are already hard to anticipate. In the context of uncertain futures, environmental decision-making requires forward-looking, anticipatory approaches, firstly, to avoid path dependency that forecloses adaptive responses and secondly, to steer transformative changes required to meet sustainability goals (Feola, 2015; Griffith et al., 2010; IPBES, 2019; Moore et al., 2018; Olsson et al., 2006). This is particularly evident as climate and other uncertainties challenge traditional planning (Boyd et al., 2015; Stafford Smith et al., 2011) and decision-making approaches (Folke et al., 2021; Gerlak et al., 2021; Mangnus et al., 2021; Quay, 2010; Stafford Smith et al., 2011). Whilst some transformations will likely be unintended and undesired, proactive and deliberate transformations towards more sustainable futures are possible (Moore et al., 2014; O'Brien, 2012; Olsson et al., 2006). As such, key questions for adaptive governance concern: how to prioritise long-term uncertain futures in current decision-making; how to motivate action before crises (Koontz et al., 2015); and how to develop methods and capacities to imagine and plan for alternative futures (Boyd et al., 2015; Wyborn et al., 2016).

Approaches to systematically anticipate uncertain futures, variously termed futures-thinking, anticipation, strategic foresight, and futuring, are therefore essential in the governance of social-ecological systems (SES), and represent an important direction for adaptive governance scholarship and practice (Cook et al., 2014; Boyd et al., 2015; Muiderman et al., 2020). *Futures-thinking* is henceforth used as an inclusive term to encompass the range of approaches. The capacity to anticipate and respond to change is central to building adaptive and transformative capacities (Boyd et al., 2015; Moore and Milkoreit, 2020; Pereira et al., 2018; Quay, 2010).

Despite growing interest within the sustainability sciences, the diversity of futures methods remains largely unknown in environmental governance (Bengston, 2019), and environmental governance research remains largely disconnected from futures-thinking (Vervoort and Gupta, 2018). Within adaptive governance scholarship, engagement with futures-thinking and methods is limited, despite some notable exceptions (Tschakert and Dietrich, 2010; Boyd et al., 2015; Nykvist et al., 2017). There is a need to understand the application, use and limitations of futures-thinking across diverse governance contexts, including the political and governance dimensions that enable or constrain futures approaches.

This chapter explores how futures-thinking methods provide capacities to proactively adapt and transform SES. We aim to highlight how futuring methods may contribute to adaptive governance, bringing together literature from adaptive governance of SES, transformations, anticipatory governance and futures-thinking. Empirical studies that explicitly and implicitly engage with the concept of futures-thinking are drawn on from biodiversity conservation, water governance and environmental governance. This targeted review draws on aspects most relevant to applying futures-thinking to environmental governance, responding to the need for greater understanding of the use and limitations of futures methods in governing SES. The next section explores the link between adaptation, transformation, and anticipation, before the third section introduces futures-thinking and methods. We review how futures-thinking methods are used in adaptive governance in the fourth section, exploring how these methods support capacities to proactively adapt and transform. We then propose considerations for adaptive governance to proactively and strategically address long-term and uncertain futures in the fifth section. To conclude, we call for expanded approaches to adaptive governance, capable of confronting long-term perspectives of future uncertainty and change, with capacities to navigate and govern processes of adaptation and transformation.

GOVERNING FUTURE CHANGE – CONCEPTUALISING THE LINK BETWEEN ADAPTATION, TRANSFORMATION, AND ANTICIPATION

Adaptive governance is an umbrella concept for approaches to governing SES that deal with uncertainty, and with decision-making processes that can anticipate, learn from, and respond to change (Hurlbert and Gupta, 2016; Wyborn, 2015). While conceptual ambiguity has been noted with related and precursor terms of adaptive management and adaptative co-management (Hasselman, 2017), adaptive governance scholarship broadly focuses on collaborative decision-making, cross-scale linkages in nested governance structures and social learning (Folke et al., 2005; Wyborn, 2015). Adaptation and transformation are understood as key capacities to deal with uncertainty and steer change, then understanding how adaptive governance can assist these capacities is central to SES scholarship (Moore et al., 2018; Patterson et al., 2017). Whilst debate exists in the literature on the distinction between adaptation and transformation, we define adaptation as "the capacity of a system to adjust its responses to changing external drivers and internal processes and stay on the current pathway" (Moore et al., 2018), whilst transformation is understood as "the capacity to create entirely new systems" (Moore et al., 2018), where "fundamental changes in structural, functional, relational, and cognitive aspects of socio-technical-ecological systems that lead to new patterns of interactions and outcomes" are achieved (Patterson et al., 2017).

Understanding how to navigate transformative change, including the need to strategically transform SES into new alternative states, is an important question for adaptive governance (Visseren-Hamakers et al., 2021). There is a broad literature on deliberate transformations with differing conceptual approaches (see Patterson et al. (2017)). The SES transformations approach is distinguished by its theoretical origins in adaptive governance and complex adaptive systems (Olsson et al., 2004; Patterson et al., 2017). SES transformations: (1) emphasise the importance of adaptiveness for transformation processes, (2) are usually place based (i.e. a watershed or region), and (3) focus on bringing together multiple types of knowledge such as local and scientific knowledge (Patterson et al., 2017). Empirical studies on SES transformations have focused on social transformations towards sustainable governance regimes (Herrfahrdt-Pähle et al., 2020; Olsson et al., 2006).

The multiscale nature of transformative change in SES is central to SES transformation scholarship, exploring the interplay of persistence, adaptability, and transformability across scales (Chaffin et al., 2014; Miller et al., 2014). For example, adaptation at one scale may be reliant or affected, upon transformation at another scale (Folke et al., 2010; Chaffin et al., 2014; Miller et al., 2014). Similarly, it is important to consider the imagined perception of change and temporal dynamics of social-ecological responses to slow and fast events at different scales. Despite this, the governance of proactively adapting and transforming requires further attention (Chaffin et al., 2016).

Distinguishing between the need and opportunity to adapt or transform is a challenge that decision-makers at different scales increasingly face (Armitage and Plummer, 2010; Curtis et al., 2014; Marshall et al., 2012). Pre-emptive action to reduce impacts of future change, including climate change, will entail decisions on adapting versus transforming. For example, should an agricultural community shift from monoculture to diversify their crops in response to changes, or should they transform to other livelihood options such as tourism? Governance capacities will be required that can support making such forward-looking decisions. Therefore, whilst the ability to understand, accommodate, and respond to change under uncertainty is foundational to adaptive governance (Folke et al., 2005; Chaffin et al., 2014), the need to more proactively plan for uncertain futures is increasingly recognised (Nykvist et al., 2017).

Within adaptive governance literatures, instances of proactive forward-looking adaptation are limited, instead focusing on responses to crises as motivations for adaptation (Koontz et al., 2015; Hurlbert and Gupta, 2016; Nykvist et al., 2017). Nykvist et al. (2017) point to the "crisis before action" trap, arguing that relying on crisis to stimulate action does not build or elevate long-lasting adaptive capacity. For example, a study of regional water governance in Sweden highlighted that crises such as flooding events evoked existing response structures, and did not result in new types of response processes (Nykvist et al., 2017). Whilst responses to a particular crisis may increase ability to deal with a future crisis of the same nature, it does not build capacity to deal with novel crises (Nykvist et al., 2017), or to prepare for slower, long-term change. Understanding how to motivate anticipatory action is thus a key question for adaptive governance scholarship and practice (Koontz et al., 2015).

The related field of anticipatory governance focuses on "governance processes in the present that seek to use anticipation to engage with uncertain futures in order to guide action in the present" (Muiderman et al., 2022). Anticipatory governance emerged in Science, Technology and Innovation Foresight programmes within governments in the 1960s, with various other traditions of anticipatory governance emerging over the last half a century, including in national security policy analyses, sustainability science, and environmental governance and policy literatures (Muiderman et al., 2022; Ramos, 2014). Within sustainability sciences, anticipatory governance is used to address adaptation challenges associated with the uncertainty of climate change in contested spaces (Serrao-Neumann et al., 2013).

Despite cross-over, distinctions can be made between adaptive governance and anticipatory governance. "Anticipation" differs from "planning" as outlined in adaptive governance models in certain regards. Key features of anticipation include addressing long-term time horizons (often 20–30 years into the future); engaging with multiple alternative futures; strategic direction setting; and addressing socio-political contexts of futures (i.e. not only climatic or technological futures). The concept of anticipatory governance is receiving increasing attention within adaptive governance literature, as it is noted to increase efficacy of policy responses to climate change and develop future solutions through participatory processes

(Hurlbert and Gupta, 2016). None-the-less, anticipatory governance systems for managing natural resources are underdeveloped, and cross-over between adaptive governance and anticipatory governance scholarship, whilst increasing, is still emerging (Boyd et al., 2015).

Given the political and contested nature of SES governance, forward-looking decisions require attention to politics and power. Preparing and planning for uncertain futures often involves parallel or contested visions of the future (Teräväinen, 2019). For example, Anderson (2010: 780) addresses the uncomfortable fact that "certain lives may have to be abandoned, damaged, or destroyed in order to protect, save or care for life" in futures dramatically altered by climate change. Conservation futures are already highlighting the highly political act of deliberate (and undeliberate) triage that arises with the recognition that not all ecosystems can be conserved in perpetuity (Wyborn et al., 2021). There are calls for more attention to be paid to disconnects between what science calls for as necessary characteristics of adaptive governance, what is politically feasible, and further, what society desires from ecosystems (Chaffin et al., 2014; Wyborn, 2015). Further, the politics of futures-thinking requires attention to the plural attitudes towards the future and temporal scales, including perspectives from Indigenous peoples and non-Western cultures (Milojević, 2002; Murphy et al., 2016; Whyte, 2017).

Embracing uncertain futures to proactively adapt and strategically transform will require both the openness and participation of adaptive governance, the long-term perspective and foresight capacities of anticipatory governance (Boyd et al., 2015), and increased attention to transformations (Patterson et al., 2017). Various disciplines have proposed ways to proactively imagine and steer future change and uncertainty. Some scholars have called for an expanded model of adaptive governance that integrates anticipatory governance, adaptive management, and adaptive co-management (Hurlbert, 2018; Hurlbert and Gupta, 2016); others are calling for a shift towards the emerging concept of transformative governance (Chaffin et al., 2016; Patterson et al., 2017; Visseren-Hamakers et al., 2021). Governing substantial yet uncertain future change will require strategies to proactively navigate adaptation and transformation within and across scales, and forward-looking methods will be key.

FUTURES-THINKING AND METHODS

Futures-thinking is a field of study and approach that considers uncertain futures in proactive, strategic, and robust ways (Slaughter, 1996). Futures-thinking explores alternative future trajectories and their implications for current decision-making (Cork, 2018; Wyborn et al., 2021), by systematically analysing drivers of change and stability (Slaughter, 2009) to imagine futures in diverse ways. Some scholars argue that futures thinking requires "futures literacy", which is defined as the capability and "skills needed to decide why and how to use their imagination to introduce the non-existent future into the present" (Miller, 2018) (see Box 5.1). Futures-thinking aims to make explicit the plurality of ideas that people have about the future, which shape how we act and make decisions in the present (Voros, 2007). Futures-thinking is used to: support policy development and action plans; build information and knowledge; build capacity and societal preparedness; test the resilience of plans across multiple alternative futures; and mobilise stakeholders (Muiderman et al., 2020; Pereira et al., 2019; Wyborn et al., 2021). Beyond this, emerging scholarship is focusing on the role of futures-thinking in transformations to sustainability (Muiderman et al., 2022). Critical and Indigenous scholars are concerned with decolonising futures-thinking, as modern futures-thinking is largely based in the Western intellectual tradition (Milojević, 2002; Nikolakis, 2020).

BOX 5.1   FUTURES LITERACY

Futures literacy is a term that has been endorsed and promoted by the United Nations Educational, Scientific and Cultural Organization (UNESCO). Futures literacy (FL) is defined as a capability whereby a "… futures literate person has acquired the skills needed to decide why and how to use their imagination to introduce the non-existent future into the present" (Miller, 2018:15). The concept emphasises that, similar to other forms of literacy, futures literacy is a skill that is universal, and teaching and learning futures literacy can be incorporated in all educational settings. The core of the capability is our individual or collective ability to "use the future" to effectively anticipate change. As such, the analytical component of FL research identifies and explores "anticipatory systems", and differentiates between two main forms of anticipation. The first is anticipation for particular desired or expected futures, which encompasses, for example, investing in the stock market or planning for two degrees temperature rise. The second anticipatory system is anticipation for emergence, which is an imaginative and exploratory approach to possible futures that is not constrained by probability or identified trends. While the former is highly dominant, it is argued that this form of anticipation also unduly limits what societies regard as possible futures. Much of the UNESCO FL agenda is therefore focused on growing capability in these more emergent forms of anticipation.

Mangnus et al. (2021) however, identify several different forms of futures thinking and practice, and point to important differences between them. They argue that "being futures literate" means being aware of, and reflexive about these different fundamental bases from which people may understand, engage with and act towards the future. While this is not incompatible with the UNESCO framework approach, Mangnus et al. (2021) draw greater attention to the philosophical, social and political implications of different ways of approaching the future.

Futures-thinking as a field proposes a shift away from a deterministic forecast of a single future, towards pluralistic approaches to explore and shape alternative futures. Developing effective strategies from a forecast of a single future is difficult in conditions of high uncertainty and complexity (Quay, 2010), as predictive forecasting cannot adequately address the uncertain, diffuse, multi-scalar drivers of change in complex SES (Bennett et al., 2003; Bengston, 2019). Whilst we cannot predict one future accurately, focusing on multiple alternative futures enables us to prepare for and embrace uncertainty (Inayatullah, 2008). Furthermore, it is assumed that futures-thinking can generate individual and societal capacities to "create futures that we desire" (Inayatullah, 2008; Slaughter, 1996). Within modes of governance, this shift can be understood as moving away from traditional "predict and plan" forecast approaches, towards a focus on futures-thinking, or foresight (Jurgilevich, 2021).

Scholars have outlined many approaches to engaging with the future, with differing aims (Anderson, 2010; Cork, 2018; Mangnus et al., 2021; Muiderman et al., 2020). Cork (2018) outlines three approaches to relating to the future, including: predictive forecasting *"what will happen if ...*"; explorative "*what might happen if ...*"; and normative "*how might futures be achieved by ...*". Explorative approaches to futuring investigate a range of possible and plausible futures as a way to address uncertainty and surprise (Anderson, 2010), aiming to build adaptive capacity and preparedness (Muiderman et al., 2020). Normative approaches focus on exploring what future is desirable, addressing how target futures may be achieved (Cork, 2018; Svenfelt et al., 2010) to co-create transformed futures (Muiderman et al., 2020). Unlike predictive forecasting, explorative and normative approaches shift away from the idea that the future can be predicted. Integrated methodologies have also been developed merging explorative and normative approaches, seeking to identify robust actions across multiple plausible futures (van Vliet and Kok, 2015; Yung et al., 2019).

Across these approaches, a vast range of anticipatory methods have been developed, with differing applications and limitations (see Box 5.2). Futures methods are used individually or in combination with other approaches. Bengston (2019) noted 34 futuring methods, and classified them across three continua, including expert-based vs participatory, quantitative vs qualitative, and evidence-based vs imagination-based (Bengston, 2019). Common methods applied to natural resources governance are scenario planning, backcasting, horizon scanning, and visioning (see Box 5.2). Participatory processes often draw on evidence-based representations of the future for stakeholders to develop shared scenarios and visions, having considered trade-offs and multiple pathways (Murphy et al., 2016). Modelling based approaches have for instance integrated scenarios with geographical information systems (GIS) for spatial planning (Haslauer et al., 2012). Applications of futures methods have been reviewed in conservation and environmental decision-making (Cook et al., 2014; Wyborn et al., 2021), ecosystem assessments (Cork, 2018), climate change adaptation (Quay, 2010), climate risk assessments (Jurgilevich, 2021), and resilience in water governance (Boyd et al., 2015).

BOX 5.2   FUTURES METHODS

Scenarios

Scenarios create alternative futures by understanding the present, identifying future uncertainty, and developing alternative futures. Scenarios are used to explore uncertainty through representing a range of 'plausible futures' that explore the implications of different trajectories in key drivers of change. There are a range of qualitative, quantitative and participatory methods used to develop scenarios, and alongside that, a large diversity of what comprises a "scenario". This includes everything from expert-led computational models (e.g. Kim et al., (2018)) to participatory processes that develop visions of the future (e.g. Pereira et al., 2018). Scenarios are used for a range of purposes, including: (1) exploratory scenarios to support agenda setting; (2) target-seeking scenarios to support policy or programme design; (3) policy-screening scenarios to support implementation; and (4) scenarios to support retrospective evaluation or policy review (see IPBES, 2016).

Backcasting

Backcasting develops pathways to a desired future state or vision, by firstly developing a normative vision of a desired future, from which pathways are developed backwards from the vision to present (Wiek and Iwaniec, 2014). Initially developed by Robinson

(Robinson, 1982) to address energy futures, the approach has been applied to develop robust water climate adaptation strategies (van der Voorn et al., 2012; van Vliet and Kok, 2015). Backcasting has also been framed more broadly as a methodological framework for transformational sustainability research (Wiek and Lang, 2016).

Horizon Scanning

Horizon scanning is used to detect signals and trends about emerging issues by drawing together diverse streams of information about current trends and conditions. This process systematically detects early signs of potentially important changes, including weak signals, wild cards, trends in consistency and change, risks, and threats (Cook et al., 2014). Horizon scanning is often a first step in scenario development, and also used as a standalone activity.

Visioning

Visioning is a process for creating a representation of a desired future or future state. A variety of methodologies and approaches to visioning have been elaborated, including Future Workshop, Community Visioning, Sustainability Solution Space, and Visioneering (Wiek and Iwaniec, 2014). Whilst most visioning methodologies call for stakeholder engagement, levels of participation vary and many methodologies have limited information and rationales for levels of stakeholder engagement (Wiek and Iwaniec, 2014).

Three Horizons Framework

The "Three Horizons" framework is a simple participatory tool that can be used to support dialogue about uncertain futures, and the strategies that might be needed to transition towards desirable futures (Sharpe et al., 2016). Participants identify "three horizons", the first (H1) representing the current state of play, or "business as usual", the third (H3) representing an emerging pattern that could, in the future, come to represent the dominant patterns of behaviour, and the second (H2) representing the transitional activities and innovations that emerge in response to the changing patterns of behaviour between H1 and H3. In exploring these three horizons, participants identify current concerns, future aspirations, inspirations that could inspire new practice, innovations needed to move towards a desirable future, and the aspects of the current system they would like to maintain.

THE CAPACITIES TO USE FUTURES-THINKING AND METHODS IN ADAPTIVE GOVERNANCE

Navigating and governing socio-political and ecological change will require capacities to enable necessary changes in policies, laws, and decision-making processes. Adaptive governance requires creating capacities to implement futures-thinking methods to: (a) engage with uncertainty and surprise; (b) develop and translate futures knowledge; (c) envision transformation; (d) enhance systems reflexivity; and (e) address contestation. We propose that whilst they are all important for proactive adaptation, certain capacities may be more important for transformation.

Engage with Future Uncertainty and Surprise

Developing scenarios of alternative futures can increase capacity to deal with future uncertainty and surprise (Boyd et al., 2015; Whitney et al., 2017). Futures methods that explore alternative futures facilitate consideration of uncertainty, complexity, and non-linear feedback dynamics (Thorn et al., 2020) (see Box 5.2). Participatory scenarios have been used to develop robust strategies that deal with uncertainty and surprise across multiple futures, including in climate change adaptation strategies (Quay, 2010), environmental policymaking (Höjer et al., 2011; Svenfelt et al., 2010), and development of water management strategies (Haasnoot and Middelkoop, 2012) (see Table 5.1). Wild cards and weak signals have also been used to proactively approach possible surprises in water services (Takala and Heino, 2017). Given that aspirations to reduce all uncertainties are illusive, futures-thinking can be used to generate understanding of uncertain futures, supporting decision-making under uncertainty (Yung et al., 2019). Yet despite decision-making under uncertainty being central for adaptive governance, action is often hindered by perceptions that more information is needed to reduce uncertainty (Boyd et al., 2015; Wyborn et al., 2021).

Generating and Translating Futures Knowledge

Futures methods build knowledge of alternative futures by developing and integrating past, present and future knowledge of SES. Scenarios and other futures methods can be used to understand SES and feedbacks, identify potential tipping points, highlight emerging threats, and identify new opportunities (Bennett et al., 2003; Cook et al., 2014; Schneider and Rist, 2014; Cork, 2018). Participatory futures methods also integrate knowledge across geographical scales and disciplines (Dufva et al., 2015; Enfors et al., 2008; Murphy et al., 2016; Thorn et al., 2020). Furthermore, the process of integrating knowledge between stakeholders can generate new social networks, including multi-level networks from local to regional scales (Dufva et al., 2015). Bennett et al. (2003) argue that participatory scenario development processes increased collaboration between scientists, managers, and stakeholders, and highlights how the procedural function of futures methods (i.e. the process of constructing scenarios) supports development of cross-sectoral and multi-level social networks. In this regard, participatory scenario construction and other futures methods may activate a "learning by planning" aspect of adaptive governance, supporting competence building, networks, and generating new information (Wiek et al., 2006). However, challenges to participatory scenario planning processes have been noted, including difficulties in: maintaining stakeholder engagement (Faysse et al., 2018; Drakes et al., 2020); finding relevant socio-economic and climate data; and, addressing contradictory interpretations of existing institutions and knowledge (Gielczewski et al., 2011).

The knowledge generated from futures methods may be used to reposition existing understanding of SES. This may include, for example, testing the implications of existing policies across multiple scenarios, understanding potential consequences of actions and adopting new perspectives of current trajectories (Dufva et al., 2015). For example, scenarios have been used to identify indicators, and highlight whether a region is developing in desirable or undesirable pathways (Enfors et al., 2008; Quay, 2010). Further, reconceptualising knowledge of the past,

Table 5.1   Futures-thinking methods that support capacities for adapting and transforming

Futures methods support capacity to …	By …	Futures methods
Engage with uncertainty and surprise	• Developing robust strategies across multiple futures (Enfors et al., 2008; Haasnoot and Middelkoop, 2012; van Vliet and Kok, 2015a) • Incorporating uncertainty in environmental policymaking (Höjer et al., 2011) • Developing flexible adaptation strategies (Quay, 2010)	Exploratory and participatory scenarios; wild cards and weak signals
Develop and integrate futures knowledge	• Generating new knowledge of SES (Bennett et al., 2003b; Wiek et al., 2006) • Integrate knowledge (Enfors et al., 2008; Thorn et al., 2020) • Integrating visions of desired futures with decisions informed by science (Meyer et al.,2016). • Increasing cross-sectoral and cross-disciplinary collaboration (Bennett et al., 2003a) • Generating novel multi-level social networks (Dufva et al., 2015; Meyer et al., 2016) • Reassessing existing knowledge (Dufva et al., 2015) • Exploring future elements/weak signals that may initiate a transition (Murphy et al., 2016, 2017; Sondeijker et al., 2006)	Scenarios; participatory scenarios; participatory visioning processes
Foster capacity to envision transformed futures	• Imagining radically different futures (Pereira et al., 2019) • Inspiring positive and transformative futures (Raudsepp-Hearne et al., 2020) • Developing imagination as a transformative capacity (Moore and Milkoreit, 2020)	Arts-based participatory approaches to visioning and scenarios; seeds approaches
Foster systems reflexivity	• Gaining understanding of others' worldviews (Dufva et al., 2015) • Making explicit the underlying values in visions of desired futures (Meyer et al., 2016; Schneider and Rist, 2014)	Participatory visioning; scenarios
Address contestation	• Illuminating key tensions across worldviews (Sandström et al., 2016) • Illuminating synergies between stakeholders (Sandström et al., 2016; Nikolakis, 2020) • Addressing power dynamics of stakeholders to create shared visions of transformative change towards sustainability (Pereira et al., 2019) • Identifying systemic causes, underlying worldviews and paradigms to ensure change is transformative (Inayatullah, 2008)	Participatory backcasting; causal layered analysis; Futures focused workshops and scenarios; arts-based participatory approaches to visioning and scenarios

present, and future also supports sustainability transformation, where scenario methods can help explore binaries of desired and undesired futures, and futures emerging from continuity of the present versus resulting from transformation (Bruckmeier, 2020).

Fostering Capacity to Envisioning Transformation

Whilst futures methods support development of robust adaptive strategies, literature on transformations and futures-thinking points to methods that generate transformative visions (see Table

5.1). Generating a vision of a transformed and desired future is recognised as an initial phase in transformation processes (Chaffin et al., 2016; Moore et al., 2014; Sondeijker et al., 2006; Wiek et al., 2006). For scenarios to capture positive transformative change, Raudsepp-Hearne et al. (2020) argue that novel sets of drivers are required that engage with cultural contexts, socio-environmental change, and trust. For example, the "Seeds of a Good Anthropocene" builds positive and plausible scenarios from inspiring real-world examples, known as "seeds", and highlights how processes of change and transformation will involve recombination of existing and novel ideas, technologies, and concepts, resulting in a "bricolage" of the old and the new (Moore and Milkoreit, 2020; Olsson et al., 2017; Pereira et al., 2018; Raudsepp-Hearne et al., 2020).

The capacity to envision transformation has been linked to other transformative capacities, such as imagination and participant agency (Moore and Milkoreit, 2020). Transformative capacity is considered to encompass adaptive capacity (defined as "the potential to mobilise existing resources for adapting to change" (Marshall et al., 2012:2)), as well as other capacities to disrupt current systems and build up alternatives (Moore et al., 2018). Despite overlap, where adaptive and transformative capacities diverge is not well understood (Moore et al., 2018; Marshall et al., 2012). The process of utilising futures methods may generate "transformative spaces" in which transformative capacities are developed and networks of support are mobilised (Moore et al., 2014; Pereira et al., 2018). For example, scholars suggest that engagement with arts-based approaches in scenario processes can trigger imagination, richer visions, and innovative actions (Pereira et al., 2019). Methods such as storytelling (Pereira et al., 2018) and wildcards aim to integrate more imagination into futures-thinking processes (Hauptman and Steinmuller, 2018). As such, futures methods may also generate transformative capacities and commitments for transformative change (Moore et al., 2014). Sharpe et al. (2016) argue that methods that simultaneously address futures uncertainty and privilege participants agency are critical for futures-thinking to support transformative change.

Futures methods can also be used to translate knowledge about future sustainability transformations into actionable pathways (Schneider and Rist, 2014). Methods such as backcasting, transition scenarios, and the Three Horizons framework can be used to develop plans and strategies towards desired futures (Inayatullah, 2008; Sharpe et al., 2016). For example, Ferguson et al. (2013) developed a strategic program for transforming Melbourne's urban water systems to a water sensitive paradigm, by analysing content from a participatory transition scenario process. However, the ability of scenarios and other futures methods to influence decision-making has been questioned, both for adaptive and transformative processes. Moore et al. (2014) note that whilst visioning and other participatory futures methods are key to transformation, implementation of transformative pathways is not assured.

Enhancing Systems Reflexivity

Systems reflexivity, the capacity to "*see, interrogate and reimagine the taken-for-granted structures that sustain current systems and people-planet relationships*", will be vital for navigating transformative change and envisioning alternative futures (Moore et al., 2018). The ability to imagine alternative futures requires capacities to interrogate current social-ecological realities (Moore and Milkoreit, 2020) and to detach from present-day reality and structures in order to imagine alternative futures. Research on participatory visioning processes suggests that the ability to influence the future is constrained when existing values, rules, institutions, and structures are taken-for-granted as preconditions for future realities (Jenssen, 2010). Many futures methods aim to illuminate stakeholders' worldviews and assumptions about current and future SES (Meyer et al., 2016; Cork, 2018; Pereira et al., 2019). However, Inayatullah (2008) notes that worldviews and values are often difficult to discern during futures-thinking processes, highlighting the importance of prioritising systems reflexivity. Futures methods can explicitly interrogate existing values and knowledge of stakeholders while reflecting on existing structures that prevent reaching desired futures (see Box 5.3).

Whilst futures-thinking processes focus on interrogating and bringing to the fore individuals' assumptions about current realities, capacities for transformative change may require deeper systemic reflexivity that focus only on social structures, and on change processes in social-ecological systems (Moore et al., 2018). This may include understanding cross-scale change process and institutions that structure social-ecological relationships (Moore et al., 2018). For example, the Three Horizons method focuses on understanding patterns of change, including helping distinguish between incremental and transformative change (Sharpe et al., 2016).

Addressing Contestation

Futures-thinking and methods provide tools to engage with contestation and trade-offs in adaptive governance contexts, as constructing visions and scenarios require working across perspectives and thinking outside of silos in order to create a complete future "world". For example, a foresight project in Chile focused on regional futures, with the aim to draw out the inherent conflicts between water users and develop pathways towards a shared desired future (Dufva et al., 2015). Similarly, participatory backcasting has been used to illuminate key tensions in worldviews and norms over highly contested forest futures, and was also used to outline synergies between Indigenous peoples and non-First Nations people (Sandström et al., 2016; Nikolakis, 2020).

The capacity to address power asymmetries across contested values, whilst also important for adaptation, may require heightened attention when aiming to develop visions for transformative change. Transformation requires lasting change in power relations (Chaffin et al., 2016), and processes of socio-political-environmental change are unlikely to arise from a single cohesive collective vision (Pereira et al., 2019; Walker et al., 2009). Pereira et al. (2019) propose that some arts-based approaches to scenario development may be well equipped to address power asymmetries (e.g. class, gender and ethnicity), by ensuring an inclusive and reflexive approach. Despite this, the political dimensions of transformation processes remain under-developed in theory (Patterson et al., 2017), and the contested nature of visioning processes are often downplayed (Späth and Rohracher, 2010).

BOX 5.3   RETHINKING BIODIVERSITY CONSERVATION
            ADAPTATION IN TIMES OF CHANGE

The Conservation Futures project implemented in Colombia developed processes to help protected area managers rethink the nature of conservation and management strategies in the context of climate change, by examining observed and expected impacts of climate change on local livelihood systems, or the provision of ecosystem services, and the implications of change for decision making in the protected area and surrounding landscapes.

Although the Conservation Futures approach is not a normative process, it can help deliberation about ecological transformation, and the future of conservation goals affected by climate impacts.

Through a dialogue-based series of activities, conservation practitioners were encouraged to anticipate ecosystem transformation and potential impacts on benefits and values, while exploring alternative management approaches. The process allowed a reflection about what people value about the protected areas, existing knowledge in use guiding decisions related with ecological transformations, and the institutional management options available. This thinking helped participants identify what can be done now to prepare for uncertain futures.

Lessons Learnt, Challenges and Limitations

Adapting protected areas to climate change require changes in how we think about management. Applying an approach such as Conservation Futures helped participants to explore adaptive and reflective management actions for protected area management. The experience in Colombia was made easier by a strong interest in understanding climate change impacts in protected areas, and a history of analysis and synthesis within all levels of management.

Implementing the approach faced communication, technical and political challenges. Scientific narratives supporting conservation goals tend to focus on preventing change, therefore, the language and concepts of accommodating ecological change are unfamiliar, often not well received. Protected areas have legal geographical restrictions affecting governance and action to certain boundaries. Overcoming the perceived need for "more and better" scientific information to deal with climate change, was a significant barrier that required discussions and deliberations to better understand where managers in Colombia were at. These approaches should be seen as long-term processes. It requires engagement to build trustful relationships, and a collective understanding of the problem. This often means having financial resources, that are not often available.

Source: See van Kerkhoff et al. (2019).

BOX 5.4   ENGAGING COMMUNITIES WITH CLIMATE CHANGE FUTURES IN THE WESTERN UNITED STATES

Projections of climate change in the Western United States suggest potentially transformative impacts on regional ecologies, economies, and livelihoods. Using an iterative scenario-building process, we engaged diverse stakeholders in two Rocky Mountain communities in a dialogue about possible landscape changes and how they might respond. The method intended to explore, rather than reduce, uncertainties, guided by four key principles (see Murphy et al. 2016):

- Explicit consideration of *social-ecological integration*;
- Recognition of continuing *uncertainty* regarding how future impacts will manifest;
- Close attention to cross-scale interactions that play out in *particular places*;
- Inclusion of *diverse knowledges* from natural and social sciences as well as communities.

The three scenarios storylines (see Table 5.2) represented plausible futures and were pegged to a 20 year timeframe to balance futures that participants could realistically envisage, while still enabling differentiation from climate impacts across the scenarios. We identified ecological features or processes of likely social concern, and then used the temperature and precipitation data to generate ecological responses using peer reviewed literature and published reports. These projections formed the basis of scenario narratives constructed to be easily readable and relatable, such that participants would be able to "see their worlds" in the storylines.

Table 5.2   Scenario storylines

Scenario	Climate Description
Some like it Hot	Warmer and drier across all seasons with perennial drought
The Seasons are a Changin'	Warmer across all seasons, earlier snowmelt, with more winter precipitation (as snow and/or rain)
"Feast or Famine"	High inter-annual climate variability, with hot, dry years followed by cool, wet years (increasing the frequency of extreme events such as floods or droughts)

In qualitative interviews, participants responded to biophysical and climatological narrative scenarios to identify risks, vulnerabilities, and possible adaptive strategies. Interviews were analysed to distil likely actions, in that many participants suggested a particular strategy. Based on this information, revised "social-ecological" scenarios weaved in aspects of social responses, and explicitly sought to depict cross-scale, cross-sectoral changes. In a final community meeting, participants from across the community discussed different responses, possible tensions, and expectations of key governance actors. The methodology effectively enabled researchers and participants to grapple with the cross-scale nature of climate impacts and other drivers of change (for example global markets), and the ways in which these were differentially understood and experienced by stakeholders. As the future unfolded in different ways across the scenarios, we were able to explore how cross-scale feedbacks between drivers of change play out in response to different variables and social responses. Finally, the method presented climate impacts in tangible ways that enabled researchers to engage with communities traditionally sceptical of climate change, which is critical to move beyond the impasse that stymies adaptation planning in much of the Western US.

Sources: See Murphy et al. (2016); Murphy et al. (2017) and Wyborn et al. (2015) for further details.

SITUATING ADAPTIVE GOVERNANCE INTO FUTURES – TOWARDS ANTICIPATORY-ADAPTIVE GOVERNANCE

In this section we explore how futures-thinking may be situated into adaptive governance.

Motivating Forward-looking and Long-term Perspectives

A common mismatch in current governance systems is where planning and funding mechanisms are dominated by short-term timescales compared with the need for long-term planning required for sustainability challenges. The timescales over which adaptations, transformations, and change processes must be planned are hard to comprehend and longer than a human lifetime (Manning et al., 2006). Such processes require collective action for the future and governance processes that enable us to think about and structure future actions over long-time horizons (Bruckmeier, 2020). Stafford Smith et al. (2011) propose the concept of a *decision lifetime* as a useful means to determine if decision-making requires dealing with alternative futures. Decision lifetimes are understood as incorporating the *lead time*, "the time it takes to make and execute a decision" and the *consequence time* "the period over which the consequences of the decision emerge" (Stafford Smith et al., 2011). Where decisions have longer decision lifetimes, a more divergent range of alternative futures must be considered (Stafford Smith et al., 2011). More broadly, this calls for shifts in governance systems away from *how* to respond to change, towards prioritising forward-looking, long-term approaches and more flexible funding mechanisms. Another approach to reconcile different temporal perceptions in planning, can be through recognising other communication practices and knowledge. For example, Indigenous peoples' conceptions of past and futures have always extended over long-time scales, including deep histories (Whyte, 2017), and further highlights the imperative for futures-thinking processes and adaptive governance to be integrated with respect for sovereignty and Indigenous laws.

Further, motivating forward-looking approaches will require a cognitive shift in governance systems towards recognising that future change will not extend as a linear outcome of past and present trends. For example, as de Loe and Plummer (cited in Armitage and Plummer, 2010) note, natural resources governance institutions remain largely structured around the concept of "stationarity", which assumes that natural systems function within a known envelop of variability (Yung et al., 2019). The predicability of this envelope is unlikely to continue into the future, further pointing to the need for futures-thinking rather than relying on forecasts based on trend extrapolations (Daniell, 2020; Yung et al., 2019). Similarly, temporal structures in dominant public policy and planning tend to focus on the near future, with assumptions that long-term positive change in SES can be addressed with incremental improvements over time (Bruckmeier, 2020), highlighting another way in which the future is assumed to be a linear extension of the past.

The ability to proactively deal with uncertainty and surprise requires conceptual and institutional structures that move beyond historically bound assumptions of the range of uncertainty and variability that is tolerable in socio-political and environmental systems. Futures methods can support this, however there is a risk that scenarios and visions are generated based upon assumptions that the future will mostly continue as a linear extension of the past. This points to the need to engage explicitly in processes that support and foster systems reflexivity capacities, for example through integrating different temporal perspectives, knowledge and memories to identify necessary transitions to achieve desired futures (Múnera-Roldán et al., 2020). Yung et al. (2019) argue that futures approaches can support such a process, whereby quantitative models that extend into mid to long-term futures (i.e., 20–50 years into the future) present a "jumping off point" for discussions about the future, "destabilising participants connection to the present".

Engaging Futures Methodologies in Adaptive Governance Contexts

There is a need for more empirical evidence to establish design guidelines for futures methods applied to SES and sustainability (Boyd et al., 2015; Wiek and Iwaniec, 2014). This section explores considerations for futures methods engagement with adaptive governance contexts.

Firstly, participatory futures-thinking methods require knowledge of SES and futures that is concurrently accessible to participation and addresses complexity. The knowledge and information required to develop scenarios and visions (i.e. the knowledge of drivers of change, etc.) needs to be comprehensible and accessible to enable participation. At the same time, methods need to engage with the complexity and uncertainty of climate change projections and other biophysical change processes (Boyd et al., 2015). This challenge has been noted by Drakes et al. (2020) who notes that participants found the process arduous and required experts to support decision-making throughout the process. As such, simpler, more accessible knowledge is required to encourage participatory engagement and avoid stakeholder intimidation in futures-thinking processes (Boyd et al., 2015; Meyer et al., 2016).

Secondly, there is a need for futures methods to address multiple geographical and institutional scales in scenarios and visions (Bennett et al., 2003; Enfors et al., 2008; Dufva et al., 2015; Drakes et al., 2020).Whilst examples of multi-scale scenarios exist (Dufva et al., 2015; Drakes et al., 2020) (also see Box 5.4), there is a risk for bias towards local scale scenarios with local level driving forces, thereby omitting fundamental global drivers (Drakes et al., 2020), and for global scenarios to ignore local realities. Scenarios can be used to conceptualise change across multiple scales through the process and the changes envisioned by the scenarios (Murphy et al., 2016; Drakes et al., 2020). There is a rich literature in adaptive governance on multi-scalar processes and interactions (Chaffin et al., 2014) that may inform futures methods, and further points to the insights that can be gained from a closer conversation between adaptive governance and futures-thinking literatures.

Thirdly, methods to anticipate futures will require processes and capacities to engage with and assemble "futures bricolage", as future change may entail a bricolage of continuity, adaptation and transformation, within and across scales (Olsson et al., 2017). Uncertain futures will likely involve recombinations of existing and novel ideas, technologies, concepts and systems (Raudsepp-Hearne et al., 2020; Sharpe et al., 2016). Specific systems elements may need to be maintained rather than transformed to provide some level of stability during transformation (Moore and Milkoreit, 2020). For example, whilst a SES may be facing multiple future social and ecological transformations, not all aspects or scales will transform. Aspects of memory and knowledge may provide essential continuity within a transformation process (Whyte, 2017; Moore and Milkoreit, 2020). Therefore, whilst transformative change is widely called for (Feola, 2015; Griffith et al., 2010; IPBES, 2019; Moore et al., 2018; Olsson et al., 2006), the role of "continuity" within transformations requires attention (Moore and Milkoreit, 2020). Future research on futures methods in adaptive governance may look to understanding how narratives of transformation, adaptation, and continuity are assembled within futures methods, and the politics of doing so in transparent and participatory ways.

Addressing Politics and Political Realities

Thinking about and governing the future fundamentally requires engagement with questioning what it is a desirable future – a subjective and contested endeavour. Given existing critiques that adaptive governance inadequately theorises power and politics (Cleaver and Whaley, 2018; Karpouzoglou et al., 2016; Visseren-Hamakers et al., 2021), it is important to stress the political realities and politics of futures-thinking when these approaches are applied in adaptive governance contexts.

Futures-thinking processes are inherently social and political, arising from and shaped by different social and political contexts and priorities, and containing underlying norms and goals (Boyd et al., 2015; Knappe et al., 2019). Futures methods can be powerful tools for empowering or excluding actors, creating new or preserving existing SES, and entrenching or shifting underlying values that shape what is considered a desirable future (Knappe et al., 2019). Making the political dimensions of futures-thinking explicit requires paying attention to: power asymmetries and inequalities; the assumptions about underlying values; and the contestation and trade-offs. Questioning who is included or excluded from futures-thinking processes; whose knowledge is included; what futures are imagined; and what measures are taken, are all starting points to address the politics of futures-thinking (Bruckmeier, 2020; Knappe et al., 2019; Smith and Stirling, 2010; Vervoort and Gupta, 2018). Further, Indigenous scholarship points to the need for more work to understand how futures methods can give voice to Indigenous futures, which is particularly pertinent in contested landscapes (Nikolakis, 2020).

Scholars have called for the "politicisation" of future making, whereby practices are broadened "towards more pluralistic and imaginative understandings of the future", rather than only approaching the future from technocratic or managerial perspectives (Knappe et al., 2019). This points to the broader need to politicise co-production and participatory processes in environmental governance, where contestation of knowledge plays a vital role in developing just futures and societal transformation (Turnhout et al., 2020). Challenges have been noted however, including difficulties engaging diverse stakeholders due to tensions between actors with different perspectives (Faysse et al., 2018), or tensions between different knowledge systems and their dissonant timescales and approaches (e.g. Indigenous Peoples practices vs 'Command-and-control' Western management),

Consideration of political realities and governance systems that enable or constrain futures-thinking within adaptive governance is required for futures-thinking to be used effectively and justly. Short-term political agendas do not currently provide the necessary demand for high quality long-term and future-focused knowledge on ecosystem functions (Nykvist et al., 2017). For example, analysis of anticipatory planning in Australia highlights a limited capacity of adaptation strategies to incorporate new science and practical lessons due to political interests and bias (Serrao-Neumann et al., 2013). Further, accounting for long-term futures is often hampered by short-term political cycles (Dewulf and Termeer, 2015), and governance systems may exclude long-term perspectives in current decision contexts (see Guillaume et al. (2017) on uncertainty as an excuse for delay). There is an increasing need for frameworks that enable decision-making under uncertainty (i.e., such as Robust Decision Making (Lempert, 2019)), including uncertain futures faced from climate change (Stafford Smith et al., 2011; Yung et al., 2019).

Embedding Futures-thinking in Governance Structures

Forward-looking decision-making needs to be iterative and embedded within governance systems (Dewulf and Termeer, 2015). There is a risk that many futures methods are applied in one-off projects. The reliance on "projects" in natural resource management has been noted by Allan (2012), who argues that projects encourage short-term planning and are strongly tied to political and financial cycles. Adaptive governance thus not only requires futures-thinking capacities, but also governance structures in place that ensure futures-thinking can be supported and prioritised. One way of "embedding" futures-thinking might be to facilitate decision-makers and managers to embrace and accept SES change rather than controlling the system (van Kerkhoff et al., 2019). Further, institutional structures are required to be able to use the insights gained from futures-thinking processes (Hoolohan et al., 2019). These insights are often complex, and research currently suggests that the impact of futures-thinking processes on decision-making and mid to long-term planning is often limited (Meyer et al., 2016). Pereira et al. (2019) identify a "chicken and egg" problem with the use of futures thinking methods, in that policy makers need to see demonstrated value to invest in these processes, yet the processes themselves need to be developed in order to articulate their potential contribution. Institutionalising futures-thinking is a key challenge and understanding of the institutional constraints to anticipatory governance remain limited.

CONCLUSION

This chapter has argued that governing future changes will entail a bricolage of continuity, adaptation, and transformation. As such, there is a need to bring together literatures on governance of transformation and adaptation. Further, understanding how futures methods can support forward-looking governance that can imagine, plan for, and navigate processes of adaptation and transformation is an important future direction for research. Futures methods can support adaptation and transformation in SES, by supporting capacities to imagine and plan for uncertain futures, including capacities to: engage with uncertainty and surprise; develop and integrate futures knowledge; envision transformation; foster systems reflexivity; and address contestation. Addressing future transformational change will require governance arrangements that enable and prioritise long-term participatory perspectives, and more robust methods for dealing with future change.

Increasing engagement between adaptive governance and futures thinking may also support development of improved futures methods. This may include: (1) addressing political contestation and socio-political context within futures-thinking processes; (2) more coherently integrating knowledge across scales to inform futures methods; and (3) developing scenarios that deal with continuity and bricolage of adaptations and transformations across scales. We identify the following areas of future work, including motivating forward-looking and long-term perspectives; engaging futures methodologies in adaptive governance contexts; addressing politics and political realities; and embedding futures thinking in governance structures. Thus, we argue that an expanded model of adaptive governance is required to foster plural, long-term perspectives of uncertain futures and transformative social and ecological change.

REFERENCES

Allan, C. 2012. Rethinking the "project": bridging the polarized discourses in IWRM. *Journal of Environmental Policy and Planning*, 143, 231–241. https://doi.org/10.1080/1523908X.2012.702012.
Anderson, B. 2010. Preemption, precaution, preparedness: anticipatory action and future geographies. *Progress in Human Geography*, 346, 777–798. https://doi.org/10.1177/0309132510362600.

Armitage, D., and Plummer, R. 2010. Adapting and transforming: governance for navigating change. In D. Armitage and R. Plummer (Eds.), *Adaptive Capacity and Environmental Governance*, pp. 287–302. Springer-Verlag, Berlin and Heidelberg. https://doi.org/10.1007/978-3-642-12194-4_14.

Bengston, D. N. 2019. Futures research methods and applications in natural resources. *Society and Natural Resources*, 3210, 1099–1113. https://doi.org/10.1080/08941920.2018.1547852.

Bennett, E. M., Carpenter, S. R., Peterson, G. D., Cumming, G. S., Zurek, M., and Pingali, P. 2003. Why global scenarios need ecology. *Frontiers in Ecology and the Environment*, 16, 322–329. https://doi.org/10.1890/1540-92952003001[0322:WGSNE]2.0.CO;2.

Boyd, E., Nykvist, B., Borgström, S., and Stacewicz, I. A. 2015. Anticipatory governance for social-ecological resilience. *Ambio*, 441, 149–161. https://doi.org/10.1007/s13280-014-0604-x.

Bruckmeier, K. 2020. Re-thinking temporal perspectives of sustainability transformation. *Economics and Sustainability* pp. 377–418. https://doi.org/10.1007/978-3-030-56627-2_9.

Chaffin, B. C., Garmestani, A. S., Gunderson, L. H., Benson, M. H., Angeler, D. G., Tony, C. A., Cosens, B., Craig, R. K., Ruhl, J. B., and Allen, C. R. 2016. Transformative environmental governance. *Annual Review of Environment and Resources*, 41, 399–423. https://doi.org/10.1146/annurev-environ-110615-085817.

Chaffin, B. C., Gosnell, H., and Cosens, B. A. 2014. A decade of adaptive governance scholarship. *Ecology and Society*, 193, 1–13. http://www.jstor.org/stable/26269646.

Cleaver, F., and Whaley, L. 2018. Understanding process, power, and meaning in adaptive governance: a critical institutional reading. *Ecology and Society*, 232. https://doi.org/10.5751/ES-10212-230249.

Cook, C. N., Inayatullah, S., Burgman, M. A., Sutherland, W. J., and Wintle, B. A. 2014. Strategic foresight: how planning for the unpredictable can improve environmental decision-making. *Trends in Ecology and Evolution*, 299, 531–541. https://doi.org/10.1016/j.tree.2014.07.005.

Cork, S. 2018. Using futures-thinking to support ecosystem assessments. *Routledge Handbook of Ecosystem Services*, 170–187. https://doi.org/10.4324/9781315775302-16.

Curtis, A., Ross, H., Marshall, G. R., Baldwin, C., Cavaye, J., Freeman, C., Carr, A., and Syme, G. J. 2014. The great experiment with devolved NRM governance: lessons from community engagement in Australia and New Zealand since the 1980s. *Australasian Journal of Environmental Management*, 212, 175–199. https://doi.org/10.1080/14486563.2014.935747.

Daniell, K. A. 2020. Water systems and disruptions: the 'old abnormal'? *Australian Journal of Water Resources*, 241, 1–8. https://doi.org/10.1080/13241583.2020.1780732.

Dewulf, A., and Termeer, C. 2015. Governing the future? The potential of adaptive delta management to contribute to governance capabilities for dealing with the wicked problem of climate change adaptation. *Journal of Water and Climate Change*, 64, 759–771. https://doi.org/10.2166/wcc.2015.117.

Drakes, C., Cashman, A., Kemp-Benedict, E., and Laing, T. 2020. Global to small island; a cross-scale foresight scenario exercise. *Foresight*, 225–6, 579–598. https://doi.org/10.1108/FS-02-2020-0012.

Dufva, M., Könnölä, T., and Koivisto, R. 2015. Multi-layered foresight: lessons from regional foresight in Chile. *Futures*, 73, 100–111. https://doi.org/10.1016/j.futures.2015.08.010.

Enfors, E. I., Gordon, L. J., Peterson, G. D., and Bossio, D. 2008. Making investments in dryland development work: participatory scenario planning in the Makanya Catchment, Tanzania. *Ecology and Society*, 132. https://doi.org/10.5751/ES-02649-130242.

Faysse, N. et al. 2018. Participatory scenario planning for sustainable irrigated agriculture when actors seldom communicate: an experiment in Morocco. *International Journal of Water Resources Development*, 346, 982–1000. doi: 10.1080/07900627.2017.1322500.

Feola, G. 2015. Societal transformation in response to global environmental change: a review of emerging concepts. *Ambio*, 445, 376–390. https://doi.org/10.1007/s13280-014-0582-z.

Ferguson, B. C., Frantzeskaki, N., and Brown, R. R. 2013. A strategic program for transitioning to a Water Sensitive City. *Landscape and Urban Planning*, 117, 32–45. https://doi.org/10.1016/j.landurbplan.2013.04.016.

Folke, C., Carpenter, S. R., Walker, B., Scheffer, M., Chapin, T., and Rockström, J. 2010. Resilience thinking: integrating resilience, adaptability and transformability. *Ecology and Society*, 154. https://doi.org/10.5751/ES-03610-150420.

Folke, C., Hahn, T., Olsson, P., and Norberg, J. 2005. Adaptive governance of social-ecological systems. *Annual Review of Environment and Resources*, 30, 441–473. https://doi.org/10.1146/annurev.energy.30.050504.144511.

Folke, C., Polasky, S., Rockström, J., Galaz, V., Westley, F., Lamont, M., Scheffer, M., Österblom, H., Carpenter, S. R., Chapin, F. S., Seto, K. C., Weber, E. U., Crona, B. I., Daily, G. C., Dasgupta, P., Gaffney, O., Gordon, L. J., Hoff, H., Levin, S. A., Lubchenco, J., Steffen, W., Walker, B. H. 2021. Our future in the Anthropocene biosphere. *Ambio*, 50, 4, 834–869. https://doi.org/10.1007/s13280 -021-01544-8.

Gerlak, A. K., Jacobs, K. L., McCoy, A. L., Martin, S., Rivera-Torres, M., Murveit, A. M., Leinberger, A. J., and Thomure, T. 2021. Scenario planning: embracing the potential for extreme events in the Colorado River Basin. *Climatic Change*, 1651–2, 1–21. https://doi.org/10.1007/s10584-021-03013-3.

Gielczewski, M. et al. 2011. How can we involve stakeholders in the development of water scenarios? Narew river basin case study. *Journal of Water and Climate Change*, 22–3, 166–179. doi: 10.2166/wcc.2011.027.

Griffith, R., Mitchell, M., Walkerden, G., Brown, V., and Walker, B. 2010. Building a framework for transformative action in the Wakool Shire, Transformation for Resilient Landscapes and Communities project working paper 1, Issue 61. https://www.csu.edu.au/__data/assets/pdf_file/0005/702860/61_Wakool_report.pdf.

Guillaume, J. H. A., Helgeson, C., Elsawah, S., Jakeman, A. J., and Kummu, M. 2017. Toward best practice framing of uncertainty in scientific publications: a review of *Water Resources Research* abstracts. *Water Resources Research*, 538, 6744–6762. https://doi.org/10.1002/2017WR020609.

Haasnoot, M., and Middelkoop, H. 2012. A history of futures: a review of scenario use in water policy studies in the Netherlands. *Environmental Science and Policy*, 19–20, 108–120. https://doi.org/10.1016/j.envsci.2012.03.002.

Haslauer, E., Biberacher, M., and Blaschke, T. 2012. GIS-based backcasting: an innovative method for parameterisation of sustainable spatial planning and resource management. *Futures*, 444, 292–302. https://doi.org/10.1016/j.futures.2011.10.012.

Hasselman, L. 2017. Adaptive management; adaptive co-management; adaptive governance: what's the difference? *Australasian Journal of Environmental Management*, 241, 31–46. https://doi.org/10.1080/14486563.2016.1251857.

Hauptman, A., and Steinmuller, K. 2018. Surprising scenarios: imagination as a dimension of foresight. In R. Peperhove, H.-L. Dienel, and K. Steinmuller (Eds.), *Envisioning Uncertain Futures*, pp. 49–68. Springer Nature, Wiesbaden. https://doi.org/10.1007/978-3-658-25074-4.

Herrfahrdt-Pähle, E., Schlüter, M., Olsson, P., Folke, C., Gelcich, S., and Pahl-Wostl, C. 2020. Sustainability transformations: socio-political shocks as opportunities for governance transitions. *Global Environmental Change*, 63, March, 102097. https://doi.org/10.1016/j.gloenvcha.2020.102097.

Höjer, M., Dreborg, K. H., Engström, R., Gunnarsson-Östling, U., and Svenfelt, Å. 2011. Experiences of the development and use of scenarios for evaluating Swedish national environmental objectives. *Futures*, 431, 1–15. https://doi.org/10.1016/j.futures.2010.02.005.

Hoolohan, C., McLachlan, C., and Larkin, A. 2019. 'Aha' moments in the water–energy–food nexus: a new morphological scenario method to accelerate sustainable transformation. *Technological Forecasting and Social Change*, 148, August, 119712. https://doi.org/10.1016/j.techfore.2019.119712.

Hurlbert, M. A. 2018. *Adaptive Governance of Disaster: Drought and Flood in Rural Areas*. Springer.

Hurlbert, M., and Gupta, J. 2016. Adaptive governance, uncertainty, and risk: policy framing and responses to climate change, drought, and flood. *Risk Analysis*, 362, 339–356. https://doi.org/10.1111/risa.12510.

Inayatullah, S. 2008. Six pillars: futures thinking for transforming. *Foresight*, 101, 4–21. https://doi.org/10.1108/14636680810855991.

IPBES. 2016. The methodological assessment report on scenarios and models of biodiversity and ecosystem services: summary for policymakers. www.iisd.ca/ipbes/ipbes3/12jan.htm.

IPBES. 2019. Summary for policymakers of the global assessment report on biodiversity and ecosystem services of the Intergovernmental Science-Policy Platform on Biodiversity and Ecosystem Services.

Jenssen, S. 2010. Municipal visions: reflexive futures between paradigm and practice. *Futures*, 424, 345–354. https://doi.org/10.1016/j.futures.2009.11.020.

Jurgilevich, A. 2021. Governance modes and epistemologies of future-oriented vulnerability assessments: example of a mixed-methods approach. *Futures*, 128, 102717. doi: 10.1016/J.FUTURES.2021.102717.

Karpouzoglou, T., Dewulf, A., and Clark, J. 2016. Advancing adaptive governance of social-ecological systems through theoretical multiplicity. *Environmental Science and Policy*, 57, 1–9. https://doi.org/10.1016/j.envsci.2015.11.011.

Khadra, R. et al. 2011. Down-scaling pan-European water scenarios to local visions in the mediterranean: the Candelaro basin case study in Italy. *Journal of Water and Climate Change*, 22–3, pp. 180–188. doi: 10.2166/wcc.2011.008.

Kim, H., Rosa, I. M. D., Alkemade, R., Leadley, P., Hurtt, G., Popp, A., van Vuuren, D. P., Anthoni, P., Arneth, A., Baisero, D., Caton, E., Chaplin-Kramer, R., Chini, L., de Palma, A., di Fulvio, F., di Marco, M., Espinoza, F., Ferrier, S., Fujimori, S., … Pereira, H. M. 2018. A protocol for an intercomparison of biodiversity and ecosystem services models using harmonized land-use and climate scenarios. *Geoscientific Model Development*, 1111, 4537–4562. https://doi.org/10.5194/gmd-11-4537-2018.

Knappe, H., Holfelder, A. K., Löw Beer, D., and Nanz, P. 2019. The politics of making and unmaking sustainable futures: introduction to the special feature. *Sustainability Science*, 14, 4, 891–898. https://doi.org/10.1007/s11625-019-00704-w.

Koontz, T. M., Gupta, D., Mudliar, P., and Ranjan, P. 2015. Adaptive institutions in social-ecological systems governance: a synthesis framework. *Environmental Science and Policy*, 53, 139–151. https://doi.org/10.1016/j.envsci.2015.01.003.

Lempert, R. J. 2019. Robust Decision Making RDM. In Marchau V., Walker W., Bloemen P., Popper S. (Eds.) *Decision Making under Deep Uncertainty*. Springer, Cham. https://doi.org/10.1007/978-3-030-05252-2_2.

Mangnus, A. C., Oomen, J., Vervoort, J. M., and Hajer, M. A. 2021. Futures literacy and the diversity of the future. *Futures*, 132. https://doi.org/10.1016/j.futures.2021.102793.

Manning, A. D., Lindenmayer, D. B., and Fischer, J. 2006. Stretch goals and backcasting: approaches for overcoming barriers to large-scale ecological restoration. *Restoration Ecology*, 144, 487–492. https://doi.org/10.1111/j.1526-100X.2006.00159.x.

Marshall, N. A., Park, S. E., Adger, W. N., Brown, K., and Howden, S. M. 2012. Transformational capacity and the influence of place and identity. *Environmental Research Letters*, 73. https://doi.org/10.1088/1748-9326/7/3/034022.

Meyer, W. S., Bryan, B. A., Summers, D. M., Lyle, G., Wells, S., McLean, J., and Siebentritt, M. 2016. Regional engagement and spatial modelling for natural resource management planning. *Sustainability Science*, 115, 733–747. https://doi.org/10.1007/s11625-015-0341-5.

Miller, R. 2018. Sensing and making sense of futures literacy: towards a futures literacy framework. In R. Miller (Ed.), *Transforming the Future: Anticipation in the 21st Century*, pp. 1–276. UNESCO, Paris.

Miller, T. R., Wiek, A., Sarewitz, D., Robinson, J., Olsson, L., Kriebel, D., and Loorbach, D. 2014. The future of sustainability science: a solutions-oriented research agenda. *Sustainability Science*, 92, 239–246. https://doi.org/10.1007/s11625-013-0224-6.

Milojević. 2002. 'Futures of education: feminist and post-Western critiques and visions', PhD thesis, University of Queensland, Australia.

Moore, M. L., and Milkoreit, M. 2020. Imagination and transformations to sustainable and just futures. *Elementa*, 81, 1–17. https://doi.org/10.1525/elementa.2020.081.

Moore, M. L., Olsson, P., Nilsson, W., Rose, L., and Westley, F. R. 2018. Navigating emergence and system reflexivity as key transformative capacities: experiences from a Global Fellowship program. *Ecology and Society*, 232. https://doi.org/10.5751/ES-10166-230238.

Moore, M. L., Tjornbo, O., Enfors, E., Knapp, C., Hodbod, J., Baggio, J. A., Norström, A., Olsson, P., and Biggs, D. 2014. Studying the complexity of change: toward an analytical framework for understanding deliberate social-ecological transformations. *Ecology and Society*, 194. https://doi.org/10.5751/ES-06966-190454.

Muiderman, K., Gupta, A., Vervoort, J., and Biermann, F. 2020. Four approaches to anticipatory climate governance: different conceptions of the future and implications for the present. *Wiley Interdisciplinary Reviews: Climate Change*, 116, 1–20. https://doi.org/10.1002/wcc.673.

Muiderman, K., Zurek, M., Vervoort, J., Gupta, A., Hasnain, S., and Driessen, P. 2022. The anticipatory governance of sustainability transformations: hybrid approaches and dominant perspectives. *Global Environmental Change*, 73, 102452. https://doi.org/10.1016/j.gloenvcha.2021.102452.

Múnera-Roldán, C., Roux, D. J., Colloff, M. J., and van Kerkhoff, L. 2020. Beyond calendars and maps: rethinking time and space for effective knowledge governance in protected areas. *Land*, 99. https://doi.org/10.3390/LAND9090293.

Murphy, D. J., Yung, L., Wyborn, C., and Williams, D. R. 2017. Rethinking climate change adaptation and place through a situated pathways framework: a case study from the Big Hole Valley, USA. *Landscape and Urban Planning*, 167, July, 441–450. https://doi.org/10.1016/j.landurbplan.2017.07.016.

Murphy, D., Wyborn, C., Yung, L., Williams, D. R., Cleveland, C., Eby, L., Dobrowski, S., and Towler, E. 2016. Engaging communities and climate change futures with Multi-scale, Iterative Scenario Building MISB in the western United States. *Human Organization*, 331, 33.

Nikolakis, W. 2020. Participatory backcasting: building pathways towards reconciliation? *Futures*. 122, 102603.

Nykvist, B., Borgström, S., and Boyd, E. 2017. Assessing the adaptive capacity of multi-level water governance: ecosystem services under climate change in Mälardalen region, Sweden. *Regional Environmental Change*, 178, 2359–2371. https://doi.org/10.1007/s10113-017-1149-x.

O'Brien, K. 2012. Global environmental change II: from adaptation to deliberate transformation. *Progress in Human Geography*, 365, 667–676. https://doi.org/10.1177/0309132511425767.

Olsson, P., Folke, C., and Hahn, T. 2004. Social-ecological transformation for ecosystem management: the development of adaptive co-management of a wetland landscape in southern Sweden. *Ecology and Society*, 94. https://doi.org/10.5751/ES-00683-090402.

Olsson, P., Gunderson, L. H., Carpenter, S. R., Ryan, P., Lebel, L., Folke, C., and Holling, C. S. 2006. Shooting the rapids: navigating transitions to adaptive governance of social-ecological systems. *Ecology and Society*, 111. https://doi.org/10.5751/ES-01595-110118.

Olsson, P., Moore, M. L., Westley, F. R., and McCarthy, D. D. P. 2017. The concept of the Anthropocene as a game-changer: a new context for social innovation and transformations to sustainability. *Ecology and Society*, 22, 2. https://doi.org/10.5751/ES-09310-220231.

Patterson, J., Schulz, K., Vervoort, J., van der Hel, S., Widerberg, O., Adler, C., Hurlbert, M., Anderton, K., Sethi, M., and Barau, A. 2017. Exploring the governance and politics of transformations towards sustainability. *Environmental Innovation and Societal Transitions*, 24, 1–16. https://doi.org/10.1016/j.eist.2016.09.001.

Pereira, L. M., Hichert, T., Hamann, M., Preiser, R., and Biggs, R. 2018. Using futures methods to create transformative spaces: visions of a good anthropocene in Southern Africa. *Ecology and Society*, 231. https://doi.org/10.5751/ES-09907-230119.

Pereira, L., Sitas, N., Ravera, F., Jimenez-Aceituno, A., and Merrie, A. 2019. Building capacities for transformative change towards sustainability: imagination in Intergovernmental Science-Policy Scenario Processes. *Elementa: Science of the Anthropocene*, 7. https://doi.org/10.1525/elementa.374.

Quay, R. 2010. Anticipatory governance: a tool for climate change adaptation. *Journal of the American Planning Association*, 764, 496–511. https://doi.org/10.1080/01944363.2010.508428.

Ramos, J. M. 2014. Anticipatory governance: traditions and trajectories for strategic design. *Journal of Futures Studies*, 191, 35–52.

Raudsepp-Hearne, C., Peterson, G. D., Bennett, E. M., Biggs, R., Norström, A. v., Pereira, L., Vervoort, J., Iwaniec, D. M., McPhearson, T., Olsson, P., Hichert, T., Falardeau, M., and Aceituno, A. J. 2020. Seeds of good anthropocenes: developing sustainability scenarios for Northern Europe. *Sustainability Science*, 152, 605–617. https://doi.org/10.1007/s11625-019-00714-8.

Robinson, J. B. 1982. Energy backcasting: a proposed method of policy analysis. *Energy Policy*, 104, 337–344. https://doi.org/10.1016/0301-42158290048-9.

Sandström, C., Carlsson-Kanyama, A., Lindahl, K. B., Sonnek, K. M., Mossing, A., Nordin, A., Nordström, E. M., and Räty, R. 2016. Understanding consistencies and gaps between desired forest futures: an analysis of visions from stakeholder groups in Sweden. *Ambio*, 45, 100–108. https://doi.org/10.1007/s13280-015-0746-5.

Schneider, F., and Rist, S. 2014. Envisioning sustainable water futures in a transdisciplinary learning process: combining normative, explorative, and participatory scenario approaches. *Sustainability Science*, 94, 463–481. https://doi.org/10.1007/s11625-013-0232-6.

Serrao-Neumann, S., Harman, B. P., and Low Choy, D. 2013. The role of anticipatory governance in local climate adaptation: observations from Australia. *Planning Practice and Research*, 284, 440–463. https://doi.org/10.1080/02697459.2013.795788.

Sharpe, B., Hodgson, A., Leicester, G., Lyon, A., and Fazey, I. 2016. Three horizons: a pathways practice for transformation. *Ecology and Society*, 212. https://doi.org/10.5751/ES-08388-210247.

Slaughter, R. 2009. The state of play in the futures field: a metascanning overview. *Foresight*, 115, 6–20. https://doi.org/10.1108/14636680910994932.

Slaughter, R. A. 1996. Futures studies: from individual to social capacity. *Futures*, 288, 751–762. https://doi.org/10.1016/0016-32879600009-2.

Smith, A., and Stirling, A. 2010. The politics of social-ecological resilience and sustainable socio-technical transitions. *Ecology and Society*, 151. https://doi.org/10.5751/ES-03218-150111.

Sondeijker, S., Geurts, J., Rotmans, J., and Tukker, A. 2006. Imagining sustainability: the added value of transition scenarios in transition management. *Foresight*, 85, 15–30. https://doi.org/10.1108/14636680610703063.

Späth, P., and Rohracher, H. 2010. "Energy regions": the transformative power of regional discourses on socio-technical futures. *Research Policy*, 394, 449–458. https://doi.org/10.1016/j.respol.2010.01.017.

Stafford Smith, M., Horrocks, L., Harvey, A., and Hamilton, C. 2011. Rethinking adaptation for a 4°C world. *Philosophical Transactions of the Royal Society A: Mathematical, Physical and Engineering Sciences*, 3691934, 196–216. https://doi.org/10.1098/rsta.2010.0277.

Svenfelt, Å., Engström, R., and Höjer, M. 2010. Use of explorative scenarios in environmental policy-making: evaluation of policy instruments for management of land, water and the built environment. *Futures*, 4210, 1166–1175. https://doi.org/10.1016/j.futures.2010.06.002.

Takala, A., and Heino, O. 2017. Weak signals and wild cards in water and sanitation services: exploring an approach for water utilities. *European Journal of Futures Research*, 51, 1–12. https://doi.org/10.1007/s40309-017-0111-y.

Teräväinen, T. 2019. Negotiating water and technology: competing expectations and confronting knowledges in the case of the Coca Codo Sinclair in Ecuador. *Water Switzerland*, 113. https://doi.org/10.3390/w11030411.

Thorn, J. P. R., Klein, J. A., Steger, C., Hopping, K. A., Capitani, C., Tucker, C. M., Nolin, A. W., Reid, R. S., Seidl, R., Chitale, V. S., and Marchant, R. 2020. A systematic review of participatory scenario planning to envision mountain social-ecological systems futures. *Ecology and Society*, 253, 1–55. https://doi.org/10.5751/ES-11608-250306.

Tschakert, P., and Dietrich, K. A. 2010. Anticipatory learning for climate change adaptation and resilience. *Ecology and Society*, 152, 11. https://doi.org/10.5751/ES-03335-150211.

Vähäkari, N., Lauttamäki, V., Tapio, P., Ahvenainen, M., Assmuth, T., Lyytimäki, J., and Vehmas, J. 2020. The future in sustainability transitions: interlinkages between the multi-level perspective and futures studies. *Futures*, 123, October 2018, 102597. https://doi.org/10.1016/j.futures.2020.102597.

van der Voorn, T., Pahl-Wostl, C., and Quist, J. 2012. Combining backcasting and adaptive management for climate adaptation in coastal regions: a methodology and a South African case study. *Futures*, 444, 346–364. https://doi.org/10.1016/j.futures.2011.11.003.

van Kerkhoff, L., Munera, C., Dudley, N., Guevara, O., Wyborn, C., Figueroa, C., Dunlop, M., Hoyos, M. A., Castiblanco, J., and Becerra, L. 2019. Towards future-oriented conservation: managing protected areas in an era of climate change. *Ambio*, 487, 699–713. https://doi.org/10.1007/s13280-018-1121-0.

van Vliet, M., and Kok, K. 2015. Combining backcasting and exploratory scenarios to develop robust water strategies in face of uncertain futures. *Mitigation and Adaptation Strategies for Global Change*, 20, 1. https://doi.org/10.1007/s11027-013-9479-6.

Vervoort, J., and Gupta, A. 2018. Anticipating climate futures in a 1.5 °C era: the link between foresight and governance. *Current Opinion in Environmental Sustainability*, 31, June 2017, 104–111. https://doi.org/10.1016/j.cosust.2018.01.004.

Visseren-Hamakers, I. J., Razzaque, J., Mcelwee, P., Turnhout, E., Kelemen, E., Rusch, G. M., Chan, I., Lim, M., Islar, M., Gautam, A. P., Williams, M., Mungatana, E., Karim, S., Muradian, R., Gerber, L. R., Lui, G., Liu, J., Spangenberg, J. H., and Zaleski, D. 2021. Transformative governance of biodiversity: insights for sustainable development. *Current Opinion in Environmental Sustainability*, 53, 20–28.

Voros, J. 2007. On the philosophical foundations of futures research. In van der Duin, P. (Ed.) *Knowing Tomorrow? How Science Deals with the Future*, pp. 69–90. Eburon Academic Publishers, Delft.

Walker, B. H., Abel, N., Anderies, J. M., and Ryan, P. 2009. Resilience, adaptability, and transformability in the Goulburn-Broken Catchment, Australia. *Ecology and Society*, 141, 284–294. https://doi.org/10.1111/j.1464-410X.1989.tb05191.x.

Whitney, C. K., Bennett, N. J., Ban, N. C., Allison, E. H., Armitage, D., Blythe, J. L., Burt, J. M., Cheung, W., Finkbeiner, E. M., Kaplan-Hallam, M., Perry, I., Turner, N. J., and Yumagulova, L. 2017. Adaptive capacity: from assessment to action in coastal social-ecological systems. *Ecology and Society*, 222. https://doi.org/10.5751/ES-09325-220222.

Whyte, K. 2017. Indigenous climate change studies: Indigenizing futures, decolonizing the Anthropocene. *English Language Notes*, 55, 1, 153-162

Wiek, A., Binder, C., and Scholz, R. W. 2006. Functions of scenarios in transition processes. *Futures*, 387, 740– English Language Notes, 551–2, 153–162. https://doi.org/10.1215/00138282-55.1-2.153766. https://doi.org/10.1016/j.futures.2005.12.003.

Wiek, A., and Iwaniec, D. 2014. Quality criteria for visions and visioning in sustainability science. *Sustainability Science*, 94, 497–512. https://doi.org/10.1007/s11625-013-0208-6.

Wiek, A., and Lang, D. J. 2016. Transformational sustainability research methodology. *Sustainability Science*, 31–41. https://doi.org/10.1007/978-94-017-7242-6.

Wyborn, C. 2015. Co-productive governance: a relational framework for adaptive governance. *Global Environmental Change*, 30, 56–67. https://doi.org/10.1016/j.gloenvcha.2014.10.009.

Wyborn, C., Louder, E., Harfoot, M., and Hill, S. 2021. Engaging with the science and politics of biodiversity futures: a literature review. *Environmental Conservation*, 1–8. https://doi.org/10.1017/S037689292000048X.

Wyborn, C., van Kerkhoff, L., Dunlop, M., Dudley, N., and Guevara, O. 2016. Future oriented conservation: knowledge governance, uncertainty and learning. *Biodiversity and Conservation*, 257, 1401–1408. https://doi.org/10.1007/s10531-016-1130-x.

Wyborn, C., Yung, L., Murphy, D., and Williams, D. R. 2015. Situating adaptation: how governance challenges and perceptions of uncertainty influence adaptation in the Rocky Mountains. *Regional Environmental Change*, 154, 669–682. https://doi.org/10.1007/s10113-014-0663-3.

Yung, L., Louder, E., Gallagher, L. A., Jones, K., and Wyborn, C. 2019. How methods for navigating uncertainty connect science and policy at the water–energy–food nexus. *Frontiers in Environmental Science*, 7, APR, 1–18. https://doi.org/10.3389/fenvs.2019.00037.

6. Spatial data, methods, and mismatches for adaptive governance research

Maija Nikkanen and Aleksi Räsänen

INTRODUCTION

Many of the problems that afflict socio-ecological systems arise from mismatches between the scale of management and the scales of the ecological processes being managed (Cumming et al. 2006). These mismatches between and within scales hinder successful governance; therefore, adaptive governance approaches should consider and analyse scales and work across them. Adaptive governance allows improvement of the fit between governance and social-ecological processes, as well as recognition of multiple relevant scales and addressing scale interactions.

Since geographical scale is one of the key scales, spatial data, approaches, and methods become crucial to understand and assess what kind of mismatches there are and how they can be analysed. Nevertheless, there is a lack of knowledge of how spatial data and methods have been used and how they could be used in adaptive governance research. We address this gap by focusing on the following objectives. We (1) provide an overview of spatial and scale mismatches, (2) ask how spatial data and methods have been used in adaptive governance and scale mismatch research, and (3) suggest what kind of spatial data and methods could advance adaptive governance literature. To keep the chapter focused and not too broad, we decided to concentrate, although not exclusively, on disaster governance. Disaster governance deals with complex socio-ecological systems involving risks, uncertainties and changing circumstances, and is thus a relevant context for applying adaptive governance (see also Chapter 15).

The three objectives form the basis for three main sections in this chapter. The following section about spatial and scale mismatches concentrates on disaster research and shows what kind of mismatches have been found and how they have been researched. After looking at mismatches, we conduct systematised literature searches to find the strand of adaptive governance literature that has specifically focused on spatial data and methods. The section focuses also on other adaptive governance literature than disaster governance, as we found that there is little adaptive disaster governance literature utilising spatial data and methods. Finally, in the last section of this chapter, we show how spatial data and methods have been used in broader disaster research literature, and how they support maintaining an up-to-date picture of the functioning and changes in socio-ecological systems, help to engage with various sources of knowledge, and include diverse stakeholders. We also propose future directions for utilising spatial data and methods in adaptive governance research.

SPATIAL INTERACTIONS AND MISMATCHES

Scale can be defined as the "spatial, temporal, quantitative, or analytical dimensions used to measure and study any phenomenon" (Cash et al. 2006, following Gibson et al. 2000). The meaning of *scale* differs between fields: in ecology, scale usually refers to spatial and temporal dimensions, whereas sociological scale includes institutions, i.e., policies and norms (Cumming et al. 2006). *Levels*, on the other hand, stand for the units of analysis that are located at different positions on a scale, such as local, regional, and global level on a spatial scale (Cash et al. 2006).

The concept of scale is strongly connected to adaptive governance, as it is characterised by polycentric and layered institutions (Ruane 2020; Fournier et al. 2016). Polycentricity allows for recognition of multiple relevant scales and improving the fit between knowledge, action, and social-ecological processes (Djalante et al. 2011). For adaptive governance, cross-level and cross-scale interactions are significant, and there rarely is a single suitable scale and level for governing a specific socio-ecological problem (Djalante et al. 2011; Termeer et al. 2010). Institutions of governance are nested, and decision-making authority is distributed between a network of actors on different levels (Ruane 2020). Consequently, adaptive governance is a useful tool in addressing scale mismatches.

A scale mismatch occurs, for example, when the scale of management is different from the scale of the processes being managed (Cumming et al. 2006). A typical case is a catchment area that extends into the territory of several countries and is managed by multiple separate institutions, while no one governs the wider entity. Mismatches can be spatial, as in the former case, or temporal: bureaucratic processes may be too slow to address rapid changes in eco-systems, or the political system may incentivise focusing on parliamentary terms instead of addressing ecological processes progressing through centuries (Blair et al. 2018; Termeer et al. 2010). Cumming et al. (2006) note that the emergence of mismatches is influenced by major socio-economic and technological changes: shifts in livelihoods, administrative structures, and technology. Scale mismatches may in turn lead to unclear division of responsibilities, lack of appropriate monitoring frameworks, and disconnection between ecological and social systems.

Termeer et al. (2010) specify how different governance systems approach scale mismatches. *Monocentric governance* sees state as the central actor and focuses on the jurisdictional scale. Scale-related problems are seen as gaps in the system, and consequently monocentric govern-ance systems attempt to solve scale mismatches through structural reforms and clarification of responsibilities. In contrast, *multilevel governance* is less centralised and more flexible: it emphasises cross-level interactions, and distributes power between the international level, regional and local authorities as well as civil society. This increases transaction costs and calls for coordination. Finally, *adaptive governance* recognises complexity and emphasises uncer-tainty. Cross-level and cross-scale interactions are significant, and scale-related problems are approached through network leadership and re- and self-organisation. In addition to spatial and jurisdictional scales, issues connected to temporal and knowledge scales are recognised. Scale issues in the adaptive governance literature can be divided roughly into two categories: cross-scale issues (e.g., existence of multiple relevant scales; for example, global data and national decision-making) and cross-level issues (e.g., short-term solutions can aggregate into long-term problems).

Over the past decades, as environmental governance has shifted from centralised approaches to more networked governance with cross-scale linkages, a similar shift has also occurred in the disaster governance section (Kapucu et al. 2010). This ongoing change has also affected disaster management, and responsibilities adopted by different actors within the disaster governance sector have been changing. State-led disaster management has given way to decentralised sharing of responsibility (Crosweller and Tschakert 2021). Combined with the increasingly important role that especially local governments play in climate change adaptation, local-level disaster management plans have come under focus (Melo Zurita et al. 2015).

Next, we will discuss different types of mismatches found in the field of disaster governance in further detail: first, the scale of governance not matching the scale of the relevant hazard for management, and second, levels of governance not interacting with each other or having different priorities.

Missing the Big Picture

There are many benefits to decentralisation of disaster governance. Local authorities have relevant knowledge on local risks and a good understanding of local needs, assets, and vulnerability. They are also often responsible for local infrastructure, preparedness, and emergency planning, that are linked to disaster response. In addition, local authorities are able to offer timely, rapid response, due to being physically close (Bae et al. 2016). However, decentralisation may also lead to scale mismatches: the small scale of governance may be unable to address large-scale, cross-scale or cross-level issues.

Often the scale of governance is too small to tackle regional or global risks. There is an obvious conflict between disaster-related processes, which are often global or encompass large areas – whether biophysical or socio-ecological – and disaster governance that is decentralised, fragmented, and divided into separate policy sectors spatial and jurisdictional scales, and phases of the hazards cycle, e.g., mitigation and response (Tierney 2012). In the decentralised framework, local government is usually tasked with mainstreaming disaster governance (Blackburn 2014). However, even when local institutions involve and communicate with the local population, they may lack the authority and power to act – the resources and enforcement capacity may be centralised and available for state level only (Ardaya et al. 2019; Blackburn 2014). Blackburn (2014) calls this incomplete decentralisation. For example, a small-scale planning system does not necessarily have a mechanism to refuse new development permits for risky areas, and planners may not have adequate knowledge of local ecosystems (Gonzalez-Mathiesen et al. 2021).

In theory, disaster governance should fit to the phenomenon that is being governed. For example, wildfire protection planning should be determined by topography and vegetation, but in practice, no actor has a mandate to act outside their area of jurisdiction – level of planning must be chosen so that there is a mandate to make things happen (Williams et al. 2012). Furthermore, planning systems for wildfire mitigation and preparedness are often splintered and not of appropriate scale to tackle wildfire risks (Abrams et al. 2016). A common problem is the disconnect between planning systems leading to a failure to recognise transmitted risk from neighbouring land ownerships – e.g., wildfires spreading from one landownership area to the nearby community (Ager et al. 2017).

Fragmentation along sectoral lines also hinders responding to multidimensional risks. Marks and Lebel (2016) describe how land and water are governed separately in Thailand, and collaboration between sectors is lacking, aggravated by rapid development incompatible with flood mitigation. Furthermore, separate state-level decision-making bodies and networks may come to different conclusions and take conflicting measures to manage continental scale hazards. An example of this was a bark beetle outbreak in a large area in western United States, when mostly state-level governance networks ended up responding in different ways, steered by their respective histories and pre-existing institutional arrangements (Abrams et al. 2021). As a further example, Nordic countries have traditionally taken a holistic approach to safety and security, focusing on network-like cooperation to improve resilience (Pursiainen 2018), but decentralisation has also contributed to creating ambiguities in responsibility sharing. In Finland, the complex allocation of power and responsibility has proved to be a recurrent hindrance when responding to emergencies and disasters, most recently during the COVID crisis (Tiirinki et al. 2020).

Conflicting Priorities, Lack of Coordination

Mismatches may also arise when levels of governance have different, sometimes even conflicting priorities. On the one hand, a state may be responsible for mitigating natural hazards, while local authorities are in charge of spatial planning and might prioritise advancing economic development (Robert and Schleyer-Lindenmann 2021). On the other hand, top-down state-level disaster recovery often focuses on housing, while local needs for everyday services are put aside (Contreras et al. 2017).

Conflicting interests may also cause legitimacy issues. Authorities at different levels of governance disagreeing on flood defence measures and national and international legislation conflicting with regional interests have been connected to citizen disengagement regarding flood preparedness in Northern Finland (Räsänen 2021). In addition, community-level views of acceptable risk management practices may differ from risk governance processes developed at larger scales. For example, the community-level expectations regarding fisheries in Fukushima have been different from risk governance processes developed at larger scales: while the national approach has focused on fixed radiation standards for produce and dispelling 'harmful rumours', the municipalities have taken a more deliberative approach of admitting remaining uncertainties and making risk management processes transparent (Mabon and Kawabe 2017).

Sometimes objectives are not in conflict, but cross-level and cross-scale interaction and coordination is lacking, which causes difficulties. Occasionally, the local level is entirely disconnected from decision-making. This may be the result of local communities being unaware of their rights and responsibilities, but sometimes there just is no formal mechanism for community input into policy design (Blackburn 2014). For example, regional wildfire preparedness planning might not account for local action at all (Abrams et al. 2016). At times practical problems, like not reimbursing travel costs, may lead to not involving local level representatives at regional level meetings. The result is top-down delivery of information, and communities not participating in disaster governance (Blackburn 2014). Blackburn (2014) also brings up the phenomenon of level-jumping: e.g., national level engaging and collaborating with local communities directly, without involving the levels between.

Overall, the above literature shows that there are multiple different types of (spatial) scale mismatches, and there have been several studies examining the interactions and mismatches. Nevertheless, the above studies have not typically utilised spatially explicit analyses. To gather evidence of how spatial data and methods have been utilised in this field of research, we provide a review in the next section.

IS THERE USE OF SPATIAL DATA AND METHODS FOR ADAPTIVE GOVERNANCE (AG)?

Spatial data references the specific geographic location of a phenomenon, event, or observation (Longley et al. 2015). Spatial data is stored, processed, integrated, and analysed in a geographic information system (GIS). Spatial data contain data, for instance, about population, borders, infrastructure, landforms, and ecosystems, and are collected in various ways, for example by surveying (active data collection by surveyors), remote sensing (e.g., satellite imagery), and mobile sensors (e.g., mobile phones). Spatial analysis methods are used to process and analyse spatial datasets to examine spatial patterns, associations, interactions, and dependencies of various phenomena. The methods range from GIS methods, such as, overlaying and merging different spatial datasets or calculating distances between points of interest to sophisticated spatial statistics methods (Longley et al. 2015).

To examine how spatial data and methods have been used in scientific adaptive governance research, we conducted a SCOPUS search with the following search syntax: ("adaptive governance" AND (*spatial* OR GIS OR "remote sensing" OR map* OR "geographic information")) on October 22, 2021. The search resulted in 57 articles with publication years ranging from 2006 to 2021.

We found that most of the articles did not use spatial data or methods. Instead, most of the articles (42 out of 57) analyse or only discuss some spatial aspects, such as fit, interactions and mismatches between spatial and other scales, the use of spatial data, spatial planning and governance, and interactions between different levels. The list shows the centrality of (spatial) scale interactions and mismatches in adaptive governance research and further justifies our choice to focus on mismatches in the previous section.

Another set of articles (eight out of 57) use spatial data but only discuss adaptive governance. Examples of different spatial datasets and analyses are GIS analyses of habitat connectivity and amount of set-aside forests in forest certification schemes (Elbakidze et al. 2011), analysis of land use/land cover change with remote sensing and other GIS data, as well as investigation of socioeconomic trends with census data (Ramos-Santiago et al. 2014), socio-ecological change monitoring with multiple spatial data streams and participatory research in a long-term socio-ecological research site (Bretagnolle et al. 2018), satellite data-based analysis of water resources and social media analysis of ecotourism (Broitman et al. 2019), climate models (Singh et al. 2020), spatially explicit surveys about willingness to pay for ecosystem services (Liu 2020), review of land use planning in the Amazon basin partly based on geospatial social and ecological data (Ruiz Agudelo et al. 2020), and spatial resilience indices and models (Assumma et al. 2021).

The seven studies that combine spatial methods with adaptive governance analysis are mostly but not exclusively related to governance and management of natural resources and include analysis of scale interactions and mismatches. The first article examines the governance of urban ecosystem services through a framework, which combines ecological patterns with social structure. The article synthesises existing research that used, on the one hand, spatial analysis of multiple data streams, such as land use/land cover patterns and bird species movements, and on the other hand, social science methods such as surveys, interviews, policy document analyses, and participatory research (Ernstson et al. 2010). The second article combines spatial analysis of a forest ecosystem with spatial analysis of conservation mandates of management bodies and thus analyses the governance system of forest resources and the fit between ecological and institutional landscape (Shkaruba and Kireyeu 2013). The third article investigates water resource governance by integrating interpretation of hydro-climatic change projections into an analysis of policy and legislative frameworks (Clarvis et al. 2014). The fourth article develops an adaptive governance model that includes analysis of spatial changes in ecosystem service values and analysis of regional governance (Ding et al. 2019). The fifth article shows how geospatial risk-based analytic tools facilitate the development of adaptive governance of wildfire risks in multi-jurisdictional landscapes (Dunn et al. 2020). The sixth article integrates spatial analysis of stormwater bills into examination of changes in governance of green infrastructure (Hsu et al. 2020). The seventh article analyses forest governance with land use/land cover change analysis, interviews, and statistics, and shows how a forest transition and related sociopolitical changes provide a window of opportunity for more adaptive forms of governance (Lorenzen et al. 2021).

All articles listed in the preceding paragraph combine the spatial analysis of ecological, environmental or – to a lesser extent – societal data with an examination of governance context. The key principles of adaptive governance are visible in multiple ways. First, the articles analyse how the focal environmental phenomenon matches – spatially, temporally, and functionally – with the jurisdictional, institutional, and management scales. Second, the studies show how the spatially and temporally dynamic socio-ecological context necessitates flexibility and learning in the forms of governance and management. Third, the articles discuss how multilevel, polycentric, and networked governance structures enable more sustainable management of natural resources whose spatiotemporal patterns seldom fit with the jurisdiction of a single administrative body.

Based on the brief review, it can be concluded that the use of spatial methods in articles that use the term adaptive governance is rare. However, our search targeted only title, abstract and keywords in the articles; therefore, there might be articles that did use the search terms in the main text. To screen how spatial methods have been used in scale mismatch and interaction literature, we conducted further searches with keywords including both GIS-related terms (GIS OR "remote sensing" OR map* OR "geographic information" OR "spatial analysis") and scale-related terms ("scale mismatch", "scale interaction"). We found two more articles that used spatial data and methods and were relevant in terms of adaptive governance. One article combines remote sensing analysis of cropland abandonment and forest-cover loss to a village level survey about household resources and constraints (Müller and Munroe 2008). The other article develops a spatial socio-ecological network analysis to examine estuary conservation to examine interactions between social and ecological units, composing, e.g., of management organisations and hydrological units (Sayles and Baggio 2017).

The nine studies summarised in the two preceding paragraphs are interdisciplinary and include analysis of integrated socio-ecological systems and show spatially how and where the social and ecological systems (mis)match and interact. The studies also show the strength of spatial data and methods to examine changes in socio-ecological systems. Nonetheless, the review also shows that while spatial analysis and GIS has been used extensively in environmental and socio-ecological research, spatial analysis is not widely utilised in adaptive governance research. We argue that spatial data and methods can be used in more versatile ways in adaptive governance research, as shown with the examples and future directions in the next section. Particularly, combining stakeholder involved research with spatial methods could foster both adaptive governance and wider socio-ecological literature.

POSSIBLE SPATIAL DATA SOURCES FOR ADAPTIVE GOVERNANCE RESEARCH

In this section, we summarise what kind of spatial data and methods have been used in broader disaster research and suggest how these approaches could further be used to advance adaptive governance research. The section is divided into two subsections: risk maps and their use, and participatory and crowdsourced data. On the one hand, hazard, vulnerability and risk maps and index-based assessments of disaster risks are widespread in the literature but they could be improved and linked to governance research in more versatile ways. On the other hand, we argue that information about human preferences and actions provided by participatory and crowdsourced data could provide new research possibilities, especially when linked with governance analysis. Even though we concentrate on these two categories, we acknowledge that there are also other types of spatial data that can be utilised in adaptive governance research.

Utilising and Improving Maps of Hazards and Risks

The disaster risk maps and geo-spatialised information about disaster management can be used in adaptive governance research in various ways. When examining disasters and disaster risk, there has been an extensive literature on mapping disaster risk and its components using various data sources. First, GIS and remote sensing have been used to map spatial patterns of hazards. For instance, digital terrain models can be used to determine the potential extent of floods (Muthusamy et al. 2021), while remote sensing data can be used to detect the observed extent of hazards and damages caused by them (Sarker et al. 2020). Second, socioeconomic, and environmental GIS data is widely used to map vulnerability and exposure to disaster risks. Examples of such data streams include geo-spatialised statistical data or survey data of social characteristics of populations (Räsänen et al. 2019), and data about building vulnerability (Pereira et al. 2020). Furthermore, GIS methods can be used to model the spatiotemporal changes in hazards, vulnerability, exposure, and risks (Landreau et al. 2021).

However, used maps and datasets are often too coarse for local disaster governance, providing an example of a scale mismatch. For example, global climate models and regional weather forecasts do not respond to local disaster risk reduction needs (Birkmann et al. 2014). This may lead to an underestimation of the potential effects of disasters (Tavares et al. 2015). When the goal is to, e.g., protect critical municipal infrastructure (Treinish et al. 2019) or create local flood or drought scenarios (Milz et al. 2018, Kundzewicz et al. 2017), information on local extremes would be more beneficial than large-scale overviews (Kundzewicz et al. 2019). A similar problem of too coarse data applies to vulnerability mapping. Vulnerability indicators are usually based on county or city-level data because of conventional census geographic units. However, the most relevant vulnerability hotspots are often small-scale, for instance specific neighbourhoods (Thompson et al. 2021, Ashley et al. 2014), and county-level indicators also do not match with experimental understandings of vulnerability and resilience (Borie et al. 2019). It has been shown that the unit of analysis and scale of measurements can directly influence the results of vulnerability assessments (Cutter and Derakhshan 2019, Räsänen et al. 2019). More accurate indicators of resilience and vulnerability would require high-resolution data which is rarely available (Chuang et al. 2018). Further analysis of spatial patterns of disaster-related phenomena could also be examined with spatial data analysis and spatial statistics methods, such as analyses of spatial (auto)correlations, spatial interpolation, spatial clustering, and spatial regression. While spatial statistics are not always utilised when the research includes spatial data, the use of such methods aids to find hot spots of disaster risk (Brandt et al. 2020), construct spatially continuous datasets, and examine spatial relationships, e.g., between disaster vulnerability and response (Wang et al. 2019).

While some studies have looked at how the disaster risk maps have been used in disaster mitigation, planning, preparedness, and response (Dunn et al. 2020), more studies could examine whether the risk maps alter the way risks are perceived and governed. In other words, risk maps provide a powerful method to visualise spatial patterns of disaster risks, but they may provide misleading or even erroneous information, of which the problems with data resolution are one example. Evaluation of the governance context and adaptive risk management could even pave the way for thorough validation and negotiation of maps. Another research avenue could look at how past governance and management decisions have altered the spatial patterns of disaster risk. For instance, longitudinal research has shown how risks change over time (Fawcett et al. 2017) but this literature has not widely analysed the role of governance in spatial risk dynamics. Nevertheless, the problem here is often the lack of long-term data about vulnerability and resilience (Chuang et al. 2018).

In addition to looking at past changes, particularly in assessments of climate-related risks, the focus should be on future risks to enable more informed adaptation. The future-oriented assessments have typically projected biophysical phenomena and hazards, such as heat and floods into the future, while projections of socio-economic factors related to disaster vulnerability and exposure have been scarcer (Jurgilevich et al. 2017). The projections of socio-economic factors typically are statistical and quantitative projections that do not assess vulnerability and exposure dynamics as a process, i.e., drivers and pathways of change (Jurgilevich et al. 2021). There has been development of dynamic adaptive policy pathways that sketch how adaptive policies affect future development trajectories (Haasnoot et al. 2013), but to the best of our knowledge, there has not been methodological development on spatially explicit adaptive policy models that would assess what kind of spatial implications policy, management, or governance decisions have and how the spatial patterns of socio-ecological phenomena such as disaster risk change in the future depending on chosen and changing policies. To develop these models or assessments, multiple different approaches could be tested, merged, and compared, including for instance agent-based, process-based, statistical and conceptual socio-ecological models, and qualitative more in-depth information about change drivers and scenario narratives. This kind of research could enable spatially explicit modelling of adaptive governance decisions into the future and construction of multiple alternative future pathways.

Participatory and Crowdsourced Data

Participatory GIS (PGIS), volunteered geographic information (VGI), and geotagged social media data have been used to supplement incomplete location-based information and to gather difficult-to-measure qualitative and experiential knowledge of different phases of the disaster management cycle. Participatory GIS offers a way to engage with local sources of knowledge, and to find suitable solutions for different contexts. This way it can be used to advance adaptive governance's objectives of combining top-down and bottom-up decision-making, inclusion of diverse stakeholders (Fournier et al. 2016) and integrating different types of knowledge (Karpouzoglou et al. 2016). In addition, collecting data directly from individuals and local communities supports observing changing situations and responding to them in a timely manner, which is a key aspect of adaptive governance.

PGIS, or Public Participatory GIS (PPGIS), is a way to extract place-based information from experts, stakeholders, or the general public, by allowing them to draw information about the focal phenomena on maps. PGIS can be seen as a solution to data scarcity (Brandt et al. 2020, Dierich et al. 2019). It can be utilised to gather hard-to-access information from experts – for example, to understand critical infrastructure interdependencies and available resources (Dierich et al. 2019). In addition, PGIS can be used to make qualitative things more tangible: when experiences, emotions, contextual details, social networks, and local spatial knowledge of hazards are marked on a map, it makes visible in ways that planners can engage with (Taylor et al. 2020). This allows more comprehensive risk mapping (Reichel and Frömming 2014; McCall and Peters-Guarin 2009) and enables transcending different scales of knowledge. Participatory mapping has been used to gather knowledge on local bushfire preparedness (Haworth et al. 2016) and flood impacts (Brandt et al. 2020). It is also beneficial for assessing local needs for warning systems, relief centres, and shelters, prioritising risks, and mapping experiences of slow-onset hazards, as well as resilience and adaptation (McCall and Peters-Guarin 2009). Furthermore, PGIS can be used as a way to communicate ideas about vulnerability and share information (Canevari-Luzardo et al. 2017), and to analyse and display how different scenarios of disasters could play out on the landscape (Voinov et al. 2018). Fruitful participatory research processes have been noted to positively contribute to the resilience knowledge of participants as well (Meyer et al. 2018), and they can lead to increased social connectedness and engagement in risk reduction (Haworth et al. 2016), improving the interaction between different levels of governance.

Voluntary geographic information (VGI) refers to georeferenced (place-based) information that members of the general public contribute to databases, i.e., it is a version of crowdsourcing (Goodchild and Li 2012). Like PGIS, VGI is used to gather diverse, local information (Haworth and Bruce 2015). While both PGIS and VGI aim to capture people's valuable spatial knowledge, include and engage citizens, and gather data efficiently, there are some differences: VGI is more focused on application and large data, while PGIS is more about processes and outcomes (Verplanke et al. 2016). VGI has been frequently used in crowdsourcing disaster and hazard management-related information (Yan et al. 2020). A notable and successful disaster-related VGI initiative has been the Humanitarian OpenStreetMap (HOT-OSM), which allows volunteers to interpret satellite imagery to draw maps of areas that lack maps or that have been changed by disasters. The project has been lauded as a tangible relief work without actually being physically present (Zook et al. 2010), providing information for, e.g., Red Cross and Red Crescent (Scholz et al. 2018). Other global VGI platforms, which enable two-way communication of disaster risk instead of top-down information sharing, include Risk Geo-Wiki focusing on flood-related spatial information, and open-source hazard management software InaSAFE (McCallum et al. 2016). VGI has also been used to map residents' preferences regarding flood evacuation shelters (Kusumo 2016).

Similar to VGI, using social media data is used to gather local information from many people. However, social media data does not quite qualify as VGI, as the users are not necessarily deliberately participating in the gathering of data. However, useful real-time information about disasters is often posted on social media: reports of victims, infrastructure damage, and requests of urgent needs (Imran et al. 2020). This allows for efficient monitoring incidents and gathering situational awareness and assessing damages (Wiegmann et al. 2021, Imran et al.

2020, Zhang et al. 2019, Resch et al. 2018), as well as keeping track of post-disaster recovery (Jamali et al. 2019). Spatial dimension is one of the most commonly used attributes of social media data, in addition to time, content, and network (Wang and Ye 2018). Consequently, social media data is a valuable method for gathering the otherwise scarce small-scale data of hazards and their impacts. The most common method for extracting location from social media is using the coordinates in message metadata (Stock 2018), as messages are geotagged when the user attaches geographical information manually, or the platform does it automatically (Phengsuwan et al. 2021). However, this approach has its limits: it reports the posting location rather than the location that the message refers to (Stock 2018). In addition, social media users often use vague, e.g., country-level geotags to mark their locations, or use nonsensical expressions, such as wonderland (Phengsuwan et al. 2021). Consequently, extracting place names from message text have been noted to provide more accurate data. Deducing location based on social media connections can also provide good results, but with limitations (Stock 2018).

Participatory and crowdsourced data are associated with some notable challenges. First, representative sampling and inclusive practices require careful deliberation (Haworth and Bruce 2015). While participatory processes aim at gathering diverse information, participants are often experts, and community engagement remains weak (Meyer et al. 2018). Likewise, while the number of projects involving citizens has increased in the EU, their quality has been questioned due to weak funding, engagement, and influence (Onencan et al. 2018). Social media data is particularly susceptible to outliers and other biases, as participation in social media is far from equal (Wiegmann et al. 2021). Social media also tends to emphasise more populous areas during disasters (Fan et al. 2020), which means that the number of messages is not a good indication of event severity (Xiao et al. 2015). Second challenge is data quality assurance and source trustworthiness (Haworth et al. 2016), including weeding out misinformation (Imran et al. 2020). Third, handling large amounts of data and extracting relevant information and summarisation into useful form can be difficult (Haworth and Bruce 2015; Imran et al. 2020). In addition, potential issues of privacy have to be taken into account (Haworth et al. 2016, Haworth and Bruce 2015).

Despite the challenges, participatory GIS and crowdsourcing can be considered as useful tools in rapid gathering of spatially explicit data, for instance about local knowledge, perceptions, and preferences, how people act before, during and after disasters, and how people use and manage natural resources. These pieces of information, collected directly from individuals, local communities, and different stakeholders, are crucial to understand and model socio-ecological systems and spatiotemporal dynamics therein. Collected GIS data also has potential to make more informed management and governance decisions and to improve interaction between governance levels.

SUMMARY AND CONCLUSION

This chapter reviewed the use of spatial methods in adaptive governance research and exemplified what kind of problems they could be used to solve in the future. The focus was on disaster governance research, which deals with complex socio-ecological systems involving risks, uncertainties and changing circumstances, and is thus a relevant context for applying adaptive governance. In the first section of this chapter, we focus on spatial interactions and mismatches as an example of a context where spatial approaches are appropriate. Scale mismatches arise when scales of governance and the physical and social world do not fit together. In disaster governance, this may lead to splintered governance that does not address large-scale problems and lack of interaction or conflicting objectives between different levels of governance. In the second section, we look at the actual use of spatial data and methods in adaptive governance literature. Based on a systematised literature review, we find that spatial methods are not commonly used in adaptive governance research, although spatial aspects, such as interactions and mismatches, are discussed regularly. In the third section, we review data and methods that have been used in disaster research and could be used in adaptive governance research. We suggest how disaster risk maps could be utilised and developed further and how participatory and crowdsourced information increases our understanding of human dimensions of disasters.

While the amount of available location-based data is increasing, its utilisation requires careful consideration. Grêt-Regamey et al. (2021) emphasise that integration of different types of data is crucial, and the best results are achieved with a balanced combination of passive sensing (e.g., remote sensing, social media data), and active sensing (e.g., participatory methods such as PGIS). When these sensing systems are in dialogue, active sensing data gives meaning and value to passively sensed data, and continuous feedback helps to connect ecological, technological, and social contexts, while enabling reacting to changes. This kind of integration of active sensing and passive sensing data has been carried out by Müller and Munroe (2008), who combined village-level household surveys with satellite image data to develop statistical models of rural land-use changes after the fall of the Soviet Union. Furthermore, a different kind of integrative approach was implemented by Sayles and Baggio (2017), who quantitatively analysed how regional and local resource management organisations collaborate to solve social and ecological scale mismatches in estuary restoration. Such successful integration of data sources and knowledge types requires active curation of sensed data, and the involvement of data users in the selection of appropriate data sources. Privacy protection should also be considered while simultaneously ensuring access to data (Grêt-Regamey et al. 2021).

Our chapter shows the multiple possibilities of spatial data for adaptive governance research. In particular, with spatially explicit data, spatiotemporal trends of socio-ecological phenomena can be monitored and projected, and spatial patterns of disaster risks and their management can be evaluated. The various spatial methods discussed in this chapter support maintaining an up-to-date picture of the functioning and changes in socio-ecological systems, taking into account scale interactions and mismatches. Spatial data and methods can illustrate and be used to examine how governance patterns have interacted with disaster risk changes in the past, and help to improve governance practices, for instance, by modelling future spatiotemporal implications of present-day governance decisions. Overall, responding to changing circumstances is the key in adaptive governance. Potential changes can be either continuous or abrupt, and often with largely unpredictable consequences. Thus, the ability to mobilise and link the necessary actors and knowledge quickly and effectively across different levels becomes crucial (Termeer et al. 2010). However, our chapter shows that spatially oriented adaptive governance research is often focused on one theme at a time. Therefore, more holistic perspectives are needed, for example by connecting multiple data streams and coupling governance analysis with the analysis of focal social and ecological processes.

REFERENCES

Abrams, J., Nielsen-Pincus, M., Paveglio, T., and Moseley, C. 2016. Community wildfire protection planning in the American West: homogeneity within diversity? *Journal of Environmental Planning and Management*, 59, 3, 557–572.

Abrams, J., Huber-Stearns, H., Steen-Adams, M., Davis, E. J., Bone, C., Nelson, M. F., and Moseley, C. 2021. Adaptive governance in a complex social-ecological context: emergent responses to a native forest insect outbreak. *Sustainability Science*, 16, 1, 53–68.

Ager, A. A., Evers, C. R., Day, M. A., Preisler, H. K., Barros, A. M., and Nielsen-Pincus, M. 2017. Network analysis of wildfire transmission and implications for risk governance. *PLoS One*, 12, 3, e0172867.

Ardaya, A. B., Evers, M., and Ribbe, L. 2019. Participatory approaches for disaster risk governance? Exploring participatory mechanisms and mapping to close the communication gap between population living in flood risk areas and authorities in Nova Friburgo Municipality, RJ, Brazil. *Land Use Policy*, 88, 104103.

Ashley, W. S., Strader, S., Rosencrants, T., and Krmenec, A. J. 2014. Spatiotemporal changes in tornado hazard exposure: the case of the expanding bull's-eye effect in Chicago, Illinois. *Weather, Climate, and Society*, 6, 2, 175–193.

Assumma, V., Bottero, M., De Angelis, E., Lourenço, J. M., Monaco, R., and Soares, A. J. 2021. A decision support system for territorial resilience assessment and planning: an application to the Douro Valley Portugal. *Science of the Total Environment*, 756, 143806.

Bae, Y., Joo, Y. M., and Won, S. Y. 2016. Decentralization and collaborative disaster governance: evidence from South Korea. *Habitat International*, 52, 50–56.

Birkmann, J., Garschagen, M., and Setiadi, N. 2014. New challenges for adaptive urban governance in highly dynamic environments: revisiting planning systems and tools for adaptive and strategic planning. *Urban Climate*, 7, 115–133.

Blackburn, S. 2014. The politics of scale and disaster risk governance: barriers to decentralisation in Portland, Jamaica. *Geoforum*, 52, 101–112.

Blair, B., Lovecraft, A. L., and Hum, R. 2018. The disaster chronotope: spatial and temporal learning in governance of extreme events. In *Governance of Risk, Hazards and Disasters*, pp. 43–64. Routledge.

Borie, M., Ziervogel, G., Taylor, F. E., Millington, J. D., Sitas, R., and Pelling, M. 2019. Mapping for resilience across city scales: an opportunity to open-up conversations for more inclusive resilience policy? *Environmental Science & Policy*, 99, 1–9.

Brandt, K., Graham, L., Hawthorne, T., Jeanty, J., Burkholder, B., Munisteri, C., and Visaggi, C. 2020. Integrating sketch mapping and hot spot analysis to enhance capacity for community-level flood and disaster risk management. *The Geographical Journal*, 186, 2, 198–212.

Bretagnolle, V., Berthet, E., Gross, N., Gauffre, B., Plumejeaud, C., Houte, S., Balderhausser, I., Monceau, K., Allier, F. Monestiez,P., and Gaba, S. 2018. Towards sustainable and multifunctional agriculture in farmland landscapes: lessons from the integrative approach of a French LTSER platform. *Science of the Total Environment*, 627, 822–834.

Broitman, B., Sproles, E., Weideman, C., Salas, S., Geldes, C., Zambra, A., Gonzalez-Silvestre, L., and Bugueño, L. 2019. Building consensus through assessment evidence from San Pedro de Atacama, Chile. In *Mainstreaming Natural Capital and Ecosystem Services into Development Policy*, pp. 121–148. Routledge.

Canevari-Luzardo, L., Bastide, J., Choutet, I., and Liverman, D. 2017. Using partial participatory GIS in vulnerability and disaster risk reduction in Grenada. *Climate and Development*, 9, 2, 95–109.

Cash, D. W., Adger, W. N., Berkes, F., Garden, P., Lebel, L., Olsson, P., Pritchard, L., and Young, O. 2006. Scale and cross-scale dynamics: governance and information in a multilevel world. *Ecology and Society*, 11, 2.

Chuang, W. C., Garmestani, A., Eason, T. N., Spanbauer, T. L., Fried-Petersen, H. B., Roberts, C. P., Sundstrom, S. M., Burnett, J. L., Angeler, D. G., Chaffin, B. C., Gunderson, L., Twidwell, D., and Allen, C. R. 2018. Enhancing quantitative approaches for assessing community resilience. *Journal of Environmental Management*, 213, 353–362.

Clarvis, M. H., Fatichi, S., Allan, A., Fuhrer, J., Stoffel, M., Romerio, F., Gaudard, L., Burlando, P., Beniston, M., Xoplaki, E., and Toreti, A. 2014. Governing and managing water resources under changing hydro-climatic contexts: the case of the upper Rhone basin. *Environmental Science & Policy*, 43, 56–67.

Contreras, D., Blaschke, T., and Hodgson, M. E. 2017. Lack of spatial resilience in a recovery process: Case L'Aquila, Italy. *Technological Forecasting and Social Change*, 121, 76–88.

Crosweller, M., and Tschakert, P. 2021. Disaster management and the need for a reinstated social contract of shared responsibility. *International Journal of Disaster Risk Reduction*, 63, 102440.

Cumming, G. S., Cumming, D. H., and Redman, C. L. 2006. Scale mismatches in social-ecological systems: causes, consequences, and solutions. *Ecology and Society*, 11, 1.

Cutter, S. L., and Derakhshan, S. 2019. Implementing disaster policy: exploring scale and measurement schemes for disaster resilience. *Journal of Homeland Security and Emergency Management*, 16, 3.

Dierich, A., Tzavella, K., Setiadi, N. J., Fekete, A., and Neisser, F. M. 2019. Enhanced crisis-preparation of critical infrastructures through a participatory qualitative-quantitative interdependency analysis approach. *ISCRAM*, May.

Ding, X., Zhou, C., Zhong, W., and Tang, P. 2019. Addressing uncertainty of environmental governance in environmentally sensitive areas in developing countries: a precise-strike and spatial-targeting adaptive governance framework. *Sustainability*, 11, 16, 4510.

Djalante, R., Holley, C., and Thomalla, F. 2011. Adaptive governance and managing resilience to natural hazards. *International Journal of Disaster Risk Science*, 2, 4, 1–14.

Dunn, C. J., D O'Connor, C., Abrams, J., Thompson, M. P., Calkin, D. E., Johnston, J. D., Stratton, R., and Gilbertson-Day, J. 2020. Wildfire risk science facilitates adaptation of fire-prone social-ecological systems to the new fire reality. *Environmental Research Letters*, 15, 2, 025001.

Elbakidze, M., Angelstam, P., Andersson, K., Nordberg, M., and Pautov, Y. 2011. How does forest certification contribute to boreal biodiversity conservation? Standards and outcomes in Sweden and NW Russia. *Forest Ecology and Management*, 262, 11, 1983–1995.

Ernstson, H., Barthel, S., Andersson, E., and Borgström, S. T. 2010. Scale-crossing brokers and network governance of urban ecosystem services: the case of Stockholm. *Ecology and Society*, 15, 4.

Fan, C., Esparza, M., Dargin, J., Wu, F., Oztekin, B., and Mostafavi, A. 2020. Spatial biases in crowd-sourced data: social media content attention concentrates on populous areas in disasters. *Computers, Environment and Urban Systems*, 83, 101514.

Fawcett, D., Pearce, T., Ford, J. D., and Archer, L. 2017. Operationalizing longitudinal approaches to climate change vulnerability assessment. *Global Environmental Change*, 45, 79–88.

Fournier, M., Larrue, C., Alexander, M., Hegger, D., Bakker, M., Pettersson, M., Crabhé, A., Mees, H., and Choryński, A. 2016. Flood risk mitigation in Europe: how far away are we from the aspired forms of adaptive governance? *Ecology and Society*, 21, 4.

Gibson, C. C., Ostrom, E., and Ahn, T. K. 2000. The concept of scale and the human dimensions of global change: a survey. *Ecological Economics*, 32, 2, 217–239.

Gonzalez-Mathiesen, C., Ruane, S., and March, A. 2021. Integrating wildfire risk management and spatial planning: a historical review of two Australian planning systems. *International Journal of Disaster Risk Reduction*, 53, 101984.

Goodchild, M. F., and Li, L. 2012. Assuring the quality of volunteered geographic information. *Spatial Statistics*, 1, 110–120.

Grêt-Regamey, A., Switalski, M., Fagerholm, N., Korpilo, S., Juhola, S., Kyttä, M., Käyhkö, N., McPhearson, T., Nollert, M., Rinne, T., Soininen, N., Toivonen, T., Räsänen, A., Willberg, E. and Raymond, C. M. 2021. Harnessing sensing systems towards urban sustainability transformation. *NPJ Urban Sustainability*, 1, 1, 1–9.

Haasnoot, M., Kwakkel, J. H., Walker, W. E., and Ter Maat, J. 2013. Dynamic adaptive policy pathways: a method for crafting robust decisions for a deeply uncertain world. Global environmental change, 23, 2, 485–498.

Haworth, B., and Bruce, E. 2015. A review of volunteered geographic information for disaster management. *Geography Compass*, 9, 5, 237–250.

Haworth, B., Whittaker, J., and Bruce, E. 2016. Assessing the application and value of participatory mapping for community bushfire preparation. *Applied Geography*, 76, 115–127.

Hsu, D., Lim, T. C., and Meng, T. 2020. Rocky steps towards adaptive management and adaptive governance in implementing green infrastructure at urban scale in Philadelphia. *Urban Forestry & Urban Greening*, 55, 126791.

Imran, M., Ofli, F., Caragea, D., and Torralba, A. 2020. Using AI and social media multimodal content for disaster response and management: opportunities, challenges, and future directions. *Information Processing & Management*, 57, 5, 102261.

Jamali, M., Nejat, A., Ghosh, S., Jin, F., and Cao, G. 2019. Social media data and post-disaster recovery. *International Journal of Information Management*, 44, 25–37.

Jurgilevich, A., Räsänen, A., and Juhola, S. 2021. Assessing the dynamics of urban vulnerability to climate change: case of Helsinki, Finland. *Environmental Science & Policy*, 125, 32–43.

Jurgilevich, A., Räsänen, A., Groundstroem, F., and Juhola, S. 2017. A systematic review of dynamics in climate risk and vulnerability assessments. *Environmental Research Letters*, 12, 1, 013002.

Kapucu, N., Arslan, T., and Collins, M. L. 2010. Examining intergovernmental and interorganizational response to catastrophic disasters: toward a network-centered approach. *Administration & Society*, 42, 2, 222–247.

Karpouzoglou, T., Dewulf, A., and Clark, J. 2016. Advancing adaptive governance of social-ecological systems through theoretical multiplicity. *Environmental Science & Policy*, 57, 1–9.

Kundzewicz, Z. W., Krysanova, V., Dankers, R., Hirabayashi, Y., Kanae, S., Hattermann, F. F., Huang, S, Milly, P. C. D., Stoffel,M., Driessen, P. P. J., Matczak, P., Quevauviller, P., and Schellnhuber, H. J. 2017. Differences in flood hazard projections in Europe: their causes and consequences for decision making. *Hydrological Sciences Journal*, 62, 1, 1–14.

Kundzewicz, Z. W., Su, B., Wang, Y., Wang, G., Wang, G., Huang, J., and Jiang, T. 2019. Flood risk in a range of spatial perspectives: from global to local scales. *Natural Hazards and Earth System Sciences*, 19, 7, 1319–1328.

Kusumo, A. N. L. 2016. Utilizing volunteered geographic information to assess community's flood evacuation shelters: case study: Jakarta. Master's thesis, University of Twente.

Landreau, A., Juhola, S., Jurgilevich, A., and Räsänen, A. 2021. Combining socio-economic and climate projections to assess heat risk. *Climatic Change, 167*,1, 1–20.

Liu, Y. 2020. The willingness to pay for ecosystem services on the Tibetan Plateau of China. *Geography and Sustainability*, 1, 2, 141–151.

Longley, P. A., Goodchild, M. F., Maguire, D. J., and Rhind, D. W. 2015. *Geographic Information Systems and Science*, 4th edition. John Wiley & Sons.

Lorenzen, M., Orozco-Ramírez, Q., Ramírez-Santiago, R., and Garza, G. G. 2021. The forest transition as a window of opportunity to change the governance of common-pool resources: the case of Mexico's Mixteca Alta. *World Development*, 145, 105516.

Mabon, L., and Kawabe, M. 2017. Making sense of complexity in risk governance in post-disaster Fukushima fisheries: a scalar approach. *Environmental Science & Policy*, 75, 173–183.

Marks, D., and Lebel, L. 2016. Disaster governance and the scalar politics of incomplete decentralization: fragmented and contested responses to the 2011 floods in Central Thailand. *Habitat International*, 52, 57–66.

McCall, M. K., and Peters-Guarin, G. 2009. Making communities safer: participatory mapping and PGIS in support of community risk assessment. Presentation at: SKI-Canada Spatial Knowledge & Information, Fernie, BC.

McCallum, I., Liu, W., See, L., Mechler, R., Keating, A., Hochrainer-Stigler, S., ... and Moorthy, I. 2016. Technologies to support community flood disaster risk reduction. *International Journal of Disaster Risk Science*, 7, 2, 198–204.

Melo Zurita, M. D. L., Cook, B., Harms, L., and March, A. 2015. Towards new disaster governance: subsidiarity as a critical tool. *Environmental Policy and Governance*, 25, 6, 386–398.

Meyer, M. A., Hendricks, M., Newman, G. D., Masterson, J. H., Cooper, J. T., Sansom, G., Gharaibeh, N., Horney, J, Berke, P, van Zandt, S., and Cousins, T. 2018. Participatory action research: tools for disaster resilience education. *International Journal of Disaster Resilience in the Built Environment*.

Milz, D., Zellner, M., Hoch, C., Radinsky, J., Pudlock, K., and Lyons, L. 2018. Reconsidering scale: using geographic information systems to support spatial planning conversations. *Planning Practice & Research*, 33, 3, 291–308.

Müller, D., and Munroe, D. K. 2008. Changing rural landscapes in Albania: cropland abandonment and forest clearing in the postsocialist transition. *Annals of the Association of American Geographers*, 98, 4, 855–876.

Muthusamy, M., Casado, M. R., Butler, D., and Leinster, P. 2021. Understanding the effects of Digital Elevation Model resolution in urban fluvial flood modelling. *Journal of Hydrology*, 596, 126088.

Onencan, A. M., Meesters, K., and Van de Walle, B. 2018. Methodology for participatory GIS risk mapping and citizen science for Solotvyno salt mines. *Remote Sensing*, 10, 11, 1828.

Pereira, S., Santos, P. P., Zêzere, J. L., Tavares, A. O., Garcia, R. A. C., and Oliveira, S. C. 2020. A landslide risk index for municipal land use planning in Portugal. *Science of The Total Environment*, 735, 139463.

Phengsuwan, J., Shah, T., Thekkummal, N. B., Wen, Z., Sun, R., Pullarkatt, D., Thirugnanam, H., Vinodi Ramesh, M., Morgan, G., James, P., and Ranjan, R. 2021. Use of social media data in disaster management: a survey. *Future Internet*, 13, 2, 46.

Pursiainen, C. 2018. Critical infrastructure resilience: a Nordic model in the making? *International Journal of Disaster Risk Reduction*, 27, 632–641.

Ramos-Santiago, L. E., Villanueva-Cubero, L., Santiago-Acevedo, L. E., and Rodriguez-Melendez, Y. N. 2014. Green area loss in San Juan's inner-ring suburban neighborhoods: a multidisciplinary approach to analyzing green/gray area dynamics. *Ecology and Society*, 19, 2.

Räsänen, A. 2021. Cross-scale interactions in flood risk management: a case study from Rovaniemi, Finland. *International Journal of Disaster Risk Reduction*, 57, 102185.

Räsänen, A., Heikkinen, K., Piila, N., and Juhola, S. 2019. Zoning and weighting in urban heat island vulnerability and risk mapping in Helsinki, Finland. *Regional Environmental Change*, 19, 5, 1481–1493.

Reichel, C., and Frömming, U. U. 2014. Participatory mapping of local disaster risk reduction knowledge: an example from Switzerland. *International Journal of Disaster Risk Science*, 5, 1, 41–54.

Resch, B., Usländer, F., and Havas, C. 2018. Combining machine-learning topic models and spatiotemporal analysis of social media data for disaster footprint and damage assessment. *Cartography and Geographic Information Science*, 45, 4, 362–376.

Robert, S., and Schleyer-Lindenmann, A. 2021. How ready are we to cope with climate change? Extent of adaptation to sea level rise and coastal risks in local planning documents of southern France. *Land Use Policy*, 104, 105354.

Ruane, S. 2020. Applying the principles of adaptive governance to bushfire management: a case study from the South West of Australia. *Journal of Environmental Planning and Management*, 63, 7, 1215–1240.

Ruiz Agudelo, C., Mazzeo, N., Díaz, I., Barral, M., Piñeiro, G., Gadino, I., Roche, I., and Acuña-Posada, R. J. 2020. Land use planning in the Amazon basin: challenges from resilience thinking. *Ecology and Society*, 25, 1.

Sarker, M. N. I., Peng, Y., Yiran, C., and Shouse, R. C. 2020. Disaster resilience through big data: way to environmental sustainability. *International Journal of Disaster Risk Reduction*, 101769.

Sayles, J. S., and Baggio, J. A. 2017. Social–ecological network analysis of scale mismatches in estuary watershed restoration. *Proceedings of the National Academy of Sciences*, 114, 10, E1776-E1785.

Scholz, S., Knight, P., Eckle, M., Marx, S., and Zipf, A. 2018. Volunteered geographic information for disaster risk reduction: the missing maps approach and its potential within the red cross and red crescent movement. *Remote Sensing*, 10, 8, 1239.

Shkaruba, A., and Kireyeu, V. 2013. Recognising ecological and institutional landscapes in adaptive governance of natural resources. *Forest Policy and Economics*, 36, 87–97.

Singh, P. K., Papageorgiou, K., Chudasama, H., and Papageorgiou, E. I. 2019. Evaluating the effectiveness of climate change adaptations in the world's largest mangrove ecosystem. *Sustainability*, 11, 23, 6655.

Stock, K. 2018. Mining location from social media: a systematic review. *Computers, Environment and Urban Systems*, 71, 209–240.

Tavares, A. O., dos Santos, P. P., Freire, P., Fortunato, A. B., Rilo, A., and Sá, L. 2015. Flooding hazard in the Tagus estuarine area: the challenge of scale in vulnerability assessments. *Environmental Science & Policy*, 51, 238–255.

Taylor, F. E., Millington, J. D., Jacob, E., Malamud, B. D., and Pelling, M. 2020. Messy maps: qualitative GIS representations of resilience. *Landscape and Urban Planning*, 198, 103771.

Termeer, C. J., Dewulf, A., and Van Lieshout, M. 2010. Disentangling scale approaches in governance research: comparing monocentric, multilevel, and adaptive governance. *Ecology and Society*, 15, 4.

Thompson, C. M., Dezzani, R. J., and Radil, S. M. 2021. Modeling multiscalar influences on natural hazards vulnerability: a proof of concept using coastal hazards in Sarasota County, Florida. *GeoJournal*, 86, 1, 507–528. 2019–2021

Tierney, K. 2012. Disaster governance: social, political, and economic dimensions. *Annual Review of Environment and Resources*, 37, 341–363.

Tiirinki, H., Tynkkynen, L. K., Sovala, M., Atkins, S., Koivusalo, M., Rautiainen, P., Jormanainen, V., and Keskimäki, I. 2020. COVID-19 pandemic in Finland: preliminary analysis on health system response and economic consequences. *Health Policy and Technology*, 9, 4, 649–662.

Treinish, L., Praino, A., Tewari, M., and Hertell, B. 2019. Predicting impacts of weather-driven urban disasters in the current and future climate. *IBM Journal of Research and Development*, 64, 1/2, 6: 1–13.

Voinov, A., Jenni, K., Gray, S., Kolagani, N., Glynn, P. D., Bommel, P., Prell, C., Zellner, M., Paolisso, M., Jordan, R., Sterling, E., Schmitt Olabisi, L,. Giabbanelli, P. J., Sun, Z., Le Page, C., Elsawah, S., BenDor, T. K., Hubacek, K., Laursen, B. K., Jetter, A., Basco-Carrera, L., Singer, A., Young, L., Brunacini, J., and P. Smajgl. A. 2018. Tools and methods in participatory modeling: selecting the right tool for the job. *Environmental Modelling & Software*, 109, 232–255.

Walker, B. B., Schuurman, N., Swanlund, D., and Clague, J. J. 2021. GIS-based multicriteria evaluation for earthquake response: a case study of expert opinion in Vancouver, Canada. *Natural Hazards*, 105, 2, 2075–2091.

Walker, G., Tweed, F., and Whittle, R. 2014. A framework for profiling the characteristics of risk governance in natural hazard contexts. *Natural Hazards and Earth System Sciences*, 14, 1, 155–164.

Wang, Z., and Ye, X. 2018. Social media analytics for natural disaster management. *International Journal of Geographical Information Science*, 32, 1, 49–72.

Wang, Z., Lam, N. S., Obradovich, N., and Ye, X. 2019. Are vulnerable communities digitally left behind in social responses to natural disasters? An evidence from Hurricane Sandy with Twitter data. *Applied Geography*, 108, 1–8.

Verplanke, J., McCall, M. K., Uberhuaga, C., Rambaldi, G., and Haklay, M. 2016. A shared perspective for PGIS and VGI. *The Cartographic Journal*, 53, 4, 308–317.

Wiegmann, M., Kersten, J., Senaratne, H., Potthast, M., Klan, F., and Stein, B. 2021. Opportunities and risks of disaster data from social media: a systematic review of incident information. *Natural Hazards and Earth System Sciences*, 21, 5, 1431–1444.

Williams, D. R., Jakes, P. J., Burns, S., Cheng, A. S., Nelson, K. C., Sturtevant, V., Brummel, R. F., Staychock, E., and Souter, S. G. 2012. Community wildfire protection planning: the importance of framing, scale, and building sustainable capacity. *Journal of Forestry*, 110, 8, 415–420.

Xiao, Y., Huang, Q., and Wu, K. 2015. Understanding social media data for disaster management. *Natural Hazards*, 79, 3, 1663–1679.

Yan, Y., Feng, C. C., Huang, W., Fan, H., Wang, Y. C., and Zipf, A. 2020. Volunteered geographic information research in the first decade: a narrative review of selected journal articles in GIScience. *International Journal of Geographical Information Science*, 34, 9, 1765–1791.

Zhang, C., Fan, C., Yao, W., Hu, X., and Mostafavi, A. 2019. Social media for intelligent public information and warning in disasters: an interdisciplinary review. *International Journal of Information Management*, 49, 190–207.

Zook, M., Graham, M., Shelton, T., and Gorman, S. 2010. Volunteered geographic information and crowdsourcing disaster relief: a case study of the Haitian earthquake. *World Medical & Health Policy*, 2, 2, 7–33.

7. Serious games as an adaptive governance method

Peter Edwards

INTRODUCTION

Natural resource management encompasses complex social-ecological challenges, including for example, climate change, water use and conservation, cultural heritage, labour, employment and working conditions, and community health. These complex challenges make decision-making extremely difficult. Without a shared understanding between decision-makers and communities (the ultimate site where governance is enacted), there is a risk that vested interests will be retained, power imbalances will be maintained and potentially exacerbated and a resulting loss of trust between communities and decision-makers will ensue.

Adaptive governance (or AG) is one proposed way to address these challenges through flexibility, sharing of resources and mutual understanding. Sharma-Wallace et al. (2018) break adaptive governance down into eight elements – collaboration, coordination, social capital, community engagement/empowerment, capacity development, linking knowledge and decision-making, leadership, and governance opportunities. Through experimenting and learning processes, adaptive governance can be used to develop flexible, more equitable shared understandings between the actors involved. One way in which to enact experimentation and experiential learning in a safe, generally consequence-free environment is through serious games.

Serious games (SGs) are games primarily intended for education and learning, rather than amusement (Abt 1987: 9). They can be entertaining, but have been specifically designed to foster learning, collaboration and knowledge (Blackett et al. 2022). These games can have physical components, e.g., boards or cards, may be solely computer-based or some combination of these. How serious games are able to provide a method to enact adaptive governance comes down to the objectives and how they are designed, providing an opportunity for bias that needs to be actively managed. The social learning that can occur through serious games (cf. Flood et al. 2018; Edwards et al. 2019a) is closely connected to Pahl-Wostl's (2009) reflections on instrumental and communicative learning in adaptive governance, in which instrumental learning is the acquisition of new knowledge or skills and communicative learning is understanding and interpreting knowledge (cf. Edwards et al. 2019a).

In addressing how serious games can be a method for enacting adaptive governance, I will go through how they can address each of the eight elements of adaptive governance (Sharma-Wallace et al. 2018). The ability of serious games to contribute to each of these elements of adaptive governance is not individual or siloed, but cut across several or all elements in similar ways. This chapter draws on the literature and our experience in building a serious game. The role of serious games in addressing each element of adaptive governance will include support from the literature, followed by observations from my own experience of designing a serious game, with others, including community members, Catchment 2030.[1]

ADAPTIVE GOVERNANCE

Adaptive governance is considered a mode of governance founded on flexibility, shared resources and mutual understanding between actors (Brunner et al. 2005; Schultz et al. 2015). A number of key characteristics of adaptive governance include adaptability (Olsson et al. 2006), collaboration (Chaffin and Gunderson 2016) and learning and experimentation (Sharma-Wallace et al. 2019). Further, Sharma-Wallace et al. (2018) found in an extensive review of adaptive governance that there were eight core elements to enacting adaptive governance – collaboration, coordination, social capital, community empowerment, capacity development, linking knowledge and decision making, and leadership, and governance opportunities. The brief explanation for each of these eight elements are as follows (a more detailed explanation can be found in Sharma-Wallace et al. (2018)):

1. *Collaboration* – includes being across multiple scales – e.g., hierarchical, geographical, issue, and actor scales. It includes interactions between a large range and diversity of actors and their perspectives. Collaboration also considers formal and informal opportunities.
2. *Coordination* – bringing together different scales to achieve desired outcomes.
3. *Social capital* – trust, familiarity and goodwill between actors. This can take a significant period of time to build.
4. *Community empowerment* – Community is where governance processes and outcomes are mediated and actualised; local engagement is vital and locals should be involved in governance planning at the earliest possible time.
5. *Capacity development* – knowledge, resources and scope for action.
6. *Link science and decision making* – The best available information on the problem and solutions needs to be available to decision makers.
7. *Leadership* – need a passionate, skilled, charismatic leader to identify the problems, bring together and coordinate actors.
8. *Windows of opportunity* – take advantage of outside events to initiate adaptive governance, e.g., natural disasters, government changes or other events (can be large or small).

Alongside these elements, adaptive governance poses a number of significant challenges or constraints, particularly around its uptake and implementation. Rijke et al. (2012) highlight that adaptive governance often has ambiguous purposes and objectives, and requires a clear identification of purpose in order to be successful. They also note constraints that include unclear contextual conditions. Other authors, including Young (2002), Cumming et al. (2006) and Chaffin et al. (2014) highlight the joint issues of complexity and uncertainty. One element of this uncertainty is what Rijke et al. (2012) identify as the effectiveness of different governance strategies. It can be difficult, if not impossible to test different strategies in the real world without potentially serious consequences. Serious games and simulation are methods that

---

[1]   The author would like to acknowledge the significant contribution of the other researchers involved in the project, as well as the Waiapu community, in developing Catchment 2030.

allow you to test, experiment, and learn in a safe space without real-world consequences. This is particularly evident in the virtual world (Williams-Bell et al. 2015; Tawadrous et al. 2013), but can be played out through different types of serious games, including in-person role-plays.

SERIOUS GAMES

There are multiple types of serious games, for example, role-playing games (Susi et al. 2007), board (Blackett et al. 2022), card-based games (Drummond et al. 2014) and computer-based or online games (cf. Katsaliaki and Mustafee 2012). These different types of serious games can have different objectives and can be designed for different purposes. Some types of games are better suited for different purposes, for example, role-playing games can be better suited for negotiation and communication outcomes. Ultimately, serious games, no matter the format, provide a safe innovation and learning space (Flood et al. 2018; Edwards et al. 2019a).

In addressing power imbalances, equity, vested interests and trust, serious games allow, to a certain extent, the dampening of power imbalances by allowing equal access for all participants, and allow for mediation, negotiation and development of conflict resolution methods (Mayer et al. 2004). By having clear objectives and a sense of conflict built into the game design, where participants are working towards a resolution, community empowerment can be built through collaboration and engagements in the game (ProActive 2009; Sharma-Wallace et al. 2018). However, Morardet et al. (2012) found that even with the inclusive nature and theoretical equal access for all participants, power imbalances do exist and can lead to the exclusion of some potential participants. Pre-existing power imbalances between potential game participants (and the game proponents) can limit both the participation in the games and the benefits that may emerge from game play (Rajabu 2007; Gourmelon et al. 2013). In Catchment 2030, the researchers attempted to manage some of the power imbalances by hosting separate game play sessions for the community, local and central government actors (cf. Hertzog et al. 2014).

Trust can be difficult to build in the course of one or even several iterations of game play. Trust is not necessarily quickly built, but can take significant time, as people gain increased knowledge of others (knowledge-based trust – see e.g. Uslaner and Brown 2005). Gourmelon et al. (2013) noted that trust and social capital are often side effects in most games, coming long after the game has finished, due to the length of time to build trust.

Serious games can be aligned with the complexity and uncertainty that are inherent in managing shared resources. Games can do this through improving collective awareness and understanding of the complexity of the problem, and fostering collaboration between game participants. Where participants in a game are given different roles than the one(s) they play in real life, or are asked to switch roles in subsequent game-plays, they can gain a more holistic understanding of the complexity and potential solutions through the lens of other stakeholders (Edwards et al. 2019a).

Games allow players to recognise and work with uncertainty, values and multiple adaptive options (Lawrence and Haasnoot 2017). They can further encourage consideration of potentially innovative, alternative ways forward (Lawrence and Haasnoot 2017), and challenge existing beliefs of what will work (Rumore et al. 2016). The key is creating an appropriate serious game that is attentive to the problems being addressed and the context in which it will be situated.

CREATING A SERIOUS GAME

In the course of an adaptive governance research project, a serious game was proposed as one method of enabling action. The game was initially designed by institutional and community researchers, and tested and further re-developed with community members and other stakeholders. Catchment 2030 was (imperfectly) designed (based on Walsh et al. 2014) to try and enable adaptive governance in a remote catchment with multiple, social, economic, ecological and cultural challenges. The working version introduced, in terms of stakeholders (characters) 'the usual suspects', new, plausible stakeholders and arranged these stakeholders in different constellations (see https://www.scionresearch.com/science/sustainable-forest-and -land-management/adaptive-governance-a-toolkit-for-action).

Based on the context and the experiences of the researchers and community, an in-person, role-playing serious game was determined to be the most effective game type for Catchment 2030. Factors that contributed to this determination included the physical infrastructure constraints placed on potential participants (e.g. poor internet connectivity) and cultural norms (Māori cultural protocols prefer kanohi ki te kanohi, or face-to-face meetings) (cf. Harmsworth 2005). The choice of game medium, however, – in person or online; board game, card game, or role-play, is very context dependent.

Elements of AG in Serious Games

The eight elements of adaptive governance (collaboration, coordination, social capital, community empowerment, capacity development, link science and decision making, leadership, and windows of opportunity) are important, as games can be designed to achieve or partially achieve each of these elements. Bringing together as many of these elements as possible within a serious game can contribute to serious games as a way to enable adaptive governance.

Collaboration

Collaboration can mean working with different people and/or in different ways, including at different scales. Serious games, and in particular role-playing games can help participants develop new ways of working with others (Souchère et al., 2010). There are different ways of introducing collaboration in role-playing games, such as getting player characters to engage with existing and new stakeholders and bringing stakeholders together in different constellations (Rumore and Susskind 2013; Barreteau et al. 2007). Serious game design can encourage open discussion and/or negotiation (Barreteau et al. 2007).

All too often, even within an organisation, different actors and teams can be working, unintentionally, at cross purposes with respect to a particular challenge. In designing a serious game, we introduced multiple ways in which participants would need to collaborate. First, individual characters were grouped according to their rough interests or by organisation. For example, three or four characters with different remits from a single organisation needed to collaborate to settle on a common goal and objectives before they were able to go out and collaborate/negotiate with other characters. Similarly, characters representing a variety of businesses were grouped together under the auspices of a 'Chamber of Commerce' or similar organisation that helped them and their businesses come up with collaborative goals and objectives. This had a mild effect of getting these characters to think and work differently than the siloed ways they were used to.

The second level of collaboration occurred when each group had collaborated on common goals and objectives. The characters in each group went 'out' to negotiate collaboration and resources with other characters and groups to help them achieve their goal. Each of the characters in their group would have to regroup throughout the exercise to ensure that they were collaboratively working towards their goals and objectives.

Coordination

Through their design and objectives, some types of role-playing games are able to achieve coordination in adaptive governance. In the literature, most games appear to be played at a single geographical scale, usually local communities (Adamatti 2009), or if across scales, at the household and community scales (cf. Barreteau et al. 2001; Morardet et al. 2012). Susskind (2010) and Dolin and Susskind (1992) have successfully run serious games across multiple scales, however these have been in specific circumstances – generally urban and focusing on a single issue, rather than complex problems that are conducive to adaptive governance approaches.

In the Catchment 2030 game, a role-playing design was adopted where players role-playing other actors were provided with different resources (roughly broken down into financial, knowledge and human resources) that would be needed to realise the groups' aspirations for their catchment. The players then networked and negotiated with other players in an attempt to get the resources needed to achieve their aspirations. This resulted in existing and innovative constellations of stakeholders and partnerships that, at times, reached across scales (local/ household, local and central government).

Players were encouraged to focus on thinking outside the box and co-designing solutions with others, leaving room for novel ideas to emerge. One way in which this was achieved was through providing characters in the game with the need to coordinate at two different scales. First, within their 'organisation' – this could have been different 'staff' from different parts of one organisation or, different characters from different organisations that needed to coordinate through a 'coordinating body'. For example, a number of business-related characters needed to coordinate their vision and aspirations through belonging to a Chamber of Commerce. The second scale where players could and should coordinate was with other groups that may have developed similar goals and aspirations to strengthen their negotiating position in getting the resources they needed. In some cases, the mere act of coordinating with like-minded characters and organisations may have provided many of the resources needed to achieve their goals.

Social capital

Social capital is not necessarily achieved through serious games, but they can be used as a way to steer players and stakeholders in a shared direction (D'Aquino et al., 2003). Serious games can be a catalyst to enhance exchanges and relationships between players outside of the games themselves. Acting as a catalyst, games can be designed to have high (or low) levels of interaction. High levels can help push participants to build social capital outside of the game.

While not directly social capital, one key objective in designing a serious game is empathy development. Chourou et al. (2021: 2) define empathy as 'the response of an individual to the witnessed experience of others.' Some people are naturally more empathetic, however, empathy can be developed over time. While studies are mixed on whether empathy promotes or maintains cooperative behaviours (Osman et al. 2018), it has been shown to help create better connections and compassion (Miller 1998; Tran 2020), particularly prosocial and pro-environmental behaviours (Berenguer 2010; Chourou et al. 2021). Making connections and building relationships can later lead to the building of bridging and bonding social capital. Putnam (2001) defines bonding social capital as the strong bonds or connections between, e.g., family members or people with similar social backgrounds. Bridging social capital consists of weaker connections that are found in relationships between different (social) groups (Meer and Tolsma 2014).

In our experience with Catchment 2030, the conditions upon which to build social capital were created. This was primarily done through bringing together real life individuals that would not normally associate with each other. For example, bringing together community members and 'backroom' staff from the local authority connected people that likely would not have connected under normal circumstances. These connections have the potential to lead to closer relationships that may even form the foundation of building trust between two groups that have historically mistrusted each other. Unfortunately, due to the short-term nature of project-based research, we were unable to track and evaluate these potential relationships over time, post-project.

Community empowerment

Serious games can be grassroots and community driven. These games allow bottom-up knowledge production and enhance the legitimacy of games, and thus empower participants to input into the planning or policy-making (Bourgoin and Castella 2011). Games are a medium that can facilitate conversations between stakeholders that normally would not communicate with each other, e.g., between communities, researchers, and decision-makers. While serious games attempt to empower stakeholders that are often disempowered, pre-existing power differentials can still be limiting (c.f. Edwards et al. 2019a). Pragmatically, Donovan (2012) notes that a well-designed game can give players a sense of control or power to the participants.

Catchment 2030 did provide a sense of control to participants by allowing them to determine their own aspirations for the catchment. Participants were then able to network and negotiate with other participants in the game to achieve their aspirations in ways that resonated with them.

While it can be difficult to empower, for example, community participants, playing Catchment 2030 did build people's confidence to approach other people/players and empower them to realise that they are able to make new connections. These new connections included those within the community and with local government staff.

Capacity development

Continuous learning is a crucial element to take into account complexity and uncertainty (Rijke et al. 2012). Role-playing serious games are commonly intended as a learning tool, and all games reviewed by Edwards et al. (2019a) had some level of learning or capacity development. Players often gain topical knowledge and understanding (cognitive learning), and have the ability to handle large amounts of technical, context and process-based information (Susskind 2010; Rumore et al. 2016). Further, normative learning (learning to adjust views and opinions) and relational learning (developing new interpersonal connections) can be gained through serious games (Aubert et al. 2018; den Haan and van der Voort 2018). Some serious games also provide the opportunity to learn about negotiation and communication (c.f. Rumore et al. 2016), while role-playing games can help players make sense of and learn about others' positions and interests. In many cases, players don't actually realise that they are learning – they are so caught up in achieving goals or competing with other players during the game (Donovan 2012).

There is some debate in the academic literature as to whether the learning from serious games is able to be retained over a long period of time (cf. Susskind 2010; Rumore et al. 2016). Donovan (2012), however, found that in corporate learning through games, there has been increased retention of knowledge. Additionally, an examination of several meta-analyses showed that serious games effectively improve learning and understanding (Donovan 2012).

Catchment 2030, as a game more focused on adaptive governance, had an underlying objective to build capacity or capability with the players. Supporting this, our research was embedded in a 'capital' model (cf. Cook and de Lourdes Melo Zurita 2019; Edwards et al. 2019b), whereby we were looking to leverage existing capacity and capability in the community and local government in different ways. Feedback from Catchment 2030 indicated that some learning took place. This included, for example, 'learning' that the problem being addressed was only the tip of the iceberg – it was actually much more complex than first imagined. Other feedback noted that the negotiation and communication skills developed and used during the game were proving to be useful in players' real world lives. Without an ongoing evaluation or follow up with participants, it can be difficult to determine whether learning has occurred and what has been learned in the course of the game.

Linking knowledge and decision-making

Serious games can link knowledge and decision-making. Games need to be balanced between providing participants with enough information to make the game playable, relevant to real-world learning, but allowing enough latitude to explore, gain further information and make decisions based on their existing and gained knowledge. This exploration also allows them to possibly change any preconceived ideas and stereotypes. Lewin's theories of organisational change helped us link the empathy of individuals with decisions around behaviour and organisational change (see Cummings et al. 2016).

Serious games can link science/information with decision-making through pre- and post-game evaluations of players. These evaluations can provide a comparison of knowledge, skills and capacity before and after the game session. One long-term study to determine the impacts on water management and decision-making used longitudinal interviews and questionnaires with participants and non-participants in Tanzania (Rajabu 2007). Rajabu (2007) found that there was improved management and decision-making in the areas where villagers had played the game, as opposed to where they had not played the game.

Leadership and governance opportunities

Games allow out of the box thinking and delivering solutions (Mayer et al. 2004) in a consequence-free environment, where things can be trialled and experimented with before attempting implementation in the real world. Susi et al. (2007) note that serious games can be used for exploring leadership challenges, there is a growing body of literature around the use of serious games for leadership development, particularly, in the corporate sector (Donovan 2012).

We seriously considered creating an opportunity to allow players in Catchment 2030 to be able to 'reset', taking advantage of a 'shock' to change or implement an ideal vision for the catchment, based on adaptive governance. In early development, we created several of these shocks or events, for example, having a storm event come through the catchment and a subsequent release of resources for rebuilding. However, we did not use these events in the game play, primarily because of the perceived cognitive overload that we believed it may cause with the players.

LIMITATIONS AND STRENGTHS OF SERIOUS GAMES FOR ADAPTIVE GOVERNANCE

Serious games that have the enactment or implementation of adaptive governance as a goal are not easy or quick to design. Working with complex, messy and wicked problems make defining clear objectives and approaches for the game(s) difficult. Nor, is developing a game a linear process. It may start out this way, however, there are multiple iterations, refinements and changes throughout the course of developing the game. There is no one 'off the shelf' serious game solution, they are quite context dependent, however, existing games could be customised to meet the needs of a particular context.

Serious games are not necessarily a panacea to enable adaptive governance or any other purpose. Designing games is an imperfect process. Balancing reality versus abstraction, present day versus future scenarios, and determining the 'right' objectives the first or even second or subsequent times is relatively difficult. In our case, it took over 18 months to get the 'team' developing the game aligned around the objectives, somewhat longer to get the community and local government staff on board, and never managed to get central government staff on board.

Human beings are not necessarily rational, and won't always 'do' what you want them to do. There are so many unknowns around human behaviour and the way that people think about complex or wicked problems, that serious games may not achieve what the proponents are hoping to achieve.

Pragmatically, it can be very difficult to facilitate and manage large groups of people. The Catchment 2030 game was played with a wide range of numbers, from approximately 15 local government officials to 30 community members and decision-makers (in separate sessions), to approximately 80 university students. Although scalable, working with smaller groups is much easier.

Serious games are not a 'quick fix' to implement adaptive governance. It can take months or years for the impact to become visible. Therefore, long-term monitoring and evaluation of the effects and impacts of the serious game need to be built into projects and the associated funding.

Notwithstanding the foregoing limitations, serious games can be an extremely useful method to help enact adaptive governance. While games can work in the abstract, in order to gain maximum traction, where possible, use a real place, real time, and real problem scenario as the basis for a serious game. However, a certain level of abstraction is needed to decouple participants from their current positions and interests.

Designing serious games for adaptive governance (among other purposes) requires a clear purpose and objectives early in the design stage. Serious game participants require a clear set of objectives and purpose as to what they are trying to achieve. Otherwise, confusion and doubt enter and the learning and reflection on, for example, interests and positions becomes secondary to any feelings of disenchantment.

In terms of pragmatic elements, the amount of time devoted to the serious game or role-play needs to be sufficient. In our experience, we found that approximately two hours was adequate, giving players time to interact and negotiate 'deals' to achieve their aspirations. While the set-up of the game is important, as much attention needs to be paid to the winding down of the role-play. The completion of post-game surveys or briefing sheets helps shift the role-play from the abstract back to real life applications. This shift can also be enabled through a facilitated verbal debrief with the players after the game has concluded.

Facilitation is crucial to the success of serious games as a method for adaptive governance. Players are being put in an unfamiliar situation, and it is very easy for them to 'get lost'. Good explanations as an introduction to the game and good facilitation throughout the game play and debrief are crucial to help keep players focused on 'achieving' the elements of adaptive governance.

REFERENCES

Abt, C. 1987. *Serious Games* (Lanham: University Press of America).

Adamatti, D. 2009. An Overview of the MABS and RPG Techniques in Natural Resources Management International Conference on Computer Engineering and Technology, 2009. ICCET '09 (Singapore: IEEE).

Aubert, A., Bauer, R. and Lienert, J. 2018. A review of water-related serious games to specify use in environmental multi-criteria decision analysis. *Environmental Modelling & Software*, 10: 64–78.

Barreteau, O., Bousquet, F. and Attonaty, J. M. 2001. Role-playing games for opening the black box of multi-agent systems: method and lessons of its application to Senegal River Valley irrigated systems. *J. Artif. Soc. Soc. Simul.*, 4: 13.

Barreteau, O., Le Page, C. and Perez, P. 2007 Contribution of simulation and gaming to natural resource management issues: an introduction. *Simulation & Gaming*, 38: 185–94.

Berenguer, J. 2010. The effect of empathy in environmental moral reasoning. *Environmental Behaviour*, 42: 110–134.

Blackett, P., FitzHerbert, S., Luttrell, J., Hopmans, T., Lawrence, H. and Colliar, J. 2022. Marae-opoly: supporting localised Māori climate adaptation decisions with serious games in Aotearoa New Zealand. *Sustainability Science*, 17: 415–431. https://doi.org/10.1007/s11625-021-00998-9.

Bourgoin, J. and Castella, J.-C. 2011. 'Pulp Fiction': landscape simulation for participatory land use planning in northern Lao PDR. *Mt. Res. Dev.*, 31: 78–88.

Brunner, R. D., Steelman, T. A., Coe-Juell, L. and Cromley C. (eds). 2005. *Adaptive Governance: Integrating Science, Policy and Decision-Making* (New York: Columbia University Press).

Chaffin, B., Gosnell, H. and Cosens, B. 2014. A dedicated of adaptive governance scholarship: synthesis and future directions. *Ecology and Society*, 19, 3: 56.

Chaffin, B. and Gunderson, L. 2016. Emergence, institutionalization and renewal: rhythms of adaptive governance in complex social-ecological systems. *Journal of Environmental Management*, 165: 81–7.

Chourou, L., Grira, J. and Saadi, S. 2021. Does empathy matter in corporate social responsibility? Evidence from emerging markets. *Emerging Markets Review*, 46: 100776.

Cook, B. and de Lourdes Melo Zurita, M. 2019. Fulfiling the promise of participation by not resuscitating the deficit model. *Global Environmental Change*, 56: 56–65.

Cumming, G. S., Cumming, H. and Redman, C. 2006. Scale mismatches in social-ecological systems: causes, consequences and solutions. *Ecology and Society*, 11, 1: 14.

Cummings, S., Bridgman, T. and Brown, K. G. 2016. Unfreezing change as three steps: rethinking Kurt Lewin's legacy for change management. *Human Relations*, 69, 1: 33–60.

D'Aquino, P., Le Page, C., Bousquet, F. and Bah, A. 2003. Using self-designated role-playing games and a multi-agent system to empower a local decision-making process for land use management: the SelfCormas experiment in Senegal. *J. Artif. Soc. Soc. Simul.*, 6: 5.

Den Haan, R.-J. and van der Voort, M. C. 2018. On evaluating social learning outcomes of serious games to collaboratively address sustainability problems: a literature review. *Sustainability*, 10: 4529.

Dolin, E. and Susskind, L. 1992. A role for simulations in public policy disputes: the case of national energy policy. *Simul. Gaming*, 23: 20–44.

Donovan, L. 2012. *The Use of Serious Games in the Corporate Sector: A State of the Art Report* (Dublin: Learnovate Centre).

Drummond, R., Brandao, A. and Salles, C. 2014. Wandea: a framework to develop card based games to help motivate programming students. 2014 Brazilian Symposium on Computer Games and Digital Environment, pp. 158–164. Doi: 10.1109/SBGAMES.2014.18.

Edwards, P., Sharma-Wallace, L., Wreford, A., Holt, L., Cradock-Henry, N., Flood, S. and Velarde, S. 2019a. Tools for adaptive governance for complex social-ecological systems: a review of role-playing games as serious games at the community-policy interface. *Environmental Research Letters*, 14, 11: 113002.

Edwards, P., Sharma-Wallace, L., Barnard, T., Velarde, S., Waremenhoven, T., Fitzgerald, G., Harrison, D., Garrett, L., Porou, T. and Pohatu, P. 2019b. Sustainable livelihoods approaches to inform government–local partnerships and decision-making in vulnerable environments. *New Zealand Geographer*, 75: 63–73.

Flood, S., Cradock-Henry, N. A., Blackett, P. and Edwards, P. 2018. Adaptive and interactive climate futures: systematic review of 'serious games' for engagement and decision-making. *Environmental Research Letters*, 13, 6: 063005.

Gourmelon, F., Chlous-Ducharme, F., Kerbiriou, C., Rouan, M., and Bioret, F. 2013. Role-playing game developed from a modelling process: a relevant participatory tool for sustainable development? A co-construction experiment in an insular biosphere reserve. *Land Use Policy*, 32: 96–107.

Harmsworth G. 2005. Good practice guidelines for working with tangata whenua and Māori organisations: consolidating our learning. *Manaaki Whenua – Landcare Research Report* LC0405/091.

Hertzog, T., Poussin, J.-C., Tangara, B., Kouriba, I. and Jamin, J.-Y. 2014. A role playing game to address future water management issues in a large irrigated system: experience from Mali. *Agriculture and Water Management*, 137: 1–14.

Katsaliaki, K. and Mustafee, N. 2012. A survey of serious games on sustainable development Winter Simulation Conference (Berlin, Germany, 9–12 December, 2012).

Lawrence, J., and Haasnoot, M. 2017. What it took to catalyse uptake of dynamic adaptive pathways planning to address climate change uncertainty. *Environmental Science & Policy*, 68: 47–57.

Mayer, I. S., Daalen, C. E. V. and Bots, P. 2004. Perspectives on policy analyses: a framework for understanding and design. *Int. J. Technol. Policy Manage.*, 4: 169–91.

Meer, T. v. d. and Tolsma, J. 2014. Ethnic diversity and its effects on social cohesion. *Annual Review of Sociology*, 40: 459–478.

Miller, J. 1998. Making connections through holistic learning. *Educational Leadership*, 56, 4: 46–48.

Morardet, S., Milhau, F. and Murgue, C. 2012. Wet-WAG, a role-playing game to support stakeholder dialogue on wetland management. WETwin Project Report 66 WetWin Project.

Olsson, P., Gunderson, L., Carpenter, S., Ryan, P., Lebel, L., Folke, C. and Holling, C. 2006. Shooting the rapids: navigating transitions to adaptive governance of social-ecological systems. *Ecol. Soc.*, 11: 18.

Osman, M., Lv, J.-Y. and Proulx, M. J. 2018. Can empathy promote cooperation when status and money matter? *Basic and Applied Social Psychology*, 40, 4: 201–218.

Pahl-Wostl, C. 2009. A conceptual framework for analysing adaptive capacity and multi-level learning processes in resource governance regimes. *Global Environmental Change*, 19, 3: 354–365.

ProActive. 2009. *Production of Creative Game-Based Learning Scenarios* (Brussels: Education and Culture DG).

Putnam, R. D. 2001. *Bowling Alone: The Collapse and Revival of American Community* (New York: Simon and Schuster).

Rajabu, K. R. M. 2007. Use and impacts of the river basin game in implementing integrated water resources management in Mkoji sub-catchment in Tanzania Agric. *Water Manage.*, 94: 63–72.

Rijke, J., Brown, R., Zevenbergen, C., Ashley, R., Farrelly, M., Morison, P. and van Herk, S. 2012. Fit-for-purpose governance: a framework to make adaptive governance operational. *Environmental Science and Policy*, 22: 73–84.

Rumore, D., Schenk, T. and Susskind, L. 2016. Role-play simulations for climate change adaptation education and engagement. *Nat. Clim. Change*, 6: 745–50.

Rumore, D. and Susskind, L. 2013. Collective climate adaptation: can games make a difference? *Solut. J.*, 4: 19–24.

Schultz, L., Folke, C., Österblom, H. and Olsson, P. 2015. Adaptive governance, ecosystem management, and natural capital. *Proc. Natl Acad. Sci.*, 112: 7369–7374.

Sharma-Wallace, L., Velarde, S., Edwards, P., Warmenhoven, T. and Pohatu, P. 2019. Exploring adaptive governance for indigenous peoples: lessons from Aotearoa New Zealand's Erosion Control Funding Programme. *Soc. Nat. Resour.*, 33, 1: 1–24.

Sharma-Wallace, L., Velarde, S. and Wreford, A. 2018. Adaptive governance best practice: show me the evidence! *J. Environ. Manage.*, 222: 174–84.

Souchère, V., Millair, L., Echeverria, J., Bousquet, F., Le Page, C., and Etienne, M. 2010. Co-constructing with stakeholders a role-playing game to initiate collective management of erosive runoff risks at the watershed scale. *Environ. Modelling Software.*, 25, 1359–70.

Susi, T., Johannesson, M. and Backlund, P. 2007. Serious games – an overview. Technical Report HS-IKI-TR-07-001. School of Humanities and Informatics, University of Skövde, Sweden.

Susskind, L, 2010, Responding to the risks posed by climate change – cities have no choice but to adapt, *Town Plan. Rev.*, 81: 217–235.

Tawadrous, M., Kevan, S., Kapralos, B. and Hogue, A. 2013. A serious game for incidence response education and training. *International Journal of Technology and the Knowledge Society*, 8, 4: 134–162.

Tran, L. 2020. Teaching and engaging international students: people-to-people connections and people-to-people empathy. *Journal of International Students*, 10, 3: xii–xvii.

Uslaner, E. and Brown, M. 2005. Inequality, trust, and civic engagement. *American Politics Research*, 33: 868–894.

Walsh, J. R., Vander Zanden, M. J. and Stanley, E. H. 2014. World of watershed management: a role-playing game. Project Resource. CIRTL Network.

Williams-Bell, F., Murhpy, B., Kapralos, B., Hogue, A. and Weckman, E. 2015. Using serious games and virtual simulation for training in the Fire Service: a review. *Fire Technology*, 51: 553–584.

Young, O. 2002. *The Institutional Dimensions of Environmental Change: Fit, Interplay and Scale* (Cambridge MA: MIT Press).

PART III

GOVERNANCE CONTEXTS AND CASE STUDIES

8. Adaptive governance in forest management

Jesse Abrams and Marine Elbakidze

INTRODUCTION AND PURPOSE

The world's forests are under intense pressure given the increasing demand for diverse forest goods and services crucial for livelihoods and economies from local to global scales, combined with the impacts of an altered climate and other drivers of global environmental change (Katila et al., 2014). A growing understanding of the complexity of forests as social-ecological systems acknowledges that their dynamics may be unpredictable, especially as they increasingly reorganise into novel 'no analogue' assemblages of species and processes (Hobbs et al., 2009; Williams and Jackson, 2007). In this context, the concept of adaptive governance can be seen to encompass a diversity of decision-making and management approaches intended to transform people's relationships with forests in pursuit of goals like social-ecological resilience, biological and cultural diversity, social learning, and the maintenance of ecosystem services (Spathelf et al., 2018). The focus on adaptive *governance* (as opposed to adaptive management or adaptive co-management) represents an emphasis on the formal and informal institutional context within which decisions are made, legitimated, implemented, and evaluated (Chaffin et al., 2014; Hasselman, 2017). Our purpose here is to analyse why conventional forest governance models have fallen out of favour in many parts of the world and to examine how adaptive governance has taken shape in diverse social-ecological settings. We use two global initiatives (Model Forests and third-party forest sustainability certification) and two national initiatives (collaborative and partnership-based governance of US national forestlands and Ecoparks in Sweden) as case examples to illustrate the variety of emerging models that fall under the banner of adaptive governance.

ON COMPLEXITY AND SIMPLIFICATION

A key feature of forest systems is their great social-ecological complexity. The ecological complexity of forests arises from their vast diversity of interacting species and processes, ranging from the daily cycles of plant respiration and photosynthesis to the annual/decadal patterns of wildfire, insects, pathogens and other disturbance agents to the processes of forest stand development and species compositional changes that may occur over centuries to millennia (Perry et al., 2008). The social dimension of forest systems is likewise highly complex. Formal forest title includes vast ownerships by national and subnational governments, large corporate estates, small- to medium-scale family ownership, community ownership, Indigenous title, and ownership by a range of NGOs, utilities, investors, and other entities. Additional layers of informal tenure include traditional patterns of forest access, 'tree tenure' (often with strong gender dimensions), community access for hunting, non-timber forest product collection, and recreation, and other uses (Katila et al., 2020; Rocheleau and Edmunds, 1997). Added to this complexity is the wide range of human interactions with and dependencies upon forests and the myriad ecosystem services they provide.

For much of the past two centuries, scientific forest management was oriented toward the simplification of forest ecosystems (Hölzl, 2010). The early history of the science of forestry was strongly influenced by German conceptions of scientific management that emerged in the eighteenth and nineteenth centuries as theories of economic rationalisation were advanced within a system of state control of resources (Lowood, 1990). Forestry's rational economic ideal took shape in the concept of *normalwald* ('normal forest') and its key component the *normalbaum* ('normal tree'), reflecting an attempt to simplify forest ecosystems in pursuit of a narrow range of outputs and making a complex system legible to state scientists (Puettmann et al., 2009; Scott, 1998). The *normalwald* model was operationalised through sustained yield forestry, which later became a general paradigm in forest management worldwide (McManus, 1999). Sustained yield forestry implies continuous production so planned as to achieve a balance between growth and harvest and has primarily been focused mainly on wood fibre production from a limited number of species considered to be of greatest commercial value. The achievement of sustained yield was in many places closely tied to state control of forestlands to eliminate species and dynamics that interfered with the rationalisation project— specifically, disturbances such as fire and insects, undesirable tree species, and especially local people and their traditional uses (Elbakidze et al., 2013; Hölzl, 2010).

In the United States, for example, the vision of sustained yield was pursued through the creation of the US Forest Service in 1905, a federal agency tasked with managing a federal estate that eventually grew to over 78 million hectares. Under the leadership of Gifford Pinchot, himself trained in the German tradition, the Forest Service worked with state and private forestry professionals to suppress forest fires, control insect outbreaks, and convert natural forests across ownership categories to fast-growing, efficient producers of wood fibre for the country's needs. Although justified as a means of forestalling the waste and destruction associated with prevailing timbering practices of the time, the fire exclusion program instituted by the US Forest Service represented a break with thousands of years of Indigenous fire use (Pyne, 1982). Native American tribal forestlands were also managed intensively by federal agencies in pursuit of the maximisation of timber volume – often over the objections of tribal members themselves and against the warnings of some nontribal scientists who recognised problems with fire elimination (Cooper, 1960; Weaver, 1947, 1959). Although it was successful at producing large quantities of wood fibre, the scientific forestry paradigm failed to acknowledge the diverse social values for forests or to consider the potentially beneficial role of fire and other disturbance processes. Social conflicts grew throughout much of the twentieth century, eventually culminating in a series of protracted protests and lawsuits in the 1990s that resulted in stronger protections for sensitive fish and wildlife species and their forested habitats (Hoberg, 2001).

In Europe, due to diversity in natural, historical, societal, and economic legacies, sustained-yield forestry has been implemented somewhat differently (Elbakidze et al., 2013). Still, almost all prevailing forest management systems have resulted in simplified forests that diminish social values, structural complexity, and biodiversity at multiple spatial scales. In Sweden, about half of the forests are owned by nonindustrial private forest owners and the rest are owned mainly by industrial forest companies, the state, and forest commons (The Swedish Forest Agency, 2010). From an economic perspective, the production of a maximum sustained yield of wood using even-aged forest management systems is the focus of current forest management. Tree retention is practiced, and set-aside areas are managed to maintain ecological, social, and cultural values of forests as providers of products that serve tourism and amenity migration demands. The primary end-user is the export-oriented forest industry focusing on value-added production for environmentally concerned markets. However, from an ecological perspective, a long history of sustained yield forest management has resulted in a critical loss of compositional, structural, and functional elements of biodiversity (Angelstam et al., 2020). Environmental organisations have strongly criticised Swedish forestry for seriously failing to meet environmental objectives connected to forests and for retaining a strong production orientation in spite of international demands for environmental protection.

By contrast, in the Russian Federation all forest is owned by the state. Since the end of the Soviet Union in 1991, forestry and the forest sector are in transition from planned to the market economy. Sustained yield forestry has remained the core concept, with the government defining the harvest level by estimation of the 'annual allowable cut' (or sustained yield) for all state forest management units. However, forest management has been characterised by some as 'wood mining' and large forested regions, particularly in the boreal zone, have been severely affected by accelerated wood harvesting in recent decades. The existing model of forestry has triggered a long-term confrontation between environmental NGOs and forest companies. The main issue driving this confrontation is continuous logging of intact forest landscapes (IFLs) which are crucial for biodiversity conservation at national and global levels. IFLs are also the primary source of wood supply in many regions of Russia and the proportion of logging within IFLs is steadily increasing, leading to their fragmentation and loss. The zoning of forests to satisfy economic, nature conservation, and social functions helps to maintain multiple values of forests in Russia. Zoning was conducted for all forests starting in 1943, and forests are currently divided into exploitation, protection, and reserve forests, the latter meaning forests not yet opened for exploitation. Protection forests are grouped into several sub-categories depending on their ecological, social, or other functions; forest companies are required to follow certain restrictions to maintain forests' social and ecological contributions. Furthermore, the forestry sector has been exposed to international pressure to develop the market economy amid the challenges of biodiversity conservation, increased use of bioenergy, and rural development. New additional challenges are the emerging uncertainty and instability linked to global economic and climate change, making prediction and control more difficult.

FORESTRY CRISES AND GOVERNANCE RESPONSES

Globally, forests have been placed under intense management and development pressure since the late nineteenth century as a result of changes in technologies and global markets. More recently, forests in many regions have begun to show the collective impacts of decades of simplification and suppression of disturbance combined with a changing climate and the global spread of invasive species (IPBES, 2018). Forests in the western US, interior British Columbia (Canada), central Europe, Russia, Australia, and Chile experienced some of their most severe wildfire, insect, and disease outbreaks on record in the late twentieth and early twenty-first centuries (Bowman et al., 2020). These events reflected complex influences of past management practices and more contemporary climatic drivers. By the end of the twentieth century, the forestry sector also faced a crisis of legitimacy as both state and private forest managers had failed to heed growing social calls to consider the broadly defined sustainability of forests.

The crisis manifested in widespread protests against harvesting in native forests combined with consumer boycotts of products and retailers linked to controversial wood production practices (Schirmer, 2013).

However, the normative interpretation of sustainability in forestry broadened beyond sustained yield when sustainable forest management (SFM) policies appeared at multiple levels from global to national, and within businesses, by the last decade of the twentieth century (Ministerial Conference on Protection of Forests in Europe (MCPFE), 1995, 1998, 2001). Forest managers in many countries claim that sustained yield forestry is an important part of SFM (Korotkov et al., 2009). Others have argued that the timber-oriented sustained yield concept is no longer appropriate (Wiersum, 1995) and that forest managers need to 'develop from being crop managers to ecosystem managers' (Farrell et al., 2000 p. 6). Additionally, there are arguments that sustained yield forestry as single-use management (Behan, 1990) changes forest composition and structure and alters the natural dynamics in forest landscapes (Bawa and Seidler, 1998; Holling and Meffe, 1996; Luckert and Williamson, 2004). As a consequence, forest ecosystems lose native species, habitats, and ecological processes, which affect ecological integrity and resilience (Farrell et al., 2000). There is also a sceptical perception of sustained yield forestry based on arguments related both to the poor rate of success in implementation of the concept in practice and to increasing demands for diverse ecosystem services from forests, which makes implementation of this concept more difficult (Clapp, 1998; Elbakidze et al., 2013; Wiersum, 1995).

Today, SFM aims at maintaining sustainable ecological, economic, social, and cultural functions of managed forests through multi-stakeholder participatory approaches (MCPFE, 1995, 1998, 2001). SFM thus encompasses key goals of maintaining the health, integrity, and biodiversity of forest ecosystems; long-term profitability; a healthy environment for local communities; and the cultural values of forest landscapes. This requires that forest managers consider the use of a broad range of ecosystem services through adaptive governance in order to be able to handle potentially conflicting demands at multiple spatial scales (Bawa and Seidler, 1998; Behan, 1990; Bouthillier, 2001; Farrell et al., 2000; Wiersum, 1995). The Montréal Process developed SFM principles for temperate and boreal forests and the MCPFE did so for European countries. There is growing interest in SFM across diverse national and cultural contexts. This is the outcome of multiple economic, technological, and cultural developments that include increasing levels of societal awareness of and concern for environmental quality; the loss of large expanses of native forests over the twentieth and early twenty-first centuries; the development of forest-based bioenergy production; and broadly recognised needs to both adapt to and mitigate climate change (Spittlehouse and Stewart, 2003).

Across country contexts, new forest governance models have emerged since the late twentieth century that share key attributes of adaptive forest governance (see more about adaptive governance in Chapter 1), such as: integration of the ecological, social, and economic dimensions of sustainability rather than a narrow focus on maximising outputs; the inclusion in decision-making of diverse state and non-state stakeholders, including many that were traditionally adversaries on forest policy issues; and an explicit focus on innovation, social learning, and adaptation. Not all of the newer governance models can be called successes. Yet many of these new approaches to forest governance were designed specifically to be more adaptive in practice, and several have been successful enough that they are now considered standard elements of the forest governance landscape at regional to global scales. Here, we take a closer look at the kinds of approaches that have characterised adaptive governance in forestry to date.

Our review focuses on forest management institutions, defined as 'commonly accepted ways of doing things' (Abers and Keck, 2013) that are legitimated and practised by key actors within a social-political setting. Processes of institutional reform are characterised by the dynamic tension between institutionalisation (implying a conservative stability in guiding principles) and innovation (implying experimentation with alternatives to prevailing rules) (Craig et al., 2017). We examine two global-scale initiatives (Model Forests and Third-Party Forest Sustainability Certification) and two national-scale initiatives (collaborative and networked governance of US national forestlands and Ecopark in Sweden). A guiding question in each case is whether (and how) the new model represents a form of adaptive governance compared to business as usual.

CASE EXAMPLES: GLOBAL INITIATIVES

Model Forests

The Model Forest concept originated in Canada in early 1990s as a response to the critics of Canada's forestry sector at the international level for unsustainable use of forest resources and multiple conflicts among different forest stakeholders within the country (Bull and Schwab, 2005). From an initial 10 Model Forests in Canada in 1992, the International Model Forest Network has grown to include more than 60 sites in over 35 countries on five continents. A Model Forest is a process designed to establish a partnership and a forum for collaboration to realise a common vision of sustainable development in a large landscape. The critical functions of a Model Forest are to test new ideas and develop innovations related to SFM, as agreed to by Model Forest partners, and to develop the adaptive capacity of the local social-ecological system to deal with uncertainty and change (LaPierre, 2002).

Model Forest creation is often triggered by conflicts among forest stakeholders on the ground. For example, the establishment of the Komi Model Forest in Russia began with a conflict between environmental NGOs and foreign forest companies regarding the use of the last remaining large intact forests in the Komi Republic – to protect or to log. In Sweden, the pioneering motivation for establishment of the Vilhelmina Model Forest was a desire to reduce or avoid conflicts among different land-use interests (nature conservation, rights of Indigenous people, and economic interests of forest companies) and foster communication among diverse groups of stakeholders. Thus, the initial motivations were influenced by the range of sustainability challenges to be solved in the particular region. In addition, a primary focus has been to build adaptive capacity in the local to regional governance system through capacity building and education. However, there are fundamental differences in how leaders identify and formulate problems and initiate dialogue among stakeholders. For example, in Sweden, the Model Forest process was led by local champions with very limited financial support. In Russia, the initiatives grew out of a political opportunity involving foreign stakeholders concerned about forest sector changes that might affect their ecological or economic interests.

In general, Model Forests in Russia and Sweden have established a new type of forest governance, moving from a top-down and sectoral approach to governance based in collaboration of stakeholders from different societal sectors and governance levels in diverse contexts. Scholars and practitioners have raised questions about the viability of Model Forests over the long term. For example, all Russian Model Forests committed to the International

Model Forest Network (2008) appeared as a result of successful timing and the combination of donors interested in Russian forest sector development and a strong local or regional champion. These factors made it possible to promote and implement new governance systems to change and improve forest management according to the desires of multiple stakeholders. The majority of the activities in the decision-making and implementation processes were initiated, facilitated and financed by foreign donors. However, as studies show (Angelstam et al., 2019; Elbakidze et al., 2010), local governance arrangements supported financially, and partly professionally, from abroad typically struggle to be adaptive in the long run, including during their 'post-project' life. For the Swedish cases, one of the main concerns is whether local governance arrangements that depend on local champions and lack reliable financial resources are adaptive in the long run when the policy entrepreneurs retire or have other reasons for withdrawing from the process.

Another issue is that Model Forests operate in diverse 'governance domains,' or governance systems on a national level, which may influence the local Model Forest initiative's ability to develop adaptive capacities. For example, there is a fragile governance system at the national level in the Russian Federation with poorly functioning institutions, non-existent property rights, widespread corruption, and low levels of social capital. In Sweden, there is a rigid governance system at the national level, in which coordination and cooperation are high. Still, responsiveness to external changes is slow and incremental due to either biased or weak feedback. Thus, the governance systems of Model Forests differ in their potential to develop and realise their adaptive capacity created by their 'governance domain' legacies.

Third-party Forest Sustainability Certification

Private third-party forest sustainability certification represents an important example of larger trends in private commodity governance that emerged across sectors in the late twentieth century (other prominent examples include certification of textiles, coffee, cacao, and seafood) (Auld, 2014; Bartley, 2007; Gulbrandsen, 2010). As a governance tool, forest certification was designed to respond to multiple social and political drivers characteristic of this particular time period: broad concerns with the environmental sustainability and social equity dimensions of the forestry sector as reflected (and amplified) in consumer boycotts of wood retailers and organised protests of logging operations; broad neoliberal currents of global market governance that emphasised voluntary and market-based solutions rather than trade barriers or other state action; and the inability of international organisations to forge consensus on global forest conservation rules, reflected most prominently in the failure to reach a binding forest agreement at the 1992 Rio Earth Summit (Cashore et al., 2004, 2017; Gulbrandsen, 2010). In the wake of the Earth Summit, a coalition of environmental NGOs, Indigenous community representatives, wood products retailers, and other stakeholders rolled out the Forest Stewardship Council (FSC) as the first widespread attempt at global private forest sustainability governance. As an alternative to state regulation, FSC's model offered to label and promote products from forests certified by independent auditors as meeting or exceeding environmental, social, and economic sustainability standards. The model is premised upon the granting of legitimacy within the marketplace for certified products and, implicitly, de-legitimising products lacking the FSC label (Bernstein and Cashore, 2007; Cashore, 2002; Schepers, 2010).

Despite the FSC's efforts to serve as the single label for responsible forestry, alternative certification schemes were established soon after the FSC rollout. In particular, the Programme for the Endorsement of Forest Certification Schemes (PEFC) has gained widespread industry support as the FSC's main competitor. As of February 2022, the FSC had certified roughly 232 million hectares in 89 countries compared with PEFC having certified about 330 million hectares in over 70 countries. Many countries have also developed national-level alternatives to FSC, driven by pressure from forest owners or from national governments themselves in response to perceived limitations of the FSC scheme (e.g., limitations on the conversion of native forest to monoculture plantations or the inability of governments to participate directly in governance of the scheme application) (Abrams et al., 2018; Burns et al., 2016; Cashore et al., 2007; Tricallotis et al., 2019). The creation of alternative certification schemes to FSC complicated the quest for legitimacy within the marketplace that originally drove the FSC model and created competitive pressure on FSC that, according to some observers, has led to a weakening of standards (Moog et al., 2015).

Overall, certification uptake has been strongest in temperate and boreal forests of the global North, whereas certification of tropical forests and within developing countries more broadly has been limited (Xu and Lu, 2021). FSC certification of native tropical forests is most common in places with existing community forest tenure systems, export-oriented wood markets, supportive public policies, and strong NGO support; for example, Bolivia was seen as an early success story for its high level of FSC certification adoption, but certified acreage has declined substantially due to shifts in both markets and forest policies (Espinoza and Dockry, 2014). A key finding from certification scholarship to date is that the legal, political, and institutional context of individual countries strongly influences the direction and success of sustainability certification, meaning that certification cannot make up entirely for state failures (Bartley, 2014). Although it was originally envisioned as an alternative to governmental regulation of forests, certification is now better seen as a complement to state action.

The key question here is whether and how third-party sustainability certification represents a form of adaptive governance compared to business as usual. For corporate, family, and public forest owners, participating in certification implies engagement with a diverse set of forestry stakeholders at multiple scales – including perspectives that might normally be excluded from decision-making (e.g., Indigenous community representatives). Whether this structure allows for robust participation and deliberation is still unclear, however (Secco and Pettenella, 2006). Moreover, third-party sustainability certification standards are socially and historically constructed phenomena that are embedded 'in local structures at firm and farm level, and in their direct environment in the community and domestic governance institutions' (Graz, 2021 p. 3). Bartley (2021) observes that local contexts, including institutions, are important in understanding challenges and limitations in implementation of transnational private governance.

The design of many certification schemes allows for continuous monitoring, feedback, and adjustment – including adjustment of the standards and criteria themselves. The participatory process of standard adjustment in light of new information represents a robust opportunity to practice adaptive governance. At the same time, the feedback process linking knowledge with a change in certification standards may be constrained by the competition among rival schemes and the consequent pressure to maintain uptake demand among forest owners. The 'downward' pressure on stringency driven by competition stands in tension with the 'upward' pressure placed by environmental and social advocacy organisations, some of whom have pulled their support of favoured schemes (or threatened to do so) due to a perceived lack of commitment to upholding the ideals of sustainability (Moog et al., 2015). Further, it should be emphasised that the adaptive potential of sustainability certification applies largely to forests enrolled in those schemes, which excludes vast areas in the tropics and other regions of conservation importance.

CASE EXAMPLES: NATIONAL INITIATIVES

Collaborative and Network Governance on US Public Lands

The emergence of collaborative and networked governance models for federal forestlands represents one of the most significant recent changes in environmental governance in the United States. Collaborative governance is characterised by the inclusion of diverse perspectives in deliberative processes designed to pursue consensus solutions to complex social and environmental dilemmas (Innes and Booher, 2010; Margerum, 2011). This approach was innovated across the western US (where the majority of federal lands are located) beginning in the 1980s and 1990s as an alternative dispute resolution mechanism during a time of pitched social and political battles over the management of national forests and other federal lands. Collaborative efforts began as representatives of wood products, labour, environmental, government, and other interests in several rural communities attempted to reach agreement on plans that would provide wood fibre to local mills and employ local people in forest management while protecting species at risk, preserving old-growth forests, and reducing the wildfire hazard to human communities (Davis et al., 2020). Several early efforts in scattered communities across the western US proved to be successful enough at reducing tensions and meeting multiple interests simultaneously that collaborative approaches became increasingly legitimised and, eventually, institutionalised over time. Nearly all national forest units had experimented with some kind of place-based collaboration by the late 1990s (Selin et al., 1997) and collaboration has been recognised and incentivised in various legislative and administrative policy changes since the 1990s (Cheng, 2006; Mattor and Cheng, 2015; Monroe and Butler, 2016; Schultz et al., 2018).

The growing scope and scale of wildfire and other disturbances on US federal forestlands has acted as a key driver of recent federal forestland policy and governance change (Schultz et al., 2021). Indeed, collaborative forestry efforts have shown the greatest success in fire-adapted landscapes, where diverse interests share common concerns regarding wildfires and other disturbances in forests altered by a century of fire suppression (Charnley et al., 2015; Platt et al. 2022). Although collaborative organisations generally lack formal authority over federal lands, their recommendations have been adopted by federal forest managers in some places as a means of experimenting with new methods and rebuilding trust between communities and land managers (Fairfax et al., 1999). Given a widespread belief that collaborative processes may avoid protracted legal conflicts over forest management, collaboration has been embraced – at least in principle – by the US Forest Service. This belief is not always well-founded in practice, however, as collaboratively designed projects are still regularly subject to legal contestation (Moseley and KenCairn, 2001; Urgenson et al., 2017).

A distinct but related governance trend entails the growth of interagency, agency-NGO, and agency-landowner partnerships as means of increasing the scope and scale of treatments designed to make forests more resilient (Bobzien and Van Alstyne, 2014; Cyphers and Schultz, 2019). Whereas collaborative approaches emphasise building trust and consensus among traditionally divergent stakeholder groups, partnership approaches emphasise planning and management coordination among traditionally isolated agencies, organisations, and forest owners. Common concerns regarding cross-boundary issues such as wildfire, invasive species, and endangered species recovery drive many of these efforts (Cyphers and Schultz, 2019; Schultz et al., 2018; Steen-Adams et al., 2022). These partnerships also serve to compensate for declining federal agency capacity through leveraging the efficiencies from partnerships and creative funding sources, and these approaches have at least the potential to shift power and influence in forest governance (Abrams, 2019). In tandem with collaborative governance efforts, partnership-oriented innovations contribute to a networked approach to national forest governance, in which the traditional monopoly of decision-making and implementation held by the Forest Service is formally conserved but informally shared with non-agency public and partners through various mechanisms (Abrams, 2019).

Returning to the question of whether and how networked and partnership-oriented governance models represent adaptive governance, it is clear that they encompass many of the principles of adaptive governance in terms of a focus on learning, relationship-building, and the creative assemblage of practice, policy, and learning/support networks at multiple scales (Butler et al., 2015; Cheng and Dale, 2020; Cromley, 2005). Through their inclusion of multiple perspectives and emphasis on integrated restoration and stewardship, they represent stark contrasts to conventional national forest governance approaches oriented around the control, simplification, and rationalisation of forest ecosystems. They contain at least the potential to encourage processes of social learning and to support the practice of adaptive management (Cheng et al., 2011; Fernandez-Gimenez et al., 2008). The question remains whether these newer governance models are adaptive in fact; that is, whether they do indeed promote learning and adaptation over time. Social learning has been observed as a key outcome of collaborative processes linked to other elements of collaborative governance including the strengthening of relations of trust among collaborative group members, as well as to the inclusion of participatory monitoring efforts (Fernandez-Gimenez et al., 2008; McIntyre and Schultz, 2020; Schultz et al., 2014).

At the same time, federal forestland collaborative and partnership efforts are often limited in their adaptive potential by a lack of formal authority and by the persistence of higher-level institutional influences (Cheng et al., 2015). Cheng et al. (2011), for example, found that most changes attributable to community-based forestry groups in the US (which include but are not limited to public lands collaborative groups) were at the operational level, with some collective-choice adaptations but relatively few constitutional-level changes. Complementary conclusions were drawn from a comparative study of four national forests affected by native bark beetle outbreaks (Abrams et al., 2021). Although responses in all four cases involved robust collaborative and partnership-oriented networks, the ability to effect adaptive outcomes was contingent upon factors outside the control of local and regional participants (Abrams et al., 2021).

Unlike the intentionally designed third-party sustainability certification and Model Forest examples, collaborative and networked governance approaches emerged through a variety of innovations and experiments at local to regional scales. Although they are supported by various policy tools and mandates, there is no cohesive program of collaborative or networked governance within the US national forest system (Davis et al., 2020); rather, these efforts represent a widespread network of ad-hoc efforts and initiatives that largely lack formal governance authority on federal lands. In addition, the pre-existing policy frameworks that guided national forest management under prior governance paradigms remain largely in place. As many scholars have observed, these attributes may limit the transformative potential of emerging models (Abrams, 2019; Abrams et al., 2017; Cheng et al., 2011, 2015; Davis et al., 2020; Wurtzebach et al., 2019).

Ecoparks on Public Lands in Sweden

Sweden's state-owned profit-based forestry company, Sveaskog Co., manages 14% (4.04 million ha) of the country's forestland. In the 1990s, Sveaskog was heavily criticised by various national government authorities for a lack of effort to reach Swedish environmental goals, particularly those related to biodiversity. In response to this criticism, Sveaskog initiated Ecoparks as a new form of multifunctional landscapes and developed a new environmental policy, adopted in 2003, stating that 20% of the company's productive forest accumulated at tree, stand, and landscape scales in each Swedish ecoregion should be managed to promote nature conservation (Dawson et al., 2017). Ecoparks cover 5% of Sveaskog's productive forests, distributed throughout Sweden with a view to creating an interconnected network of forest landscapes with high conservation values. A minimum of 50% of total area of each Ecopark is set aside for biodiversity conservation purposes, whilst the remainder is actively managed by sustainable, selective harvesting methods in order to restore mixed forest habitats tailored to the characteristics of individual landscapes. The first Ecopark opened in 2003, and today a total of 37 Ecoparks cover 175,000 hectares of forest, of which over 100,000 hectares are protected through binding 50-year nature protection contracts.

Development and implementation of the Ecopark concept relied on support from local landowners, forestry entrepreneurs, national policymakers, and other stakeholders. Ecoparks have become experimental laboratories aimed at investigating responses of forest ecosystems to a variety of novel management approaches. Active experimentation has been based on developing a 'best guess' hypothesis, implementing it as well as possible, and carefully monitoring results in order to evaluate ongoing utility. The Ecopark staff integrated learning cycles in different ways, including by directly modifying implementation processes, increasing the available knowledge base upon which to structure implementation visions and plans, modifying leadership characteristics and approaches, and slowly altering underlying institutional and regulatory frameworks (Dawson et al. 2017). Whilst ecological benefits dominated the early stage of the Ecopark concept vision, during the implementation phase the focus was on identification and making visible the social benefits and public utility of Ecopark's outcomes. Many of the social benefits are related to recreation, sense of place, and community relations. The clear identification of the socioeconomic value of Ecoparks was an important factor in gaining the support of key decision-makers, who were often situated within traditional development institutional frameworks or in positions of economic accountability.

Additionally, Ecopark staff developed and employed a variety of pedagogical materials with which they communicated their visions and plans. These materials were vital for enabling decision-makers and other stakeholders to understand the implications of complex long-term plans more intuitively and to include other perspectives. Sveaskog also invested significant resources in obtaining and integrating informal knowledge, establishing informal spaces such as workshops, field trips, and excursions and participating in a variety of networks where informal knowledge was gathered and shared. Although the Ecopark leaders enjoy a great deal of control regarding the development of initial visions and plans, implementation remains highly dependent on obtaining sufficient support from decision-makers and stakeholders who provide essential inputs in terms of funding, personnel, access, and various kinds of knowledge.

CROSS-CUTTING THEMES

The cases examined here, while disparate, all represent a divergence from conventional forest governance and management models for state-owned, private, and other forestland ownership categories. Common elements across the profiled models include the following: (1) explicit attempts to integrate and reconcile multiple interests and values for forests; (2) inclusion of stakeholders from different societal sectors and governance levels in deliberative decision-making processes; (3) linking local-scale governance processes with those operating at meso (e.g., regional) or macro (e.g., national) scales; (4) the integration of knowledges (e.g., scientific, professional, and local) into adaptive processes for forest management; and (5) institutional flexibility that allows the governance processes themselves to adapt over time.

The profiled models were all innovated in response to social, ecological, or combined socioecological crises: for the Model Forests and Ecoparks, social discord over particular areas of forestland led to the development of new governance models that were then expanded to other forests. Intergovernmental accords were the initial focus for resolving conflicts over the global governance of high conservation value forests; due to a lack of progress in those forums, key actors developed third-party sustainability certification as an alternative and the broad approach has since been applied worldwide under various specific models. Collaborative and networked governance of US public lands arose in response to both political crises (in which routine forest management decisions regularly ended up mired in legal challenges) and to the increasing scope and scale of wildfires and insect and disease outbreaks (Schultz et al., 2021).

Importantly, the models that emerged in response to these varied crises did so only through the creative agency of individuals acting within their respective networks. Many of the initial pilot programmes within these initiatives relied heavily upon individual 'champions' that worked to align actors and interests, engage in problem-solving, and advocate for resources and recognition. Consistent with scholarship on institutional work (Battilana and D'Aunno, 2009), new institutions associated with adaptive forest governance were actively constructed through embedded human agency. However, the reliance upon a small number of champions can also be a weakness for the long-term persistence of innovative governance models. Many early examples of success have been challenged in their long-term sustainability as key champions move on and as initial networks of funding and organisational support decline.

The models profiled here also confronted broadly similar challenges, many of them related to challenges overcoming the influence of pre-existing institutions. Third-party sustainability certification, for example, is limited by its voluntary nature and by the important role played by governments in setting the stage for sustainable forest management – as well as the more active government roles in promoting or impeding particular certification schemes (Abrams et al., 2018; Hackett, 2013; Lister, 2011). Despite being formally recognised in selected policies, collaborative and networked governance approaches on US public lands are limited by the persistence of forest planning and management institutions, grounded largely in mid-century paradigms of public administration. Model Forests have shown substantial promise in transforming conflicts, but this approach has likewise been limited in many countries by an inability to reform both formal forest policies and informal institutions such as corruption and weak state capacity. Adaptive governance innovations thus confront the tensions between institutional flexibility and rigidity (Craig et al., 2017), in many cases showing greater success in reforming operational- and collective choice-level institutions at local scales than at reforming collective-choice and constitutional-level institutions at higher scales.

CONCLUSION

Conventional forest governance models limited decision-making to state scientists (on state-owned lands) or to formal title holders (on private lands) and conventional management approaches emphasised the simplification of forest systems in the service of optimising a narrow range of outputs. While these approaches have contributed to the production of timber and other wood products valuable to society, their sustainability in an age of rapid social and ecological change has been called into question. An emphasis on simplification, calculation, and control is a poor fit for the 'no analogue' present and future of forests under the combined pressures of climate change, biological invasions, forest structure and process alteration, fragmentation, and competing societal demands. Over a short time-period, adaptive governance has been transformed from an academic concept to an actionable paradigm through the experimentation and innovation of individuals and networks in varied forest environments.

Still, important questions remain for the future of adaptive forest governance. To what extent will promising models be able to flourish without substantive institutional change at broader constitutional and collective-choice levels? Will the institutionalisation of emerging models risk undermining the creative capacities that allow for experimentation and adaptation? How will these models be sustained as key champions and start-up support wane over time? How will models that rely upon the unpaid involvement of volunteer forest stakeholders ensure that key voices are not excluded due their economic, political, or cultural marginalisation? Answering these and related questions will be essential as adaptive governance approaches continue to evolve.

REFERENCES

Abers, R. N., and Keck, M. E. 2013. *Practical Authority: Agency and Institutional change in Brazilian Water Politics.* Oxford University Press.

Abrams, J. 2019. The emergence of network governance in US National Forest administration: causal factors and propositions for future research. *Forest Policy and Economics,* 106, 101977.

Abrams, J., Huber-Stearns, H., Bone, C., Grummon, C., and Moseley, C. 2017. Adaptation to a landscape-scale mountain pine beetle epidemic in the era of networked governance: the enduring importance of bureaucratic institutions. *Ecology and Society,* 224, 22.

Abrams, J., Huber-Stearns, H., Steen-Adams, M., Davis, E. J., Bone, C., Nelson, M. F., and Moseley, C. 2021. Adaptive governance in a complex social-ecological context: emergent responses to a native forest insect outbreak. *Sustainability Science,* 16, 1, 53–68.

Abrams, J., Nielsen, E., Diaz, D., Selfa, T., Adams, E., Dunn, J. L., and Moseley, C. 2018. How do states benefit from nonstate governance? Evidence from forest sustainability certification. *Global Environmental Politics,* 18, 3, 66–85.

Angelstam, P., Elbakidze, M., Axelsson. R., Khoroshev, A., Pedroli, B., Tysiachniouk, M., and Zabubenin, E. 2019. Model forests in Russia as landscape approach: demonstration projects or initiatives for learning towards sustainable forest management? *Forest Policy and Economics,* 101, 96–110.

Angelstam, P., Manton, M., Green, M., Jonsson, B. G., Mikusiński, G., Svensson, J., and Sabatini, F. M. 2020. Sweden does not meet agreed national and international forest biodiversity targets: a call for adaptive landscape planning. *Landscape and Urban Planning,* 202, 103838.

Auld, G. 2014. *Constructing Private Governance: The Rise and Evolution of Forest, Coffee, and Fisheries Certification.* Yale University Press.

Bartley, T. 2007. Institutional emergence in an era of globalization: the rise of transnational private regulation of labor and environmental conditions. *American Journal of Sociology,* 113, 2, 297–351.

Bartley, T. 2014. Transnational governance and the re-centered state: sustainability or legality? *Regulation and Governance*, 8, 1, 93–109.

Bartley, T. 2021. Power and the practice of transnational private regulation. *New Political Economy*. doi: 10.1080/13563467.2021.1881471.

Battilana, J., and D'Aunno, T. 2009. Institutional work and the paradox of embedded agency. In T. B. Lawrence, R. Suddaby, and B. Leca (eds.), *Institutional Work: Actors and Agency in Institutional Studies of Organizations*, pp. 31–58. Cambridge University Press.

Bawa, K., and Seidler, R. 1998. Natural forest management and conservation of biodiversity in tropical forests. *Conservation Biology*, 12, 46–55.

Behan, R. W. 1990. Multiresource forest management: a paradigmatic challenge to professional forestry. *Journal of Forestry*, 88, 12–18.

Bernstein, S., and Cashore, B. 2007. Can non-state global governance be legitimate? An analytical framework. *Regulation and Governance*, 1, 4, 347–371.

Bobzien, C., and Van Alstyne, K. 2014. Silviculture across large landscapes: back to the future. *Journal of Forestry*, 112, 5, 467–473.

Bouthillier, L. 2001. Quebec: the consolidation and the movement towards sustainability. In M. Howlett, (ed.) *Canadian Forest Policy*, pp. 237–278. University of Toronto Press.

Bowman, D. M. J. S., Kolden, C. A., Abatzoglou, J. T., Johnston, F. H., van der Werf, G. R., and Flannigan, M. 2020. Vegetation fires in the Anthropocene. *Nature Reviews Earth and Environment*, 110, 500–515. https://doi.org/10.1038/s43017-020-0085-3.

Bull, G., and Schwab, O. 2005. Communities and forestry in Canada: a review and analysis of the model forest and community-forest programs. In R. G. Lee and D. R. Field (eds.), *Communities and Forests: Where People Meet the Land*, pp. 176–192. Oregon State University Press.

Burns, S. L., Yapura, P. F., and Giessen, L. 2016. State actors and international forest certification policy: coalitions behind FSC and PEFC in federal Argentina. *Land Use Policy*, 52, 23–29.

Butler, W. H., Monroe, A., and McCaffrey, S. 2015. Collaborative implementation for ecological restoration on US public lands: implications for legal context, accountability, and adaptive management. *Environmental Management*, 55, 3, 564–577.

Cashore, B. 2002. Legitimacy and the privatization of environmental governance: how non-state market-driven (NSMD) governance systems gain rule–making authority. *Governance*, 15, 4, 503–529.

Cashore, B., Auld, G., and Newsom, D. 2004. *Governing Through Markets: Forest Certification and the Emergence of Non-state Authority*. Yale University Press.

Cashore, B., Auld, G., and Newsom, D. 2017. Legitimizing political consumerism: the case of forest certification in North America and Europe. In M. Micheletti, A. Follesdal, and D. Stolle (eds.), *Politics, Products and Markets: Exploring Political Consumerism Past and Present*, pp. 181–199. Transaction Publishers.

Cashore, B., Egan, E., Auld, G., and Newsom, D. 2007. Revising theories of nonstate market-driven (NSMD) governance: lessons from the Finnish forest certification experience. *Global Environmental Politics*, 7, 1, 1–44.

Chaffin, B. C., Gosnell, H., and Cosens, B. A. 2014. A decade of adaptive governance scholarship: synthesis and future directions. *Ecology and Society*, 19, 3, 56.

Charnley, S., Poe, M. R., Ager, A. A., Spies, T. A., Platt, E. K., and Olsen, K. A. 2015. A burning problem: social dynamics of disaster risk reduction through wildfire mitigation. *Human Organization*, 74, 4, 329–340.

Cheng, A. S. 2006. Build it and they will come? Mandating collaboration in public lands planning and management. *Natural Resources Journal*, 46, 4, 841–858.

Cheng, A. S., and Dale, L. 2020. Achieving adaptive governance of forest wildfire risk using competitive grants: insights from the Colorado Wildfire Risk Reduction Grant Program. *Review of Policy Research*, 37, 5, 657–686.

Cheng, A. S., Danks, C., and Allred, S. R. 2011. The role of social and policy learning in changing forest governance: an examination of community-based forestry initiatives in the US. *Forest Policy and Economics*, 13, 2, 89–96.

Cheng, A. S., Gerlak, A. K., Dale, L., and Mattor, K. 2015. Examining the adaptability of collaborative governance associated with publicly managed ecosystems over time: insights from the Front Range Roundtable, Colorado, USA. *Ecology and Society*, 20, 1, 35.

Clapp, R. A. 1998. The resource cycle in forestry and fishing. *Canadian Geographer/Le Géographe Canadien*, 42, 2, 129–144.

Cooper, C. F. 1960. Changes in vegetation, structure, and growth of southwestern pine forests since white settlement. *Ecological Monographs*, 30, 2, 129–164.

Craig, R. K., Garmestani, A. S., Allen, C. R., Arnold, C. A. T., Birgé, H., DeCaro, D. A., Fremier, A. K., Gosnell, H., and Schlager, E. 2017. Balancing stability and flexibility in adaptive governance: an analysis of tools available in US environmental law. *Ecology and Society*, 22, 2, 3. https://doi.org/10.5751/ES-08983-220203.

Cromley, C. M. 2005. Community-based forestry goes to Washington. In R. D. Brunner, T. A. Steelman, L. Coe-Juell, C. M. Cromley, C. M. Edwards, and D. W. Tucker (eds.), *Adaptive Governance: Integrating Science, Policy, and Decision Making*, pp. 221–267. Columbia University Press.

Cyphers, L. A., and Schultz, C. A. 2019. Policy design to support cross-boundary land management: the example of the Joint Chiefs Landscape Restoration Partnership. *Land Use Policy*, 80, 362–369.

Davis, E. J., Hajjar, R., Charnley, S., Moseley, C., Wendel, K., and Jacobson, M. 2020. Community-based forestry on federal lands in the western United States: a synthesis and call for renewed research. *Forest Policy and Economics*, 111, 102042. https://doi.org/10.1016/j.forpol.2019.102042.

Dawson, L., Elbakidze, M., Angelstam, P., and Gordon, J. 2017. Governance and management of landscape restoration at multiple scales: learning from successful environmental managers in Sweden. *Journal of Environmental Management*, 197, 24–40.

Elbakidze, M., Angelstam, P., Sandström, C., and Axelsson, R. 2010. Multi-stakeholder collaboration in Russian and Swedish Model Forest initiatives: adaptive governance towards sustainable forest management? *Ecology and Society*, 15, 2, 14.

Elbakidze, M., Andersson, K., Angelstam, P., Armstrong, G., Axelsson, R., Doyon, F., Hermansson, M., Jacobsson, J., and Pautov, Y. 2013. Sustained yield forestry in Sweden and Russia: how does it correspond to sustainable forest management policy? *Ambio*, 42, 160–173.

Espinoza, O., and Dockry, M. J. 2014. Forest certification in Bolivia: a status report and analysis of stakeholder perspectives. *Forest Products Journal*, 63, 3–4, 80–89. https://doi.org/10.13073/FPJ-D-13-00086.

Fairfax, S. K., Fortmann, L. P., Hawkins, A., and Huntsinger, L. 1999. The federal forests are not what they seem: formal and informal claims to federal lands. *Ecology Law Quarterly*, 25, 630–646.

Farrell, E., Fuhrer, E., Ryan, D. Andersson, F., Huttl, R. and Piussi, P. 2000. European forest ecosystems: building the future on the legacy of the past. *Forest Ecology and Management*, 132, 5–20.

Fernandez-Gimenez, M., Ballard, H., and Sturtevant, V. 2008. Adaptive management and social learning in collaborative and community-based monitoring: a study of five community-based forestry organizations in the western USA. *Ecology and Society*, 13, 2, 4. https://doi.org/10.5751/ES-02400-130204.

Graz, J. H. 2021. Grounding the politics of transnational private governance: introduction to the special section. *New Political Economy*. doi:10.1080/13563467.2021.1881472.

Gulbrandsen, L. H. 2010. *Transnational Environmental Governance: The Emergence and Effects of the Certification of Forests and Fisheries*. Edward Elgar.

Hackett, R. 2013. From government to governance? Forest certification and crisis displacement in Ontario, Canada. *Journal of Rural Studies*, 30, 120–129.

Hasselman, L. 2017. Adaptive management; adaptive co-management; adaptive governance: what's the difference? *Australasian Journal of Environmental Management*, 24, 1, 31–46. https://doi.org/10.1080/14486563.2016.1251857.

Hobbs, R. J., Higgs, E., and Harris, J. A. 2009. Novel ecosystems: implications for conservation and restoration. *Trends in Ecology and Evolution*, 24, 11, 599–605.

Hoberg, G. 2001. The emerging triumph of ecosystem management: the transformation of federal forest policy. In C. Davis (ed.), *Environmental Politics and Western Public Lands*, pp. 55–86. Westview Press.

Holling, C. S., and Meffe, G. K. 1996. Command and control and the pathology of natural resource management. *Conservation Biology*, 10, 328–337.

Hölzl, R. 2010. Historicizing sustainability: German scientific forestry in the eighteenth and nineteenth centuries. *Science as Culture*, 19, 4, 431–460. https://doi.org/10.1080/09505431.2010.519866.

IPBES. 2018. The IPBES regional assessment report on biodiversity and ecosystem services for Europe and Central Asia. M. Rounsevell, M. Fischer, A. Torre-Marin Rando, and A. Mader (eds.), Secretariat of the Intergovernmental Science-Policy Platform on Biodiversity and Ecosystem Services, Bonn, Germany.

Innes, J. E., and Booher, D. E. 2010. *Planning with Complexity: An Introduction to Collaborative Rationality for Public Policy*. Routledge.

Katila, P., Galloway, G., de Jong, W., Pacheco, P., and Mery, G. (eds.). 2014. *Forests Under Pressure: Local responses to global issues* (IUFRO World Series Vol. 32). IUFRO.

Katila, P., McDermott, C., Larson, A., Aggarwal, S., and Giessen, L. 2020. Forest tenure and the Sustainable Development Goals: a critical view. *Forest Policy and Economics*, 120, 102294. https://doi.org/10.1016/j.forpol.2020.102294

Korotkov, V., Leinonen, T., Palenova, M., Filipchuk, A. and Nesterenko, Y. 2009. Towards sustainable and intensive forest management in Northwest Russia. *Working Papers of the Finnish Forest Research Institute* 107.

LaPierre, L. 2002. Canada's Model Forest Program. *Forestry Chronicle* 78, 5, 613–617.

Lister, J. 2011. *Corporate Social Responsibility and the State: International Approaches to Forest Co-regulation*. UBC Press.

Lowood, H. E. 1990. The calculating forester: quantification, cameral science, and the emergence of scientific forestry management in Germany. In T. Frängsmyr, J. L. Heilbron, and R. E. Rider (eds.), *The Quantifying Spirit in the 18th Century*, pp. 315–342. University of California Press.

Luckert, M. K., and Williamson, T. 2004. Should sustained yield be part of sustainable forest management? *Canadian Journal of Forest Research*, 35, 356–364.

Margerum, R. D. 2011. *Beyond Consensus: Improving Collaborative Planning and Management*. MIT Press.

Mattor, K. M., and Cheng, A. S. 2015. Contextual factors influencing collaboration levels and outcomes in national forest stewardship contracting. *Review of Policy Research*, 32, 6, 723–744.

McIntyre, K. B., and Schultz, C. A. 2020. Facilitating collaboration in forest management: assessing the benefits of collaborative policy innovations. *Land Use Policy*, 96, 104683.

McManus, P. 1999. Histories of forestry: ideas, networks and silences. *Environment and History*, 5, 2, 185–208. https://doi.org/10.3197/096734099779568344.

MCPFE. 1995. Pan-European criteria and indicators for sustainable forest management. Retrieved 10 August, 2011, from http://www.fao.org/docrep/004/AC135E/ac135e09.htm.

MCPFE. 1998. Third Ministerial Conference on the Protection of Forests in Europe. 2–4 June, Lisbon. Retrieved 20 October 2010, from http://www.mcpfe.org/.

MCPFE. 2001. Criteria and indicators for sustainable forest management of the MCPFE. International expert meeting on monitoring, assessment and reporting on the progress towards Sustainable Forest Management, Yokohama, 5–8 November 2001, Yokohama, Japan.

Monroe, A. S., and Butler, W. H. 2016. Responding to a policy mandate to collaborate: structuring collaboration in the Collaborative Forest Landscape Restoration Program. *Journal of Environmental Planning and Management*, 59, 6, 1054–1072. https://doi.org/10.1080/09640568.2015.1053562.

Moog, S., Spicer, A., and Böhm, S. 2015. The politics of multi-stakeholder initiatives: the crisis of the Forest Stewardship Council. *Journal of Business Ethics*, 128, 3, 469–493.

Moseley, C., and KenCairn, B. 2001. Problem solving or social change? The Applegate and Grand Canyon Forest Partnerships. In R. K. Vance, C. B. Edminster, W. W. Covington, and J. A. Blake (eds.), *Ponderosa Pine Ecosystems Restoration and Conservation: Steps Toward Stewardship*, pp. 121–129. USDA Forest Service Rocky Mountain Research Station.

Perry, D. A., Oren, R., and Hart, S. C. 2008. *Forest Ecosystems* (2nd edn). Johns Hopkins University Press.

Platt, E., Charnley, S., Bailey, J. D., and Cramer, L. A. 2002. Adaptive governance in fire-prone landscapes. *Society and Natural Resources*. https://doi.org/10.1080/08941920.2022.2035872.

Puettmann, K. J., Coates, K. D., and Messier, C. C. 2009. *A Critique of Silviculture: Managing for Complexity*. Island Press.

Pyne, S. J. 1982. *Fire in America: A Cultural History of Wildland and Rural Fire*. Princeton University Press.

Rocheleau, D., and Edmunds, D. 1997. Women, men and trees: gender, power and property in forest and agrarian landscapes. *World Development*, 25, 8, 1351–1371.

Schepers, D. H. 2010. Challenges to legitimacy at the Forest Stewardship Council. *Journal of Business Ethics*, 92, 2, 279–290.

Schirmer, J. 2013. Environmental activism and the global forest sector. In E. Hansen, R. Panwar, and R. Vlosky (eds.), *The Global Forest Sector: Changes, Practices, and Prospects*, pp. 203–235. CRC Press.

Schultz, C. A., Abrams, J. B., Davis, E. J., Cheng, A. S., Huber-Stearns, H. R., and Moseley, C. 2021. Disturbance shapes the US forest governance frontier: a review and conceptual framework for understanding governance change. *Ambio*, 50, 12, 2168–2182.

Schultz, C. A., Coelho, D. L., and Beam, R. D. 2014. Design and governance of multiparty monitoring under the USDA Forest Service's Collaborative Forest Landscape Restoration Program. *Journal of Forestry*, 112, 2, 198–206.

Schultz, C. A., McIntyre, K. B., Cyphers, L., Kooistra, C., Ellison, A., and Moseley, C. 2018. Policy design to support forest restoration: the value of focused investment and collaboration. *Forests*, 9, 9, 512.

Scott, J. C. 1998. *Seeing Like a State: How Certain Schemes to Improve the Human Condition Have Failed*. Yale University Press.

Secco, L., and Pettenella, D. 2006. Participatory processes in forest management: the Italian experience in defining and implementing forest certification schemes. *Schweizerische Zeitschrift Fur Forstwesen*, 157, 10, 445–452.

Selin, S. W., Schuett, M. A., and Carr, D. S. 1997. Has collaborative planning taken root in the national forests? *Journal of Forestry*, 95, 5, 25–28.

Spathelf, P., Stanturf, J., Kleine, M., Jandl, R., Chiatante, D., and Bolte, A. 2018. Adaptive measures: integrating adaptive forest management and forest landscape restoration. *Annals of Forest Science*, 75, 2, 55. https://doi.org/10.1007/s13595-018-0736-4.

Spittlehouse, D. L., and Stewart, R. B. 2003. Adaptation to climate change in forest management. *BC Journal of Ecosystems and Management*, 4, 1, 1–11.

Steen-Adams, M. M., Abrams, J. B., Huber-Stearns, H. R., Bone, C., and Moseley, C. 2022. Leveraging administrative capacity to manage landscape-scale, cross-boundary disturbance in the Black Hills: what roles for federal, state, local, and nongovernmental partners? *Journal of Forestry*, 120, 1, 86–105.

The Swedish Forest Agency. 2010. *Forest Statistic Yearbook*. Jönköping: Skogsstyrelsen.

Tricallotis, M., Kanowski, P., and Gunningham, N. 2019. The drivers and evolution of competing forest certification schemes in the Chilean forestry industry. *International Forestry Review*, 21, 4, 516–527.

Urgenson, L. S., Ryan, C. M., Halpern, C. B., Bakker, J. D., Belote, R. T., Franklin, J. F., Haugo, R. D., Nelson, C. R., and Waltz, A. E. M. 2017. Visions of restoration in fire-adapted forest landscapes: lessons from the Collaborative Forest Landscape Restoration Program. *Environmental Management*, 59, 2, 338–353. https://doi.org/10.1007/s00267-016-0791-2.

Weaver, H. 1947. Fire – nature's thinning agent in ponderosa pine stands. *Journal of Forestry*, 45, 6, 437–444. https://doi.org/10.1093/jof/45.6.437.

Weaver, H. 1959. Ecological changes in the ponderosa pine forest of the Warm Springs Indian Reservation in Oregon. *Journal of Forestry*, 57, 1, 15–20. https://doi.org/10.1093/jof/57.1.15.

Wiersum, K. F. 1995. 200 Years of sustainability in forestry: lessons from history. *Environmental Management*, 19, 321–329.

Williams, J. W., and Jackson, S. T. 2007. Novel climates, no-analog communities, and ecological surprises. *Frontiers in Ecology and the Environment*, 5, 9, 475–482.

Wurtzebach, Z., Schultz, C., Waltz, A. E. M., Esch, B. E., and Wasserman, T. N. 2019. Adaptive governance and the administrative state: knowledge management for forest planning in the western United States. *Regional Environmental Change*, 19, 8, 2651–2666. https://doi.org/10.1007/s10113-019-01569-6.

Xu, L., and Lu, A. J. 2021. Forest certification in developing countries: current status and hindrances to its adoption within a macro-framework. *International Forestry Review*, 23, 1, 105–126.

9. Adaptive governance for marine environments: methods, challenges, and lessons for ocean fisheries

Barbara Quimby

INTRODUCTION

For centuries, many perceived oceans to be inscrutable and infinite. In 1883, T. H. Huxley stated: "I believe, then, that the cod fishery ... and probably all the great sea fisheries, are inexhaustible: that is to say that nothing we do seriously affects the number of fish. And any attempt to regulate these fisheries seems ... to be useless." (Kurlansky, 1998). Some of Huxley's contemporaries disagreed (Sims and Southward, 2006); yet for a century on, the expansive size of oceans, their diversity and unpredictability, and their cross-scale interdependency and interactions, made governance seem impossible. By the mid-20th century, changes in technology increased the range and depth of ocean exploitation, and the illusion of limitless oceans and marine fisheries was dispelled by collapsing stocks and increasing conflicts over resources. Efforts by the United Nations to create governance systems for expansive marine environments had focused on centralised, "command and control" approaches that proved inadequate for dynamic marine settings. By the 1990s, the collapse of Northern Atlantic cod fisheries that Huxley perceived to be interminable highlighted the need for a more responsive governance approach (McCay and Finlayson, 1995).

Yet oceans present many challenges to coordinated governance. Marine environments encompass twice the surface area of terrestrial biomes on Earth, across latitudes from arctic to tropical zones. In addition, the marine context is multidimensional, including the entire water column from sea floor to surface, with physical processes (e.g. currents) and biological processes (e.g. species migration) occurring and interacting across scales, all made increasingly unpredictable by climate change (Greenhill et al., 2020; Jeffers, 2010). In marine fisheries, climate change is shifting the habitats and patterns of fish stocks, increasing uncertainty and creating pressure on governance to adapt quickly (Pinsky et al., 2021). In addition, the social and political dimensions of marine spaces have been undervalued in marine research (Levine et al., 2015), with poor attention to cultural meaning and power relationships. In spite of their importance to livelihoods, food systems, and community well-being, marine environments have frequently been conceptualised as "wild" or "unoccupied" spaces, overlooking existing institutions and governance histories (Fabinyi and Barclay, 2022).

The scale, diversity, and unpredictability of marine social-ecological systems, and in particular marine fisheries, have inspired and informed conceptualisations of adaptive governance. Adaptive governance (AG) is a framework for addressing uncertainty and change with institutions and policy processes that reflect the social context (Chaffin et al., 2014; Dietz et al., 2003; Folke et al., 2005). As discussed in other chapters of this book, at the centre of AG strategies is a process of knowledge sharing, learning and experimentation, and responding rapidly to changing social-ecological systems, as well as governance failures. In developing these strategies, Dietz et al (2003) examine the cod fishery and identify a lack of information about changes in the system as a contributor to poor governance adaptability, informing the need for stakeholder participation and knowledge-sharing between decision-makers and resource users. The scale of marine governance has also informed conceptualisations of nested and cross-scale institutional arrangements, drawing inspiration from the strengths of traditional, self-organised, and polycentric governance of small-scale fisheries, such as in the Pacific (Folke et al., 2005). In turn, governance designed to address uncertainty and change aligns with the realities of vast, diverse, data-poor marine fisheries, and since the introduction of its key principles nearly two decades ago, AG has been adopted in contexts across the globe. Yet while they are theoretically a good match, the nascent state of marine governance institutions, challenges of spatial size and social-ecological complexity, and realities of power-sharing and stakeholder engagement leave room for improvement.

This chapter provides a synthesis of the literature on AG in marine contexts. Relevant literature was identified with a non-systematic use of Scopus and Google Scholar searches that included "adaptive governance" and "marine", "ocean", and "coastal", as well as by reviewing the literature cited in selected papers. First, I discuss the history and diversity of institutional arrangements of marine governance. Second, I outline the challenges to developing effective adaptive marine governance, particularly for capture fisheries. Third, I evaluate how effectively AG has been implemented and how it has responded to sudden social and ecological shocks in diverse marine contexts. While issues such as pollution (Vince and Hardesty, 2017) and renewable energy development (Wright, 2015) are also important for marine governance, I focus on fisheries because of their unique challenges for institutional diversity and "fit", stakeholder participation, and responsiveness to a dynamic, living natural resource. This synthesis highlights the benefits of, and future directions for, adaptive marine governance.

HISTORY OF MARINE GOVERNANCE: A BRIEF OVERVIEW

Freedom of the Seas

Prior to the 20th century, ocean governance was generally limited to near-shore environments, as an extension of terrestrial territories. Based on the concept of "freedom of the seas" (*Mare Liberum*) introduced in Europe in the early 17th century, spaces beyond the coastline were unclaimed and unregulated (Steinberg, 2001). This openness allowed for unfettered travel and trade on the high seas – the marine spaces that are outside of the governance zones. However, colonial expansion and industrialisation led to a need to establish ownership and authority of coastal waters. State and colonial governments claimed navigable waters below the high-tide mark, erasing traditional tenure in coastal lagoons and bays and limiting the formal authority and control of local actors.

Law of the Sea and Exclusive Economic Zones (EEZs)

By the mid-20th century, there was a shift from "freedom of the seas" to recognition of the need to address resource management conflicts in the oceans. A significant step in ocean governance was adoption of the United Nations Convention on the Law of the Sea (UNCLOS)

40 years ago. Signed by 164 parties, the law establishes three types of governance zones: the traditionally recognised territorial seas up to 12 nautical miles from shore; a contiguous zone of 24 nautical miles, which serves as a customs zone in which countries have the right to regulate use, and a 200 nautical mile Exclusive Economic Zone (EEZ). This convention helped to clarify governance relationships and responsibilities and created an international tribunal and other procedural organisations to address issues on the high seas. In the United States, most coastal states and territories have jurisdiction over an area of 3 nautical miles from the baseline (high water mark); Texas, Florida, and Puerto Rico were granted larger 9-mile jurisdictions. Municipalities also have jurisdiction over coastal spaces above the high-water mark and can therefore influence integrated coastal marine governance. In other nations, state jurisdictions can overlap with or legally integrate customary tenure boundaries and Indigenous governance structures.

In establishing jurisdictions over previously unregulated ocean commons, UNCLOS stimulated governments to consider how to regulate, develop, and conserve resources within their territories (Wright, 2015). The creation of EEZs shifted control of previously open common-pool resources like fisheries to coastal states; Pacific Island nations in particular became "ocean-rich", with exclusive access to key resources including tuna stocks (Hannesson, 2008). The agreement also explicitly tasks governments with responsibility for the sustainable management of their marine territories, requiring more information and new governance tools. Yet, there remain vast marine spaces outside of these territories, and the interrelatedness of marine environments, varying social and political contexts, and more recently, the effects of climate change on ocean environments and fisheries, combine to produce several challenges for marine governance.

Collaborative Marine Governance Arrangements

The Law of the Sea catalysed the development of new marine governance systems that can become the basis for AG. The need to create cross-scale governance has led to many forms of hybridised and cooperative institutional arrangements at different scales, including regional transboundary governance, marine protected areas and marine managed areas, and co-management.

The expansiveness and interconnectedness of marine settings has inspired large-scale governance approaches for "seascapes" and "regional seas", that include networked, transboundary governance approaches (Fidelman et al., 2012). The UN Sustainable Development Goals identify the importance of strengthening capacity at the regional level (UN 2015), and there are now at least 25 global governance organisations for regional ecosystem-based management (Mahon and Fanning, 2019); yet their effectiveness and integration varies, with Indigenous (regionally-driven) frameworks proving most useful. Even in the European Union, where there is an established shared legal framework, fully integrated regional marine governance is slow to develop in practice (Soma et al., 2015). There are also several regional fisheries management organisations (RFMOs); these focus on specific transboundary fisheries and species, rather than spatial areas.

Marine reserves existed prior to UNCLOS, but the new agreement and a rise in the establishment of terrestrial protected areas and national parks inspired the creation of similar marine protected areas (MPAs) (Humphreys and Clark, 2020; IUCN, 2008). MPAs vary in size, from large-scale (LSMPAs) to networked locally-managed marine areas (Govan, 2009; Gruby et al., 2021). MPAs frequently use an ecosystem-based management approach (Brown et al., 2013); however, MPAs have been criticised for providing a technocratic governance solution that emphasises quantitative economic and environmental measures over cultural complexity and social equity outcomes (De Santo, 2013; Humphreys and Clark, 2020), undercutting good governance. Researchers suggest ongoing evaluation of MPAs to address the dynamic effects of policy interactions in marine fisheries contexts and avoiding disruptions to local livelihoods and cultural needs (Gruby et al., 2021; McCay and Jones, 2011). MPAs have also been criticised for implementing a top-down structure; in response, some incorporate co-management approaches discussed below, with varied success (Brown et al., 2013).

Community-based approaches to fisheries management have flourished in the past few decades, in response to the failures of centralised, top-down governance approaches (Jentoft et al., 2010). While locally focused approaches show advantages in flexibility and responsiveness, it is crucial that they be incorporated into a nested, multiscale approach for dynamic and interdependent marine environments. Adaptive co-management, characterised as the operationalisation of AG that centres bottom-up, community-focused approaches (Olsson et al., 2004), has become a common strategy for small-scale fisheries and coastal management (Hunter et al., 2018; Quimby and Levine, 2018; Weeks and Jupiter, 2013). Traditional Indigenous institutions and culture are frequently incorporated into AG approaches in the Pacific to enhance responsiveness to change and rule compliance (Cohen et al., 2015; Quimby and Levine, 2021). Still, these hybridised approaches do not guarantee knowledge and power sharing across scales, nor equitable participation and outcomes for all community members (Aswani and Ruddle, 2013; Kleiber et al., 2017).

IMPLEMENTING ADAPTIVE GOVERNANCE FOR MARINE FISHERIES

Emergent collaborative governance arrangements for marine environments still struggle to address several issues; in particular: the allocation of access and use rights, conservation and protection of resources from overexploitation, monitoring and enforcement, and adaptation to changing ocean contexts (Haas et al., 2021; Wright, 2015). Theoretically, AG presents a way forward; however, there are several challenges to developing effective adaptive marine governance, particularly in marine fisheries (see Table 9.1).

Institutional Variety

As discussed earlier, the variety of marine environments and their socio-political histories have led to several different forms of institutional design that may form the basis of AG. Environmental governance includes the institutions (e.g., laws, rules, and norms), regulatory processes, and mechanisms for conflict resolution that are created and used by actors to shape actions and outcomes around the use and protection of natural resources (Chaffin et al., 2014; Lemos and Agrawal, 2006). Multilevel governance that effectively connects governance arrangements across local, national, regional, and global scales is important for common-pool resource management (Ostrom, 2005). While some scholars believe marine governance has developed a "sectoral and fragmented approach" (Kelly et al., 2018) that fails to address the interactions and interdependencies of marine ecosystems, others suggest that there are path-

Table 9.1   Challenges of adaptive marine governance

Strategies for adaptive governance (Dietz et al. 2003)	Social-environmental challenges of marine fisheries
Institutional Variety – including local social norms, laws, and markets (Folke et al., 2007)	Lack of "fit" for large-scale/transboundary governance
	Species-specific policy approaches
	Poor recognition of existing institutions and social and cultural dimensions of fisheries
	Rapid fluctuations in markets and fish stock distribution
Stakeholder Participation	Wide spatial distribution and diversity of stakeholders
	Self-organisation
	Procedural equity and gender inclusion
Power Sharing and Nested Authority	Cross-scale institutional integration
	Colonial histories and existing hierarchical governance
	Procedural equity

ways forward for better cross-scale integration (Fanning and Mahon, 2020). As Fabinyi and Barclay (2022) discuss in their examination of marine fisheries governance, "new" governance efforts do not occur in a void, but are instead overlaid and integrated with the pre-existing social and institutional context. AG is an opportunity to turn that existing institutional diversity into a strength through cross-scale linkages and polycentric arrangements that create redundancies and reflect the specific social-environmental context.

Governance "fit" is especially challenging for transboundary governance (Chaffin et al., 2014; Wilson, 2006). Matching governance to ecological scales has driven transboundary efforts; yet not only are marine spatially vast, but they are also interconnected with coastal spaces and governance institutions (Steinberg, 2013; Partelow et al., 2020). Preconceptions of marine spaces as historically unoccupied and ungoverned can also obscure the existing human dimensions of an area (Bennett et al., 2015). Tuda et al. (2019) assess the potential for AG in the coastal waters that extend between Kenya and Tanzania by examining the current governance institutions and processes to identify enabling (or constraining) characteristics for developing AG. The area provides ecological continuity, with critical habitat for biodiversity, including coral reefs, mangroves, and seagrass used by dugongs and turtles. As such, local artisanal fishers move across national borders with seasonal variation. Through surveys of members of 81 organisations involved in coastal and marine management, including local community groups, NGOs, and government agencies, the authors conclude that strong networks and collaborative relationships exist to support knowledge-sharing with resource managers. However, these networks are highly centralised, narrowing the diversity of knowledge conveyed, and there is a lack of policy structure (rules) to guide managers, resulting in a lack of adaptive action. The study also notes that the function of any new governance system will depend on how well it reflects the region's significant social and cultural diversity.

Inadequate integration of existing formal and informal institutions – including social norms, markets, and Indigenous political processes – can reduce adaptive capacity. Social norms and informal institutions can be used in regulating behaviours in fisheries, but inadequate attention to actors' experiences and relationship to a dynamic social-environmental system has limited their use for improving flexibility and adaptive capacity (de la Torre-Castro and Lindström, 2010; Knudsen, 1995). Markets and economic pressures can also provide fishers with incentives for conservation or overexploitation; however, fishers are often more flexible than governance institutions. For example, Aguilera et al. (2015) examine the flexibility of small-scale commercial fishers in California, who easily shift between sardine, anchovy, and squid, depending on fishers' perceptions of the availability or depletion of stocks; however, governance intransigence can hamper their adaptability. The authors suggest that species-specific regulatory processes permitting for different fisheries should recognise their interconnectedness, enabling greater adaptability to a highly variable, multi-species fishery.

Polycentric institutions have been embraced by commons theorists (Andersson and Ostrom, 2008) and offer another opportunity for organisational variety. Polycentric systems are considered to have several key strengths that support AG. First, a nested, cross-scale arrangement of semi-autonomous groups facilitates institutional fit to dynamic social-ecological systems (Folke et al., 2005). They also provide redundancies that can mitigate failures by any single actor or policy, in contrast with centralised approaches (Ostrom et al., 1999). Polycentric institutions can also be a way to "scale up" governance approaches, build on the strengths of local organisations and customary tenure while enabling coordination and knowledge-sharing across multiple jurisdictions or environments, from local to national or transboundary regional scales (see Carlisle and Gruby (2018) and Tuda et al. (2021)). However, the benefits of polycentricity are not a given, and there is a lack of empirical studies to examine their outcomes for marine AG.

Stakeholder Participation

Participation of diverse stakeholders – the individuals, organisations, and communities involved in a specific marine context – is fundamental to knowledge-sharing, informed decision-making, and policy implementation. Stakeholder participation is a key part of AG and widely recognised as a critical contributor to adaptability (Jentoft et al., 2010; Reed et al., 2018). However, the push to include local communities and stakeholders is very recent and contradicts traditional, established institutional models of top-down governance, creating tension in efforts to implement effective AG. Historical governance outcomes, such as the failures of past top-down governance, can create distrust between stakeholders. Further, the socio-political context can present difficulties for procedural and distributional equity. Gendered bias about livelihoods and hierarchical social norms has led to the exclusion and underrepresentation of women in knowledge-sharing and decision-making (Gustavsson et al., 2021; Kleiber et al., 2017; Schoeffel, 1985). While governance solutions have traditionally focused on institutional arrangements, this has led to inadequate technocratic solutions, and there is a critical need to increase attention to the agency of actors who are engaging with these institutions (Haas et al., 2021).

Identifying and recruiting stakeholders for participation in marine AG is complicated by scale, type of activity, and their relationship to different local and global value chains and markets. Spatially, the people engaged in a marine fishery can be distributed widely across multiple communities, and their presence and activities in a particular area will fluctuate over seasons and with the movement of species. Assumptions about engaged participants can also be subverted by scale, with staff from national agencies or international NGOs playing key roles in governance processes, in spite of not being local. Participation in decision-making and governance actions is also shaped by social dimensions, especially power relationships: who has the power to decide which groups or individuals should be invited to participate, and what their roles should be, informs the fairness and inclusiveness of any governance exercise (St. Martin, 2006).

In large-scale fisheries management, stakeholders are primarily engaged through formal organisations and institutions. In Europe, Regional Advisory Councils (RACs) were introduced in 2002 to increase stakeholder participation; however, an evaluation of the RAC for Pelagic fisheries in the North East Atlantic region identifies a need for decentralisation of decision-making and increased prioritisation of stakeholder input (Coers et al., 2012). In small-scale fisheries, efforts to identify participants have sometimes relied on limited indicators, such as boat ownership, that obscures social value and labour relationships – for example, subsistence fishers, and the people (often women) engaged in processing catch. In marine settings, AG also requires recognition of where different scales and practices of fishing intersect to support strong, representative participation. Chandra (2011) provides an illustration of the need for inclusion of stakeholders from many different fisheries sectors, including artisanal, commercial, and aquaculture workers, in Fijian coastal resource governance.

Bottom-up participation through self-organisation is a principle for common-pool resource governance, and a common consideration for small-scale fisheries governance (Mahon et al., 2008; Tam et al., 2021). Self-organisation through formal and informal social networks of individuals and groups is considered key for learning, trust-building and knowledge-sharing (Folke et al., 2005; Plummer et al., 2013). Self-organisation can originate from existing social networks or be facilitated with institutional support (Ayers and Kittinger, 2014). Communication through these groups can support social learning. Social learning is an iterative process of learning, knowledge creation, and building a shared understanding of phenomena in the world, that can support adaptive behaviours (Reed et al., 2010). For example, the creation of informal or semi-formal forums can facilitate knowledge-sharing and trust-building. In the United States, a Community Fisheries Action Roundtable was created by a non-profit resource centre to bring together full-time fishers from different commercial fisheries, particularly those working within the nearshore, state-managed waters of Maine. Research by Brewer (2013) finds that facilitating these meetings and workshops is expensive; however, the outcome was significant social learning among fisherman and more positive interactions with management institutions.

However, in large transboundary fisheries, an emphasis on technical solutions can overshadow learning. For example, Rubio et al. (2021) examine social networks in Basque tuna fisheries to understand how communication among stakeholders influences their choice of adaptation strategies. The authors found that communication was strong throughout the fishery and inclusive of many different types of actors, including government agents, NGO representatives, and fishing industry leaders. Many of these actors connected through a Regional Fisheries Management Organization for Atlantic tuna fisheries (ICCAT) and governance institutions at national and local scales. While there was regular communication between groups and across scales, actors focused less on learning than other strategies for adaptive capacity, such as organisational structure and agency. The authors suggest that raising the profile of actors with more holistic approaches to adaptation could increase knowledge-sharing and overall adaptive capacity.

In this way, institutional arrangements can affect stakeholder engagement and recognition; yet procedural equity, the capacity for stakeholders to participate in and lead decision-making processes, is also driven by the specific social-political context. There are several criteria for assessing and fostering procedural equity in small-scale fisheries (Bennett et al., 2020; Zafra-Calvo et al., 2017). Institutional arrangements can counter the exclusion of women and actively include diverse actors and perspectives (Frangoudes and Gerrard, 2018; Gustavsson et al., 2021; Kleiber et al., 2017). However, in an analysis of MPA processes, Horigue et al (2016) find that the governance context, the socioeconomic and political processes and pressures, are the key drivers of participation. Fisheries governance can organise policy instruments to create limits on catch quotas or total allowable catch, regulate fishing effort such as gear and vessel types or licenses, and operational limits such as seasonal closures (Basurto and Nenadovic, 2012). These policies have direct effects on livelihoods and well-being. Therefore, explicit attention to equity in decision-making, management actions, and distributional outcomes is necessary for sustainable and adaptable governance (Bennett et al., 2020; Quimby and Levine, 2018).

Power Sharing and Nested Authority

As other chapters in this book discuss, AG requires thoughtful attention to conceptualisations of power and practices of power-sharing at all scales of AG. Coherence across nested institutions, even at smaller scales, can be inhibited by unique historical and social factors of each context. Evans et al. (2011) consider the "messiness" of developing AG for small-scale fisheries in Kenyan coastal waters. Although the fishery is under the control of a single nation, governance includes multiple scales of institutions and actors. While this model implements adaptive management strategies of nested authority across scales, they can become disjointed and lose coherence as institutions at different scales respond to different pressures. Evolving social networks and institutional arrangements influence how knowledge is gained and shared, and in turn how well governance structures and actors are able to learn and respond to change. Using multiple data collection methods including surveys, interviews, and participant observation, the authors find that at the local level, fishers' ecological knowledge primarily informs their decision-making, and due to historical conflicts over an MPA design, they are wary of top-down state interventions. State level organisation is equally stymied by a focus on inland spaces and poor representation of stakeholders in decision-making. In all, the authors find that lack of trust and cooperation between stakeholders, the pressures of poverty, and the persistence of centralised decision-making processes are inhibiting AG.

Given the theoretical roots of AG in the empirical evidence of traditional environmental governance, a transition from local to polycentric AG would seem simple; however, Carlisle and Gruby (2018) demonstrate the difficulties in shifting power to a larger organisational structure. This study is a qualitative case study of a small-scale fishery governance system in Palau as it transitioned from community-based to polycentric governance. They consider how polycentric the system is, what are the enabling conditions, and what are the outcomes for institutional fit, mitigating risk through redundancy, and adaptive capacity. In all, the shift to polycentric governance weakened local power and control and created a "top-heavy" structure strongly influenced by NGO actors, which had some negative outcomes, including greater social tolerance of rule violations. They suggest that if the original governance structure was centralised and the process decentralising power, outcomes may have differed. Overall, the AG outcomes were mixed. The new polycentric system demonstrated some advantageous characteristics, such as willingness by actors to experiment with new policies and strategies when old approaches failed. However, there was also reduced engagement by actors who resented the influence of external actors, reducing the potential for knowledge-sharing and learning.

ADAPTIVE MARINE GOVERNANCE AND RESPONSE TO CRISIS

This section discusses three case studies of AG in marine settings that experienced a significant crisis or shock. The scales and contexts of each example are different, as are the institutional, social, and environmental stressors they experience. In all, they reveal the importance of social networks and their integration with governance institutions for adaptive capacity and resilience.

Österblom and Folke (2013) provide an examination of remote, transboundary adaptive governance in the Southern Ocean that reveals the important interplay between actors (individuals and groups) and structures (institutions and organisations) in the governance processes. The authors examine how a large-scale AG system (the Commission for the Conservation of Antarctic Marine Living Resources- CCAMLR) emerged for the Southern Ocean, a remote environment outside national boundaries. This transnational organisation was specifically formed to address illegal, unreported, and unregulated (IUU) fishing. Drawing on data from qualitative interviews, quantitative surveys, and social network analysis, they find that when the organisation struggled with a crisis (due in part to poor fit between regional environmental challenges and new transnational institutions), informal "shadow" networks filled the gap until formal structures could adapt. In this way, actors enabled fast adaptation, while the institutional structures supported the slower development of trust and legitimacy. The authors emphasise the need to consider both institutions and agency in assessing the functionality and outcomes of AG.

Another recent study elucidates the response of AG in a small-scale fishery to an unprecedented driver of social and economic change, the COVID-19 Pandemic. Pedroza-Gutiérrez et al. (2021) examined coastal fisheries and tourism based in villages of the Yucatan Peninsula, in the states of Campeche and Yucatan. In March of 2020, the fishery was suddenly closed; distribution channels were restricted, both local and export markets became unavailable, and seafood freezing plants locked down for several months. Analysis of interview data reveals that individuals quickly used their knowledge and social networks to cope, first with the full closure of ports, and later with the precipitous drop in market demand. Most fishers turned to catching for household consumption and or sharing with the community, with minimal sales through "friend-to-friend" networks reaching to neighbouring communities. Interestingly, illegal fishing decreased during this period, which the authors attribute to "social cohesion" and mutual respect for the circumstances, although the lack of open markets likely also contributed. The government solicited feedback from fishers to develop plans for implementing safety measures while supporting the reopening of the fishery with new local marketing. Critically, the authors identify new organisational and governance structures created in response to changes in market demand, social contacts, and other rapid shifts in the socioeconomic environment. Overall, while they found that most adaptation occurred at the individual level, with fishers making decisions based on their own knowledge and situation, the experience has also driven "learning and innovation" to build resilience within local social networks and implement new adaptive strategies at state and national levels informed by fishers' experience.

In Vanuatu, Eriksson et al. (2017) describe how AG approaches embedded in customary tenure and community-based fisheries management enabled quick responses to multiple environmental crises. After experiencing multiple shocks, including a tropical cyclone and earthquake event that destroyed reefs used for fishing, local communities experienced losses to their livelihoods and infrastructure, as well as food shortages that increased pressure on local fisheries. In response, community leaders responded by temporarily lifting fishing restrictions in some areas. Government agencies encouraged and supported these openings, and took additional actions, such as the establishment of a women's market and distribution of new fishing gear. While the researchers do not address knowledge-sharing, they found that individuals relied on existing knowledge and skills, and found high social capital enabled the community's responses.

DISCUSSION

Adaptive governance approaches have demonstrated many strengths for addressing uncertainty and change in marine environments, including socially and environmentally driven shocks. The particular strengths of AG in marine settings include institutional design that can be configured for vast spaces, with cross-scale linkages that reflects/responds to organisational diversity and multiplicity at different levels. Fisheries AG has found particular relevance for settings with co-management structures that integrate local social networks and traditional institutions.

However, for its institutional strengths, AG also encounters some challenges for implementation and practice. Social learning and self-organisation to support trust building and knowledge-sharing are more challenging for large-scale AG efforts, due to the high transaction costs and difficulty identifying all relevant stakeholders. Lack of participation and representation from diverse fishing interests can reduce knowledge-sharing and trust. Fisheries are also experiencing a loss of knowledge and adaptive capacity due to the "greying of the fleet", as experienced fishers retire (Haugen et al., 2021). Large and small AG schemes continue to struggle with the issues of conflict and power-sharing raised by Dietz et al. (2003). When AG is embedded in institutions informed by traditional social hierarchies or colonial legacies, it can reduce procedural equity and adaptive capacity (Quimby and Levine, 2021). Overall, an emphasis on technical fixes and policies that overlook implementation and issues of power distribution can reduce the effectiveness of AG.

Fortunately, marine AG practitioners and theorists are exploring how to improve integration across scales of policy and planning (Greenhill et al., 2020). To improve social learning, Pedroza-Gutiérrez (2021) encourages AG to facilitate learning networks, which can diversify knowledge sources and support self-organisation to respond to crisis. These informal social connections compliment governance structures and actions, providing flexibility in times of rapid change. Effective participation and power sharing can also be supported by centring communities and fishers in the early stages of AG planning and conceptualisation, and reflecting on power relations in institutional processes (Cleaver and Whaley, 2018). De la Torre-Castro (2012) suggests viewing governance as embedded in social processes, in order to increase the focus on actors and equitable outcomes rather io technocratic solutions. Additionally, new frameworks for increasing procedural and distributional equity can help to address shortfalls of marine AG (Bennett et al., 2020; Gurney et al., 2021).

AG in marine environments will also benefit from creating more space to experiment and innovate. For example, Partelow et al. (2020) suggest building a broader governance toolbox and complimenting AG approaches with other theoretical frameworks, in order to better customize AG to the needs of a specific coastal marine context. There is also a push to reconsider how we conceptualize marine environments: "wet ontologies" for theorising dynamic aquatic environments beyond social-ecological systems provides a way to decouple marine governance from terrestrial standards and assumptions (Steinberg and Peters, 2015). Moving forward, there are opportunities to build on the established institutional strengths of marine AG and incorporate more context-specific, actor and practise-centred approaches.

CONCLUSIONS

This chapter presents a unique synthesis of the literature to examine the implementation, challenges, and responses of adaptive governance to diverse marine environments. Although AG was developed with marine contexts in mind, there are limited studies of adaptive marine governance and crisis outcomes beyond institutional analysis. This synthesis demonstrates that the application of AG at regional and local scales around the globe has yielded some positive results for social and environmental adaptation to complex, unpredictable pressures and needs. However, the implementation in diverse marine fisheries elucidate several lessons for improving the AG framework for addressing uncertainty and complexity.

Formal institutional structures are important for providing legitimacy and support for governance and can be designed to support inclusive and equitable stakeholder participation. However, fostering institutional variety across scales that adequately incorporate the socio-cultural and political context and recognize existing Indigenous and local institutions overemphasis is key to avoiding technocratic approaches. Stakeholder participation at every stage is also challenging but vital; in many of the examples shown here, adaptive capacity was enabled through informal learning networks and inventive strategies by individual actors. Power sharing for large and transboundary governance areas requires more attention to ensure procedural equity across scales. Still, AG has proven to be sustainable and responsive in the face of social and ecological crises. In all, new institutional arrangements that recognise existing social and political dimensions, support social learning and equity, and move beyond conceptualisations of empty, ahistorical seas, will enable more integrated and responsive marine AG.

REFERENCES

Aguilera, S. E., Cole, J., Finkbeiner, E. M., Le Cornu, E., Ban, N. C., Carr, M. H., Cinner, J. E., Crowder, L. B., Gelcich, S., and Hicks, C. C. 2015. Managing small-scale commercial fisheries for adaptive capacity: insights from dynamic social-ecological drivers of change in Monterey Bay. *PloS One*, 10, 3, e0118992.

Andersson, K., and Ostrom, E. 2008. Analyzing decentralized resource regimes from a polycentric perspective. *Policy Sciences*, 41, 1, 71–93.

Aswani, S., and Ruddle, K. 2013. Design of realistic hybrid marine resource management programs in Oceania. *Pacific Science*, 67, 3, 461–476. Research Library. https://doi.org/10.2984/67.3.11.

Ayers, A., and Kittinger, J. 2014. Emergence of co-management governance for Hawai'I coral reef fisheries. *Global Environmental Change*, 28, 251–262. https://doi.org/10.1016/j.gloenvcha.2014.07.006.

Basurto, X., and Nenadovic, M. 2012. A systematic approach to studying fisheries governance. *Global Policy*, 3, 2, 222–230. https://doi.org/10.1111/j.1758-5899.2011.00094.x.

Bennett, N. J., Calò, A., Di Franco, A., Niccolini, F., Marzo, D., Domina, I., Dimitriadis, C., Sobrado, F., Santoni, M.-C., Charbonnel, E., Trujillo, M., Garcia-Charton, J., Seddiki, L., Cappanera, V., Grbin, J., Kastelic, L., Milazzo, M., and Guidetti, P. 2020. Social equity and marine protected areas: perceptions

of small-scale fishermen in the Mediterranean Sea. *Biological Conservation*, 244, 108531. https://doi
.org/10.1016/j.biocon.2020.108531.

Bennett, N. J., Govan, H., and Satterfield, T. 2015. Ocean grabbing. *Marine Policy*, 57, 61–68. https://
doi.org/doi:10.1016/j.marpol.2015.03.026.

Brewer, J. F. 2013. From experiential knowledge to public participation: social learning at the
Community Fisheries Action Roundtable. *Environmental Management*, 52, 2, 321–334. https://doi
.org/10.1007/s00267-013-0059-z.

Brown, N., Gray, T., and Stead, S. M. 2013. *Contested Forms of Governance in Marine Protected Areas*.
Routledge.

Carlisle, K. M., and Gruby, R. L. 2018. Why the path to polycentricity matters: evidence from fisheries
governance in Palau. *Environmental Policy and Governance*, 28, 4, 223–235. https://doi.org/10.1002/
eet.1811.

Chaffin, B. C., Gosnell, H., and Cosens, B. A. 2014. A decade of adaptive governance scholarship:
synthesis and future directions. *Ecology and Society*, 19, 3. https://doi.org/10.5751/ES-06824-190356.

Chandra, A. 2011. A deliberate inclusive policy (DIP) approach for coastal resources governance:
a Fijian perspective. *Coastal Management*, 39, 2, 175–197.

Cleaver, F., and Whaley, L. 2018. Understanding process, power, and meaning in adaptive governance:
a critical institutional reading. *Ecology and Society*, 23, 2, 49. https://doi.org/10.5751/ES-10212
-230249.

Coers, A., Raakjær, J., and Olesen, C. 2012. Stakeholder participation in the management of North East
Atlantic pelagic fish stocks: the future role of the Pelagic Regional Advisory Council in a reformed
CFP. *Marine Policy*, 36, 3, 689–695. https://doi.org/10.1016/j.marpol.2011.10.017.

Cohen, P. J., Evans, L., and Govan, H. 2015. Community-based, co-management for governing
small-scale fisheries of the Pacific: a Solomon Islands' case study. In S. Jentoft and R. Chuenpagdee
(Eds.), *Interactive Governance for Small-Scale Fisheries: Global Reflections*. pp. 39–59. Center for
Maritime Research.

De La Torre-Castro, M. 2012. Governance for sustainability: insights from marine resource use in a tropical setting in the Western Indian Ocean. *Coastal Management*, 40, 612–633.

de la Torre-Castro, M., and Lindström, L. 2010. Fishing institutions: addressing regulative, normative
and cultural-cognitive elements to enhance fisheries management. *Marine Policy*, 34, 1, 77–84.
https://doi.org/10.1016/j.marpol.2009.04.012.

De Santo, E. M. 2013. Missing marine protected area (MPA) targets: how the push for quantity over
quality undermines sustainability and social justice. *Journal of Environmental Management*, 124,
137–146. https://doi.org/10.1016/j.jenvman.2013.01.033.

Dietz, T., Ostrom, E., and Stern, P. C. 2003. The struggle to govern the commons. *Science*, 302, 1907.

Eriksson, H., Albert, J., Albert, S., Warren, R., Pakoa, K., and Andrew, N. 2017. The role of fish and
fisheries in recovering from natural hazards: lessons learned from Vanuatu. *Environmental Science
and Policy*, 76, 50–58. https://doi.org/10.1016/j.envsci.2017.06.012.

Evans, L. S., Brown, K., and Allison, E. H. 2011. Factors influencing adaptive marine governance in
a developing country context. *Ecology and Society*, 16, 2. *JSTOR*. http://www.jstor.org.ezproxy1.lib
.asu.edu/stable/26268893.

Fabinyi, M., and Barclay, K. 2022. Fisheries governance. In M. Fabinyi and K. Barclay (Eds.),
Asia-Pacific Fishing Livelihoods. pp. 65–90. Springer International Publishing. https://doi.org/10
.1007/978-3-030-79591-7_4.

Fanning, L., and Mahon, R. 2020. Governance of the global ocean commons: hopelessly fragmented
or fixable? *Coastal Management*, 48, 6, 527–533. https://doi.org/10.1080/08920753.2020.1803563.

Fidelman, P., Evans, L., Fabinyi, M., Foale, S., Cinner, J., and Rosen, F. 2012. Governing large-scale
marine commons: contextual challenges in the Coral Triangle. *Marine Policy*, 36, 1, 42–53. https://
doi.org/10.1016/j.marpol.2011.03.007.

Folke, C., Pritchard Jr, L., Berkes, F., Colding, J., and Svedin, U. 2007. The problem of fit between
ecosystems and institutions: ten years later. *Ecology and Society*, 12, 1, 30.

Folke, C., Hahn, T., Olsson, P., and Norberg, J. 2005. Adaptive governance of social-ecological systems.
Annual Review of Environment and Resources, 30, 1, 441–473. https://doi.org/10.1146/annurev
.energy.30.050504.144511.

Frangoudes, K., and Gerrard, S. 2018. (En)gendering change in small-scale fisheries and fishing communities in a globalized world. *Maritime Studies*. https://doi.org/10.1007/s40152-018-0113-9.

Govan, H. 2009. *Status and Potential of Locally-Managed Marine Areas in the South Pacific: Meeting nature conservation and sustainable livelihood targets through widespread implementation of LMMAs* (Study Report Component 3A-Project 3A3 Institutional Strengthening and technical support). SPREP/WWF/WorldFish-Reefbase/CRISP. https://pipap.sprep.org/content/status-and -potential-locally-managed-marine-areas-south-pacific-meeting-nature-conservation.

Greenhill, L., Kenter, J. O., and Dannevig, H. 2020. Adaptation to climate change–related ocean acidification: an adaptive governance approach. *Ocean and Coastal Management*, 191, 105176. https://doi .org/10.1016/j.ocecoaman.2020.105176.

Gruby, R. L., Gray, N. J., Fairbanks, L., Havice, E., Campbell, L. M., Friedlander, A., Oleson, K. L. L., Sam, K., Mitchell, L., and Hanich, Q. 2021. Policy interactions in large-scale marine protected areas. *Conservation Letters*, 14, 1, e12753. https://doi.org/10.1111/conl.12753.

Gurney, G. G., Mangubhai, S., Fox, M., Kiatkoski Kim, M., and Agrawal, A. 2021. Equity in environmental governance: perceived fairness of distributional justice principles in marine co-management. *Environmental Science and Policy*, 124, 23–32. https://doi.org/10.1016/j.envsci.2021.05.022.

Gustavsson, M., Frangoudes, K., Lindström, L., Ávarez, M. C., and de la Torre Castro, M. 2021. Gender and Blue Justice in small-scale fisheries governance. *Marine Policy*, 133, 104743. https://doi.org/10 .1016/j.marpol.2021.104743.

Haas, B., Mackay, M., Novaglio, C., Fullbrook, L., Murunga, M., Sbrocchi, C., McDonald, J., McCormack, P. C., Alexander, K., Fudge, M., Goldsworthy, L., Boschetti, F., Dutton, I., Dutra, L., McGee, J., Rousseau, Y., Spain, E., Stephenson, R., Vince, J., … Haward, M. 2021. The future of ocean governance. *Reviews in Fish Biology and Fisheries*. https://doi.org/10.1007/s11160-020-09631 -x.

Hannesson, R. 2008. The exclusive economic zone and economic development in the Pacific island countries. *Marine Policy*, 32, 6, 886–897. https://doi.org/10.1016/j.marpol.2008.01.002.

Haugen, B. I., Cramer, L. A., Waldbusser, G. G., and Conway, F. D. L. 2021. Resilience and adaptive capacity of Oregon's fishing community: cumulative impacts of climate change and the graying of the fleet. *Marine Policy*, 126, 104424. https://doi.org/10.1016/j.marpol.2021.104424.

Horigue, V., Fabinyi, M., Pressey, R. L., Foale, S., and Aliño, P. M. 2016. Influence of governance context on the management performance of marine protected area networks. *Coastal Management*, 44, 1, 71–91. Environment Complete.

Humphreys, J., and Clark, R. W. E. 2020. A critical history of marine protected areas. In J. Humphreys and R. W. E. Clark (Eds.), *Marine Protected Areas*. pp. 1–12. Elsevier. https://doi.org/10.1016/B978 -0-08-102698-4.00001-0.

Hunter, C. E., Lauer, M., Levine, A., Holbrook, S., and Rassweiler, A. 2018. Maneuvering towards adaptive co-management in a coral reef fishery. *Marine Policy*, 98, 77–84. https://doi.org/10.1016/j .marpol.2018.09.016.

IUCN. 2008. *Establishing Marine Protected Area Networks: Making it Happen*. IUCN World Commission on Protected Areas.

Jeffers, J. 2010. Climate change and the Arctic: adapting to changes in fisheries stocks and governance regimes. *Ecology Law Quarterly*, 37, 3, 917–977. JSTOR.

Jentoft, S., McCay, B. J., and Wilson, D. C. 2010. Fisheries co-management: improving fisheries governance through stakeholder participation. In R. Q. Grafton, R. Hilborn, D. Squires, M. Tait, and Meryl. J. Williams (Eds.), *Handbook of Marine Fisheries Conservation and Management*. pp. 675–686. Oxford University Press.

Kelly, C., Ellis, G., and Flannery, W. 2018. Conceptualising change in marine governance: learning from transition management. *Marine Policy*, 95, 24–35. https://doi.org/10.1016/j.marpol.2018.06.023.

Kleiber, D., Frangoudes, K., Snyder, H., Choudhry, A., Cole, S. M., Soejima, K., Pita, C., Santos, A., Mcdougall, C., Petrics, H., and Porter, M. 2017. promoting gender equity and equality through the small-scale fisheries guidelines: experiences from multiple case studies. In S. Jentoft, R. Chuenpagdee, M. Barragán-Paladines, and N. Franz (Eds.), *The Small-Scale Fisheries Guidelines* (Vol. 14). Amsterdam University Press. 10.1007/978-3-319-55074-9_35.

Knudsen, S. 1995. Fisheries along the Eastern Black Sea Coast of Turkey: informal resource-management in small-scale fishing in the shadow of a dominant capitalist fishery. *Human Organization*, 54, 4, 437–448.

Kurlansky, M. 1998. *Cod: A Biography of the Fish that Changed the World*. Penguin Books.

Lemos, M. C., and Agrawal, A. 2006. Environmental governance. *Annual Review of Environment and Resources*, 31, 1, 297–325.

Levine, A., Richmond, L. S., and Lopez-Carr, D. 2015. Marine resource management: culture, livelihoods, and governance. *Applied Geography*, 59, 56–59.

Mahon, R., and Fanning, L. 2019. Regional ocean governance: polycentric arrangements and their role in global ocean governance. *Marine Policy*, 107, 103590. https://doi.org/10.1016/j.marpol.2019.103590.

Mahon, R., McConney, P., and Roy, R. N. 2008. Governing fisheries as complex adaptive systems. *Marine Policy*, 32, 1, 104–112. https://doi.org/10.1016/j.marpol.2007.04.011.

McCay, B. J., and Finlayson, A. 1995. The political ecology of crisis and institutional change: the case of the Northern Cod. Annual Meeting of the American Anthropological Association, Washington, DC, November 15.

McCay, B. J., and Jones, P. J. S. 2011. Marine protected areas and the governance of marine ecosystems and fisheries. *Conservation Biology*, 25, 6, 1130–1133.

Olsson, P., Folke, C., and Berkes, F. 2004. Adaptive comanagement for building resilience in social-ecological systems. *Environmental Management*, 34, 75–90. https://doi.org/10.1007/s00267-003-0101-7.

Ostrom, E. 2005. *Understanding Institutional Diversity*. Princeton University Press.

Ostrom, E., Burger, J., Field, C., Norgaard, R., and Policansky, D. 1999. Revisiting the commons: local lessons, global challenges. *Science*, 284, 278–282. https://doi.org/10.1126/science.284.5412.278.

Österblom, H., and Folke, C. 2013. Emergence of global adaptive governance for stewardship of regional marine resources. *Ecology and Society*, 18, 2, 1–13.

Partelow, S., Schlüter, A., Armitage, D., Bavinck, M., Carlisle, K., Gruby, R. L., Hornidge, A.-K., Le Tissier, M., Pittman, J. B., Song, A. M., Sousa, L. P., Văidianu, N., and Van Assche, K. 2020. Environmental governance theories: a review and application to coastal systems. *Ecology and Society*, 25, 4. https://doi.org/10.5751/ES-12067-250419.

Pedroza-Gutiérrez, C., Vidal-Hernández, L., and Rivera-Arriaga, E. 2021. Adaptive governance and coping strategies in the Yucatan Peninsula coasts facing COVID-19. *Ocean & Coastal Management*, 212, 105814. https://doi.org/10.1016/j.ocecoaman.2021.105814.

Pinsky, M. L., Fenichel, E., Fogarty, M., Levin, S., McCay, B., St. Martin, K., Selden, R. L., and Young, T. 2021. Fish and fisheries in hot water: what is happening and how do we adapt? *Population Ecology*, 63, 1, 17–26. https://doi.org/10.1002/1438-390X.12050.

Plummer, R., Armitage, D. R., and de Loë, R. C. 2013. Adaptive comanagement and its relationship to environmental governance. *Ecology and Society*, 18, 1, 21. https://doi.org/10.5751/ES-05383-180121.

Quimby, B., and Levine, A. 2018. Participation, power, and equity: examining three key social dimensions of fisheries comanagement. *Sustainability*, 10, 9, 3324. escholarship.org/uc/item/76z69144. https://doi.org/10.3390/su10093324.

Quimby, B., and Levine, A. 2021. Adaptive capacity of marine comanagement: a comparative analysis of the influence of colonial legacies and integrated traditional governance on outcomes in the Pacific. *Regional Environmental Change*, 21, 1, 10. https://doi.org/10.1007/s10113-020-01730-6.

Reed, M. S., Evely, A. C., Cundill, G., Fazey, I., Glass, J., Laing, A., Newig, J., Parrish, B., Prell, C., Raymond, C., and Stringer, L. C. 2010. What is social learning? Response to Pahl-Wostl 2006 "The Importance of Social Learning in Restoring the Multifunctionality of Rivers and Floodplains." *Ecology and Society*, 15, 4, r1.

Reed, M. S., Vella, S., Challies, E., de Vente, J., Frewer, L., Hohenwallner-Ries, D., Huber, T., Neumann, R. K., Oughton, E. A., Sidoli del Ceno, J., and van Delden, H. 2018. A theory of participation: what makes stakeholder and public engagement in environmental management work? *Restoration Ecology*, 26, S1, S7–S17. https://doi.org/10.1111/rec.12541.

Rubio, I., Hileman, J., and Ojea, E. 2021. Social connectivity and adaptive capacity strategies in large-scale fisheries. *Ecology and Society*, 26, 2. https://doi.org/10.5751/ES-12395-260242.

Schoeffel, P. (Ed.) 1985. Women in the fisheries of the South Pacific. In *Women in Development in the South Pacific: Barriers and Opportunities,* pp. 156–175. Australian National University.

Sims, D. W., and Southward, A. J. 2006. Dwindling fish numbers already of concern in 1883. *Nature*, 439, 7077, 660–660. https://doi.org/10.1038/439660c.

Soma, K., van Tatenhove, J., and van Leeuwen, J. 2015. Marine governance in a European context: regionalization, integration and cooperation for ecosystem-based management. *Marine Governance in European Seas: Processes and Structures of Regionalization*, 117, 4–13. https://doi.org/10.1016/j.ocecoaman.2015.03.010.

St. Martin, K. 2006. The impact of "community" on fisheries management in the US Northeast. *Geoforum*, 37, 2, 169–184. https://doi.org/10.1016/j.geoforum.2005.05.004.

Steinberg, P. E. 2013. Of other seas: metaphors and materialities in maritime regions. *Atlantic Studies*, 10, 2, 156–169.

Steinberg, P. E. 2001. *The Social Construction of the Ocean*. Cambridge University Press.

Steinberg, P., and Peters, K. 2015. Wet ontologies, fluid spaces: giving depth to volume through oceanic thinking. *Environment and Planning D: Society and Space*, 33, 2, 247–264. https://doi.org/10.1068/d14148p.

Tam, J., Waring, T., Gelcich, S., Chan, K. M. A., and Satterfield, T. 2021. Measuring behavioral social learning in a conservation context: Chilean fishing communities. *Conservation Science and Practice*, 3, 1, e336. https://doi.org/10.1111/csp2.336.

Tuda, A. O., Kark, S., and Newton, A. 2021. Polycentricity and adaptive governance of transboundary marine socio-ecological systems. *Ocean & Coastal Management*, 200, 105412.

Tuda, A. O., Kark, S., and Newton, A. 2019. Exploring the prospects for adaptive governance in marine transboundary conservation in East Africa. *Marine Policy*, 104, 75–84.

Vince, J., and Hardesty, B. D. 2017. Plastic pollution challenges in marine and coastal environments: from local to global governance. *Restoration Ecology*, 25, 1, 123–128. https://doi.org/10.1111/rec.12388

Weeks, R., and Jupiter, S. D. 2013. Adaptive comanagement of a marine protected area network in Fiji. *Conservation Biology*, 27, 6, 1234–1244. JSTOR.

Wilson, J. A. 2006. Matching social and ecological systems in complex ocean fisheries. *Ecology and Society*, 11, 1, 263–284. 8gh.

Wright, G. 2015. Marine governance in an industrialised ocean: a case study of the emerging marine renewable energy industry. *Marine Policy*, 52, 77–84. https://doi.org/10.1016/j.marpol.2014.10.021.

Zafra-Calvo, N., Pascual, U., Brockington, D., Coolsaet, B., Cortez-Vazquez, J. A., Gross-Camp, N., Palomo, I., and Burgess, N. D. 2017. Towards an indicator system to assess equitable management in protected areas. *Biological Conservation*, 211, 134–141.

10. Adaptive governance in open data ecosystems: experiences and insights on the role of sociotechnical arrangements
Cancan Wang

INTRODUCTION

In the past decade, the accelerating development and deployment of data infrastructure has reinstated *open data* movements across the globe to make public data accessible for various socio-economic gains, including increased transparency, efficiency of public services, innovation, and entrepreneurship (Corrales-Garay et al., 2019; Janssen et al., 2012). With these promises come uncertainties, such as the ambition of innovation around open data-based applications, and complexities in coordinating a large-scale open data ecosystem that involves citizens, communities, policy makers, institutions, and private actors.

The uncertainties and complexities are challenging for existing governance approaches. On the one hand, the control-oriented governance approach that is oriented towards stability through command-and-control measures, such as defining, enforcing, and monitoring data activities, often fails to respond in a timely manner to the evolving sociotechnical complexities around open data across jurisdictional boundaries (Wang and Staykova, 2019). On the other hand, the community-driven approach that emerges from informal networks while capable of addressing ad hoc contextualised situations through fast learning, can also suffer from issues such as representation or transfer of knowledge in its long-term transition to more stable governance form (Wang et al., 2020).

Adaptive governance (Chaffin et al., 2014; Dietz et al., 2003) that was originally introduced as an alternative governance approach to address large-scale problems in socioecological systems in a flexible, responsive, yet stable manner, is therefore particularly relevant for examining the governance in complex sociotechnical systems such as open data ecosystems (Janssen and van der Voort, 2016; Wang et al., 2017). In this study, I follow the development of the open data movement in Shanghai between 2015 and 2020 and the local governance experiences to exemplify how the concept of adaptive governance can help envision a new form of data governance that can potentially strike a balance between change and stability and learning and control.

Resonating with the existing discussion on stability and change in adaptive governance (Chaffin and Gunderson, 2016), the findings suggest that while informal networks are important in the learning process across open data ecosystem, continuous experimentations of governance form play a critical role in addressing the need for control as complexities of ecosystem evolve. Foregrounding the role of technology, this study particularly brings attention to the mediating role of *daily* communication technologies, and how actors in the ecosystem strategically use them as an experimental field for governance. Moreover, I also emphasise the role of data resource as a governance subject in shaping the choice of governance form in the long run. I argue that long-term choice of governance form is largely influenced by the different views of data as a social resource.

In the following, I will start by introducing open data, the challenges it brings to the current governance approaches, and how the current understanding of adaptive governance in socio-technical system may help to relieve the open data related governance challenges. Drawing on critical institutionalism, I present our conceptualisation of adaptive governance in open data ecosystem as a process of institutional bricolage on governance form that is contingent on the logics of data as a governance subject, and constituted by sociotechnical arrangements around identity, working norms, decision-making authority, and ownership. Based on a longitudinal study on the governance of a local open data ecosystem in Shanghai, I explore the concept adaptive governance empirically through four questions: What are the governance dilemmas in the open data ecosystem? How did adaptive governance emerge in an open data ecosystem and address this dilemma? How to understand adaptive governance as a sociotechnical arrangement? What can we learn about adaptive governance by looking into the context of sociotechnical ecosystem? In this case study, I follow the change in the governance form of the open data ecosystem and the practices lead up to these changes as the main empirical subject. Looking at the governance practices, I draw on three primary data sources that were collected between 2015–2020: my participant observation in the offline meetups and online chats and in-depth as well as semi-structured interviews with leaders in the open data ecosystem.

Along this line, this study contributes to the understanding of adaptive governance by exemplifying its manifestation in an open data ecosystem and bringing new insights to its conceptualisation by foregrounding the mediating role of sociotechnical arrangements (i.e., people's engagement with daily communication technologies and data as a social resource), which is relevant for understanding the adaptive governance of socioecological systems as well.

BACKGROUND

Open Data and Governance Challenges

Technology development has always been a challenging object of governance due to its uncertainties and complexities (Mandel, 2009; Moor, 2005). While the uncertainties are associated with the potential benefits and risks of technologies, the complexities have to do with the range of actors and how they are implicated in the conceptualisation, development, and implementation of technology.

Today, one of the prevalent examples of uncertain and complex technological development can be found in information technology. In the past decades, we have seen an exponential growth of internet-based, data driven technologies, such as big data, machine learning and artificial intelligence. With the prevalence of these data-based technologies, the open data movement, which advocates that data can be accessed, used, or shared by anyone, came into being amidst different ideas of data as a social resource (Baack, 2015; Hess and Ostrom, 2006). The open data movement is influenced by two paralleled movements: big data and open source; each advocate for a different view of data ownership, knowledge, and the agency and rights of human actors. On the one hand, open data is related to big data, which focuses on how big data technologies and algorithms generate knowledge using the digital traces of systems and people's behaviours. Data generated this way are often not re-contextualised into the experience of everyday life, thus impede data generators to act in an agentic manner. Data in this context is commonly processed by specific organisations or actors and considered as privately owned assets. They are used for generating values that benefit the data utilisers, such as companies and governments (Kitchin, 2014; LaValle et al., 2011; Wamba et al., 2015). On the other hand, open data is closely associated with the open-source movement, which is fundamentally concerned with rights to access and distribution of knowledge. Different from the focus in big data, open source focuses on voluntary participation and collaboration, granting access to the source code of software and incorporating contributions from potentially everyone. In this sense, the generated data, especially the ones through public service, are considered a shared social resource at a societal level (Willinsky, 2005).

These divergent movements provide a complex picture of who owns data and data infrastructure as important social resources in the emerging open data ecosystem. As data is processed through a diverse and evolving range of actors, depending on how data is created, mediated, and used, these actors may perceive themselves as the owner of the data thus entitled to decide on the data-related standards. For example, when citizens use a public service, citizens, government, and private service providers may all feel like they are the legitimate owner of data resources. This also means that actors, each from their own perspective, may have different perceptions of data related benefits and risks, and thus engage in different ways of controlling the flow of data. Private entities may be interested in opening their data as a way of generating value for innovation that can be converted into market benefits, while NGOs may be interested in ensuring the citizens' rights and privacy are not infringed. In addition, open data also concerns technical infrastructure that needs to be coordinated at a societal level, such as how data infrastructure is set up, what types of data should be open, in what way and to which degree data should be open. Divergence in the perception of technical needs and standards by different data actors thus can create obstacles for open data to materialise at a large scale.

Governance of an open data ecosystem, that is the ways of coordinating resources and decision-making around open data at a societal level, thus presents a quandary for existing governance approaches, including: (1) the good governance approaches perspective which focuses on the principles of a properly functioned state and government operations; (2) the New Public Management approach that focuses on efficiency and efficacy by involving non-state actors and introducing private management principles to government operations; (3) the corporate IT governance approach that focuses on the control of data as an asset via designed distribution of decision-making rights and accountability to generate future profits; (4) multi-level governance that distributes the decision-making power vertically across bureaucratic structures within government and horizontally across boundaries of government agencies and non-government organisations and actors; and (5) network governance that emphasises the use of informal networks within a social system (Osborne, 2010; Wang, 2019).

The good governance approach and the new public management approach take a specific stance by focusing on either government operations or involving non-state actors, thus failing to capture the complexity in the range of actors and the evolving nature of open data as an emerging sociotechnical system. Corporate IT governance approach that focuses on command and control assumes the existence of closed range of stakeholders and considers data primarily as privately owned resources – assets. Although multi-level governance takes into consideration the range of involved actors in a sociotechnical system, its focus on enforcing structures and process design does not address the rapid changes associated with sociotechnical systems.

Network governance, though focusing on the emergent coordination practices among informal social networks, neglects the interaction with formal control mechanisms such as regulation and bureaucracy.

The emerging open data ecosystem, thus, requires a balancing act that supports continuous learning about the stakeholders' interests and interactions as well as the ownership of data and data infrastructure while keeping control of technical needs and sharing standards. Recently, there has been an increasing focus on developing alternative governance philosophy for sociotechnical systems, that is adaptive governance that focuses on governing complex systems. Below I will briefly describe the origin of adaptive governance in the context of a socioecological system and explain why adaptive governance is a suitable philosophy for an open data ecosystem.

Adaptive Governance in Sociotechnical Systems

Adaptive governance is a governance philosophy that addresses how humans cope with forms of complexity and uncertainty in socioecological systems (Brunner et al., 2005; Chaffin et al., 2014; Chaffin and Gunderson, 2016; Cleaver and Whaley, 2018; Juhola and Westerhoff, 2011). Overall, adaptive governance argues for an *experimental* approach, which consists of testing policy as hypotheses, *learning* from the test and adapting according to changing contexts. Adaptive governance systems focus on *resilience* instead of *efficiency* and are characterised by emerging and evolving networks of stakeholders that promote social learning, power sharing and flexible institutions capable of accommodating and responding to changes and uncertainties arising from both environmental and social sources. Overall, adaptive governance scholars argue against the *command-and-control* approaches to manage complexity and uncertainty in socioecological system.

Recently, adaptive governance has been introduced to address sociotechnical complexity and uncertainty in the context of digital government (Janssen and van der Voort, 2016; Wang et al., 2017). The proponents argue that in the face of rapid technological development, there are increasing demands from stakeholders and digital technologies to which existing governance mechanisms need to adapt. For instance, while technological innovation requires some freedom in legislation for trial and error without liability, technologies also pose risks that are difficult to foresee but require timely control. Existing control-oriented governance mechanisms such as legislation and procedures are reactive and inflexible, and lagging behind the expectations of businesses and citizens, posing requests for governments to transform their way of engaging with technological development.

Adaptive governance scholars have made prescriptions on how adaptive governance can help to balance between the demands of different stakeholders in the digital realm, by focusing on social learning through decentralised bottom-up decision-making, efforts to mobilise internal and external capabilities, "wider participation to spot and internalise developments, and continuous adjustments to deal with uncertainty" (Janssen and van der Voort, 2016, p. 4). Some have proposed that adaptiveness in the governance of public digital transformation can arise from the decoupling of decision-making power and accountability between public and private stakeholders (Wang et al., 2017). Some focused on how adaptive governance is increasingly mediated by information and communication technologies, such as social media in crisis response (Chatfield and Reddick, 2017) and large-scale collaborations (Wang et al., 2020). Some also embarked on how adaptiveness in regulation can arise from decoupling between liability and accountability (Wang and Staykova, 2019) as well as decentralisation (Hong and Lee, 2018).

Nonetheless, less attention has been given to the specific technological context such, as an open data ecosystem, and how adaptive governance can address different logics of data as a resource. This question is particularly important for the development of adaptive governance as a concept, as the foundation of adaptive governance is built upon public resources as commons (Hess and Ostrom, 2006; Ostrom, 1990). To engage with this inquiry, it is important to understand not only how adaptive governance principles are manifested but also how different governance practices interplay with different views of data as a resource.

UNDERSTANDING ADAPTIVE GOVERNANCE AS INSTITUTIONAL BRICOLAGE

This study draws on the approach of critical institutionalism (Cleaver and Koning, 2015; Cleaver and Whaley, 2018) to understand governance as collective arrangements that are subject to human contingency and "a mix of economic, emotional, moral and social rationalities informed by different logics and world-views" (Cleaver and Koning, 2015, p. 4). I specifically use the concept of institutional logics and institutional bricolage as sense-making devices to conceptualise the emergence of governance arrangements in an open data ecosystem.

As I have mentioned previously, the idea of open data is influenced by several paralleled movements including big data and open source. These movements gave rise to distinctive views of data as a social resource, and how it should be governed accordingly. From an institutional logics perspective, "socially-constructed, historical patterns of material practices, including assumptions, values, beliefs and rules" (Thornton et al., 2012, p. 2) provide actors with guidelines for how to make decisions on particular issues, determine which of these issues demand managerial attentions, and frame possible solutions (Gawer and Phillips, 2013; Thornton, 2002). Similarly, actors in an open data ecosystem may have different imaginaries and practices of data depending on their professional or individual experiences. For instance, during my fieldwork in the Shanghai open data ecosystem, I have observed two divergent views of data as a social resource among my informants: data as private assets for generating financial values (Birch and Muniesa, 2020), and as commons shared between relevant actors in the society (Beckwith et al., 2019).

Subsequently, these views influence how actors consider data as a governance subject by framing what they consider as data associated issues, and how these issues should be solved appropriately in terms of sources of legitimacy, authority, collective identity as well as norms, attention, and strategy (Thornton et al., 2012). For instance, some of my informants who are members of an open knowledge community considered data as a community resource that is meant to be freely used by citizen groups. Thus, they would see a municipality's interests in owning and controlling open data infrastructure as detrimental for its development, and demand power sharing and flexible institutions that can accommodate diverse and changing needs in citizens' data practices. By contrast, some members in a municipality may consider data as a resource with economic value that a municipality controls with expectations of future profit through data-driven innovation. Following this thought, they may be inclined to structure and execute decision-making rights in a certain way to ensure data generates economic values expectedly. Moreover, individuals may also subscribe to different institutional logics or engage in institutional work that changes collective identities and practice over time.

In this sense, when a new sociotechnical phenomenon such as open data emerges, while there may be a governance void initially, as actors interact with data and amongst each other, different data imaginaries and practices may arise and be mobilised to consider data a governance subject. As a result, actors may be up against varying demands of "appropriate" governance arrangements, following particular views and practices of data.

In this context, adaptive governance therefore can be understood as how actors adapt to these fragmented demands by creatively blending, layering, and piecing together ways of coordinating resources in response to daily challenges in an open data ecosystem. The concept institutional bricolage (Cleaver and Koning, 2015) particularly sheds light on adaptative governance as a process where people, consciously and non-consciously, assemble and reshape institutional arrangements around resource coordination and decision-making. It brings our attention to the daily practices where experimentation of governance arrangements takes place. Looking into how people relate to the sociotechnical world, power dynamics and technology of control in particular help us to understand how governance experimentations are shaped through people's daily practices.

More specifically, people have cultivated different ways to order their social and technological worlds in daily practices. These ways of ordering the worlds shape how people assemble governance arrangements by influencing what they consider as the appropriate sources of authority and identity. For instance, people can choose certain governance arrangements out of pragmatic or strategic needs. But people's emotions, symbolic world views and moral considerations can also be sources for legitimising their choice of governance arrangements.

As assembling governance arrangement is a collective action that often involves multiple actors in an ecosystem, the exercise of the actor's agency can also be shaped by the power dynamics people perceive among themselves. The power dynamics can take place, for instance, between power attributed through regulations and organisational functions, power adhering to professional expertise and political roles, power accompanied by possession of resources, and power emerged through the informal interactions between actors. This also means that the variability in people's identities can enable people's negotiation over their access and rights to resources, discourses, and meanings, as well as representation and participation, and in this way shape the assemblage of the governance arrangements.

In addition, technology is also an important actor for shaping governance arrangements (Forsberg, 2018), especially given that today communication and coordination are increasingly mediated through information technologies such as social media (e.g., Slack) or collaborative technologies (Teams). While actors can use these technologies for social learning and expanding networks, they can also use them to exercise varying extent of control (Wang et al., 2020).

In our case, the governance form of the open data ecosystem in Shanghai shifted from community to corporate. Rather than viewing such transition as an abrupt change, in this paper, I look at it as an accumulation of contextualised daily experimentation. Next, I zoom in on the transition in the governance form by unfolding the bricolage work that went into these transitions. I illustrate how adaptive governance is effective in addressing the initial void of data governance as well as the competing logics of data and governance demands over time.

ADAPTIVE GOVERNANCE OF THE OPEN DATA ECOSYSTEM IN SHANGHAI

Open Data in Shanghai

Before I unfold the emergence of adaptive governance arrangements in the open data ecosystem in Shanghai, I start by briefly introducing the development of open data in Shanghai, and why I consider the empirical context relevant for exploring the concept of adaptive governance empirically.

In 2015, Shanghai was among the first municipalities in China to experiment with different ways to promote and utilise open government data, among which one major effort was to establish a municipal level contest – Shanghai Open Data Applications (SODA) – to award the best applications developed using open government data. At the time, the local open data landscape was almost empty, with very few distributed grassroot online groups on open data and open knowledge. The goals of the contest were to foster a unifying community of open data advocates, tap the potential benefits of open data in service and product development, and experiment with new ways of governance (Gao, 2018).

The contest was organised in 2015 by an interest group, made up by seven actors from municipal government, IT industry, Non-governmental Organisations (NGOs) and research institutes, who got to know each other through an open data seminar that took place the year before. Although the contest had substantial involvement of government officials from the local municipality, it was not officially funded or owned by Shanghai Municipality. Rather, the contest heavily relied on the interest group members and their networks, especially the ones with existing grassroot open data groups online. The connection and coordination that went into organising the contest were made possible through collaborative platforms such as WeChat, where people across organisations or distance can discuss and work together online.

Following the success of the contest in 2015, the Shanghai Municipality decided to continue the project annually, with an increasing number of local municipal bureaus and businesses agreeing to share data through the contest. In 2016, four of the actors founded a company S to manage the operation of the contest. Subsequently, the four actors became shareholders of the company. In 2017, the four shareholders founded a new company D to restructure the share distribution among them. They do by having company S and two shareholders of S re-invested in the new company, leaving some room for a fifth shareholder.

I found the governance of the open data ecosystem in Shanghai interesting for illustrating adaptive governance for three reasons. First, the open data ecosystem in Shanghai was characterised by a governance void due to its nascency, thus providing a relevant case to understand how actors do bricolage work to establish governance arrangements and adapt over time in response to sociotechnical changes. Second, China provides an interesting institutional context where experimental governance, that is, central policymaking relying on experiences of the local governance experiment, is foregrounded as a way to address uncertainty related to emerging technologies (Heilmann, 2008; Wang and Staykova, 2019). In this way, one can argue social actors' bricolage work is invited to address the governance void in a new sociotechnical phenomenon such as open data. Nonetheless, it is also expected that these bricolage governance work may be formalised into state policies over time, presenting another condition for adaptation. Third, open data as a phenomenon is increasingly relevant to the management of natural resources, as big data analytics are increasingly used for monitoring resource usage or environmental impacts. Understanding the dilemma and response in the governance of open data can also shed light on the advancement in understanding the governance of socioecological systems.

2015–2020: Evolving Development and Governance Arrangements

Initial stage

In 2015, the local actors' primary focus was to find out how to identify, build and mobilise resources and capacities for organising open data in Shanghai, as there was no large-scale open government data initiative held in China prior to that. The local actors' ambition at the time was to focus on government data and use contest as an experimental form to test out what are the landscape of actors, their demands, needed resources and capacities, as well as the potential barriers and benefits for involved parties.

To do so, two first movers – Zhang, the Chief Executive Officer (CEO) of a state-owned enterprise and Gao, the director of the first open data NGO in China – who met each other in an open data workshop funded by the World Bank, set out to scout and assemble a group of people to organise the first open data contest in China. They reached out through their professional networks, including Zhang's former colleagues in the local government, Gao's online network of open data enthusiasts in the country, and people they met in the open data workshop. Zhang and Gao established contacts with a few practitioners who endorsed the value of open data, and who had data-related expertise, resources, or capacities. An unusual trait of this assemblage is that it not only included actors who are in leadership positions in their organisations, such as, section heads in local government, heads of research centres in university, CEOs of state-owned enterprise. It also involved start-ups, small and medium enterprises (SMEs) and NGOs. Zhang regarded this choice of involvement as *community building* based on relevant expertise and shared interests rather than organisational affiliations.

Zhang and Gao built the open data community by connecting newcomers in a chat group on a popular messaging application – WeChat. The chat group was named as "open data advocates", and soon became a space for knowledge sharing and remote work, where people dropped important files, introduced relevant contacts, and socialised with each other. This group was particularly important for the members to form a collective identity outside their affiliated workplace and to create shared work norms that help to make things happen within a short period of time. For instance, a start-up CEO initially anticipated government actors to follow a 9 to 5 schedule and "prefer meetings over actions". He was surprised to see that everyone in the group worked around the clock and acted as "an entrepreneur".

In addition, as interactions between members are visible in the chat group, persistent presence in the chat group became a sign of commitment, and an important consideration for the distribution of decision-making power in the group. The members who constantly contributed to the chat group soon gained more significance in making operational decisions. The online chat also made members' preferences and engagement of involvement in different tasks more visible. Subsequently, people started to identify different actors' roles in the ecosystem: government actors were better at bringing contacts and brokering data sources; start-ups were strong and efficient in coming up with solutions to store data and ensure data security; NGOs had a wide knowledge about international success cases of open data applications; university research centres were good at conceptualising and developing a narrative around open data appropriate for the local context.

From the discussion, the members considered contest as a means to discover stakeholder groups, explore possible data-driven outcomes and connect the stakeholders in the open data ecosystem. Because of the collective participation in organising the contest, the contest is viewed as a shared product where all the involved members can claim ownership. For this reason, the members decided not to engage any public or private sponsorship to avoid a particular party claiming ownership of their collective efforts. The resources used for organising the contest are instead "borrowed" via the members' networks. Some members brought in their own organisational resources, such as an employee or an event venue, to help to organise the contest.

In parallel to the digital arrangements in the chat group on WeChat, the members also engaged in other types of symbolic work, which helped to unite different views around open data and its potential benefits. For instance, the abbreviation of the open data contest, SODA, is drawn on by some of the stakeholders to present a worldview where data-related uncertainty symbolises growth rather than chaos. In the official narratives and news reports of the contest, the abbreviation SODA is viewed as a metaphor for data: Just like soda water is still when it is bottled, data is the same. But once the bottle is open, data can release "smart energy" once it is open, just like the opened soda. The metaphor of SODA particularly helped the municipal actors, who were initially afraid of the "destructive chaos" caused by open data, to establish a positive imaginary of open data, and recognised the legitimacy of the community-driven data application contest as an effective way to map out data-related resources in the early stage of the open data movement. The metaphor also helped to establish the relevance of open data for the non-data professionals in the group by showing data can also be understood as a common artefact.

Overall, the emergent *community building* practices in- and out-side the chat group helped to cope with the initial governance void in the nascent open data ecosystem. These practices helped to establish ways of working and coordination, roles, and decision-making structure among the members. The technical features of the digitalised chat group, including its name and group member setup, acted as a materialised frame of reference to which the members can relate their identity as an open data advocate, and sustain their relations in the emerging open data ecosystem. The community-driven governance practices proved to be effective for organising the ecosystem through contest: within three months, the members had convinced local governments, public institutions, and private companies to share 10 transportation-related datasets with the public through the contest. These available datasets drew more than 800 teams and more than 500 proposals across the country to attend the contest. The contest resulted in applicable proposals for new business models, policy guidance, and service or product solutions for data providers.

Expansion stage

Following the success of the contest in 2015, the members refocused the new contests on the expansion of the open data ecosystem, including widening the themes of the shared dataset from transportation to city safety and other social issues, attracting more public bureaus, government agencies, and private organisations to the open data ecosystem and making their datasets available to the public. Meanwhile, government agencies and companies have also become more interested in the membership of the contest with different offers of sponsorship to financially support the contest. After the contest in 2015, the members at the time conducted an evaluation on the organisation of the contest and decided to keep the membership in chat group open in the spirit of "open" data. This also means, with new offers and membership requests, newcomers (such as leaders in different levels of government) are invited into the chat group to share relevant information and participate in day-to-day discussion and decision-making.

With newcomers there also came tensions, which revolved around working norms, membership, and decision-making. These tensions were made visible in the chat group. Soon after the new members from district governments were invited into the chat group, the existing members realised the newcomers did not engage in the same way. For instance, the members from district government were not aware that they were expected to give immediate feedback on the documents that people shared in the group. As one of the members recalled, "I just don't understand what they [new members] are doing sometimes. There is one time we agreed to write a campaign article together. I finished the draft and put it in the group, expecting them to comment on it. But they dragged for days to respond, and when they responded I don't even think we are on the same page."

These miscommunications reportedly slowed down the work and created a lot of frustrations in the group. After some time, some old members got together and decided to solve this issue by dividing the chat group into two: one with the old members from 2015; and the other one with everyone including the newcomers that came later. While daily decisions were made in the new group, critical decisions were discussed in the 2015 group first, and then forwarded to the new group for plenum discussion. In doing so, all the members were involved in decision-making, while the tasks could also be completed within a limited period.

Similarly, some members also found the involvement of high-level government officials in decision-making cycle "tricky" because they were "too busy to be involved in every petite discussion", yet "their opinions are important". To solve this dilemma, the members strategically invited high-level government officials into the chat groups, to ensure the high-level government officials were informed about the process and could grant permission to the tasks by giving a "silent agreement". In this way, the members managed to combine the community-driven, participatory decision-making with the hierarchical, bureaucratic decision-making structure. Through these strategic engagements with WeChat groups, the members managed to accommodate different demands of authority and membership. Following the split of groups, the 2015 chat group was renamed into SODA Organising Committee, gradually formalising the roles of the members. This also means that a centre-periphery structure in the open data ecosystem started to emerge.

After the open data movement started to expand to other Chinese cities, the movement soon attracted national attention, with a policy push to make the municipalities the main drivers of growth in open data ecosystems. In January 2018, Shanghai alongside four other municipal governments, i.e., Beijing, Zhejiang, Fujian, and Guizhou, had been appointed as a pilot municipality for open data. Contest and open data portal are especially seen as main instruments to stimulate the growth of a local open data ecosystem. The experiences of organising SODA therefore made the members of the open data ecosystem in Shanghai a "hot commodity", and they were, in fact, asked to organise open data application contests for other municipalities.

Meanwhile, there was an increasing tension around the ownership of the SODA contest, including the data sources that were made open, the data infrastructures that supported the contest, and the data applications generated by the contestants. As the talk around equal ownership was still prevalent, some actors started to use different references to assert their ownership of the open data contest. For instance, a private actor who managed the chat group, used the administrator status in the chat group as a reference for ownership of the network. Another private actor who built the data storage systems for the open data contest, referred to the data storage system as their stake in the contest ownership, in their talk with an investment company. Rumours like these travelled across the ecosystem and started to unsettle actors in the ecosystem in terms of contest ownership. These unsettlements especially came from the public actors, who were concerned about the private interests that drove the claim of ownership.

With the increased internal concerns over ownership and the external requests to purchase organising services for open data application contests, four of the original committee members of SODA 2015 (i.e., affiliated with the private sector and NGOs) set up a joint-stake company S. The company was described as an open data service company that design and deliver open data contests for local municipalities and was overseen by a board that consisted of the four original committee members. After the company was established, the company S signed a service contract with the Shanghai Municipality, becoming a private service provider for local open data contest SODA. The introduction of corporate as way to govern the open data ecosystem subsequently changed the relationship between these members and the rest of the ecosystem: the company S privately owned the organising service of open data contest, and the municipal government owned the product of the open data contest. This also means that the open data contest became publicly funded. And the Shanghai municipal government's role had been reduced to overseeing the progress of the contest and brokering local government data within the Shanghai open data ecosystem.

As the founders of company S explored how to generate profit as a service provider for open data contests to sustain the company, the four board members also wanted to bring back the "openness" of the open data ecosystem into the company structure. Attempting to embrace the evolving range and changing roles of the actors in the open data ecosystem, the four founders of company S decided to change the share distribution between the board members and leave room for future newcomers. To do so, the founding members established a new company D. The company S reinvested in the new company D with another two original founders of S, making a total of three shareholders of D. The three shareholders together held 80% of the shares of D, with the additional 20% share was set-aside for the potential new stakeholders in the future. Before that, the 20% share was entrusted to the CEO of D.

DISCUSSION

What are the Governance Dilemmas in the Open Data Ecosystem?

The evolving governance arrangement of open data ecosystem in Shanghai reveals different views of data ownership at play, that is, *asset* and *commons*. Over time, the two logics of data ownership enact different imaginaries of appropriate governance arrangements for the local actors in the open data ecosystem, each driven by an archetypical source of legitimacy and authority, such as, community, state, and market. Nonetheless, these imaginaries of governance arrangements were not always consistent with each other and created conflicts in practice when confronted with each other.

If we look at the local actors' discourses around open data, they arguably share a value of data commons, that is, data is a shared resource in the society. Following this value, the actors' governance preferences often underline the commitment to community value, as well as voluntary and cooperative engagement in the governance of the open data ecosystem. The actors were expected to contribute to the development of open data ecosystem on a voluntary basis in pursuit of shared interests and values, despite their varying professional and organisational interests.

As data becomes enacted into practice through various data related processes and systems in relation to brokering, organising, maintaining, storing, processing, and analysing data, local actors also inevitably developed a view of data resources as private assets that are generated through their investment of expertise and resources. Following these developments, the actors' governance preferences also involve control-oriented ways of working and distributing roles and decision-making rights.

While the rhetoric of the commons are used by some actors to advocate for data sharing, the governance dilemmas that come with a group of people using a shared resource remain in the dark (Purtova, 2017). In our case, the governance dilemma of open data lays in the tension between appropriation and provision. That is, actors in the ecosystem tend to believe their access to the benefits of open data depends on their perceived ability to provide data. Thus, as their involvement deepens in the ecosystem, they are increasingly interested in claiming ownership to secure their benefits for investing in open data. The issue here is that the resource boundary of data is far less than clear. For instance, the value of data source is dependent on the technologies that generate, store, process and analyse them, as well as the people that use, operate, and maintain these technologies. Depending on how data is created, mediated, and used, all the actors in an ecosystem may perceive themselves as owner of data sources or part of the infrastructure that sustain the value of the data sources.

The divergent views of data ownership therefore create a governance dilemma when actors link their access to the benefits of data to their perceived ownership of data resource: On the one hand, the health of open data ecosystem depends on actors' voluntary participation and their contributions of data related expertise and resources. On the other hand, actors may only be interested in sharing their resources when they can secure their benefits or avoid certain risks. The governance dilemma in open data ecosystem thus concerns how to encourage actors to share data resources while preserving their individual interests in securing benefits of open data.

Future studies can verify and enrich the understanding of governance dilemma by looking into other open data ecosystems across the world. The studies can also deepen the understanding of the governance dilemma by investigating what motivates the actors to contribute to an open data ecosystem. From the perspective of critical institutionalism, to answer this question, one may pay attention to the actors' shifting positions in the open data ecosystem such as a citizen, a knowledge expert or an organisational employee, their logics of data as a governance subject and the corresponding motivations. Open data researchers may also identify the boundary conditions that drive the actors to shift their positions and mobilise different logics of data to justify their participation in open data.

How did Adaptive Governance Emerge in an Open Data Ecosystem and Address this Dilemma?

In this case, when open data was first introduced into Shanghai, it was approached as a new phenomenon with no precedent, and with divergent influences from government, market, and civil society. In response to this governance void, our informants attempted to create a community arrangement by engaging in a series of practices that connect the actors' interests. These practices include creating a shared view of open data using the metaphor of SODA, forming a common identity of open data advocate, and creating a unique work routine.

The introduction of community as a governance arrangement was initially possible due to the distributed domain expertise and access to open data infrastructure across the ecosystem. The community arrangement was effective enough to support the ideation, implementation, and operation of the first open data contest in Shanghai. Nonetheless, as the expertise and access to open data infrastructures started to centralise on a few key stakeholders and the contest model started to take place, clashes between community- and state-driven governance practices start to clash. These clashes were not only reflected as disagreements in who should have the authority to decide on what it means to be open and who has access to data sources and infrastructures, but also as differences in working routines and tropes of discourses around data.

In response to the varying and fragmented demands about how to govern open data, our informants creatively used the online collaborative platform as a governance *avatar* to test out the possibilities of carrying out the open data movement without the actors' consensus on the extent of control and types of ownership. For instance, our informants engaged with a *divide and dissent* approach to create separate closed groups to accommodate different needs for knowledge sharing and decision making. These separate closed groups also make disagreements and differences in work styles less visible to newcomers in the ecosystem, thus creating a sense of coherent community that is attractive for the newcomers to engage.

As the competition between state- and community-driven governance practices intensified, the pro-community actors brought the *divide and dissent* approach offline as a long-term structural design. The actors who did not agree with the increasingly established state-driven data governance practices, borrowed the organisational form of corporate to take a circuitous route to guard non-government actors' access to data resources by privatising parts of data infrastructure and using the private data ownership as a leverage for exchange.

To better understand the emergence of adaptive governance, future studies should investigate if there are other organising logics of data aside from community, state, and market, and how actors mobilise these logics to create different combination of governance arrangements that enhance the adaptive capacity of the ecosystem. Along this line of inquiry, it is also important for future studies to investigate whether divide and dissent is an effective approach for coping with the everchanging needs and demands within an expanding open data ecosystem, and how the approach may manifest in other contexts.

How to Understand Adaptive Governance as Sociotechnical Arrangements

The use of knowledge sharing technology is an important dimension in the adaptive governance arrangement that emerged in our case. This is because learning is core for the adaptive governance of an open data ecosystem, and the use of knowledge sharing technology has the potential to shape the way and the extent to which actors learn. From an ecosystem perspective, the adaptative capacity of the governance arrangements largely depend on human actors' learning about the latest technical advancement as well as the available resources and needed capacities to deal with the changes. The use of knowledge sharing technology therefore can potentially increase the learning capacities across the ecosystem. Given knowledge sharing technology is also based on the possibilities for actors to make connections and interact with each other, it can also potentially help to create a shared sense of community and identity, which may lead to the institutionalisation of governance practices in the long run.

Nonetheless, from an individual actor's perspective, each actor in the ecosystem has their own expertise, assumptions, interests, and ways of working in their engagement with open data, which are not always congruent with each other. This means that they may not always be willing to share knowledge to the same extent. In fact, they may be interested in controlling and even constraining knowledge sharing, depending on their perceived power dynamics with others in the ecosystem, potentially harming the adaptive capacity of the ecosystem. In addition, through actors' interactions, knowledge sharing technology can also make visible the differences in actors' ways of working therefore revealing divergence or disagreement in actors' interests or intentions. Given the prevalent use of information technologies in collaboration today, it would be interesting for open data researchers to identify the sociotechnical arrangements of learning that are deployed in an ecosystem. These sociotechnical arrangements also provide adaptive governance scholars a new range of experimentation venues to observe how learning and control are balanced through digitally medicated governance practices.

In our case, our informants tactfully engage with the tension between facilitating and constraining knowledge exchange in order to create a shared sense of community while preserving the interests and capacity of each actor. These tactics helped to solve issues rapidly without delving into disagreement in assumptions and interests. For instance, our informants engaged in bricolage work on governance in their daily operations working with open data, marking ownership contingently in different scenarios where data resource could mean database or data storage systems. However, this also means there are fundamental differences in the boundaries of data sources and views of data ownership that are not reconciled. One thing that remains puzzling in our case is how actors in the ecosystem who are prone to data-sharing ended up privatising their organising capabilities for open data initiatives to increase their leverage to convince newcomers. Future research could investigate further how privatisation of data resources is used creatively as a way to guard the public access to data resources and what the implications are there for the constructed nature of data as a resource.

What Can We Learn About Adaptive Governance by Looking into the Context of Sociotechnical Ecosystem?

It is important to emphasise that the governance of socioecological systems is increasingly mediated by technologies (Forsberg, 2018; Kooij et al., 2015), especially digital technologies. For instance, information and communication technologies (ICT), such as, social media or collaborative platforms, are used for knowledge sharing and coordination to assist collaborators between human actors in disaster relief. Data analytics and Internet of Things (IoT) are also used for sustainable management of commons, such as, monitoring the use of natural resources. As environmental and climate crises become imminent, policy initiatives, such as green transition put greater emphasis on data auditing of natural resources usage. This increasing focus on data also means the governance of socioecological systems not only concerns governance *via* IT (i.e., ICT), but also governance *of* IT (i.e., data).

This dual focus on IT means that we need to take sociotechnical complexity into consideration in the discussion of adaptive governance of socioecological systems. As I have shown in the case of open data ecosystem, sociotechnical complexity in adaptive governance manifests along two dimensions: the boundary of data as a social resource and the use of knowledge sharing technology, together they have implications for theorising adaptive governance in terms of digitised governance subject, involved data actors and knowledge needs, digital learning mechanism and experimentation venue.

Digitised governance subject
The increasing *datafication* of natural resource management invites questions about the subject of adaptive governance: as natural resources, individual and organisational behaviours become inevitably digitised through different sensing and tracing methods. Our understanding of and interaction with natural resources is increasingly mediated through the imaginaries and practices of data as a resource. From a critical institutionalism perspective, in this study, I understood governance as collective arrangements that are subject to human contingency and a mix of rationalities informed by different logics. Adaptive governance, in this sense, refers to an adaptation process where actors respond to fragmented demands by creatively combining ways, or logics, of coordinating resources in daily practice. Following this line of inquiry, I argue that adaptive governance scholars need to take into consideration the various data logics at play and investigate the relation between data logics and actors' governance responses in socioecological systems. In the context of an open data ecosystem, I have showcased that at least two different data logics – data as commons and assets – are at play, generating divergent governance demands. Adaptive governance scholars should further investigate what are the implications for adaptive governance arrangements in the face of divergent data logics in daily practices.

Involved data actors and knowledge needs
Considering the effects of datafication also means to recognise data-related stakeholders in the governance of socioecological systems, including data industry, experts, bureaucrats, and activists. This is important for the understanding of adaptive governance, as one of its primary foci is to achieve resilience through wide learning across emerging and evolving networks of stakeholders. Given the importance of learning and networking in adaptive governance, taking into consideration the participation of data-related stakeholders in the socioecological systems also requires adaptive governance scholars to rethink the required networks and knowledge needs to enhance the adaptive capacity of a governance arrangement. It could be interesting to understand what kind of knowledge sources data workers utilise to create, process, and use the data generated in natural resources management, and how the choice or the lack of knowledge sources for data worker shapes the corresponding governance arrangements in a socioecological system.

Digital learning mechanism and experimentation venue
With the expanding network and the increasing penetration of digital technology in our daily (work) life, learning across a network is inevitably mediated through digital platforms, be it social media, collaborative platform, or even conferencing applications. In the open case

study, I have demonstrated that the use of these networking and sharing technologies also shapes the emergent adaptive governance arrangement. It does so, not because of the technology itself, but the interaction between the actors and the learning technologies: depending on the actor's role, and subsequent expectations, they may perceive the technologies for different purpose – enabling or constraining learning and use these technologies strategically. This is critical for the understanding of adaptive governance, as existing adaptive governance scholarship argues for an experimental approach that builds upon learning from testing policy as hypotheses in a new context. With the prevalence of knowledge sharing technologies, learning can take place at a much smaller, daily scale. Focusing on the knowledge sharing technology, it is thus important for adaptive governance scholars to identify the effective sociotechnical arrangements around learning, and their implications for the emergent adaptive governance arrangements.

CONCLUSION

In this study, I demonstrated how adaptive governance in an open data ecosystem emerged from the need to fill in the governance void in the beginning to coping with different demands of data logics afterwards. Our findings suggest community-driven governance practices emerged as an effective way to identify distributed resources for building data infrastructure and experiment with unique governance practices that are suitable for the development in the open data ecosystem. Nonetheless, as the initial governance practices start to stabilise, overlaps and clashes between the emergent and existing governance practices become more visible to actors. Our informants coped with these competing governance practices, using a "divide and dissent" approach that allows them to accommodate differences while carrying on the work needs to be done. This divide and dissent approach was tested through its virtual avatar on a collaborative platform and later materialised into separate companies that aimed at using private ownership to guard non-government actors' access to data resources. These insights from the case study are relevant for understanding the adaptive governance of a socioecological system by drawing attention to the duality of IT in adaptive governance: governance via knowledge sharing technology and data governance. Based on these insights, I put forward a research agenda for open data scholars, focusing on the data logics that are at play in an open data ecosystem, the associated governance dilemma and coping mechanism, the sociotechnical learning arrangements, and their consequences for the form of adaptive governance. I also argue that the case on open data ecosystem has implications for theorising adaptive governance, by putting forward the two dimensions of IT involvement in adaptive governance: governance *via* IT (i.e., ICT), but also governance *of* IT (i.e., data). As datafication of natural resources management intensifies, the dual focus on IT requires adaptive governance scholars to address digitised governance subject, involved data actors and knowledge needs, digital learning mechanisms and experimentation venue.

REFERENCES

Baack, S. 2015. Datafication and empowerment: how the open data movement re-articulates notions of democracy, participation, and journalism. *Big Data & Society*, 2, 2, 2053951715594634. https://doi.org/10.1177/2053951715594634.

Beckwith, R., Sherry, J., and Prendergast, D. 2019. Data flow in the smart city: open data versus the commons. In *The Hackable City*, pp. 205–221. Springer.

Birch, K., and Muniesa, F. 2020. *Assetization: Turning Things into Assets in Technoscientific Capitalism.* MIT Press.

Brunner, R. D., Steelman, T. A., Coe-Juell, L., Cromley, C. M., Tucker, D. W., and Edwards, C. M. 2005. *Adaptive Governance: Integrating Science, Policy, and Decision Making.* Columbia University Press.

Chaffin, B. C., Gosnell, H., and Cosens, B. A. 2014. A decade of adaptive governance scholarship: synthesis and future directions. *Ecology and Society*, 19, 3, 56.

Chaffin, B. C., and Gunderson, L. H. 2016. Emergence, institutionalization and renewal: rhythms of adaptive governance in complex social-ecological systems. *Journal of Environmental Management*, 165, 81–87.

Chatfield, A. T., and Reddick, C. G. 2017. All hands on deck to tweet #sandy: networked governance of citizen coproduction in turbulent times. *Government Information Quarterly*. https://doi.org/10.1016/j.giq.2017.09.004.

Cleaver, F., and Koning, J. de. 2015. Furthering critical institutionalism. *International Journal of the Commons*, 9, 1, 1–18. https://doi.org/10.18352/ijc.605.

Cleaver, F., and Whaley, L. 2018. Understanding process, power, and meaning in adaptive governance. *Ecology and Society*, 23, 2.

Corrales-Garay, D., Ortiz-de-Urbina-Criado, M., and Mora-Valentín, E.-M. 2019. Knowledge areas, themes and future research on open data: a co-word analysis. *Government Information Quarterly*, 36, 1, 77–87. https://doi.org/10.1016/j.giq.2018.10.008.

Dietz, T., Ostrom, E., and Stern, P. C. 2003. The struggle to govern the commons. *Science*, 302, 5652, 1907–1912.

Forsberg, P. 2018. Technology as integrated into institutions: expanding the list of actors affecting institutional conditions of cooperation. *International Journal of the Commons*, 12, 1.

Gao, F. 2018.. Driving urban innovation with open data: the birth of the Shanghai model. *Paris Innovation Review*, May, 7. http://parisinnovationreview.com/articles-en/driving-urban-innovation-with-open-data-the-birth-of-the-shanghai-model.

Gawer, A., and Phillips, N. 2013. Institutional work as logics shift: the case of Intel's transformation to platform leader. *Organization Studies*, 34, 1035–1071. https://doi.org/10.1177/0170840613492071.

Heilmann, S. 2008. From local experiments to national policy: the origins of China's distinctive policy process. *The China Journal*, 59, 1–30.

Hess, C., and Ostrom, E. (Eds.). 2006. *Understanding Knowledge as a Commons: From Theory to Practice.* MIT Press.

Hong, S., and Lee, S. 2018. Adaptive governance and decentralization: evidence from regulation of the sharing economy in multi-level governance. *Government Information Quarterly*, 35, 2, 299–305. https://doi.org/10.1016/j.giq.2017.08.002.

Janssen, M., Charalabidis, Y., and Zuiderwijk, A. 2012. Benefits, adoption barriers and myths of open data and open government. *Information Systems Management*, 29, 4, 258–268.

Janssen, M., and van der Voort, H. 2016. Adaptive governance: towards a stable, accountable and responsive government. *Government Information Quarterly*, 33, 1, 1–5.

Juhola, S., and Westerhoff, L. 2011. Challenges of adaptation to climate change across multiple scales: a case study of network governance in two European countries. *Environmental Science & Policy*, 14, 3, 239–247.

Kitchin, R. 2014. *The Data Revolution: Big Data, Open Data, Data Infrastructures and Their Consequences.* SAGE.

Kooij, S. van der, Zwarteveen, M., and Kuper, M. 2015. The material of the social: the mutual shaping of institutions by irrigation technology and society in Seguia Khrichfa, Morocco. *International Journal of the Commons*, 9, 1, 129–150. https://doi.org/10.18352/ijc.539.

LaValle, S., Lesser, E., Shockley, R., Hopkins, M. S., and Kruschwitz, N. 2011. Big data, analytics and the path from insights to value. *MIT Sloan Management Review*, 52, 2, 21–32.

Mandel, G. N. (2009. Regulating emerging technologies. *Law, Innovation and Technology*, 1, 1, 75–92.

Moor, J. H. 2005. Why we need better ethics for emerging technologies. *Ethics and Information Technology*, 7, 3, 111–119. https://doi.org/10.1007/s10676-006-0008-0.

Osborne, S. 2010. The (new) public governance: a suitable case for treatment? In Osborne, S. (Ed.) *The New Public Governance. Emerging Perspectives on the Theory and Practice of Public Governance*, pp. 1–15. Routledge.

Ostrom, E. 1990. *Governing the Commons: The Evolution of Institutions for Collective Action*. Cambridge University Press.

Purtova, N. 2017. Health data for common good: defining the boundaries and social dilemmas of data commons. In *Under Observation: The Interplay between eHealth and Surveillance*, pp. 177–210. Springer.

Thornton, P. H. 2002. The rise of the corporation in a craft industry: conflict and conformity in institutional logics. *Academy of Management Journal*, 45, 1, 81–101.

Thornton, P. H., Ocasio, W., and Lounsbury, M. 2012. *The Institutional Logics Perspective: A New Approach to Culture, Structure, and Process*. Oxford University Press on Demand. https://books .google.com/books?hl=zh-CN&lr=&id=xPlagJzFm2AC&oi=fnd&pg=PP1&dq=the+institutional+ logics+perspective&ots=xMBgbjrN2_&sig=bYfp8m9EZEpgsgcb8a5GOxD90NE.

Wamba, S. F., Akter, S., Edwards, A., Chopin, G., and Gnanzou, D. 2015. How 'big data' can make big impact: findings from a systematic review and a longitudinal case study. *International Journal of Production Economics*, 165, 234–246.

Wang, C. 2019. *Becoming Adaptive through Social Media: Transforming Governance and Organizational Form in Collaborative E-government*. Copenhagen Business School.

Wang, C., Medaglia, R., and Jensen, T. B. 2020. When ambiguity rules: the emergence of adaptive governance (in)congruent frames of knowledge sharing technology. *Information Systems Frontiers*. https://doi.org/10.1007/s10796-020-10050-3.

Wang, C., Medaglia, R., and Zheng, L. 2017. Towards a typology of adaptive governance in the digital government context: the role of decision-making and accountability. *Government Information Quarterly*. https://doi.org/10.1016/j.giq.2017.08.003.

Wang, C., and Staykova, K. 2019. Decoupling accountability and liability: case study on the interim measures for the opening of public data in Shanghai. *Naveiñ Reet: Nordic Journal of Law and Social Research*, 9, 275–298.

Willinsky, J. 2005. The unacknowledged convergence of open source, open access, and open science. *First Monday*, 10, 8. https://doi.org/10.5210/fm.v10i8.1265.

11. Policy experimentation in the construction of ecological civilisation in China

Ping Huang and Linda Westman

INTRODUCTION

Human society is facing unprecedented challenges of climate change, energy shortages and environmental degradation. The United Nations Sustainable Development Goals represent a global consensus on the urgency to seek more sustainable modes of development. As a response to ecological crises, China is promoting the national strategy of ecological civilisation.

Integrated into China's core national agenda in 2018, ecological civilisation refers to establishing sustainable production and consumption patterns, achieving human–human, human–nature and nature–society harmony, and emphasising the interdependence, mutual reinforcement and coexistence of human society and the natural environment (Zhang et al., 2011). Nevertheless, building ecological civilisation entails fundamental transitions of socio-ecological systems, which poses considerable complexity and uncertainty to governing processes and outcomes. Various approaches to adaptive governance are hence adopted by the government in the construction of ecological civilisation in China.

The scholarship on adaptive governance, with roots in ecosystems theory, has not been widely applied in China. On a first glance, it may even seem that the Chinese political system, characterised by top-down control, centralised policy making, and regulative policy instruments, is ill suited to this mode of governance. Yet, such superficial interpretations obscure a long tradition of what can be understood as adaptive governance in China, inherited from the Mao era (Xue et al., 2018; Heilmann and Perry, 2020). Policy experimentation is a key component of China's adaptive governance. According to Heilmann (2008a: p. 3), policy experimentation is "a policy process in which experimenting units try out a variety of methods and processes to find imaginative solutions to predefined tasks or to new challenges that emerge during experimental activity." This chapter presents a historical and systematic account of China's approaches to policy experimentation in the construction of ecological civilisation. It reveals three key characteristics of adaptive governance of ecological civilisation, namely of pragmatism, incrementalism and verticality.

The remainder of this chapter proceeds as follows. The next section presents a review of the literature on adaptive governance. The following section reviews China's tradition of adaptive governance and explores how these approaches are being adopted in building ecological civilisation and discusses the main characteristics of adaptive governance. Conclusions are drawn in the final section.

LITERATURE REVIEW

The concept of adaptive governance emerged from the literature on social-ecological systems (SES), as a response to the problem of how to govern socio-environmental issues characterised by complexity, multi-scalar interaction, and uncertainty (Chaffin et al., 2014). SES studies, which are fixed in ecological research, complexity studies and systems theory, introduced the concept of adaptive capacity. According to this scholarship, this term represents "the ability of [a] system to remain in a stability domain, as the shape of the domain changes" (Gunderson, 2000: p. 435). This means that a given socio-ecological system with a high adaptive capacity, or adaptability, is able to respond and change when exposed to different kinds of pressures whilst maintaining essential system functions. The notion of adaptive capacity is closely linked to that of resilience. For example, Walker et al. (2004: p. 4) understand adaptability in the context of SES as "the capacity of actors in a system to influence resilience". This definition stresses human agency (of individuals and groups) as a special property of socio-ecological (as opposed to ecological) systems; it is the collective ability to manage resilience which determines if a system will pass into "an undesirable system regime" when exposed to external or internal stressors (Walker et al., 2004).

Theories on adaptive management and adaptive governance draw directly on this tradition of thinking. Adaptive governance was first coined by Dietz et al. (2003) to capture the governance of complex socio-ecological systems. Building on a solid SES tradition, this early definition was coupled with multiple features assumed necessary to deliver effective governance of natural resources. First, adaptive governance needs to be informed by and provide reliable information. This is necessary because socio-environmental problems tend to involve multi-layered, unpredictable, and constantly shifting dynamics; without accurate and reliable information, policy makers will not be able to make appropriate and effective decisions (Dietz et al., 2003). Adaptive governance must also be able to cope with conflict. As is well understood in the literature on environmental politics, environmental challenges always involve multiple perspectives and social interests. In the governance of socio-ecological systems, differences in power, values, or philosophical principles likewise shape ways of viewing and managing any given problem (Dietz et al., 2003). In addition, adaptive governance needs to involve some level of rule compliance, which, according to Dietz et al. (2003), is necessary to maintain order. Further, provision of physical and technical infrastructure facilitates the management of natural resources. Being able to cope with change – especially in the long term – is another requirement of adaptive governance, as socio-ecological systems are in a constant state of flux. Dietz et al. (2003) also propose three strategies for adaptive governance, including reliance on deliberative processes, nested structures of decision making (because socio-environmental challenges transcend administrative boundaries), and institutional variety (of both structures and instruments of governance).

From this foundation, numerous successive studies expanded on the concept of adaptive governance and examined the conditions that enable successful processes and outcomes. For example, drawing on broader insights from SES scholarship, social dimensions that enable adaptive governance include self-organisation (through social networks), opportunities for social learning, interaction among multiple social groups and forms of knowledge, the existence of trust or other forms of social capital, and the ability to manage uncertainty (Folke et al., 2005). Other scholars identify opportunities of participation and deliberation, the presence of polycentric and multi-layered institutions, and accountable authorities as key to successful adaptive governance (Lebel et al., 2006). As the concept of adaptive capacity was developed in parallel with that of transformation, adaptive governance has also been studied in relation to its ability to support transformative change. Features of adaptive governance that enable transformation include self-organisation, political leadership, the strategic use of windows of opportunity, mobilisation of social networks across scales of action and knowledge domains, and collaborative learning (Olsson et al., 2004; 2006).

Reflecting on the state of knowledge on adaptive governance a decade after Dietz et al. coined the concept, Chaffin et al. (2014) conclude that research on this phenomenon has developed into a consolidated body of work. Adaptive governance emerged as an alternative to top-down, command control, linear notions of governance. It came to represent possibilities for complex and uncertain ecosystem dynamics to be governed through community-driven processes that integrate science-based monitoring with social learning. Other key elements of adaptive governance that crystallised through this decade of research were the need for governance arrangements to align with the scale of an environmental problem (the problem of "fit") and the need for "institutions and organisations to be nested across levels of govern-ance, structured with multiple centres of power, redundant in function, and connected across space and time through networks" (Chaffin et al., 2014: p. 8). These problems of institutional structure have been amply investigated in research on multilevel and network governance, polycentricity, and orchestration. Following these insights, we regard adaptive governance as processes of policy formulation and implementation based on continuous learning and exper-imentation. In these processes, government authorities revise and evaluate policy objectives and practices, ensure that policies can be continuously improved with the development of science and technology, and enable a dynamic policy environment (Xue et al., 2018).

In their review, Chaffin et al. (2014) also point to areas that remain obscure in the schol-arship on adaptive governance. For instance, questions on normative orientation embedded in the literature are underexplored; while the literature carries implicit assumptions about striving for sustainable outcomes, it is unclear how value conflicts inherent in such outcomes are resolved. Cleaver and Whaley (2018) follow a similar direction of inquiry when engaging with power dynamics of adaptive governance, suggesting that the reformulation of institutions required in adaptive governance processes likely will reproduce entrenched social relations, resulting in unanticipated outcomes (such as the reproduction of the status quo). These obser-vations reflect concerns in the scholarship on resilience and transformations, which has been criticised for a lack of attention to politics, power, agency, and epistemological assumptions (Cote and Nightingale, 2012; Blythe et al., 2018).

Despite this critical engagement, there is to date little reflection on how the concept of adaptive governance may translate into a diversity of political settings shaped by different values and cultural practices. Translating debates on adaptive governance into China implies not only applying the concept in a non-democratic political system, but also in a society with forms of social organisation, worldviews, and environmental ethics distinct from the settings in which the concept was developed (Huang et al., 2021; Westman and Huang, forthcoming). As we explore in this chapter, the translation of adaptive governance to politics in China not only raises practical questions (what does it mean on the ground?) but also opens new theoretical directions (how do lessons from China inspire new conceptualisations of adaptive governance?)

EXPERIMENTING WITH ECOLOGICAL CIVILISATION IN CHINA

China's Tradition of Adaptive Governance

China has a long tradition of adaptive governance (Xue et al., 2018). According to Heilmann and Perry (2020), the resilience of the communist regime of China – its ability to respond to crises, execute profound socio-environmental change, and simultaneously evolve – can be understood as a form of adaptive capacity. Specific governance techniques that display such capacity include recognition of perpetual change, managing tensions, experimentation, and ad-hoc interventions (Heilmann and Perry, 2020: p. 3). Heilmann and Perry propose these characteristics as a direct counterargument against the conventional understanding of communist, authoritarian regimes; rather than being locked into rigid, administrative systems, China's communist state is flexible and able to cope with uncertainty.

Heilmann and Perry (2020) trace the approaches of adaptive governance of the Communist Party of China (CPC) to the early communist movements in the 1920s. The founders of the CPC, including Mao Zedong, were greatly influenced by the American pragmatic philosopher John Dewey and his theory of experimenting to obtain scientific knowledge (Heilmann and Perry, 2020: p. 77). The CPC's experimental governance manifested first in its policies of land reforms in some areas in China and later in the governance of the country after the founding of the People's Republic of China (Bell, 2016). Pragmatism, experimentation, and scientific development were core to Mao's political philosophy and practice and further became core governing strategies of CPC (Schoon, 2014; Schmalzer, 2016).

After Mao's death in 1976, pragmatism became mainstream again (after the political turmoil of the Great Leap Forward and the Cultural Revolution) in an era of reform and opening up led by CPC leader Deng Xiaoping. This new era was characterised by well-known slogans such as "practice is the sole criterion for testing truth", "groping for stones crossing the river", and "no matter if it's a black cat or a white cat, as long as it catches mice it's a good cat", particularly in the policy domains of economic development. China has, since then, made unprecedented achievements in economic development. Within merely three decades, China's GDP grew from 191 billion US dollars in 1980 to 6,087 billion US dollars in 2010. China has eliminated the problem of absolute poverty in 2020, by lifting over 100 million of its rural population out of poverty (The Diplomat, 2021). Despite radical transformations, the economic reform proceeded incrementally, learning from and guided by experiences gained from policy experimentation (Lin et al., 2003). As noted by Heilmann (2008a: p. 2), the economic miracle of China was made to happen by an unusual adaptive capacity of the government "to try out alternative approaches to overcome long-standing impediments to economic development, tackle newly emerging challenges, and grasp opportunities when they open up".

An important approach to CPC's adaptive governance is the so-called "from point to area" (*you dian ji mian*), with the designation of a variety of "experimental points" and "experimental zones" (*shi dian*) in different policy domains (Heilmann, 2008a). The key idea is to experiment novel policies in certain policy domains and their social, economic and political implications, before replicating them at a larger scale (Heilmann, 2008b). At the end of the 1980s, the approach of policy experimentation was fully institutionalised by the central government. For instance, within the National Commission for Economic Structural Reform, a high-level Bureau for Comprehensive Planning and Experimental Points was established in 1988. As for experimental zones, the most well-known and successful example is the designation of the city of Shenzhen as a Special Economic Zone. Within three decades, Shenzhen has grown from a fishing village to an international city and a hub for technological innovation. In 2018, for the first time, Shenzhen's GDP overtook that of its neighbour Hong Kong. Entering the Xi era, approaches to adaptive governance continue to be used in different arenas of governance in China, including urban restructuring (Schoon, 2014), sustainability transitions (Huang and Liu, 2021) and water management (Li et al., 2020). A very recent examples of national experimental zones is the designation of Shenzhen as a pilot demonstration area of socialism with Chinese characteristics.

A quite unique feature of China's policy experimentation is the dynamic central-local interactions (Miao and Lang, 2015). This pattern is observed by scholar Sebastian Heilmann (2008a; 2008c) during China's economic reform, termed as "experimentation under hierarchy". As explained by Heilmann (2008c), experimentation under hierarchy is "a process of policy generation that legitimises local initiative while maintaining ultimate hierarchical control" (p. 1), guaranteed by the authority of the central government on the one hand and the decentralisation of more power to local governments on the other. According to Tsai and Dean (2014), within a hierarchical political system, the central government of China granted local governments more autonomy to experiment novel policies at the local level, and successful and feasible local reforms are then implemented at a larger scale. As depicted by Heilmann (2008b: p. 29):

> It is [...] the volatile yet productive combination of decentralised experimentation with ad hoc central interference, resulting in the selective integration of local experiences into national policy-making, that is the key to understanding China's policy process.

Within this hierarchical pattern of policy experimentation, while local actors become initiators of many reforms, the ultimate control over policy formulation still rests upon the central government (Heilmann, 2008c). In the case of eco-city initiatives in two Chinese cities, Miao and Lang (2015) identify the importance of hierarchical support from the central government.

In next sub-section, we delineate the approaches of adaptive governance in the construction to ecological civilisation in China.

Policy Experimentation in Building Ecological Civilisation

In China's practices of adaptive governance in the construction of ecological civilisation, the main approach applied is abovementioned policy *experimentation*, particularly through the designation of experimental units and pilot/demonstration zones. Although ecological civilisation officially became a national strategy of China in 2007, after the endorsement of the notion by the former president Hu Jintao, China's practices of ecological demonstration started long before that.

As early as 1995, the Ministry of Ecology and Environment (MEE) (then the State Environmental Protection Administration) issued the "Notice on Carrying out the Pilot Work of National Ecological Demonstration Zone Construction",[1] which marked the launch of the construction of ecological pilot/demonstration zones in China. In the same year, the MEE published a long-term plan for the demonstration work, the "Outline of the Construction of

---

[1]   http://www.mee.gov.cn/gkml/zj/wj/200910/t20091022_171869.htm.

National Ecological Demonstration Zone (1996–2050)".[2] In this plan, a three-phase workplan was laid out for the construction of National Ecological Demonstration Zone:

- First phase (1996–2000): The key task is the construction of experimental units; The main target is to build 50 demonstration zones nationwide.
- Second phase (2001–2010): The key task is the promotion of ecological demonstration in key regions; The main target is to select 300 regions for ecological demonstration and build 350 demonstration zones with various types and characteristics.
- Third phase (2011–2050): The key task is the nationwide promotion of ecological demonstration; The main target is to make the total area of the demonstration zones reach about 50% of the country's land area.

This first generation of ecological pilot/demonstration zones were officially called "Experimental Unit for the Construction of National Ecological Demonstration Zone" (*quanguo shengtai shifanqu jianshe shidian*). As shown in Table 11.1, from 1996 to 2004, a total of 452 experimental units were designated for the construction of National Ecological Demonstration Zones. All the experimental units had to be evaluated based on a series of indicators, such as energy consumption per unit of GDP, forest cover rate and air quality.[3] Only those experimental units that passed the evaluation would be officially named as a National Ecological Demonstration Zone. For instance, in 2002, the MEE revealed that three experimental units, including Baotou city in the Inner Mongolia Autonomous Region, Bozhou city in Anhui province and Loudi city in Hunan province, were evaluated as unqualified to further the ecological demonstration work.[4] It was stressed that the MEE would conduct regular evaluations and make adjustments to the experimental units where the demonstration work had not been progressing well.

In 2002, the MEE published an article on its website, which presented an overview of the situation of the designated experimental units for the construction of National Ecological Demonstration Zones and summarised the main experiences and the lessons learned (Table 11.2).[5]

In 1999, the MEE launched a new program for ecological demonstration, namely the "National Ecological Construction Demonstration Area", which we regard as the second generation of ecological pilot/demonstration zones in China. According to the MEE, the project of "National Ecological Construction Demonstration Area" encompasses the demonstration programs of "Ecological Province", "Ecological City", "Ecological County", "Ecological Town", "Ecological Village" and "Ecological Industrial Park". This new scheme can be viewed as an updated program of the previous scheme of National Ecological Demonstration Zone.[6] The first batch of ecological provinces was nominated as early as 1999, to the two provinces of Hainan and Jilin.[7] Nevertheless, the work of National Ecological Construction Demonstration

---

[2] http://www.mee.gov.cn/gkml/zj/wj/200910/t20091022_171869.htm.

[3] https://www.mee.gov.cn/gkml/zj/bgt/200910/t20091022_173751.htm.

[4] http://www.mee.gov.cn/gkml/zj/wj/200910/t20091022_172103.htm.

[5] http://sthj.chengdu.gov.cn/cdhbj/zrbhq/2007-05/25/content_0114d85205c6417c9572f6 16c3f4f541.shtml.

[6] https://www.mee.gov.cn/gkml/hbb/bwj/201205/t20120529_230531.htm.

[7] http://www.mee.gov.cn/gkml/zj/jh/200910/t20091022_173148.htm; http://www.mee.gov.cn/gkml/zj/jh/200910/t20091022_173162.htm.

Table 11.1   *Experimental unit for the construction of National Ecological Demonstration Zone*

Year	Group of experimental units	Number of experimental units
1996	First batch	69
1997	Second batch	31
1998	Third batch	6
1999	Fourth batch	40
2000	Fifth batch	57
2001	Sixth batch	12
2002	Seventh batch	106
2003	Eighth batch	87
2004	Ninth batch	44
Total		452

Table 11.2   *Experiences gained from the construction of National Ecological Demonstration Zone*

Demonstration experience	Description	Demonstration Zone
The model of ecological poverty alleviation	Turning ecological and environmental advantages into economic advantages to achieve poverty alleviation and prosperity	Taishun county, Zhejiang Chishui, Guizhou
The model of urban–rural integration	Combining urban and rural economic development with the construction of small towns in rural areas	Yizheng, Jiangsu Liyang, Jiangsu Wenjiang county, Sichuan Pi county, Sichuan
The model of ecological agriculture	Combining agricultural production with environmental protection to achieve a virtuous circle	Dongxiang county, Jiangxi Xinfeng county, Jiangxi Ningdu county, Jiangxi Tonghai county, Yunnan
The model of ecological tourism	Combining tourism development with the conservation of ecological system	Dujiangyan, Sichuan Huangshan, Anhui
Plain ecological restoration	Focusing on the management of sandy land	Neihuang county, Henan Feng county, Jiangsu
Ecological Restoration in Mountainous Areas	Focusing on the greening of barren hills	Huguan county, Shanxi Qi county, Henan Jinzhai county, Anhui
"Gongcheng" model	Combining mountain development with ecological protection	Gongcheng county, Guangxi

Area was not fully rolled out until 2003, when the "Indicators for the Construction of Ecological County, Ecological City, and Ecological Province (trial)" was promulgated.[8] Later in 2004, the "Planning Outline for the Construction of Ecological County and Ecological City (trial)" was released. Until 2013, a total of 16 provinces/autonomous regions/municipalities (including Fujian, Zhejiang, Liaoning, and Tianjin) had carried out the construction of Ecological Province, and more than 1,000 cities/districts/counties had carried out the construc-

---

[8]   http://www.mee.gov.cn/gkml/zj/wj/200910/t20091022_172195.htm.

tion of Ecological City and Ecological County, of which 92 cities and counties (districts) had been awarded the title of National Ecological Construction Demonstration Area.[9]

In October 2013, the official renaming of the above "Ecological Construction Demonstration Area" to the "Ecological Civilisation Construction Demonstration Area" marked the birth of the third generation of ecological pilot/demonstration zones in China.[10] This decision, made by the central government, resonates with the wider "ecological shift" in China's national agenda, namely of the construction of ecological civilisation. As early as in 2005, the State Council issued the "Decision on Implementing the Scientific Outlook on Development and Strengthening Environmental Protection",[11] in which it was mentioned to "advocate ecological civilisation". Later in 2007, the MEE issued the "Guiding Opinions on Strengthening the Initiation of Ecological Demonstration",[12] in which "cultivating ecological civilisation" was listed as one of the key tasks of ecological demonstration. Ever since, the MEE started to pilot ecological civilisation construction in a small number of areas, under the name of "National Experimental Unit for the Construction of Ecological Civilisation" (Guojia Shengtai Wenming Jianshe Shidian). For instance, in 2009, 12 counties and cities were designated as the "National Experimental Unit for the Construction of Ecological Civilisation".[13] This can be viewed as a measure of probing and testing before the full rollout of demonstration work of ecological civilisation construction. Before the promulgation of the "Indicators for National Ecological Civilisation Construction Pilot/Demonstration Area (trial)" in 2013, which provided guidance for the demonstration work of ecological civilisation construction, five batches of experimental units had been designated. The experiences gained from these experimental units had undoubtedly informed the selection and validation of indicators.

Nevertheless, with the elevation of ecological civilisation construction as a national strategy, different departments rushed into the setting up of new pilot/demonstration projects. For instance, aside from the demonstration projects under the supervision of MEE, another demonstration scheme called the "Pilot Demonstration Area of Ecological Civilisation" was jointly set up by six departments, including the National Development and Reform Commission (NDRC), the Ministry of Finance, the Ministry of Land and Resources, the Ministry of Water Resources, the Ministry of Agriculture, and the State Forestry Administration.[14] Nevertheless, the lack of coordination and standardisation of various forms of pilot schemes might lead to a waste of financial resources and increase management and supervision costs, which has also been uncovered in other low-carbon projects in China (see for instance: Khanna et al., 2014). In response to the relatively chaotic situation, in 2016, the General Office of the CPC Central Committee and the General Office of the State Council jointly issued the "Opinions on Establishing a Unified and Standardised National Ecological Civilisation Pilot Zone".[15] It specified that without the approval of the CPC Central Committee and the State Council, multiple levels of government departments should no longer establish or approve new pilot and demonstration projects under the name of "ecological civilisation construction". Ever since, all

---

9   https://news.12371.cn/2015/10/12/ARTI1444583725438941.shtml.
10   https://sthjt.nmg.gov.cn/stbh2021/stsfcj_8114/202108/P02021082.577650281164.pdf.
11   http://www.gov.cn/zwgk/2005-12/13/content_125680.htm.
12   http://www.mee.gov.cn/gkml/zj/wj/200910/t20091022_172455.htm.
13   https://www.mee.gov.cn/gkml/hbb/bh/201004/t20100409_187990.htm.
14   http://www.gov.cn/zwgk/2013-12/13/content_2547260.htm.
15   http://www.xinhuanet.com/politics/2016-08/22/c_1119434724.htm.

Table 11.3   *Designated demonstration zones for ecological civilisation construction*

Year	Group	Program	
		National Demonstration City/County for Ecological Civilisation Construction	Practice and Innovation Base for "Lucid Waters and Lush Mountains are Invaluable Assets"
2017	First batch	46	13
2018	Second batch	45	16
2019	Third batch	84	23
2020	Fourth batch	87	35
2021	Fifth batch	100	49
Total		362	136

the demonstration projects for ecological civilisation construction have been integrated to the scheme of Demonstration Area for Ecological Civilisation Construction, under the supervision of the MEE. The first batch of demonstration zones was announced in 2017. Till the end of 2021, a total of 498 demonstration zones have been nominated for ecological civilisation construction (Table 11.3, Figure 11.1).

The Socio-economic Circumstances Behind Different Stages of Ecological Policy Experimentation

As shown in Figure 11.2, the demonstration work of ecological construction in China has experienced three phases of development, with the evolution of national ecological title from the Experimental Unit for the Construction of National Ecological Demonstration Zone to the National Ecological Construction Demonstration Area and eventually to the Demonstration Area for Ecological Civilisation Construction.[16] Table 11.4 provides a summary of the key policies of the three phases of ecological experimentation.

Different phases in ecological demonstration work have had a different focus, which is in line with the broader social and economic circumstances of the country.

In the late 1990s, after a decade of rapid economic development, the ecological and environmental problems in China were increasingly prominent. Therefore, during the first phase (1995–1999), a key focus was ecological restoration and pollution control in key areas that had experienced severe ecological degradation and damage, particularly in the vast rural areas (Wang et al., 2021). This explains why most experimental units during the first phase were at the county level. Nevertheless, less than two decades after the reform and opening up policy in 1979, the top priority of China at that time was still economic development, and environmental protection was a rather marginalised issue in the political agenda.

Moving to the second phase (1999–2013), environmental issues became more and more urgent in China. In 2000, the State Council issued the "Outline for National Ecological Environment Protection".[17] Later in 2002, the MEE published the "Tenth Five-Year Plan for National Ecological Environmental Protection".[18] In 2005, the State Council released the "Decision on Implementing the Scientific Outlook on Development and Strengthening

---

[16]   青海省生态环境厅-生态文明建设示范市县区 (qinghai.gov.cn).
[17]   http://www.gov.cn/gongbao/content/2001/content_61225.htm.
[18]   https://www.mee.gov.cn/gkml/zj/wj/200910/t20091022_172089.htm.

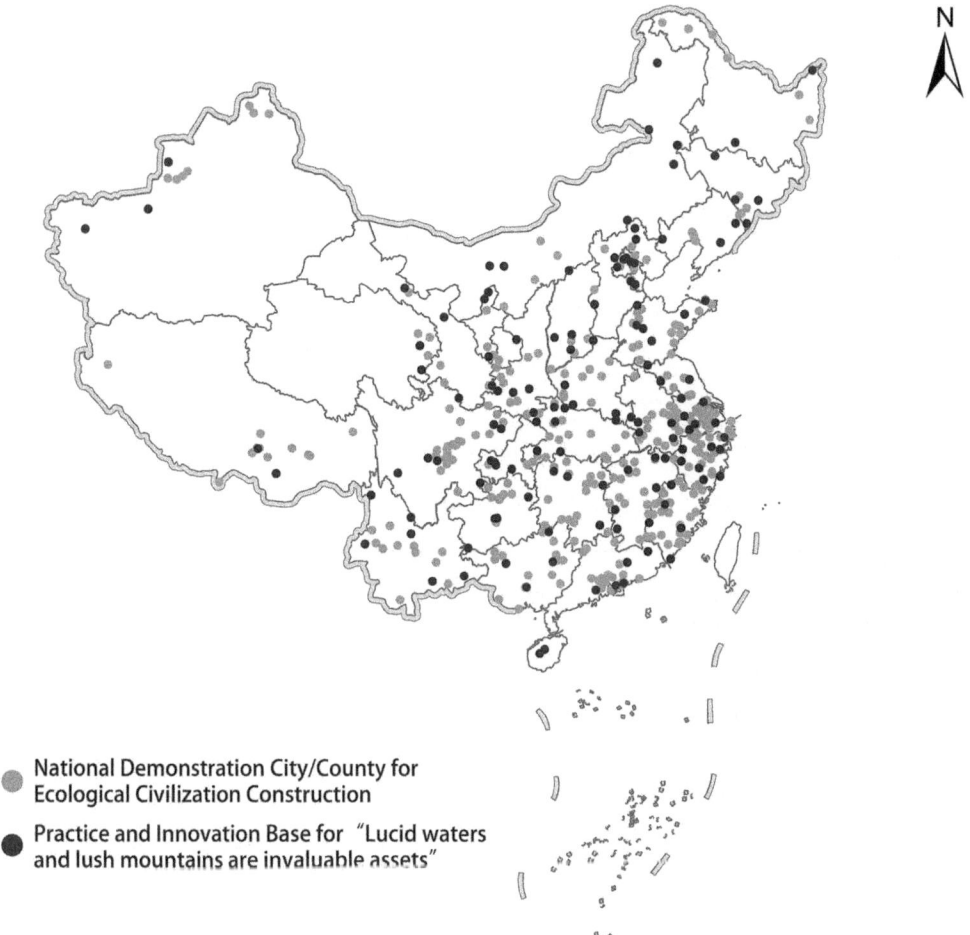

N

National Demonstration City/County for Ecological Civilization Construction

Practice and Innovation Base for "Lucid waters and lush mountains are invaluable assets"

Figure 11.1   The spatial distribution of the 498 designated "Ecological Civilisation Construction Demonstration Area"

Environmental Protection",[19] which for the first time placed ecological protection in an equally important strategic position as economic development (Wang et al., 2021). In the "Outline of the Eleventh Five-Year Plan for National Economic and Social Development (2006–2010)", the emphasis was placed on natural restoration, and the focus of promoting ecological protection and construction was to shift from post-treatment to pre-protection (Wang et al., 2021).

Since 2013, the elevation of ecological civilisation as a national strategy signals the political will to promote structural changes of the nation's production and consumption systems. In 2013, China's total trade volume ranked first in the world, becoming the world's largest trading nation (Woetzel, 2019). In 2019, China's per capita GDP exceeded US$10,000 (CGTN, 2020). Meanwhile, issues of climate change and ecological conservation are gaining

---

[19]   http://www.gov.cn/zwgk/2005-12/13/content_125680.htm.

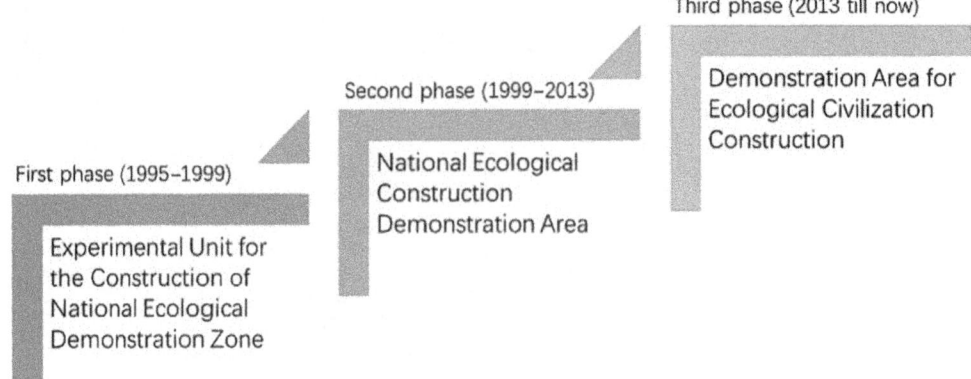

Figure 11.2   *Three phases of ecological demonstration in China*

Table 11.4   *Key policies of ecological experimentation in China*

Year	Policy	Department
1995	Notice on Carrying out the Pilot Work of National Ecological Demonstration Zone Construction (including the "Outline of the Construction of National Ecological Demonstration Zone (1996–2050)")	Ministry of Ecology and Environment
2003	Indicators for the Construction of Ecological County, Ecological City, and Ecological Province (trial)	Ministry of Ecology and Environment
2004	Planning Outline for the Construction of Ecological County and Ecological City (trial)	Ministry of Ecology and Environment
2005	Decision on Implementing the Scientific Outlook on Development and Strengthening Environmental Protection	State Council
2007	Guiding Opinions on Strengthening the Initiation of Ecological Demonstration	Ministry of Ecology and Environment
2013	Indicators for National Ecological Civilisation Construction Pilot/ Demonstration Area (trial)	Ministry of Ecology and Environment
2013	Decision on Implementing the Scientific Outlook on Development and Strengthening Environmental Protection	Ministry of Ecology and Environment
2016	Opinions on Establishing a Unified and Standardised National Ecological Civilisation Pilot Zone	General Office of the CPC Central Committee; General Office of the State Council

increasing momentum in international politics. The focus of ecological experimentation has shifted to systematic and comprehensive ecological transformation. For instance, as mentioned, under the experimentation scheme of the "National Demonstration City/County for Ecological Civilisation Construction", there are two key projects, namely the "National Demonstration City/County for Ecological Civilisation Construction" and the "Practice and Innovation Base for 'Lucid Waters and Lush Mountains are Invaluable Assets'". While the National Demonstration City/County for Ecological Civilisation Construction focuses on integrating ecological civilisation into the overall regional development, the main task of the Practice and Innovation Base for "Lucid Waters and Lush Mountains are Invaluable Assets" is to explore effective ways to transform lucid waters and lush mountains into invaluable assets, improve the supply level and guarantee ability of ecological products, and innovate the system and mechanism for realising ecological value. In policy experimentation during this phase, a key task is the institutional construction of ecological civilisation, including local legislation, standardisation, and reform in the cadre assessment system.

It is noteworthy that there are no clearcut boundaries between different phases, because demonstration projects in the previous stage might take a long-term to finally conclude and often extend to the next stage. For instance, although the second phase started in 1999, the last batch of National Ecological Demonstration Zones of the first phase was evaluated and named as late as in 2011.[20] In the next subsection, we discuss the main characteristics of adaptive governance in the construction of ecological civilisation in China.

The Characteristics of Policy Experimentation in the Construction of Ecological Civilisation

Pragmatism: "treatment in accordance with local condition" (*yin di zhi yi*)

China is a country with huge regional disparity. In the course of policy experimentation, the formulation and implementation of policy often needs to adapt to local conditions. As can be seen, during the first phase, the experiences gained from the construction of National Ecological Demonstration Zone were highly diverse and localised (see Table 11.2). This indicates that in policy experimentation of ecological civilisation, local governments are assigned substantial autonomy to experiment with whatever works to solve local problems within local contexts. Similarly, in the program of the "Pilot Demonstration Area of Ecological Civilisation" led by NDRC, the formulation of the main tasks of each demonstration area was in alignment with the characteristics of local endowments, geographical environment and economic stages. For instance, for the coastal city Dalian in Liaoning province, one of the emphases was placed on establishing an ecological protection compensation system for land and sea coordination; while for the border city Mudanjiang in Heilongjiang province, the focus was on exploring a foreign cooperation mechanism for ecological civilisation construction.[21]

Incrementalism: "from point to area"

China's policy experimentation of ecological civilisation construction also exhibits the features of incrementalism. The different focuses of varying stages indicate the need to align ecological experimentation with broader national and international circumstances, to always prioritise the "primary contradictions" while putting aside the secondary ones, which is a pragmatic governance logic of the CPC inherited from Maoist thought (Westman and Huang, forthcoming). Although the government tends to formulate long-term planning (e.g., the "Outline of the Construction of National Ecological Demonstration Zone (1996–2050)"), the actual implementation of the planning is assigned substantial flexibility. The approach of probing and testing and an error-correcting mechanism (e.g., the un-qualification of some experimental units in 2002) always ensure the capacity of governance structures and processes to adapt to new situations and to address new challenges. As mentioned, the key idea of the policy experimentation is the so-called "from point to area", in which institutional, technical, and financial incentives are first experimented in different regions, and the policy innovations

---

[20]   https://www.mee.gov.cn/gkml/hbb/bgg/201111/t20111102_219484.htm.
[21]   https://www.ndrc.gov.cn/fggz/hjyzy/stwmjs/201601/t20160112_1161166.html?code=&state=123.

that work at the local level are then evaluated and selectively integrated into national policy-making for implementation at a larger scale. For instance, in November 2020, building upon the experiences gained from the demonstration projects, the central government released the "National Ecological Civilisation Experimental Zone Experience Promotion List", which included 90 replicable and promotable reform initiatives and experiences for the construction of ecological civilisation.

Verticality: vibrant local–central interactions
As mentioned, China's policy experimentation is practised under a hierarchical political system. Likewise, the ecological experimentation involves governments and policy makers at different levels of the political system. The governing process reveals significant verticality in China's adaptive governance, represented by vibrant local–central interactions. During the initial phase, the central government has very little experience in ecological governance. The set-up of experimental units at the local level (particularly counties and villages) provided valuable inputs for further policy formulation, particularly for the top-level design of ecological civilisation construction in the following stages. Since 2010, a series of policies have been formulated and issued by the central government regarding ecological civilisation, including the "Opinions on Accelerating the Construction of Ecological Civilisation" (2015), the "Overall Plan for the Reform of Ecological Civilisation System" (2015) and the "Measures for Evaluating and Assessing the Objectives of Ecological Civilisation Construction" (2016). These documents specified the overall objectives, visions, key tasks, and institutional arrangements for the construction of ecological civilisation, put forward a systematic plan for the institutional construction of ecological civilisation, and established an assessment mechanism for comprehensive evaluation of Party and government leaders. They in turn provide the general guidance for further ecological civilisation experimentation at the local level.

DISCUSSION

From China's policy experimentation of ecological civilisation, we can see that there exist both similarities and differences between the concept of adaptive governance adopted in China and that developed in the SES literature. In the SES literature, the characteristics of adaptive governance encompass elements such as deliberative processes, interaction/coordination across nested scales of action, institutional heterogeneity, self-organisation, social learning, accountability, and trust (Dietz et al., 2003; Folke et al., 2005; Olsson et al., 2006). In China, the notion of adaptive governance does reflect some of these characteristics, including in particular policy experimentation, coping with change, ad-hoc adjustments, reflexivity and learning, up-scaling lessons (Heilmann and Perry, 2020). Nevertheless, the chapter also shows that the definition and interpretation of adaptive governance is not limited to a certain assemblage of elements as identified in the SES literature.

With a long tradition of adaptive governance characterised by approaches such as "probing and testing" and "from point to area" (Heilmann, 2008a), China's practice of adaptive governance challenges the stereotype views of adaptive governance. For instance, there have always been hidden assumptions about the need for adaptive governance to encompass elements of democratic performance, especially participation and deliberation. This has in a sense excluded many political systems from the debate. This chapter shows that instead of being bonded to democratic regimes, the notion of adaptive governance *per se* can adapt to different circumstances, particularly different settings of institutions. This is not to say that important elements such as participation, deliberation, polycentricity and heterogeneity of institutions are absent in China's adaptive governance, but manifest in different, possibly more invisible, forms (see for instance: Huang and Liu, 2021). Further empirical study would be required to determine their nature and degree of presence in this context.

Overall, China's practice of building ecological civilisation points towards the presence of different forms or styles of adaptive governance, manifest in key characteristics of pragmatism, incrementalism, and verticality. This indicates a need for serious engagement with contexts that are less familiar in the adaptive governance scholarship (e.g., those beyond liberal democracies). Such research could provide a deeper understanding of how varieties of adaptive governance can work in practice.

CONCLUSION

Adaptive governance has implicitly been understood as associated with democratic regimes. These assumptions are so deep that they often remain invisible in research (although sometimes the link is spelled out, e.g., DeCaro et al., 2017). For many, China's political system features command-and-control and authoritarianism, and the narrative of adaptive governance is irrelevant or inapplicable to the country. In fact, assumptions on the inflexible nature of communist regimes have already been challenged by the research on adaptive governance in China (see for instance: Xue et al., 2018; Heilmann and Perry, 2020). We suggest through this chapter that different styles of adaptive governance exist and that several features of adaptive governance clearly operate within the Chinese system. A historical and systematic account of China's approaches of policy experimentation in the construction of ecological civilisation reveals three key characteristics of China's adaptive governance, namely of pragmatism, incrementalism and verticality. Being pragmatic implies the adaption to diverse local conditions, which is imperative for a country with huge regional disparity; being incremental is a way of minimising political risks and social disruption (Heilmann, 2008c), particularly for a ruling party that prioritises social stability (Westman and Huang, forthcoming); while the vertical interactions between local and central governments represent a cyclic mechanism of policy innovation, evaluation, and learning. Adaptivity constitutes a core feature of adaptive governance. The notion of adaptive governance has been evolving and will continue to evolve with the input of governance practices in a variety of contexts including China.

REFERENCES

Bell, D. A. (2016). *The China Model*. Princeton University Press.

Blythe, J., Silver, J., Evans, L., Armitage, D., Bennett, N. J., Moore, M.-L., Morrison, T. H. and Brown, K. (2018). The dark side of transformation: latent risks in contemporary sustainability discourse. *Antipode*, 50(5), 1206–1223.

CGTN (2020). China's GDP per capita just passed $10,000, but what does this mean? Available from: https://news.cgtn.com/news/2020-01-17/China-s-GDP-per-capita-just-passed-10-000-but-what-does -this-mean--NkvMWAMYNO/index.html.

Chaffin, B. C., Gosnell, H., and Cosens, B. A. (2014). A decade of adaptive governance scholarship: synthesis and future directions. *Ecology and Society*, 19(3).

Cleaver, F., and Whaley, L. (2018). Understanding process, power, and meaning in adaptive governance. *Ecology and Society*, 23(2).

Cote, M., and Nightingale, A. J. (2012). Resilience thinking meets social theory: situating social change in socio-ecological systems (SES) research. *Progress in Human Geography*, 36(4), 475–489.

DeCaro, D. A., Chaffin, B. C., Schlager, E., Garmestani, A. S. and Ruhl, J. B. (2017). Legal and institutional foundations of adaptive environmental governance. *Ecology and Society*, 22(1), 1.

Dietz, T., Ostrom, E. and Stern, P. C. (2003). The struggle to govern the commons. *Science*, 302(5652), 1907–1912.

Folke, C., Hahn, T., Olsson, P., and Norberg, J. (2005). Adaptive governance of social-ecological systems. *Annu. Rev. Environ. Resour.*, 30, 441–473.

Gunderson, L. H. (2000). Ecological resilience: in theory and application. *Annual Review of Ecology and Systematics*, 31(1), 425–439.

Heilmann, S. (2008a). Policy experimentation in China's economic rise. *Studies in Comparative International Development*, 43, 1–26.

Heilmann, S. (2008b). From local experiments to national policy: the origins of China's distinctive policy process. *The China Journal* (59), 1–30.

Heilmann, S. (2008c). Experimentation under hierarchy: policy experiments in the reorganization of China's state sector, 1978–2008. CID Working Paper Series.

Heilmann, S. and Perry, E. J. (eds) (2020). *Mao's Invisible Hand*. BRILL.

Huang, P. and Liu, Y. (2021). Toward just energy transitions in authoritarian regimes: indirect participation and adaptive governance. *Journal of Environmental Planning and Management*, 64(1), 1–21.

Huang, P., Westman, L. and Castán Broto, V. (2021). A culture-led approach to understanding energy transitions in China: the correlative epistemology. *Transactions of the Institute of British Geographers*.

Khanna, N., Fridley, D., and Hong, L. (2014). China's pilot low-carbon city initiative: a comparative assessment of national goals and local plans. *Sustainable Cities and Society*, 12, 110–121.

Lebel, L., Anderies, J. M., Campbell, B., Folke, C., Hatfield-Dodds, S., Hughes, T. P. and Wilson, J. (2006). Governance and the capacity to manage resilience in regional social-ecological systems. *Ecology and Society*, 11, 1, 1–21.

Li, J., Lei, X., Qiao, Y., Kang, A. and Yan, P. (2020). The water status in China and an adaptive governance frame for water management. *International Journal of Environmental Research and Public Health*, 17(6), 2085.

Lin, J. Y., Cai, F., and Zhou, L. (2003). *The China Miracle. Development Strategy and Economic Reform*. Chinese Univ. Press.

Miao, B. and Lang, G. (2015). A tale of two eco-cities: experimentation under hierarchy in Shanghai and Tianjin. *Urban Policy and Research*, 33(2), 247–263.

North D. C. (1990). *Institutions, Institutional Change and Economic Performance*. Cambridge University Press.

Olsson, P., Folke, C., Galaz, V., Hahn, T., and Schultz, L. (2007). Enhancing the fit through adaptive co-management: creating and maintaining bridging functions for matching scales in the Kristianstads Vattenrike Biosphere Reserve, Sweden. *Ecology and Society*, 12(1), 28. http://www.ecologyandsociety.org/vol12/iss1/art28/.

Olsson, P., Folke, C., and Hahn, T. (2004). Social-ecological transformation for ecosystem management: the development of adaptive co-management of a wetland landscape in southern Sweden. *Ecology and Society*, 9(4).

Olsson, P., Gunderson, L. H., Carpenter, S. R., Ryan, P., Lebel, L., Folke, C., and Holling, C. S. (2006). Shooting the rapids: navigating transitions to adaptive governance of social-ecological systems. *Ecology and Society*, 11(1).

Schmalzer, S. (2016). *Red Revolution, Green Revolution*. University of Chicago Press.

Schoon, S. (2014). Chinese strategies of experimental governance: the underlying forces influencing urban restructuring in the Pearl River Delta. *Cities*, 41, 194–199.

The Diplomat. (2021). How successful was China's poverty alleviation drive? https://thediplomat.com/2021/09/how-successful-was-chinas-poverty-alleviation-drive/

Tsai, W. H. and Dean, N. (2014). Experimentation under hierarchy in local conditions: cases of political reform in Guangdong and Sichuan, China. *The China Quarterly*, 218, 339–358.

Walker, B., Holling, C. S., Carpenter, S. R., and Kinzig, A. (2004). Resilience, adaptability and trans-formability in social–ecological systems. *Ecology and Society*, 9(2).

Wang Xiahui, He Jun, Mu Xuejie, Zhu Zhenxiao, Chai Huixia, Liu Guihuan, Rao Sheng and Zhang Xiao (2021). 20 years of ecological protection and restoration in China: retrospect and prospect. *Chinese Journal of Environmental Management*, 13, 5, 85–92. (trans. 王夏晖, 何军, 牟雪洁, 朱振肖, 柴慧霞, 刘桂环, 饶胜 and 张箫 (2021). 中国生态保护修复 20 年: 回顾与展望. 中国环境管理, 13(5), pp. 85–92.)

Wang, J., Zhang, S., and Zhang, Q. (2021). The relationship of renewable energy consumption to finan-cial development and economic growth in China. *Renewable Energy*, 170, 897–904.

Westman, L. and Huang, P. (2022). Ecological civilization: a historical perspective on environmental policy narratives in China. *IQAS*. Under review.

Woetzel, J. (2019). China and the world: inside the dynamics of a changing relationship. https://www.mckinsey.com/~/media/mckinsey/featured%20insights/china/china%20and%20the%20world%20inside%20the%20dynamics%20of%20a%20changing%20relationship/mgi-china-and-the-world-full-report-june-2019-vf.ashx.

Xue, L., Weng, L. and Yu, H. (2018). Addressing policy challenges in implementing Sustainable Development Goals through an adaptive governance approach: a view from transitional China. *Sustainable Development*, 26(2), 150–158.

Zhang, W., Li, H., and An, X. (2011). Ecological civilisation construction is the fundamental way to develop low-carbon economy. *Energy Procedia*, 5, 839–843.

12. The role of adaptive governance in climate mitigation and adaptation: a local perspective[1]

Grete K. Hovelsrud and Hege Westskog

THE BACKDROP: WHY ADAPTIVE GOVERNANCE

Local governments worldwide are increasingly acknowledged as key actors in handling climate change challenges (Amundsen et al., 2018) by increasingly taking major responsibility for climate change adaptation and mitigation (Burch et al., 2014; Bulkeley, 2015; Kasa et al., 2018). In fact, local governments address greenhouse gas (GHG) emission sources such as transportation and buildings within their jurisdiction (Bulkeley and Betsill, 2005), and adaptation measures are predominantly local because climate change impacts are first and foremost felt at the local level (e.g., Hovelsrud and Smit (2010) and references therein; Smit and Pilifosova IPCC (2001)).

We approach the issues of climate change through the notion of wicked problems (Rittel and Webber, 1973; McConnell, 2018). Wicked problems are described as multi-causal and complex spanning organisational boundaries and responsibilities, generally with no common understanding of the cause of the problems or the solutions (McConnell, 2018; Verweij et al., 2011). As the understanding and acceptance of the climate change problem as human-made has increased, its wickedness first and foremost pertains to the complexity of the problem, the multiple solutions, and the context dependent impacts.[2] To address wicked problems, many scholars hold that there is a need for changing behaviour, perceptions, mindsets, and/or world-views (Head, 2018; O'Brien and Sygna, 2013). As aptly described by Lempert et al. (2004, p. 2): "Climate change is associated with radically diverse decision contexts, geographic scales, and time scales. It comprises many different types of policy problems involving many different types of actors, and thus is not even theoretically optimisable". This does not preclude the major differences in complexity and scale of climate mitigation versus climate adaptation.

Mitigation of GHG is by default a global policy issue where international and national agreements and strategies take centre stage, while climate adaptation occurs at the local level and is therefore predominantly handled by local and regional authorities, albeit within a national policy context. Regardless of governance scale the wickedness of both remains.

---

[1]   The authors wish to thank all the informants involved in our case studies for sharing their thoughts and experiences. We are also grateful for the support from the Research Council of Norway grant nos. 207522, 258979, 295704, and EU Horizon 2020 Grant no. 869154 FACE-IT to conduct the research relevant for this chapter. We obtained permission from the Norwegian Center for Research Data (NSD) to conduct this research. We have followed their guidelines for data management and protection.

[2]   McConnell (2018) describes three possible approaches to wicked problems: (i) pessimistic (little/nothing to do with them); (ii) optimistic (visionary leaders may make a difference and help handle the problems), (iii) pragmatic (reforms may lead to progress in handling wicked problems). To do so there is a need of better knowledge, involving of third parties, better consultations, collaborative leadership, better management strategies and smart framing of the problems.

In addition, uncertainties about environmental and societal impacts add to the complexity of climate change (Westskog et al., 2017). Further, questions of how mitigation and adaptation as increasingly interrelated can and should be handled, point to core discussions of the role of societal change in cutting emissions and adapting. The discussions span the dimensions of whether we need a radical transformation to reach a low emission and robust climate-adapted society or whether incremental changes in our societal structures are sufficient (IPCC, 2012; O'Brien, 2012; Termeer et al., 2017). Finally, climate change issues are highly intertwined with other environmental challenges and are often in conflict. The heated debates on the extensive windmill park development in pristine nature, in Norway, illustrates this well. The dual nature of windmill parks is deeply disturbing for the public, including Indigenous peoples; windmills are both a green renewable source of energy and responsible for irreversible destruction of nature (Sæþórsdóttir and Ólafsdóttir, 2020; Sovacool et al., 2019; Normann, 2021).

Faced with the wickedness of climate change, top-down and technocratic governance approaches are believed to be insufficient (Cumming et al., 2006; Chaffin et al., 2014). Instead, involvement of all parties, better consultations, and collaborative leadership are crucial elements for addressing wicked problems (Mc Connell, 2018), including climate mitigation and adaptation. This implies more flexibility in decision making and a higher degree of collaboration between relevant actors (Berkes, 2008; Dietz et al., 2003; Folke et al., 2002; McConney et al., 2007; Olsson et al., 2004; Westskog et al., 2020). Adaptive governance and its sister concept adaptive co-management are approaches that emphasise these qualities (Plummer and Fennel, 2009). This entails flexibility through both learning and adaptation as new knowledge and experiences arise and autonomy to adapt policies and measures to the local context, as well as collaboration through shared decision making and authority, and pluralism and communication between a diverse set of actors. In this way, adaptive governance and adaptive co-management approaches present an opportunity for local governments to handle complex climate change problems.

In this chapter, we investigate the role of adaptive governance in climate change mitigation and adaptation efforts, in the context of multi-level governance. Our theoretical approach, outlined in the next section, is informed by a literature review of the concepts of adaptive governance and adaptive co-management. Through reanalyses of two case studies on climate change mitigation and adaptation efforts we map out the potential weaknesses and opportunities of adaptive governance strategies to handle climate change. We conclude with some reflections on salient prerequisites for adaptive governance to work on the local level.

THEORETICAL APPROACH

Adaptive governance has largely been associated with natural resource use and environmental challenges in response to failures in addressing these issues by a top-down oriented management structure (Olsson et al., 2004; Armitage et al., 2007, Folke et al., 2005; Chaffin et al. 2014; Greenhill et al., 2020). Increasingly, climate change adaptation is addressed through the lens of adaptive governance (e.g., Munaretto et al., 2014; van Buuren et al., 2015; Smith and Lawrence, 2018). When it comes to climate mitigation the lack of engagement with adaptive governance is striking. Some exceptions are found in studies of land-use and transport planning and adaptive climate governance of urban resilience (Boyd and Juhola, 2015; Eshuis and

Gerrits, 2021; Westskog et al., 2020), but to the best of our knowledge there are few applications of the adaptive governance framework in climate mitigation processes.

Adaptive governance is defined and applied in different ways and is at times used in connection with "good governance" or "adaptive co-management" (Plummer and Baird, 2013, p. 633). While the concept adaptive unites them, the terms governance and management have different analytical connotations. Management provides strategies for handling, for example, an ecosystem or a resource, while governance pertains to the "broader social contexts of creating conditions for social coordination that enables management" (Olsson, 2007, p. 268). Adaptive governance provides the general structures and processes through which adaptive co-management could be exercised. Alternatively, adaptive governance is described as the enabler of adaptive co-management (Folke et al., 2002).

Adaptive governance pertains to implementation of multi-level governance systems (Bulkeley and Betsill, 2005; Bulkeley and Kern, 2006; Boyd and Folke, 2011), underlining the need for flexibility in governance adaptability to the local context, and over time (Westskog, et al., 2017; Chaffin et al., 2014; Sharma-Wallace et al., 2018). These aspects are central to climate change governance and management, being conducted within a multi-level system of international, national, regional, and local government levels, often including formal frameworks.

There is no linear or one-way relationship between governance and management. Instead, the two are to a large extent interlinked through the need to test, learn, and adapt with new knowledge and experience. Common to both adaptive governance and adaptive co-management is *inter alia* the emphasis on learning from experience and the inclusion of different knowledge systems, participants and societal scales, shared responsibility for governing and managing common goal goals, and tailoring the process to local context (Ruitenbeek and Cartier, 2001; Folke et al., 2002; Olsson et al., 2004; Pomeroy et al., 2004; Westskog et al., 2017). We distinguish between the two with the recognition that they, through the term adaptive, share descriptive and operational elements. We focus on the governance aspects of climate change but will draw on adaptive co-management lessons and frameworks when relevant. We apply the definition of adaptive governance suggested by Westskog et al. (2020, p. 555): "the interactive process through which societies are steered towards collectively negotiated objectives, allowing for learning and adjustments of objectives, policies and measures as new knowledge arises." This definition is inspired by that of Ansell and Torfing (2016, p. 4), but Westskog et al. (2020) highlight collaboration and flexibility in their approach to adaptive governance, which are pivotal for our empirically based study.

We investigate three central aspects of adaptive governance in the context of climate change: collaboration and shared decision making across actors, organisations, and scales; flexibility (with learning as new knowledge and experiences emerge); and context sensitivity. The two case studies are re-analysed according to these three theoretical concepts to expose weaknesses and strengths of adaptive governance. In turn, the reanalyses of the two cases provide new theoretical knowledge and thereby contribute to theory building. Our iterative discussion of empirically based findings and theoretical concepts is set up to inform and move theory forward.

Our empirical material shows that neither the national authorities nor the local decision makers in the two cases have the necessary knowledge, authority, or interest to fully address the climate change problem on their own. This calls for collaborative efforts. Climate change governance engages with uncertainties about future climate, the impacts and the effects of measures and policy instruments to reduce emissions and adapt to its consequences (Boyd and Juhola, 2015; Greenhill et al., 2020; Lempert et al., 2004). This requires flexibility to change as new knowledge and experiences arise and to take advantage of knowledge and awareness generated through collaboration (Westskog et al., 2017; 2020; Fitchett, 2014; Fidel et al., 2014). Finally, the impacts of climate change and the effects of instruments implemented to reduce emissions often differ across different local contexts (Westskog et al., 2017; Tørnblad et al., 2013). This underscores the need to be both attentive to and inclusive of the local context in governing climate change, as we have learned from studies of climate adaptation (Hovelsrud and Smit, 2010; Karlsson and Hovelsrud, 2020; Dannevig et al., 2020).

Adaptive governance approaches have been criticised as wishful thinking (Cleaver and Whaley, 2018) overlooking issues of power, institutional contexts and cultural factors that inhibit adaptive governance as a "good governance" approach (Chaffin et al., 2014). *Power* dimensions are apparent in the processes that generate benefits to some and costs to others (Cleaver and Whaley, 2018) and through different capacities to act by the parties in an adaptive governance process (King, 2005). Westskog et al. (2020) show how adaptive governance is framed by underlying power structures within climate mitigation policies. These power structures align with levels of government with different authorities, which in turn influence adaptive governance processes, exemplified in the multi-level governance agreements on transport and land-use development (see below). The role of different actors and institutional levels in an adaptive governance process is also shaped by the different and formalised institutional contexts.

Introducing flexibility through adaptive governance to formalised institutions is challenging. The process of making governance adaptive rests on the presupposition that institutions can be adjusted to fit human-nature challenges, such as climate change (Van Hecken et al., 2015). This is echoed in a study of climate adaptation in the Netherlands by Van Buuren and colleagues (2015, p.10). They conclude: "The reason why it is difficult to develop flexible arrangements has especially to do with the institutional context in which it has to happen … . The rule of law and principles of good governance (legality, judicial protection, equality) are part of this context and set boundaries on the application of flexible arrangements."

Finally, *cultural factors* shape how adaptive governance processes are formed and understood. Established institutional cultures (Hall et al., 2014) with different and potentially conflicting human values (Dietz et al, 2003) could inhibit successful adaptive governance processes. Dannevig et al. (2020) show through case studies that culturally sensitivity boundary work increases the likelihood of developing climate policies that are salient and relevant. When climate policy rests on saliency, legitimacy, and relevance the likelihood of adherence increases. We argue that the linkages to adaptive governance are clear. Thus, if scientific climate change knowledge is to motivate action and change in society, it must be framed and conveyed in ways that resonate with people's livelihoods, world views and cultural bias (Dannevig and Hovelsrud, 2016; Meadow et al., 2015).

EMPIRICAL INSPIRATIONS: TWO NORWEGIAN CASE STUDIES

To illustrate and discuss the opportunities and challenges with adaptive governance of climate change, we reanalyse two local level case studies from Norway (Westskog et al., 2017; Westskog et al., 2020). The first addresses climate change adaptation efforts and the second climate change mitigation in terms of land-use and development of climate friendly transport solutions through planning. We apply the three aspects of adaptive governance outlined above that intersect with the climate change problem: (1) collaboration and shared decision making; (2) flexibility, and (3) context sensitivity. These are discussed in relation to the two empirical case studies we offer as salient examples.

Case 1: Climate Change Adaptation Efforts

Our first reanalysis is of a case study that addressed climate adaptation efforts in the Vestfold County in Norway (now part of Vestfold and Telemark County) (Westskog et al., 2017). The study was initiated by researchers together with the Vestfold County Governor to increase attention to the need for climate adaptation in the County's municipalities. The researchers participated in the planning of the municipal dialogue seminars on climate adaptation, and subsequently observed the process. In addition to observing the dialogue seminars, the study involved in depth interviews and document analyses, in 12 of 14 municipalities, into how they addressed the need for climate adaptation measures. The County Governor assisted in recruiting the informants for these investigations. In most cases, we interviewed the Chief Municipal Executive and officials responsible for emergency planning and preparedness, and spatial planning. We also conducted interviews with the County Governor and the Norwegian Directorate for Civil Protection. In total we conducted 29 interviews (see Westskog et al., 2017 for description of methods). The dialogue seminar arranged by the County Governor of Vestfold included all 14 municipalities and took place after the interview data were gathered. The researchers participated as observers.

Adaptive governance is relevant to this case study in two ways. Firstly, and to reiterate, climate change (including climate adaptation) is a wicked problem that best can be solved through dialogue-oriented decision making where collaboration between relevant parties, shared decision making, flexibility and context sensitivity are key. How exposed and sensitive municipalities are to climate change vary, and one size does not fit all when it comes to designing strategies and measures to handle the challenges (Hovelsrud and Smit, 2010; Westskog et al., 2017). This requires attention to each municipal context and being cognizant of flexibility in measures, resources, and planning strategies. Further, the uncertainty of climate change impacts requires the tailor-made measures to be flexible as new knowledge and experience develop. Full inclusion of different competences in decision-making processes requires dialogue, collaboration, and iteration, through co-production of knowledge between levels of government, local actors and often researchers (Greenhill et al., 2020; Dannevig et al., 2019; Bremer and Meisch, 2017; Hegger et al., 2012; Dilling and Lemos, 2011). Secondly, the County Governor's intention with the dialogue process clearly resembles elements of adaptive governance processes. Most relevant parties participated in the planning and the dialogue process. At least at the outset, the intention was to develop a shared understanding of the problem and how it could be handled. The County Governor clearly signalled that he was to be considered an equal partner and not the only one with decision-making powers. Below we address the challenges and opportunities of adaptive governance from the perspective of the three central concepts introduced above.

Collaboration and shared decision making: Common challenges and the role of different government levels in addressing climate change adaptation may be revealed through collaboration, shared decision-making and dialogue processes between policy makers and administrative staff within and between municipalities, the national authorities, and researchers. The different conditions the municipalities face are shaped by physiography, human and economic resources, networks, knowledge and how the work is organised, which in turn have implications for climate change adaptation. In our case study, the dialogue process revealed that critical knowledge about quick clay slides and flooding urgently needed for planning in some of the municipalities has yet to be developed by state agencies. Thus, the dialogue process created space for cognitive and relational learning about the specific conditions, needs and local context to be included the development of the county's work on climate adaptation (see also Baird et al., 2014).

However, the pre-defined role of the different governmental levels was shown to restrict further development of collaboration on equal terms. The County Governor himself struggled with combining the role of overseeing and controlling the municipal work on climate adaptation and being a partner to the municipalities in their work. This was caused by a combination of the municipalities perceiving the County Governor to be higher in the governmental hierarchy, and by the County Governor being cautious about providing context specific advice that could be interpreted as interfering with the autonomy of municipalities. Further, a major challenge for adaptive governance processes within climate change adaptation is the lack of resources both to participate and to operationalise the outcomes of the processes. This is particularly true for smaller municipalities, which lack sufficient human and financial resources to deal with climate adaptation and civil protection. Sometimes the tasks to follow up climate adaptation polices are dedicated to officials that already are fully occupied with other pressing tasks. Some municipalities even question their own autonomy and responsibilities within this policy area and note that climate adaptation is too serious to be handled singlehandedly. They therefore call for increasing involvement by the state and the regional government levels to assist with prioritising municipal resources and possible measures. Not surprisingly, the municipalities also underline the need for more economic resources to be allocated from the national level.

Flexibility to include new knowledge and experience: Climate change adaptation has become a field of study where researchers often are heavily involved in providing advice and data to authorities in terms of flood maps, quick clay and landslide risks and estimates of the likelihood of extreme events. In Norway, flood- and landslide maps are developed by NVE (the Norwegian Water Resources and Energy Directorate) for regions and municipalities that are at risk for such events. These maps are updated according to the most recent data available, as risk areas change. Such updated and dynamic maps increase the flexibility in decision-making and development of measures that are easier to implement. We argue that the availability and applicability of risk maps presents an opportunity and a solid foundation for developing an adaptive governance framework for climate adaptation.

Conversely, this opportunity is challenged by the access to such knowledge for municipalities. Many municipalities do not have access to the relevant knowledge partly because the state officials who possess this knowledge have limited capacity to share and inform, and partly because it is difficult to locate the knowledge in the first place. Here, we have found a difference between larger municipalities with more dedicated resources and wider networks on climate adaptation, and smaller ones with less resources. The lack of human and financial resources is a barrier for smaller municipalities in terms of not having time to develop and maintain networks for climate adaptation. Another significant barrier is the negligible inclusion of locally relevant knowledge about such risks as quick clay in the national mapping exercises. This is particularly the case when the risks are not perceived as life threatening. This loops back to limited resources. Mapping areas with life-threatening risks are prioritised, leaving other areas unmapped. In the long run, and as climate change alter the conditions, this will create new challenges.

Context sensitivity: Our study shows that there is a clear need to be attentive to different municipal contexts in governance processes. To ensure that governance is *adaptive*, we argue that it is imperative to pay attention to the differences in how municipalities plan and implement their adaptation efforts. It is also critical to understand the context for why there are differences in available human and financial resources.

The problem is that the national policies, including guidelines and requirements, on climate adaptation are top-down and designed to be applicable to all types of municipalities. The local variations and needs are not addressed or included. The result is that municipalities translate these general guidelines and requirements to fit their own context at the risk of failing to include local concerns and conditions. This in turn may result in a sub-optimal approach to local adaptation, or as shown by Westskog et al. (2017), with too little or too much adaptation as the outcome. Too little adaptation reduces municipalities preparedness for future climate challenges, while too much implies a waste of limited resources that could be used for other pressing tasks. Several of the municipalities note the need for more contextual coordination of adaptation across municipalities, such as creating networks with municipalities that face similar adaptation challenges and municipal structures to coordinate cross-municipal learning. This could be an important role for the Country Governor, and an opportunity to create a bridge from the municipal to the national governance level.

Case 2: Climate Mitigation – Developing a Climate Friendly Transport System at the Local Level

Our second re-analysis is of a case study addressing urban contractual agreements (referred to as urban growth agreements) between the national, regional, and local government levels to obtain a more climate friendly transport system (Westskog et al., 2020). The study focused on three city regions in Norway that negotiate urban growth agreements (Oslo, Stavanger and Trondheim). The study was qualitative, based on 37 interviews with relevant representatives across municipal, regional, and national government levels and included both administrative officials and politicians. To better cover the process of negotiations two sets of interviews were conducted with roughly one year in between. The negotiation processes in the different city regions aimed at obtaining what is termed the zero-growth goal meaning that all growth in passenger transport in urban areas should be by public transport, cycling and walking (MoT, 2013). The state funds up to 50 per cent of the costs for constructing new public transport infrastructure. Different types of policy instruments (e.g., toll roads, improved public transport, more climate friendly land-use planning) are planned and implemented in major cities as part of these agreements. Through the urban growth agreements all government levels are committed and officials and politicians at all levels are represented in the negotiations. The parties of these agreements meet regularly to negotiate terms and requirements in the city regions. However, critics of the negotiation processes argue that decisions are taken outside the city council, the main democratic institution at the local level, and thus run the risk of not representing the views of the council. For further details on urban growth agreements, see Westskog et al. (2020).

The process of establishing urban growth agreements resembles that of adaptive governance since the parties have a shared commitment to reach the zero-growth goal and have flexibility to adapt policies to the local context and over time. Three central aspects of adaptive governance described above are used as a point of departure for the analyses and presentation of our results.

Collaboration and shared decision making: Over the years the lack of proper coordination between the national, regional, and state levels with respect to transport and land-use planning has been striking in Norway (Westskog et al., 2020). The urban growth agreements, containing adaptive governance elements, provide an opportunity to coordinate the plans and actions of the different government levels, for example, when new state-run hospitals and national and regional highways and railroads are planned and need coordination with the local level's land-use and transport infrastructure. The shared responsibility between relevant parties of the zero-growth goal enables coordination.

Shared decision-making across government levels emerges as the foundation for establishing the framework for the urban growth agreements. However, the power dynamics between the national and municipal levels challenge shared decision-making. The state with the main financial powers is considered higher in the government hierarchy than the regional and local levels. Additionally, the national level leads these negotiations. These aspects prompted several of the representatives to question the prospects of having real influence over the negotiated results. Further, the state was perceived to be equipped with a non-negotiable mandate anchored in the national policy documents, illustrating the challenges that may arise when the different representatives have roles attached to power inequalities. Such differences in power may highly likely inhibit the needed dialogue and collaborative aspects of adaptive governance. Also, multi-level governance processes, particularly those that are defined outside the formal democratic processes at the local level, may challenge both the local democracy and the legitimacy of adaptive governance outcomes. Although elected representatives from the municipal councils participated in the negotiations, the rapid speed and that the negotiations where not fully open in the interest of efficiency, impeded proper involvement by the electives of the municipal councils.

Flexibility to include new knowledge and experience: The conditions for introducing policies and measures for a more climate friendly transport and land-use development vary across cities because of factors, such as former land-use developments, characteristics of the public transport system and demographic differences. Negotiations signify flexibility in that such activity inherently contains a certain openness for different views and possibilities. This is partially illustrated by the re-negotiations and adjustments to the urban growth agreements, based on experiences with the original agreement. The main adjustment resulted in the inclusion of new partner municipalities from the city regions, such as in Trondheim, where three neighbouring municipalities were included. Increased coordination of land-use and transport planning across more municipalities in the same region creates a greater likelihood for reaching the shared zero growth goal, representing a win-win situation for each municipality and for the region. The flexible process opens for additional re-negotiations in the future.

While involvement of more relevant actors in the agreements is important for the effectiveness of transport and land-use planning, it is also more demanding when it comes to coordination of parties and resources used. Additionally, the inadvertent exclusion of relevant municipalities, due to pre-set criteria, is a tangible risk. This was the case in the Trondheim region, where municipalities without railway-stops were excluded from the agreement, even though they plan for transport and land use. The absence of a railway-stop as a concrete and excluding factor adds yet another dimension to participation and reflects a lack of flexibility. This mirrors the first case study on climate change adaptation, where lack of resources and coordinating abilities may inhibit participation by all relevant parties in an agreement. Many of our informants questioned whether the national level carries the necessary flexibility to include new experiences and knowledge. This is a legitimate concern. The national level of government is guided and limited by policies agreed upon in the Norwegian Parliament and is not at the liberty of negotiating beyond the stipulation in politically approved policies. The National Transport Plan is a case in point that is found at times to inhibit the needed flexibility to act. This in turn, we argue, may obstruct the *adaptiveness* of the governance processes.

Context sensitivity: The goal of the urban growth agreements is the establishment of transport and land-use measures at the local level for municipalities to reach the broader zero-growth goal. In theory, the municipal and the regional authorities can choose which measures to implement and how. The policies and measures are part of the negotiations and may include menus with different policy choices relevant to the local context, and outline suggestions for how to reach and implement the goals through the different instruments.

The fierce protests against both toll roads and the level of tolls have occurred in some of the city regions. Toll roads and increasing tolls were implemented by the municipal government with the dual purpose of reaching the zero-growth goal for the regions through reducing the use of private fossil burning cars and to cover their share of the costs for developing public transport infrastructure. The national government pays a share of the costs and requires the municipalities to do the same. The municipalities therefore need the income from toll roads to cover their share of the costs of building much needed infrastructure. It is only in theory that the toll roads can be avoided. The municipalities are locked in a national system that reduces their freedom to make necessary and context sensitive decisions. The way the local context is interwoven in already established structures and institutions constitutes a barrier for adaptive governance.

OPPORTUNITIES AND WEAKNESSES OF ADAPTIVE GOVERNANCE IN MULTI-GOVERNANCE STRUCTURES

Our reanalysis of the two case studies illustrates adaptive governance practices within multi-level governance structures and the potential opportunities and weaknesses that are significant for understanding adaptive governance in the two case studies. These are discussed here and summarised in Table 12.1. Firstly, collaboration through adaptive governance reveals common challenges and needs, as well as providing opportunities for coordination of plans and actions across government levels. Secondly, flexibility allows for new data and research results to be included in decision-making processes, with subsequent adjustments to policies and measures. Finally, adaptive governance facilitates attention to the local context, which highly likely will lead to more effective responses to the climate change problem.

Conversely, our analysis shows that adaptive governance, as a governing approach, comes with processual and structural weaknesses that may inhibit the ability to deal with complex decision-making problems. We have identified four such salient weaknesses. First, the different government levels have predefined roles and unequal power, which may affect collaboration on equal terms; flexibility in decision-making and ability to be context sensitive.

Table 12.1   *A summary of the opportunities and weaknesses of adaptive governance*
emerging from reanalysing two case studies

Aspects of adaptive governance	Opportunities	Weaknesses
Collaboration and shared decision making	• Reveal common challenges and roles • Reveal needs of different actors • Better coordination of plans and actions across levels	• Pre-defined roles hinder collaboration • Power dynamics inherent in different roles and levels • Lack of resources to involve in adaptive governance processes • Adaptive multi-level governance processes may challenge the democratic processes at the local level
Flexibility over time	• Provide the newest and available research data to practitioners to learn and adapt • Adjust policies and measures as new experiences and knowledge arise	• Differential access to knowledge • Adjustments over time may require more resources both human and financial • Flexibility as new knowledge arise may be inhibited by pre-defined roles
Context sensitivity	• Attention to different contexts when policies and measures are planned and implemented will likely increase success	• National policies, guidelines and requirements designed in general way to be applicable for all types of municipalities • Context sensitivity hindered by already established structures and institutions

Second, access to relevant knowledge may vary between the actors involved, leaving some with a disadvantage that creates barriers for collaborating on equal terms. Third, adaptive governance processes, as illustrated here, are often carried out outside the formal democratic channels, which raise concerns about the legitimacy of the processes. Finally, adaptive governance processes are often demanding significant financial and human resources. The lack of resources likely affects proper and equal involvement by all parties and the ability to change as new knowledge and experiences arise. These weaknesses raise the question of how adaptive governance processes may be designed to realise its full potential in addressing wicked decision-making problems.

Ultimately the success of adaptive governance processes is restricted by how current governance structures are formed and carried out. Adaptive governance situated within a governance system designed as top-down and technocratic clearly has its limits (Cumming et al., 2006; Chaffin et al., 2014). Top-down governance approaches do not readily lend themselves to dialogue processes that involve actors across scale. Our results illustrate that more room is needed for national governments to facilitate and be catalysts for adaptive decision-making processes rather than leading by command and control.

Our case studies point to five factors that are to be acknowledged for adaptive governance to be successful:

1. Time is key in adaptive governance processes. Dialogue processes need time to develop, and it is essential that they are anchored in democratic decision-making forums. Our case study on urban growth agreements illustrates the need for establishing legitimacy through democratic channels, which would require sufficient time to materialise (Westskog et al., 2020).
2. Involvement of relevant parties is also critical for gaining access to different types of knowledge and perspectives and allows for necessary coordination across actors and

geographical borders, illustrated in the case study of urban growth agreements. Our case study on climate change adaptation also illustrates how management and governance of wicked problems may be entangled and closely linked in adaptive governance processes. The County Governor manages the governance signals from the national authorities and in our case operationalised these through an adaptive governance process (which could also be designated as an adaptive co-management process) involving both the political and administrative level in the different municipalities to address climate change adaptation issues in the county.

3. Alignment of national and municipal goals. National requirements and regulations need sufficient flexibility to align with a fluid local context. This combined with inclusion of local knowledge and expertise increases efficiency and applicability of national policy measures. This is illustrated in our case study of climate adaptation.

4. Access to sufficient human and financial resources and relevant knowledge is at the heart of successful adaptive governance. Without enough people to locate and assess relevant knowledge and to participate in dialogues the adaptive governance potential is reduced. Financial and human resources are required for both developing expertise and participation.

5. Successful adaptive governance includes nested multilevel structures acknowledging the different governance roles. This enables flow and reciprocity between the institutions and upholds local democracy. The intricate relationships between power hierarchies (in our case the County Governor and municipalities) emerge in negotiation processes. The County Governor is both a partner in reaching a common goal (zero-growth) and a supervising authority with the power to object to municipal planning (both transport and land use planning). A partnership across governance levels may therefore potentially threaten the local democracy.

CONCLUDING REMARKS

Framing climate change as a wicked problem we have in this chapter explored and analysed the role of adaptive governance in climate mitigation and adaptation efforts in a multi-level governance setting, from the local level perspective. The re-analyses of our two cases studies have provided us with the tools to illustrate multi level adaptive governance processes and identify both opportunities and weaknesses in its potential to handle climate change problems.

The wickedness of climate change points to three factors for why adaptive governance is important. First, all levels of government are in theory responsible for addressing climate change, but in practice it is unclear who is to do what, when and how. Second, society and analysts grapple with whether climate change requires fundamental or incremental changes, whether we need to significantly change our behaviour or rely on technology, and whether we need degrowth or enhance green growth. Third, the way climate change is inextricably linked to environmental problems associated with land use is suggestive of the goal conflicts between different government levels. Additionally, the inherent discrepancies between environmental concerns and climate change create dissonance in people and policy makers, which increases the wickedness of the problem. This may beg the question whether we need new institutions outside the democratic channels to handle the wickedness of climate change, because of the rapid response that is required measured against a slow-moving democracy. But we caution the suggestion to circumvent democracy as a praxis, even in the case of climate change, because it could take hold in other policy areas.

The wickedness of climate change is exacerbated at the local level when, as is currently the case, the broader policy-scape and grounds for decisions are unclear. The local level is after all where the most important decisions about climate change are taken and implemented. It is also the level where the most profound and deep knowledge about local nature and society is situated. On the other hand, reciprocity and flow of knowledge and expertise between the equally important levels of government are required. For adaptive governance to work it requires that we rethink the roles and responsibilities between the different government levels, including entrepreneurial efforts. For adaptive governance of climate change to be fully transformative in terms of changing the governance processes and enabling the way we collectively make decisions we may have to rethink the current system characteristics, which perpetuates an insufficient top-down and technocratic approach to climate change mitigation and adaptation.

REFERENCES

Amundsen, H., G. K. Hovelsrud, C. Aall, M. Karlsson, and H. Westskog. 2018. Local governments as drivers of societal transformation: towards the 1.5°C ambition. *Current Opinion in Environmental Sustainability*, 31, 23–29.

Ansell, C., and Torfing, J. (Eds.). 2016. *Handbook on Theories of Governance*. Edward Elgar Publishing.

Armitage D., Berkes, F., and Doubleday, N. 2007. *Adaptive Co-Management: Collaboration, Learning, and Multi-level Governance*, University of British Columbia Press.

Baird, J., Plummer, R., Haug, C., and Huitema, D. 2014. Learning effects of interactive decision-making processes for climate change adaptation. *Global Environmental Change*, 27, 51–63.

Berkes, F. 2008. *Sacred Ecology*. 2nd edn. Routledge.

Boyd, E., and Juhola, S. 2015. Adaptive climate change governance for urban resilience. *Urban Studies*, 5, 27, 1234–1264.

Boyd, E. and Folke, C. 2011. Conclusions: adapting institutions and resilience. In E. Boyd and C. Folke (Eds.), *Adapting Institutions. Governance, Complexity and Social-Ecological Resilience* (pp. 264–280). Cambridge University Press.

Bremer, S., and Meisch, S. 2017. Co-production in climate change research: reviewing different perspectives. *Wiley Interdisciplinary Reviews: Climate Change*, 8, 6, e482.

Bulkeley, H. 2015. Can cities realise their climate potential? Reflections on COP21 Paris and beyond. *Local Environment*, 20, 11, 1405–1409.

Bulkeley, H., and Betsill, M. 2005. Rethinking sustainable cities: multilevel governance and the 'urban' politics of climate change. *Environmental Politics*, 14, 1, 42–63.

Bulkeley, H. and Kern, K. 2006. Local government and the governing of climate change in Germany and the UK. *Urban Studies*, 43, 12, 2237–2259.

Burch, S., Shaw, A., Dale, A., and Robinson, J. 2014. Triggering transformative change: a development path approach to climate change response in communities. *Climate Policy*, 14, 4, 467–487.

Chaffin, B. C., Gosnell, H., and Cosens, B. A. 2014. A decade of adaptive governance scholarship: synthesis and future directions. *Ecology and Society*, 19, 3.

Cleaver, F., and Whaley, L. 2018. Understanding process, power, and meaning in adaptive governance: a critical institutional reading. *Ecology and Society*, 23, 2.

Cumming, G., Cumming, D. H., and Redman, C. 2006. Scale mismatches in social-ecological systems: causes, consequences, and solutions. *Ecology and Society*, 11, 1.

Dannevig, H. G. K., Hovelsrud, G. K., Hermansen, E. A. T., and Karlsson, M. 2020. Culturally sensitive boundary work: a framework for linking knowledge to climate action. *Environmental Science & Policy* 112, 405–413. https://doi.org/10.1016/j.envsci.2020.07.002.

Dannevig, H., Groven, K., Hovelsrud, G. K., Lundberg, A. K., Bellerby, R. G., Wallhead, P., and Labriola, M. 2019. A framework for agenda-setting ocean acidification through boundary work. *Environmental Science & Policy*, 95, 28–37.

Dannevig, H. and Hovelsrud, G. K. 2016. Understanding the need for adaptation in a natural resource dependent community in Northern Norway: issue salience, knowledge and values. *Climatic Change*, 135, 2, 261–275.

Dietz, T., Ostrom, E., and Stern, P. C. 2003. The struggle to govern the commons. *Science*, 302, 5652, 1907–1912.

Dilling, L., and Lemos, M. C. 2011. Creating usable science: opportunities and constraints for climate knowledge use and their implications for science policy. *Global Environmental Change*, 21, 2, 680–689.

Eshuis, J., and Gerrits, L. 2021. The limited transformational power of adaptive governance: a study of institutionalization and materialization of adaptive governance. *Public Management Review*, 23, 2, 276–296.

Fidel, M., Kliskey, A., Alessa, L., and Sutton, O. O. P. 2014. Walrus harvest locations reflect adaptation: a contribution from a community-based observation network in the Bering Sea. *Polar Geography*, 37. 48-68.

Fitchett A. 2014. Adaptive co-management in the context of informal settlements. *Urban Forum*, 25, 355–374.

Folke, C., Carpenter, S., Elmqvist, T., Gunderson, L., Holling, C. S., and Walker, B. 2002. Resilience and sustainable development: building adaptive capacity in a world of transformations. *AMBIO*, 31, 5, 437–441.

Folke, C., Hahn, T., Olsson, P., and Norberg, J. 2005. Adaptive governance of social-ecological systems. *Annual Review of Environment Resources*, 30, 441–473.

Greenhill, L., Kenter, J. O., and Dannevig, H. 2020. Adaptation to climate change–related ocean acidification: an adaptive governance approach. *Ocean and Coastal Management*, 191, 105176.

Hall, K., Cleaver, F., Fanks, T. and Maganga, F. 2014. Capturing critical institutionalism: a synthesis of key themes and debates. *European Journal of Development Research*, 26, 1, 71–86.

Head, B. W. 2018. Forty years of wicked problems literature: forging closer links to policy studies. *Policy and Society*, 38, 2, 180–97.

Hegger, D., Lamers, M., Van Zeijl-Rozema, A., and Dieperink, C. 2012. Conceptualising joint knowledge production in regional climate change adaptation projects: success conditions and levers for action. *Environmental Science & Policy*, 18, 52–65.

Hovelsrud, G. K., West, J., and Dannevig, H. 2015. Exploring vulnerability and adaptation narratives among fishers, farmers and municipal planners in Northern Norway. 194–212. In O'Brien, K. and E. Selboe (Eds.) *The Adaptive Challenge of Climate Change*, Cambridge University Press.

Hovelsrud, G. K. and Smit, B. (Eds.) 2010. *Community Adaptation and Vulnerability in the Arctic Regions.* Springer Publishers.

IPCC (Intergovernmental Panel on Climate Change). 2012. Glossary of terms. In V. Barros et al. (Eds.) *Managing the Risks of Extreme Events and Disasters to Advance Climate Change Adaptation* (pp. 555–564). Cambridge University Press.

Karlsson, M. and Hovelsrud, G. K. 2020. 'Everyone comes with their own shade of green': negotiating the meaning of transformation in Norway's agriculture and fisheries sectors. *Journal of Rural Studies*, https://doi.org/10.1016/j.jrurstud.2020.10.032.

Kasa, S., Westskog, H., and Rose, L. E. 2018. Municipalities as frontrunners in mitigation of climate change: does soft regulation make a difference? *Environmental Policy and Governance*, 28, 2, 98–113.

King, A. 2005. Structure and agency. Chapter 10 in A. Harrington (Eds.) *Modern Social Theory: An Introduction*. Oxford University Press.

Lempert R., Nakicenovic, N., Sarewitz, D., and Schlesinger, M. 2004. Characterizing climate-change uncertainties for decision makers. *Climatic Change*, 65, 1–9.

McConnell, A. 2018. Rethinking wicked problems as political problems and policy problems. *Policy and Politics* 46, 1, 165–180.

McConney, P., Mahon, R., and Pomeroy, R. 2007. Challenges facing coastal resource co-management in the Caribbean. In D. Armitage, F. Berkes, and N. Doubleday (Eds.), *Adaptive Co-management: Collaboration, Learning, and Multi-level Governance* (pp. 105–124). UBC Press.

Meadow, A. M., Ferguson, D. B., Guido, Z., Horangic, A., Owen, G., and Wall, T. 2015. Moving toward the deliberate coproduction of climate science knowledge. *Weather, Climate and Society*. 7, 2, 179–191. DOI: https://doi.org/10.1175/WCAS-D-14-00050.1.

MoT, Ministry of Transport. 2013. White paper no. 26 (2012–2013), National Transport Plan 2014–2023.

Munaretto, S., Siciliano, G., and Turvani, M. E. 2014. Integrating adaptive governance and participatory multicriteria methods: a framework for climate adaptation governance. *Ecology and Society*, 19, 2.

Normann, S. 2021. Green colonialism in the Nordic context: exploring Southern Saami representations of wind energy development. *Journal of Community Psychology*, 49, 1, 77–94.

O'Brien, Karen. 2012. Global environmental change II: from adaptation to deliberate transformation. *Progress in Human Geography*, 36, 5, 667–676.

O'Brien, Karen and Linda Sygna. 2013. Responding to climate change: the three spheres of transformation. Proceedings of Transformation in a Changing Climate, 19–21, University of Oslo, Norway.

Olsson, P. 2007. The role of vision in framing adaptive co-management processes: lessons from Kristianstads Vattenrik, Southern Sweden. In D. Armitage, F. Berkes, and N. Doubleday (Eds.), *Adaptive Co-management: Collaboration, Learning, and Multi-level Governance* (pp. 268–285). UBC Press.

Olsson, P., Folke, C., and Berkes, F. 2004. Adaptive comanagement for building resilience in social–ecological systems. *Environmental Management*, 34, 1, 75–90.

Plummer, R., and Baird, J. 2013. Adaptive co-management for climate change adaptation: considerations for the Barents Region. *Sustainability*, 5, 2, 629–642.

Plummer, R., and Fennell, D. A. 2009. Managing protected areas for sustainable tourism: prospects for adaptive co-management. *Journal of Sustainable Tourism*, 17, 2, 149–168.

Pomeroy, R. S., McConney, P., and Mahon, R. 2004. Comparative analysis of coastal resource co-management in the Caribbean. *Ocean and Coastal Management*, 47, 9–10, 429–447.

Rittel, H. W., and Melvin M. Webber. 1973. Dilemmas in a general theory of planning. *Policy Sciences*, 4, 2, 155–169.

Ruitenbeek, J., and Cartier, C. M. 2001. The invisible wand: adaptive co-management as an emergent strategy in complex bio-economic systems (Vol. 34). Bogor, Indonesia: Center for International Forestry Research.

Sharma-Wallace, L., Velarde, S. J., and Wreford, A. 2018. Adaptive governance good practice: show me the evidence! *Journal of Environmental Management*, 222, 174–184.

Smit, B., Pilifosova, O. and others 2001. Adaptation to climate change in the context of sustainable development and equity. In McCarthy, J. J., Canziani, O., Leary, N. A., Dokken, D. J. and White, K. S., (Eds.), *Climate Change 2001: Impacts, Adaptation and Vulnerability. IPCC Working Group II* (pp. 877–912). Cambridge University Press.

Smith, K., and Lawrence, G. 2018. From disaster management to adaptive governance? Governance challenges to achieving resilient food systems in Australia. *Journal of Environmental Policy and Planning*, 20, 3, 387–401.

Sovacool, B. K., Martiskainen, M., Hook, A., and Baker, L. 2019. Decarbonization and its discontents: a critical energy justice perspective on four low-carbon transitions. *Climatic Change*, 155, 4, 581–619.

Sæþórsdóttir, A. D., and Ólafsdóttir, R. 2020. Not in my back yard or not on my playground: residents and tourists' attitudes towards wind turbines in Icelandic landscapes. *Energy for Sustainable Development*, 54, 127–138.

Termeer, Catrien J., Art Dewulf, and G. Robbert Biesbroek. 2017. Transformational change: governance interventions for climate change adaptation from a continuous change perspective. *Journal of Environmental Planning and Management*, 60, 4, 558–76.

Tørnblad S., Westskog, H. and Rose, L. E. 2013. Does location matter? Public acceptance of restrictive policy measures at the local level. *Journal of Environmental Policy and Planning*, 16, 37–54.

Van Buuren, A., Keessen, A. M., Van Leeuwen, C., Eshuis, J., and Ellen, G. J. 2015. Implementation arrangements for climate adaptation in the Netherlands: characteristics and underlying mechanisms of adaptive governance. *Ecology and Society*, 20, 4.

Van Hecken, G., J. Bastiaensen, and C. Windey. 2015. Towards a power-sensitive and socially-informed analysis of payments for ecosystem services (PES): addressing the gaps in the current debate. *Ecological Economics*, 120, 117–125.

Verweij, M., Ney, S. and Thompson, M. 2011. *Clumsy Solution for a Wicked World*. Palgrave Macmillan.

Westskog, H., Hovelsrud, G. K., and Sundqvist, G. 2017. How to make local context matter in national advice: towards adaptive comanagement in Norwegian climate adaptation. *Weather, Climate, and Society*, 9, 2, 267–283.

Westskog, H., Amundsen, H., Christiansen, P., and Tønnesen, A. 2020. Urban contractual agreements as an adaptive governance strategy: under what conditions do they work in multi-level cooperation? *Journal of Environmental Policy and Planning*, 22, 4, 554–567.

13. Adaptive and anticipatory governance in urban adaptation to climate change

Alexandra Jurgilevich

INTRODUCTION

Urban adaptation as a policy problem is characterised by complexity and uncertainty. As a complex policy problem, it requires both an overarching strategic approach, as well as possible "breaking down" into smaller efforts (Hurlbert and Gupta, 2015). Here, the principles of adaptive governance are useful, i.e. namely polycentricity, multi-level and multi-actor governance, carried out in a coordinated and collaborative manner (Chaffin et al., 2014; Sharma-Wallace et al., 2018). Urban adaptation is often approached as a built environment problem whereas larger societal and economic drivers are not that well taken into account, thus adaptation either stays in a physical domain, or the efforts are carried out in silos (Birkmann et al., 2010; Olazabal and Ruiz De Gopegui, 2021).

The second challenge related to urban adaptation is uncertainty – here the principles of both adaptive and anticipatory governance are key. More specifically, anticipatory governance encourages stepping away from deterministic planning and moving towards anticipating a multitude of possible futures and planning robustly across them (Fuerth, 2009; Vervoort and Gupta, 2018). This governing approach requires institutional flexibility, where adaptive governance principles are a critical enabling resource. More specifically, approaching urban adaptation through the lens of adaptive governance means the creation of resilient institutional structures that allow flexibility and are less deterministic, as well as institutional context that creates space and enables the emergence of anticipatory adaptation, as well as integration of it into urban planning. Additionally, while anticipatory and adaptive governance theories support monitoring and evaluation, adaptive governance enables it by promoting learning processes and continuous participation and collaboration (Sharma-Wallace et al., 2018).

In this chapter, I join the argument that urban adaptation to climate change presents a window of opportunity to re-think and re-assess our current governance approaches (Sanchez Rodriguez et al., 2018). The chapter explores how adaptive governance addresses complexity and need for the institutional dynamics necessary for a paradigmatic shift towards a more flexible, resilient and forward-looking urban adaptation that does not compartmentalise climate change to a land use and built environment problem, but links it to broader socio-economic development (Birkmann et al., 2014). Furthermore, this chapter explores the complementarity of adaptive and anticipatory governance principles in addressing uncertainty.

INSTITUTIONAL DYNAMICS AND CURRENT URBAN ADAPTATION CONTEXT

Dynamics means a "process or pattern of change, growth or activity" (Merriam-Webster, 2021), and that includes not only large transformational changes, but also small incremental changes over a period of time. Institutions include both established organisations, as well as established practices, laws and norms (Young, 2010). Institutional dynamics is an inherent trait of institutions governing socio-ecological systems, which manifests in evolving and changing in pursuit of realising their potential or making adjustments to stay compatible with changing conditions, both biophysical and socio-economic (Young, 2010). Institutional dynamics in governing socio-ecological systems takes the form of both incremental changes and gradual adjustments, as well as non-linear, abrupt, possibly transformational and far-reaching (Young, 2010). It is dependent on the constant interaction between the governed system (in this case urban adaptation) and governing system (actors and institutions), or more specifically in monitoring of the governed system by the governing system as well as responsiveness of the governing system to the changes (Bettini et al., 2013).

Adaptation, as a policy problem, means adjustment to actual or expected climate change, and one of its main goals is to avoid or reduce potential harm (IPCC, 2014). Urban adaptation and institutional arrangements to steer it can be organised differently. Most often adaptation is vertically passed from the national level to local, often to the existing structures, where it is usually planned as a stand-alone strategy ("dedicated") or is integrated into work of other departments of urban planning ("mainstreamed") (Anguelovski and Carmin, 2011; Bulkeley and Tuts, 2013; Cortekar et al., 2016; Reckien et al., 2019). Mainstreaming as a policy implementation process is often approached as vertical (delegated from national to local/sectoral), and horizontal – across sectors (Nunan et al., 2012; van den Berg and Coenen, 2012). Sometimes only horizontal mainstreaming is considered to be "true" mainstreaming (Dovers and Hezri, 2010). It needs to be noted that in practice the cases are not so clear-cut and feature both delegation and cooperation (Rauken et al., 2015). In all cases, adaptation is often passed as a mandate to existing institutions and structures not all of which are designed to address such a challenge. Often, at the local level institutions are established to address specific areas of work (e.g., infrastructure, water, safety and preparedness, housing, social services and healthcare) (Patterson and Huitema, 2018). Adaptation as a policy problem, however, encompasses many areas of planning (Dovers and Hezri, 2010). When urban adaptation strategies are passed on to the existing institutional structures, incompatibility can be observed if adaptation is approached not only as a built environment effort, but includes social and economic aspects, requiring institutional flexibility.

The complexity and multi-faceted character of this policy problem means that there needs to be a coordinated effort both in the planning as well as in the implementation (Rauken et al., 2015). This means that horizontal mainstreaming is essential to avoid conflicting agendas, work in silos, conflicts in resource allocation and threats of maladaptation (Bowyer et al., 2015; Rauken et al., 2015). This is especially the case if we are talking about anticipatory adaptation (Boyle et al., 2011). In these cases, adaptive governance is essential in supporting institutional flexibility and dynamics necessary for these structures to be able to fulfil and sustain their mandates (Patterson and Huitema, 2018; Young, 2010). Thus, there is a need for the adaptive governance to take place, as there is a need for institutions that function across sectors with regards to planning, prioritisation, and resource allocation (Sanchez Rodriguez et al., 2018). While there has been notable progress in urban adaptation, and in fact, many cities have established working groups or cross-cutting organisations for climate change adaptation, very often urban adaptation is still characterised as fragmented (Den Uyl and Russel, 2017; O'Brien and O'Keefe, 2013; Pilli-Sihvola et al., 2018), which means that horizontal main-streaming is lagging behind.

With regards to uncertainty, both changing biophysical and socio-economic conditions present a challenge and have implications for governance and urban planning. Even though climate prediction science has advanced to reduce prediction uncertainty, it is still impossible to eliminate it completely (IPCC, 2018). Climate change is happening faster than previously thought, thus institutions have to function in high uncertainty (IPCC, 2018). Also, the socio-economic conditions are constantly changing, e.g., population growth and structure, population distribution, urbanisation, external changes that cause perturbations in economy, can possibly pose challenges to the existing urban governance structures if they are not used to function in conditions of change and uncertainty. This requires certain adjustments in govern-ance approaches. More specifically, policy innovation and new tools addressing uncertainty are needed and started to emerge to address the issue (Walker et al., 2013). Additionally, uncertain and changing context means that adaptation planning, and implementation need to be constantly revised, and this requires capacity building in terms of monitoring, evaluation, and adjustment.

ADAPTIVE AND ANTICIPATORY GOVERNANCE IN ADDRESSING UNCERTAINTY

There are two dominant approaches in governance and planning with regards to how future is taken into account: foresight and forecast (Fuerth, 2009; Quay, 2010). Forecast as a futures research tradition broadly speaks to the "prognosis" tradition (Cuhls, 2003; Inayatullah, 2008; Masini, 2006). It builds on the empirical past and present data and seeks to predict the way forward. Its underlying assumption is that "something is changing" (Masini, 2006). Forecasting gives basis to rationalistic planning and governance, also called "predict and plan" (Quay, 2010). Predict and plan governance uses prediction and thus aims for tackling identified problems but can also take up scenarios with a backcasting approach to be used in strategic planning, i.e. envisioning the future and planning to achieve the desired vision. Rationalistic governance and planning and strong reliance on forecasting is a predominant approach to identifying climate risks and planning adaptation (Jurgilevich et al., 2017). However, with the rapidly changing biophysical and socio-economic conditions, this approach to adaptation is too limiting and rigid (Jurgilevich, 2021b). More specifically, it is not well suited to govern in conditions of rapid change, high uncertainty, long temporal horizons and highly complex problems (Fuerth, 2009; Quay, 2010; Vervoort and Gupta, 2018), all of which are characteristic of adaptation to climate change (Hurlbert and Gupta, 2015).

The alternative approach to forecasting is foresight, and it forms the basis for scenario planning, strategic planning, and anticipatory governance. In contrast to forecast-driven governance, which seeks to "prepare" for these changes (Cuhls, 2003), foresight-driven governance has a stronger agency and is driven by a principle that the future can or must be changed (Cuhls, 2003; Masini, 2006). Thus, foresight explores a multitude of possible developments, in contrast to forecast that seeks to find what is the probable among possible futures. With that, foresight-driven governance relies on flexible tools and strategies. There is a multitude of more well-known governance tools and policy instruments that serve foresight purposes, such as no-regret strategies, use of worst case scenarios, contingency plans (Fuerth, 2009; Quay, 2010). In the urban context, such tools and strategies should take into account socio-economic dynamics (e.g., urbanisation, migration, demographic change, urban sprawl) in addition to several scenarios of climatic changes (Birkmann et al., 2010; Jurgilevich, 2021b). New approaches are also emerging indicating that anticipatory governance is taking stronger positions in climate risk management and adaptation, such as e.g., dynamic adaptive policy pathways (DAPP) (Kwakkel et al., 2015).

One of the important departing points to understanding governance approaches with regards to how the future is taken into account is the approach to uncertainty. Often, in natural and social sciences, and also in vulnerability and risk literature, uncertainty is approached as something that can and should be reduced by gathering and processing more information (McDaniel and Driebe, 2005). This rather deterministic approach is traceable in forecast-driven planning and governance. The other way to approach uncertainties is to acknowledge that there are situations and policy problems where uncertainties are not statistical in nature and cannot be reduced by data gathering and processing (Walker et al., 2013). The solution here is to accept uncertainty and approach governance through anticipatory (with regards to future) and adaptive (with regards to flexibility) lenses. Anticipatory governance promotes navigating uncertainty with the use of flexible tools and policies, such as contingency plans, no-regret strategies, the use of a multitude of scenarios and constant monitoring and adjustment (Fuerth, 2009). Anticipatory governance specifically includes also constant re-visioning of policy against the implementation progress and against how the future unfolds, in contrast to prediction-driven governance that doesn't presuppose monitoring and is rather reactive towards the changes than anticipating (Quay, 2010). Adaptive governance in its turn also promotes the choices of reversible interventions and constant monitoring, and additionally puts focus on the facilitation of broad collaboration and learning, encouraging transparency and reflexivity in highlighting the limitations of the knowledge upon which the policy choices are made (Cooney and Lang, 2007), thus supporting the shift towards foresight-driven governance. A good practice example integrating the principles of anticipatory and adaptive governance in urban adaptation is Shanghai Master Plan for "Flexible Adaptation: To keep in mind the uncertainty of urban development, improve the multi-scenario planning strategy, create a new flexible functional layout model, establish the space reserving mechanism and constant evaluation and adjustment mechanism, and construct a flexible spatial strategy and management mechanism" (Olazabal and Ruiz De Gopegui, 2021, p. 6).

In many cases, administrations still function in forecasting mode and bringing forward flexible tools for adaptive and anticipatory governance has been challenging (Lawrence and Haasnoot, 2017). New foresight-driven tools have emerged to assist the shift towards adaptive and anticipatory governance, for example, contingency plans, no-regret strategies, use of worst-case scenarios (Fuerth, 2009; Quay, 2010), and more comprehensive approaches such as dynamic adaptive policy pathways (DAPP) (Haasnoot et al., 2013), robust decision-making (RBM) (Lempert, 2019) and assumption-based planning (ABP) (Dewar, 2002), have been developed. However, these approaches, relying on adaptive and anticipatory principles, face challenges in the uptake, as they challenge the norms of decision-making and planning. For example, Lawrence and Haasnoot (2017) have studied what it takes to catalyse the uptake of DAPP approaches in New Zealand at the local level flood management using serious gaming.

Serious gaming facilitated by external knowledge brokering enabled cognitive, normative, and relational learning, creating space for the change of "static" practices towards adaptive "dynamic" governance (Lawrence and Haasnoot, 2017). The success in further sustaining of adaptive and anticipatory governance principles is dependent on relational learning, among other factors, which refers to the greater understanding of views of others, greater cooperation, and codification (Lawrence and Haasnoot, 2017). Overall, strong cooperation across stakeholders and scales, as well as effective coordination are critical for sustaining adaptive governance (Sharma-Wallace et al., 2018). Relational learning is critical also for improved horizontal mainstreaming (Lawrence and Haasnoot, 2017), however, established learning practices are still lagging behind in large cities (Olazabal and Ruiz De Gopegui, 2021).

INFORMATION SUPPLY FOR URBAN ADAPTATION

Both adaptation and urban planning activities are forward-looking in their core and can and ideally should go hand-in-hand. Hazards cannot be reduced or targeted with adaptation, but people's exposure and vulnerability can be reduced through urban planning and adaptation efforts (Jurgilevich et al., 2021). More specifically, urban adaptation and urban planning can and should reduce enhanced exposure and increase people's adaptive capacity (Jurgilevich et al., 2021). Enhanced exposure means features of physical environment that make people more vulnerable to climate change impacts, including permeable surfaces, climate resilience of residential stock and critical infrastructure, green and blue infrastructure, among others. Adaptive capacity in its turn refers to people's material and social situation, and that relates to social and health care services, as well as broader determinants of welfare (Jurgilevich et al., 2021; Kazmierczak, 2015). Urban adaptation relies on the information on climate risks and vulnerabilities, which is most often collected with risk and vulnerability assessments (Adger et al., 2018).

Currently, most vulnerability and risk assessments are focused on measuring vulnerability through indices and mapping them (Adger et al., 2018; Birkmann et al., 2010; Fekete, 2012; Jurgilevich et al., 2017). These assessments collect information on past, current and future risks, and are most often presented as maps of indices. Most often, these assessments show what are the hot-spots of risk and vulnerability based on the aggregation of indicators, giving information on locations where specific adaptation measures need to be prioritised (Jurgilevich et al., 2017). If the indices are disaggregated, they tell us what indicators increase vulnerability. Overall, such assessments can be characterised as static – examining a state of risk or vulnerability at a certain point in time (Ford et al., 2018; Jurgilevich et al., 2017). Vulnerability and risk research has long been criticised for the static and deterministic approaches to assessments, and this has implications for the users of this information: namely static and deterministic assessments do not provide enough information to plan urban adaptation based on anticipatory and adaptive governance principles (Dilling et al., 2015; Ford et al., 2018; Mcdowell et al., 2016).

Dynamic risk and vulnerability assessments are emerging to respond to this need, focusing on the processes and causes of vulnerability (Fawcett et al., 2017; Jurgilevich et al., 2021; Lede et al., 2021), following the human/political ecology tradition of vulnerability research (Cutter, 1996). The rationale is to provide information on the mechanisms and processes behind vulnerability development, and thus address the root causes of risk and vulnerability, building on adaptive governance and providing insights for anticipatory adaptation (Jurgilevich et al., 2021), especially with regards to monitoring, evaluation and adjustment of adaptation. It should be noted that while some dynamic assessments utilise a number of scenarios catering for the need to account for a multitude of future developments, in practice, they may fall short of explaining the mechanisms of vulnerability and risk development and rather assess vulnerability in different points in the future according to different scenarios, i.e. following deterministic approaches. Overall, there is a need of broadening and deepening the scope of risk and vulnerability assessments that would supply usable information for anticipatory adaptation and adaptive governance, and that would include a deeper investigation of socio-economic determinants and processes influencing vulnerability development (Jurgilevich, 2021a). This would presuppose the inclusion of other types of knowledge than scientific, such as expert and local, to investigate the interdependent socio-economic processes driving urban vulnerabilities (Jurgilevich, 2021b). This is also important from the adaptive governance perspective as it enhances stakeholder collaboration across sectors and scales (Brunner et al., 2005). The use of such information in urban adaptation would promote strategic urban adaptation and urban planning that enhances citizens' resilience and adaptive capacity.

Additionally, there is a certain divide between adaptation and vulnerability research. Adaptation research has long strengthened the importance of it serving also broader societal goals – increasing welfare, social cohesion, environmental integrity and pursuing Sustainable Development Goals (SDGs) (Brown and Eriksen, 2012; Sanchez Rodriguez et al., 2018). Furthermore, exactly SDGs in urban planning are suggested to be a "unifying" goal that can help overcome resource and agenda conflict, fragmentation, and work in silos (Sanchez Rodriguez et al., 2018). The vulnerability and risk assessment literature is rather focused on providing specific assessments of risk areas or vulnerable groups of people, and less so on linking this information to adaptation and risk management (Bowyer et al., 2015; Räsänen et al., 2017), and even less so to anticipatory adaptation, sustainable development and sustainable urban planning (Brown and Eriksen, 2012). Following adaptive governance principles and linking urban adaptation with broader socio-economic development and capacity building, and using adaptive governance methods in doing so (by promoting stakeholder engagement, participation and coordinated collaboration, as well as other types of knowledge in addition to scientific) can be a fruitful path to follow in re-thinking and re-assessing existing governance approaches (Cooney and Lang, 2007).

WAYS FORWARD: ANTICIPATORY AND ADAPTIVE GOVERNANCE FOR URBAN ADAPTATION

Urban adaptation presents a window of opportunity to re-think and re-assess our current policy-making and urban planning with regards to three issues: (a) approaches to futures and uncertainty; (b) institutional context; (c) integrated vs. compartmentalised planning. Societies and countries with an overall high level of welfare, social cohesion, have higher adaptive capacity and lower risk to suffer from the impacts of climate change (Pilli-Sihvola et al., 2018). Urban vulnerability to climate change is to a large extent a consequence of how our society functions, how our cities are planned, and how our policies are designed and implemented (Jurgilevich, 2021a). That is why anticipatory adaptation should target vulnerability addressing its root causes, and urban planning should be built around the awareness of vulnerability development. This means, that all sectors of urban planning, including infrastructure, housing, social and health care services, construction, environment – all can contribute to anticipatory adaptation by taking into account vulnerability causes and its future development, relying on the principles of adaptive and anticipatory governance and promoting relational learning to enhance coordination, horizontal mainstreaming, avoiding conflicting agendas and resource competition (Lawrence and Haasnoot, 2017; Sanchez Rodriguez et al., 2018).

Additionally, a certain change in thinking about the future is needed. More specifically, this refers to giving up the idea of predicting and preparing for one specific scenario, and changing the governance thinking towards flexibility, anticipation, and constant monitoring and evaluation (M&E) of not only policy and biophysical conditions, but also of the socio-economic context (Fuerth, 2009; Quay, 2010; Vervoort and Gupta, 2018; Young, 2010). Establishing mechanisms of monitoring and evaluation, as well as continuous learning, following the principles and methods of adaptive and anticipatory governance are critical in sustaining flexible and robust urban adaptation, these are, however, largely lagging behind (Olazabal and Ruiz De Gopegui, 2021).

A change is needed on the science side as well. Risk and vulnerability assessments should deepen and broaden in scope (Jurgilevich, 2021a), and engage more with the roots of vulnerability research (Ford et al., 2018), and specifically with the human/political ecology tradition (Cutter, 1996). Understanding the broader socio-economic determinants of vulnerability, as well as processes and mechanisms of its development, provides information for anticipatory adaptation and its adaptive steering, by engaging multiple sectors in a coordinated manner as well as allowing understanding of triggers and tipping points of changes, where intervention is required (Lawrence and Haasnoot, 2017; Sanchez Rodriguez et al., 2018).

CONCLUSION

In the light of pandemic, the United Nations Development Programme (UNDP) has proposed a Triple-A (AAA) governance: adaptive, anticipatory and agile (Wiesen, 2020). Agile here refers to innovation, experimentation, responsiveness to feedback, allowing for instructive patterns and learning (Spitz, 2020). The suitability of a Triple-A governance has been suggested for climate change adaptation as well, while highlighting the pursuit of SDG in governance objectives and processes (Wiesen, 2020). The framework is promising in addressing climate change more broadly and urban adaptation in conditions of complex problems, need for horizontal mainstreaming, high uncertainty, and long-term horizons. More specifically, urban adaptation can benefit from anticipatory governance principles and tools by shifting away from deterministic prediction towards exploring a range of changes and planning adaptation that is robust across them (Birkmann et al., 2010). There is a need for the establishment of monitoring and evaluation mechanisms, central to adaptive governance, in order to ensure timely revision of adaptation measures and plans (Olazabal and Ruiz De Gopegui, 2021). Institutional dynamics is critical here to ensure responsiveness of institutions to the changes in governed systems (Bettini et al., 2013). Finally, adaptive governance can aid in broadening and deepening the scope of urban adaptation from built environment and land use problem towards broader socio-economic sustainable development, importantly in a collaborative and coordinated manner (Sanchez Rodriguez et al., 2018). These changes require paradigmatic shifts both on the practice side with regards to being more responsive to new governance approaches, as well as on the science side with regards to what kind of information we supply for further use, i.e. shifting from fragmented prediction towards broader foresight.

REFERENCES

Adger, N., Brown, I., and Surminski, S. (2018). Advances in risk assessment for climate change adaptation policy. *Philosophical Transactions of the Royal Society A: Mathematical, Physical and Engineering Sciences*, 376(2121). https://doi.org/10.1098/rsta.2018.0106.

Anguelovski, I., and Carmin, J. A. (2011). Something borrowed, everything new: innovation and institutionalization in urban climate governance. *Current Opinion in Environmental Sustainability*, 3(3), 169–175. https://doi.org/10.1016/j.cosust.2010.12.017.

Bettini, Y., Brown, R., and De Haan, F. J. (2013). Water scarcity and institutional change: lessons in adaptive governance from the drought experience of Perth, Western Australia. *Water Science and Technology: A Journal of the International Association on Water Pollution Research*, 67(10), 2160–2168. https://doi.org/10.2166/WST.2013.127.

Birkmann, J., Garschagen, M., Kraas, F., and Quang, N. (2010). Adaptive urban governance: new challenges for the second generation of urban adaptation strategies to climate change. *Sustainability Science*, 5(2), 185–206. https://doi.org/10.1007/s11625-010-0111-3.

Birkmann, J., Garschagen, M., and Setiadi, N. (2014). New challenges for adaptive urban governance in highly dynamic environments: revisiting planning systems and tools for adaptive and strategic planning. *Urban Climate*, 7, 115–133. https://doi.org/10.1016/J.UCLIM.2014.01.006.

Bowyer, P., Brasseur, G. P., and Jacob, D. (2015). The role of climate services in adapting to climate variability and change. In W. Leal Filho (Ed.), *Handbook of Climate Change Adaptation* (pp. 533–550). Springer Berlin Heidelberg. https://doi.org/10.1007/978-3-642-38670-1_29.

Boyle, M., Dowlatabadi, H., Boyle, M., and Dowlatabadi, H. (2011). Anticipatory adaptation in marginalized communities within developed countries. *Advances in Global Change Research*, 42, 461–473. https://doi.org/10.1007/978-94-007-0567-8_34.

Brown, K., and Eriksen, S. H. (2012). Sustainable adaptation to climate change. *Sustainable Adaptation to Climate Change*. https://doi.org/10.4324/9781849776912/SUSTAINABLE-ADAPTATION-CLIMATE-CHANGE.

Brunner, R. D., Steelman, T., Coe-Juell, L., Cromley, C. M., Edwards, C. M., and Tucker, D. W. (2005). *Adaptive Governance: Integrating Science, Policy, and Decision Making*. Columbia University Press.

Bulkeley, H., and Tuts, R. (2013). Understanding urban vulnerability, adaptation and resilience in the context of climate change. *Local Environment*, 18(6), 646–662. https://doi.org/10.1080/13549839.2013.788479.

Chaffin, B. C., Gosnell, H., and Cosens, B. A. (2014). A decade of adaptive governance scholarship: synthesis and future directions. *Ecology and Society*, 19(3). https://doi.org/10.5751/ES-06824-190356.

Cooney, R., and Lang, A. T. F. (2007). Taking uncertainty seriously: adaptive governance and international trade. *European Journal of International Law*, 18(3), 523–551. https://doi.org/10.1093/EJIL/CHM030.

Cortekar, J., Bender, S., Brune, M., and Groth, M. (2016). Why climate change adaptation in cities needs customised and flexible climate services. *Climate Services*, 4, 42–51. https://doi.org/10.1016/j.cliser.2016.11.002.

Cuhls, K. (2003). From forecasting to foresight processes? New participative foresight activities in Germany. *Journal of Forecasting*, 22(2–3), 93–111. https://doi.org/10.1002/for.848.

Cutter, S. L. (1996). Vulnerability to environmental hazards. *Progress in Human Geography*, 20(4), 529–539. https://doi.org/10.1177/030913259602000407.

Den Uyl, R. M., and Russel, D. J. (2017). Climate adaptation in fragmented governance settings: the consequences of reform in public administration. *Environmental Politics*, 27(2), 341–361. https://doi.org/10.1080/09644016.2017.1386341.

Dewar, J. A. (2002). *Assumption-based Planning: A Tool for Reducing Avoidable Surprises*. Cambridge, Cambridge University Press, pp. 248.

Dilling, L., Daly, M. E., Travis, W. R., Wilhelmi, O. V., and Klein, R. A. (2015). The dynamics of vulnerability: why adapting to climate variability will not always prepare us for climate change. Wiley Interdisciplinary Reviews: *Climate Change*, 6(4), 413–425. https://doi.org/10.1002/wcc.341.

Dovers, S. R., and Hezri, A. A. (2010). Institutions and policy processes: the means to the ends of adaptation. Wiley Interdisciplinary Reviews: *Climate Change*, 1(2), 212–231. https://doi.org/10.1002/WCC.29.

Fawcett, D., Pearce, T., Ford, J. D., and Archer, L. (2017). Operationalizing longitudinal approaches to climate change vulnerability assessment. *Global Environmental Change*, 45(May), 79–88. https://doi.org/10.1016/j.gloenvcha.2017.05.002.

Fekete, A. (2012). Spatial disaster vulnerability and risk assessments: challenges in their quality and acceptance. *Natural Hazards*, 61(3), 1161–1178. https://doi.org/10.1007/s11069-011-9973-7.

Ford, J. D., Pearce, T., McDowell, G., Berrang-Ford, L., Sayles, J. S., and Belfer, E. (2018). Vulnerability and its discontents: the past, present, and future of climate change vulnerability research. *Climatic Change*, October, 1–15. https://doi.org/10.1007/s10584-018-2304-1.

Fuerth, L. S. (2009). Foresight and anticipatory governance. *Foresight*, 11(4), 14–32. https://doi.org/10.1108/14636680910982412.

Haasnoot, M., Kwakkel, J. H., Walker, W. E., and ter Maat, J. (2013). Dynamic adaptive policy pathways: a method for crafting robust decisions for a deeply uncertain world. *Global Environmental Change*, 23(2), 485–498. https://doi.org/10.1016/J.GLOENVCHA.2012.12.006.

Hurlbert, M., and Gupta, J. (2015). The split ladder of participation: a diagnostic, strategic, and evaluation tool to assess when participation is necessary. *Environmental Science & Policy*, 50, 100–113. https://doi.org/10.1016/J.ENVSCI.2015.01.011.

Inayatullah, S. (2008). Six pillars: futures thinking for transforming. *Foresight*, 10(1), 4–21. https://doi.org/10.1108/14636680810855991.

IPCC. (2014). Annex II: Glossary. In Core Writing Team, R. Pachauri, and L. Meyer (Eds.), *Climate Change 2014: Synthesis Report. Contribution of Working Groups I, II and III to the Fifth Assessment Report of the Intergovernmental Panel on Climate Change* (pp. 117–130). IPCC. https://www.ipcc.ch/pdf/assessment-report/ar5/syr/AR5_SYR_FINAL_Glossary.pdf.

IPCC. (2018). Global warming of 1.5°C: an IPCC Special Report on the impacts of global warming of 1.5°C above pre-industrial levels and related global greenhouse gas emission pathways, in the context of strengthening the global response to the threat of climate change. IPCC – SR1.5, 2(October), 17–20. www.environmentalgraphiti.org.

Jurgilevich, A. (2021a). Urban futures and climate change: understanding vulnerability dynamics. Dissertationes Schola Doctoralis Scientiae Circumiectalis, Alimentariae, Biologicae, University of Helsinki.

Jurgilevich, A. (2021b). Governance modes and epistemologies of future-oriented vulnerability assessments: example of a mixed-methods approach. *Futures*, 128, 102717. https://doi.org/10.1016/J.FUTURES.2021.102717.

Jurgilevich, A., Räsänen, A., Groundstroem, F., and Juhola, S. (2017). A systematic review of dynamics in climate risk and vulnerability assessments. *Environmental Research Letters*, 12(1), 013002. https://doi.org/10.1088/1748-9326/aa5508.

Jurgilevich, A., Räsänen, A., and Juhola, S. (2021). Assessing the dynamics of urban vulnerability to climate change. *Environmental Science & Policy*, 125, 32–43. https://doi.org/10.1016/J.ENVSCI.2021.08.002.

Kazmierczak, A. (2015). Analysis of social vulnerability to climate change in the Helsinki Metropolitan Area Final report. www.hsy.fi.

Kwakkel, J. H., Haasnoot, M., Walker, W. E., Lourenço, C., Rovisco, A., Dessai, S., Moss, R., Petersen, A., Kwakkel, J. H., Haasnoot, M., and Walker, W. E. (2015). Developing dynamic adaptive policy pathways: a computer-assisted approach for developing adaptive strategies for a deeply uncertain world. *Climatic Change*, 132, 373–386. https://doi.org/10.1007/s10584-014-1210-4.

Lawrence, J., and Haasnoot, M. (2017). What it took to catalyse uptake of dynamic adaptive pathways planning to address climate change uncertainty. *Environmental Science & Policy*, 68, 47–57. https://doi.org/10.1016/J.ENVSCI.2016.12.003.

Lede, E., Pearce, T., Furgal, C., Wolki, M., Ashford, G., and Ford, J. D. (2021). The role of multiple stressors in adaptation to climate change in the Canadian Arctic. *Regional Environmental Change*, 21(2), 1–13. https://doi.org/10.1007/S10113-021-01769-Z.

Lempert, R. J. (2019). Robust Decision Making (RDM). *Decision Making under Deep Uncertainty*, 23–51. https://doi.org/10.1007/978-3-030-05252-2_2.

Masini, E. (2006). Rethinking futures studies. *Futures*, 38(10), 1158–1168. https://doi.org/10.1016/j.futures.2006.02.004.

McDaniel, R. R. J., and Driebe, D. J. (2005). Uncertainty and surprise in complex systems. In *Uncertainty and Surprise in Complex Systems*. Springer-Verlag. https://doi.org/10.1007/B13122.

Mcdowell, G., Ford, J., and Jones, J. (2016). Community-level climate change vulnerability research: trends, progress, and future directions. *Environmental Research Letters*, 11(3), 0. https://doi.org/10.1088/1748-9326/11/3/033001.

Merriam-Webster. (2021). *Merriam-Webster Dictionary*. https://www.merriam-webster.com/dictionary/dynamics.

Nunan, F., Campbell, A., and Foster, E. (2012). Environmental mainstreaming: the organisational challenges of policy integration. *Public Administration and Development*, 32(3), 262–277. https://doi.org/10.1002/PAD.1624.

O'Brien, G., and O'Keefe, P. (2013). Managing adaptation to climate risk: beyond fragmented responses. *Managing Adaptation to Climate Risk: Beyond Fragmented Responses*, 1–217. https://doi.org/10.4324/9780203836910.

Olazabal, M., and Ruiz De Gopegui, M. (2021). Adaptation planning in large cities is unlikely to be effective. *Landscape and Urban Planning*, 206. https://doi.org/10.1016/J.LANDURBPLAN.2020.103974.

Patterson, J. J., and Huitema, D. (2018). Institutional innovation in urban governance: the case of climate change adaptation. *Journal of Environmental Planning and Management* https://doi.org/10.1080/09640568.2018.1510767.

Pilli-Sihvola, K., Harjanne, A., and Haavisto, R. (2018). Adaptation by the least vulnerable: managing climate and disaster risks in Finland. *International Journal of Disaster Risk Reduction*, 31, 1266–1275. https://doi.org/10.1016/j.ijdrr.2017.12.004.

Quay, R. (2010). Anticipatory governance. *Journal of the American Planning Association*, 76(4), 496–511. https://doi.org/10.1080/01944363.2010.508428.

Räsänen, A., Jurgilevich, A., Haanpää, S., Heikkinen, M., Groundstroem, F., and Juhola, S. (2017). The need for non-climate services: empirical evidence from Finnish municipalities. *Climate Risk Management*, 16. https://doi.org/10.1016/j.crm.2017.03.004.

Rauken, T., Mydske, P. K., and Winsvold, M. (2015). Mainstreaming climate change adaptation at the local level. *Local Environment*, 20(4), 408–423. https://doi.org/10.1080/13549839.2014.880412.

Reckien, D., Salvia, M., Pietrapertosa, F., Simoes, S. G., Olazabal, M., De Gregorio Hurtado, S., Geneletti, D., Krkoška Lorencová, E., D'Alonzo, V., Krook-Riekkola, A., Fokaides, P. A., Ioannou, B. I., Foley, A., Orru, H., Orru, K., Wejs, A., Flacke, J., Church, J. M., Feliu, E., … Heidrich, O. (2019). Dedicated versus mainstreaming approaches in local climate plans in Europe. *Renewable and Sustainable Energy Reviews*, 112, 948–959. https://doi.org/10.1016/J.RSER.2019.05.014.

Sanchez Rodriguez, R., Ürge-Vorsatz, Di., and Barau, A. S. (2018). Sustainable Development Goals and climate change adaptation in cities. *Nature Climate Change*, 8(3), 181–183. https://doi.org/10.1038/s41558-018-0098-9.

Sharma-Wallace, L., Velarde, S. J., and Wreford, A. (2018). Adaptive governance good practice: show me the evidence! *Journal of Environmental Management*, 222, 174–184. https://doi.org/10.1016/J.JENVMAN.2018.05.067.

Spitz, R. (2020). The future of strategic decision-making. *Journal of Futures Studies*. https://jfsdigital.org/2020/07/26/the-future-of-strategic-decision-making/.

van den Berg, M., and Coenen, F. (2012). Integrating climate change adaptation into Dutch local policies and the role of contextual factors. *Local Environment*, 17(4), 441–460. https://doi.org/10.1080/13549839.2012.678313.

Vervoort, J., and Gupta, A. (2018). Anticipating climate futures in a 1.5 °C era: the link between foresight and governance. *Current Opinion in Environmental Sustainability*, 31, 104–111. https://doi.org/10.1016/J.COSUST.2018.01.004.

Walker, W. E., Haasnoot, M., and Kwakkel, J. H. (2013). Adapt or perish: a review of planning approaches for adaptation under deep uncertainty. *Sustainability*, 5(3), 955–979. https://www.mdpi .com/2071-1050/5/3/955/htm.
Wiesen, C. (2020). Anticipatory, adaptive and agile governance is key to the response to COVID-19. UNDP in the Asia and the Pacific. *UNDP*. https://www.asia-pacific.undp.org/content/rbap/en/home/ presscenter/articles/2020/anticipatory--adaptive-and-agile-governance-is-key-to-the-respon.html.
Young, O. R. (2010). Institutional dynamics: resilience, vulnerability and adaptation in environmental and resource regimes. *Global Environmental Change*, 20(3), 378–385. https://doi.org/10.1016/J .GLOENVCHA.2009.10.001.

14. Towards adaptive property: legal design for a climate-affected future

Daniel Fitzpatrick

INTRODUCTION

Emerging concepts of adaptive law broadly describe regulatory approaches that avoid rigid *ex ante* solutions to complex socio-ecological problems (Cosens et al. 2020, Soininen et al., this book). Attributes of adaptive law include the flexibility to accommodate self-organisation through scale-sensitive systems of resource governance (Cole 2011, Marshall 2009). But how can such a legal regime apply to property in land? Conventional formulations of property law seek stability of expectations through state-sanctioned entitlements that set out permitted and proscribed uses of resources. The primary aim is a hierarchical system of rights based on certainty of expectations rather than adaptability in the face of uncertainty. When, therefore, should property law allow for flexibility rather than certainty in the face of current risks such as environmental disruption? Is there a case for re-visiting orthodox formulations of stability/flexibility trade-offs in property law to meet the challenges of climate change? This chapter considers these questions as a contribution to broader debates over adaptive law for a climate-affected future.

For the economic analysis of property, the flexibility of property law primarily derives from the divisibility and distribution of proprietary rights through market bargaining (Harper 2014). Property law allows for flexibility because bundles of proprietary rights may be separated, combined, and alienated to parties who value the right(s) the most. This capacity to transact property rights facilitates adaptive market responses to complex social-ecological problems (Barnes 2013). The ensuing market-based perspective privileges the stability or standardising functions of property law because they provide a secure foundation for efficient bargaining. In this conception, influenced by the work of Ronald Coase, the key role for law is to define initial allocations of property rights through simple easy-to-understand rules, and then to reduce the transaction costs of property through mechanisms such as public systems for recording rights or transactions relating to land (Merrill and Smith 2001). Adjustments to rights through regulatory mechanisms beyond market bargaining – including decentralised systems of community-based resource governance – are only appropriate in circumstances of market failure (Calabresi and Melamed 1972).

The ensuing vision of property places government systems of public administration at the apex of a stable and hierarchical system of proprietary rights to land. But does this vision match the descriptive reality of property in much of the world today? Drawing on adaptive governance frameworks, this chapter argues that the reality of global property regimes is better described as polycentric rather than hierarchical. Polycentricity includes circumstances where property rights not only derive from sovereign grant, recorded in state systems of land administration; but also take the form of proprietary relationships secured through social norms, informal agreements, and private acts of coordination beyond the control or reach of the state

(Fitzpatrick and Monson 2021). The illustrative example is informal property systems in the Global South. As will be described, informal property systems include 75% or more of the world's population that are not recorded in government systems of land administration. These circumstances of informality highlight government failures in the definition, delineation, and recordation of property rights in land. The extent of government failure in relation to property is central to the phenomenon of property system polycentricity, and to the development of normative frames for adaptive property law.

This chapter further provides evidence that polycentric property systems respond to environmental disruption in heterodox, extra-legal and scale-sensitive ways. Case studies of catastrophic disasters in Indonesia and the Philippines identify acts of self-organisation, where decentralised components of a complex property system respond at scale to disruption without instruction or supervision from a central organising authority (Fitzpatrick and Compton 2021). This evidence of autonomous self-organisation highlights a key effect of polycentricity – that law is one of several scale-specific constructs for the governance of property in land. The chapter argues that design principles for adaptive property law become apparent once there is better descriptive recognition of polycentricity in relation to property. In particular, the chapter suggests that the normative trade-offs of property law design for a future of climate disruption may be extended to include the potential for adaptive capacity on the part of governance structures beyond the state. Taking climate mobility as the primary example, the chapter suggests that the more people that are forced to move because of environmental disruption, the greater the extent to which adaptive capacity becomes a variable in the context-specific design of property law.

The chapter proceeds as follows. First, there is a brief introduction to adaptive law as a product of scholarship on adaptive governance. The discussion notes the challenges of applying adaptive concepts to private law, as opposed to environmental or administrative law, because the focus in areas such as contracts, corporations and property tends to be more certainty than adaptability. Second, there is an outline of conventional approaches to property law design that have the effect of privileging certainty over adaptability. These approaches adopt hierarchical frames based on government allocation and recordation of property in land. Yet, comparative evidence of informal land sectors in the Global South suggest that global property systems are better viewed as polycentric rather than hierarchical. Third, the chapter suggests that polycentricity is essential to understanding property system responses to environmental disruption as multiple components of a disrupted system adapt and reconfigure in heterodox scale-sensitive ways. The discussion includes case studies from Haiti, Indonesia and the Philippines. Fourth, the chapter outlines a normative frame for adaptive property law. The illustrative examples are (1) rules of possession as a source of property in land; and (2) legal accommodation of community-based land tenure systems.

ADAPTIVE LAW

Concepts of adaptive governance first emerged in environmental studies as a critique of steady-state assumptions of equilibrium in biological systems (Holling 2001). These assumptions generated 'command-and-control' management responses that focused on maintenance of equilibrium stability, and restoration of equilibrium in the event of disturbance (Holling 1973). In 1973, CJ Holling identified a contrasting possibility – that complex biological systems have the potential for multiple equilibrium states (Holling 1973, pp. 2–3).[1] Transitions among stability states occur in unpredictable ways as each system has an absorptive threshold for disturbance. Absorptive thresholds are a function of the resilience of a system, which involves the capacity to retain core structures, processes, and functions through processes of self-organisation in the face of disturbance. Adaptive governance therefore describes an approach that accommodates self-organisation across multiple scales of human responses to social-ecological disturbance (Chaffin et al. 2014).

Derived from studies in adaptive governance, the notion of adaptive law involves regulatory approaches that avoid rigid or prescriptive solutions to complex socio-ecological problems (Cosens et al. 2021, Cosens et al. 2020). Broadly speaking, adaptive law may be described in terms of 'laws built to learn', or laws that seek to 'row but not steer' (Bennear and Coglianese 2013, Wiener 2017, Ayres and Braithwaite 1994). These concepts have produced a rich stream of scholarship, particularly in relation to environmental and administrative law – which are areas of law that readily lend themselves to data-driven processes of ongoing monitoring, review, and adjustment (see e.g., Adler 2016, Craig et al. 2017, Craig and Ruhl 2014). However, less has been written on adaptive forms of private law, involving person-to-person rather than state-citizen interactions. Although private law also allows for self-organisation – in the form of legal instruments such as contracts or corporations – there is more often a concern for certainty than adaptability in legal frameworks for person-to-interaction. This concern for certainty is evident in legal mechanisms for the enforcement of contracts, and – as discussed in this chapter – in relation to property rights relating to land. In this sense, the following discussion of property law highlights a key normative question relating to adaptive law (Chapter 3 (Soininen et al.) in this *Handbook*). When should law accommodate adjustments to private rights through adaptive acts of self-organisation where there are corresponding increases in the costs of regulatory uncertainty?

CONVENTIONAL HIERARCHIES OF PROPERTY LAW

Twentieth-century theories of development highlight the significance of secure property rights to economic performance (O'Driscoll and Hoskins 2003). Secure property rights in land divert resources from conflict to investment in the productive use of land. Secure rights in land support impersonal exchange and transfers to higher valuer users. Virtuous cycles develop where transfers to higher-value users provide further incentives for investment, production, and markets for capital and credit. Some economists even identify secure property rights as the primary determinant of differences between rich and poor nations (Cooter and Schaefer 2009). For example, Douglass North and Robert Thomas present data that attribute variations in economic performance to the presence (or absence) of property rights institutions (North and Thomas 1973). Perhaps best-known of all, Hernando de Soto describes an alleged US$9.3 trillion of 'dead capital' in the global South, as a result of informal property systems, and urges formalisation of property rights as key to improved economic performance (de Soto 2000).

For economic theorists of property, baseline preferences for standardised packages of property rights are necessary to encourage stability of expectations for users of land. Standardised

---

[1]   *See for* identifying the potential for multiple stability states in systems subject to constant change.

property rights and rules provide for *ex ante* identification of permitted and proscribed behaviour. Broadly speaking, optimal outcomes are more likely if participants can identify and value entitlements in advance of interactions over land (Merrill and Smith 2000). For example, the stable character of a rule of freehold ownership plays a particular role in facilitating gains from trade, and markets for housing, capital and credit. The authoritative allocation of ownership by the state not only provides optimal reductions in the information and exchange costs of property but may also serve to prevent 'tragedies of the commons' because the owner has incentives to monitor resource use and exclude outsiders (Merrill and Smith 2011). The exemplar is programs of systematic land titling in the Global South, which are predicated on assumptions that titling reduces the costs of information, exchange, and exclusion through simple packages of proprietary information (Fitzpatrick 2006).

The primary property theory rationale for standardised property regimes is that, unlike rights in contract, property rights in land are good 'against the world'; and, as a result, require rules that reduce the costs of information for a broad class of potential violators or transactors (Merrill and Smith 2000). Simple 'bright-line' messages are necessary, as a baseline for the design of property rules, because of the cost of information for a broad audience that would otherwise have to understand a range of permitted uses, or deal with multiple interest-holders in a resource (Merrill and Smith 2000). A baseline preference for bright-line formulations of property law thus arises from the cost of communicating information: all else being equal, complex flexible rules suit smaller audiences (e.g., contracting parties) and simple inflexible rules suit large audiences (e.g., property transactors, violators, and enforcers). These considerations provide the basis for conventional approaches to stability/flexibility trade-offs in the design of property law. That is: the calculus of rule design only tilts towards flexibility where the ensuing efficiency benefits outweigh the increased costs of interpreting and applying flexible rules (Smith 2009).

The treatment of community-based land tenure regimes illustrates conventional approaches to stability/flexibility trade-offs in property law design. As a general rule, relatively flexible community land tenure norms can be adopted without a great deal of standardisation when the audience is limited, or there are low informational demands on the prospective audience (Smith 2009, pp. 13, 21, 30). However, in cases of community norms relating to property in land, the potential audience is often extensive as those interested in purchasing, valuing, or using land can extend far beyond the members of a local community and can include state interests in taxation or the provision of services or infrastructure. This broad audience will incur significant costs in identifying property interests under community-based regimes. Judges, bureaucrats, and other sources of interpretive authority will also face informational costs in the process of ascertaining and interpreting localised community norms (Smith 2009, pp. 21–22). The leading property theorist Henry Smith thus suggests that where efficient but information-rich customs are recognised by law, either the process of communicating property information is made more costly for remote third parties, or the custom must be stripped of its informational complexity through a process of modification and standardisation (Smith 2009, see also Smith 2003).

THE POLYCENTRICITY OF GLOBAL PROPERTY SYSTEMS

For economic theorists, it follows that the hierarchical design of property law is more likely than other institutional options to provide optimal reductions in the information and exchange costs of property, and the social costs of resource competition. The baseline preference is standardised packages of entitlements, which most commonly emerge from systems of state grant and public systems of land administration. For the costs of information, the registration of titles or transactions by the state reduces the burden of determining what is being exchanged. For the costs of exchange, documentary requirements such as notarisation reduces fraud and uncertainty in the land market (Merrill and Smith 2011). It is only when the overall costs of resource access are lower that there is a case for alternative, more flexible legal regimes. While this chapter focuses on (1) rules of possession and (2) community land tenure systems as alternatives to government systems of land administration, other types of flexible or 'fuzzy' legal regimes relating to property include *ex post* acts of judicial adjustment to property allocations through application of standards such as reasonableness or good faith.[2]

Economic analysis of this kind foregrounds the state as the apex source or controller of property in land. As noted, a leading example is programmes of systematic land titling in the Global South, which are predicated on assumptions that governments can replace heterodox community-based systems with standardised forms of public administration; and that titling of its nature provides benefits, which ensure voluntary transitions to government land administration from community-based land tenure systems. As a result of economic theories that link secure property to economic performance, the World Bank alone has financed more than 170 projects throughout the world since the 1980s. Yet, the results of systematic land titling have been mixed. While there are clear success stories, there are also instances where the winner-takes-all nature of land titling creates conflict rather than certainty in relation to land, particularly where the central government lacks the capacity to enforce formal land titles through coercive means (Von Benda-Beckmann 1995). More fundamentally, government systems of land title administration often fail to replace popular preferences for community-based systems even where those involved have legal rights to their land (Fitzpatrick 2016).

In 2014, a World Bank/International Federation of Surveyors report commented that:

> The ability of the current land administration paradigm to quickly scale up to engage the excluded 75 percent of the world's population is impossible. It is time to rethink how land rights are recorded and managed (Enemark et al. 2014).[3]

Broadly speaking, there are two types of people who are disassociated from government systems of land administration. First, there are those who are excluded by the operation of law. This category includes well over a billion people who live in urban informal settlements UN-Habitat (2013), or on rural land subject to claims of state ownership (UN-Habitat 2013, pp. 7–8). Comparative evidence suggests that many of these informal settlers have been using or occupying the land for generations (UN-Habitat 2003). Second, there are those who choose

---

[2]   An example considered in this volume is the judicial application of reasonableness requirements for water withdrawals in United States law: see Chapter 3 (Soininen et al.) in this *Handbook*.

[3]   *See also* Enemark and McLaren (2017).

not to engage with formal land administration systems. This category includes very large numbers of titleholders who have received registered titles but choose not to register subsequent transfers or transactions (see e.g., Reerink 2009, Nguyen 2006, Coldham 1979). These people eschew the notarisation or documentation requirements of property law in favour of other types of documents such as letters, receipts, affidavits, and contracts of sale witnessed by local government officials (Bordreaux and Aligia 2007, Struyk et al. 2000, Rabé et al. 2007, Durand-Lasserve and Royston 2002).

These global circumstances merit a descriptive label of polycentricity rather than hierarchy. Polycentricity in this sense describes governance regimes on a spectrum between 'fully integrated institutions that impose regulation through comprehensive, hierarchical rules', and 'highly fragmented collections of institutions with no identifiable core and weak or non-existent linkages between regime elements' (Keohane and Victor 2011). While there is a wide variety of global property systems – with some highly fragmented and others more hierarchical – a common thread is the extent to which informal property systems continue to coexist with formal regimes of property law notwithstanding global programs of land titling. For the purposes of this chapter, then, polycentric property regimes not only encompass rights to land derived from the state and recorded in government systems of land administration; but also, durable proprietary relationships secured through social norms and localised documentation in urban informal settlements and rural regimes of customary land tenure.

THE PANARCHY OF PROPERTY: LAND RIGHTS AND ENVIRONMENTAL DISRUPTION

The polycentricity of global property systems provides an essential starting point for understanding the effects of environmental disruption on complex property systems (Gunderson and Holling 2002, Holling 2001). From a disaster risk perspective, people who are not recorded in land registration systems are disproportionately vulnerable to exclusion from shelter and livelihoods assistance in circumstances of displacement because they lack rights or documentation in the eyes of the state (UN-Habitat 2010, pp. 82–84). Numerous disaster studies report the exclusion of landlessness and undocumented persons because they are unable to prove eligibility for assistance, or experience entrenched forms of pre-disaster discrimination (for summary, see Fitzpatrick 2007). The consistent result is that landless and undocumented persons are disproportionately represented in residual caseloads of victims without access to safe shelter and sustainable solutions to displacement. In these circumstances, transitional shelters after displacement become long-term informal settlements in locations that are typically exposed to further natural hazards.

Haiti provides a telling example of polycentric property and disaster vulnerability. Prior to the 2010 earthquake, around 70% of residents in the capital – Port-au-Prince – lived in informal settlements. Less than 5% of Haiti was covered by geospatial information systems. There was little or no official data on hazards or exposure. Land administration systems were dysfunctional and affected by fraud and corruption. After the earthquake, humanitarian actors experienced considerable challenges in identifying eligible persons for assistance. Transitional shelters were populated by victims of poverty, as well as disaster. The government sought to remove people from camps and transitional shelters because they were located on land owned by others, including the state. However, government processes did not provide durable solutions for camp and shelter residents, in large part because they were landless and undocumented prior to the disaster. As a result, a number of victims remain without shelter 10 years after the earthquake (Fan 2010).

The correlations between property informality and disaster vulnerability in the Haiti case are consistent with literature on adaptive governance that identifies the costs of fragmentation in governance systems characterised by polycentricity (Biddle and Baehler 2019). Julia Black summarises these costs to include coordination challenges arising from the absence of a global controller; systemic problems of fragmentation among law, norms, and other components of a regulatory system; and constraints on oversight and accountability arising from multiple decision-making sources (Black 2008). At the same time, it is also important to recognise the embedded inevitability of polycentricity in global property systems – that desirable or not the process of securing property in circumstances of environmental disruption takes place across multiple scale-sensitive sites of governance interaction (Ostrom 2010, Ostrom 1999, Aligica and Tarko 2012). As the following case studies suggest, some of these scale-sensitive processes may be resistant to *ex post* legal attempts at standardisation or replacement through public systems of land administration. While the overall result may be costly, the answer is not necessarily legal attempts at standardisation through government fiat, but a recognition that law may have to accommodate proprietary 'facts-on-the-ground' that are embedded in extra-legal systems of governance.

PROPERTY AND DISASTERS: EXAMPLES FROM INDONESIA AND THE PHILIPPINES

Fitzpatrick and Compton provide examples of property system polycentricity in contexts of disasters from the Philippines and Indonesia (Fitzpatrick and Compton 2021). The first, from the Philippines, concerns Super Typhoon Haiyan. There are on average around 20 typhoons per year in the Philippines. At the time the strongest storm to have ever made landfall, Typhoon Haiyan had a disproportionate effect on informal users and occupiers of land. These groups included fisherfolk and farmers in rural areas, and informal settlers in both rural and urban communities. Even before Typhoon Haiyan struck, there were large numbers of informal, undocumented, or illegal landholders in the Philippines. According to the 2007 Census, there were 62,187 tenant households and 11,462 informal settler households out of a total of 804,991 households in Region VIII alone (Philippine Stat. Authority 2007). A further 251,480 households lived rent-free on land with the consent of the landowner (Philippine Stat. Authority 2007). Most tenant households lacked formal documentation of their rights to land. In total, therefore, 32% of the population of Region VIII in 2007 fell into the category of 'landless'.

Soon after the disaster, the government published the Reconstruction Assistance on Yolanda: Build-Back-Better plan (RAY plan). The RAY plan proposed resettlement of 205,128 households on the basis of a 40 m no-build zone (National Economic and Development Authority 2013). The RAY plan framed relocation in terms of risk reduction and building back better (Yonetani 2014). Yet, in the post-disaster context, there was no reasonable prospect that relocation could provide timely shelter solutions for the displaced, and that prohibitions on return could be enforced in circumstances of denial of shelter assistance. Tacloban City, the capital of Region VIII, provides an example. To implement central government policy, the Tacloban

City legislature passed an ordinance establishing a no-build zone within 40 m of waterways and the sea (Philippines Ordinance 2013). The proposed relocation site in Tacloban North was set to house 15,000 households, with a completion date of 2018. By July 2016, a mere 700 families had relocated to Tacloban North with a number of households subsequently returning to prohibited hazard zones because of the costs of housing and limited access to services, including the provision of piped water. These displaced coastal residents returned to re-build informal settlements, notwithstanding government classifications of no-build zones, because they did not receive assistance, or were unable to afford housing and services in the relocation settlements (see further Sherwood et al. 2015, Thomas 2015).

In Indonesia, the Indian Ocean tsunami disaster of 2004 damaged or destroyed almost all land-related records, and obscured or obliterated large numbers of boundary markers (Haroen et al. 2005). The first response to property uncertainty took the form of community land mapping, which commenced as a heterodox process of boundary demarcation by survivors. The government then sought a hierarchical response – to standardise community mapping through a World Bank-designed land titling project (World Bank 2005). However, as Fitzpatrick and Compton illustrate, the prescribed templates of the titling project had little effect on heterodox practices of community mapping and were too late to form the tenurial basis for house reconstruction. Moreover, even where households received new title certificates, a clear majority continued to prefer community-based methods of land administration over the mandatory registration requirements of Indonesian land law. The Indonesia case-study therefore illustrates circumstances where community processes responded more rapidly than law, formed the basis for house reconstruction, and involved a degree of extra-legal re-configuration of rights and boundaries to land.

The Philippines and Indonesia cases involved post-disaster alterations to relationships with land through community-based land governance systems without instruction or permission from governments. Those affected settled on land owned by others. They sub-divided land and altered boundaries. They re-built on land designated as 'no-build' zones. In circumstances of human mobility, their proprietary activity had adaptive elements where entitlements were re-configured to support restoration of shelter and livelihoods. Most significantly, these adaptive changes to relationships with land occurred at a faster rate than government responses – in part because land law was fixed and highly formalist in nature. As a result, the case studies illustrate durable proprietary responses to disasters which were beyond the control of law and centralised government action. This potential for autonomous adaptation highlights the key polycentric characteristic that community and family-based systems for determining entitlements to land coexist with broader-scale systems based on law and public land administration.

CLIMATE MOBILITY AND POLYCENTRIC PROPERTY SYSTEMS

To turn now to climate change: how will climate-related human mobility interact with polycentricity in global property systems? In 2019, an Intergovernmental Panel on Climate Change (IPCC) report set out a number of high confidence forecasts for climate-land interactions. Climate zones will shift poleward in mid- to high-latitudes, and upward in regions of higher elevation. Tropical areas will develop new hot zones (Jia et al. 2019). Some regions will receive increased precipitation, while others experience more extreme or prolonged droughts (Jia et al. 2019, p. 137). There will be increases in desertification due to decreases in dryland soil cover (Jia et al. 2019, p. 142). Some extreme weather and climate events will increase in frequency or intensity (Jia et al. 2019, p. 133). In combination with IPCC forecasts of rising sea levels – up to 0.44 m above 1990 levels by the 2090s – there are also high confidence forecasts of climate-induced increases in human mobility (Bindoff et al. 2007). Human mobility is a key climate risk as hazards interact with exposure and vulnerability to induce people to move from their homes.

Although increases in human mobility arise under all IPCC projections, the nature, form, and intensity of land competition vary according to a range of variables – including types of land use as well as rates of bioclimatic impacts and responses by land tenure systems (Tilman et al. 2011, Foley et al. 2011). To begin with types of land use: the IPCC sets out 2015 estimates that around 71% of global ice-free land is now subject to some form of human land use (Valentini 2019). The largest category of used land is grazing land (around 37%), followed by crop land (12%). Perhaps surprisingly, dense human settlements only take up around 1% of global ice-free land – increasing to around 7% once 'village' settlements are included (Valentini 2019, p. 560). These types of land use are exposed to different types of climate hazards – which then affects decisions by people to move from their land. For example, village areas are disproportionately more likely than dense urban settlements to be subject to food security challenges. Grazing and crop lands are more likely to be subject to ground water stress. Dense urban settlements are more likely to be subject to water quality challenges.

Land tenure regimes provide a further variable that affect climate impacts and decisions to move. Although global land tenure data is incomplete, there are indicators of polycentric tenure regimes for different areas of land use. For example, urban areas are more likely to be subject to private property regimes than areas such as grazing lands. However, as noted, it is also the case that around 850,000 urban residents live in informal settlements (UN-Habitat 2013, UN Secretary-General 2001, IAEG 2002). In agricultural areas, there are estimates that smallholder farmers use most of the world's arable land but hold legal rights to less than 20% of global farming areas (Grain 2014, Lowder et al. 2014). Much of the balance is legally held by governments or agribusiness interests under concessions granted by the state (Lowder et al. 2014, see also Cotula 2012). In forest areas, there are estimates that only around 15% of global forest lands are owned by, or designated for, local communities and Indigenous peoples, typically under collective property regimes (Cotula 2012, p. 17). A further 73% is claimed as government owned or administered (Rights and Resources Initiative 2014), with much of this land also subject to commercial concessions (Rights and Resources Initiative 2014, p. 17).

The upshot is that climate-related human mobility will involve complex interactions among climate impacts, types of land-use, and polycentric systems of land tenure. These circumstances highlight the challenges of hierarchical models for property law design that assume government capacity to provide *ex ante* solutions to resource coordination problems through public systems of land administration. The incapacity of some governments to control human mobility with respect to land is only likely to increase in a climate-affected future. How, then, to design more adaptive property law solutions to emerging challenges such as climate mobility? The starting point is to recognise limits on the adaptive capacity of governments as sources of property security in circumstances of human mobility. In the case of informal settlements, state-centred rules do not provide security or certainty for poor migrant households that are unable to afford the formality requirements of registration, that transact rights to land through mechanisms outside government administrative systems, and that engage in extra-legal acts of re-possession or adjustments to parcel boundaries after forced population displacement.

PROPERTY LAW DESIGN FOR A CLIMATE-AFFECTED FUTURE

This chapter has shown that hierarchical assumptions of sovereign state authority over property contrast sharply with the polycentric reality of many postcolonial property systems. A key implication for adaptive law is that, while hierarchical property laws assume a state capable of controlling human relationships with land, the polycentric nature of proprietary governance may result in property systems that are disassociated from the state, and resist replacement by legal institutions of the state. The results include costly forms of disaster vulnerability as informal or illegal landholders are unable to access formalised mechanisms for land and housing and are labelled as illegal for self-help settlement on land without authority from the government (Morin et al. 2016).

The phenomenon of polycentricity in global property systems highlights an important challenge for adaptive formulations of private law. Adaptive public laws such as environmental regulation or administrative law may assume a centrality for government regulation because they govern state-citizen interactions. Private law, however, involves person-person interactions for which government regulation forms one of several potential governance constructs. Other governance mechanisms include relational networks, social norms, and other bases for private coordination; and as described in this chapter these non-state mechanisms may compete, substitute, and even disassociate from, government sources of regulatory control. Recognising the inevitability of this type of private law polycentricity – particularly in areas of contested sovereignty in the Global South – provides a starting point for formulating adaptive perspectives in areas such as property law.

Once we recognise context-specific limits on governments as providers of property security, it is easier to formulate adaptive capacity as an aim of property law. Given the adaptive limits of governments, the stability/flexibility trade-offs of property law design for a future of environmental disruption may be extended to include the potential for adaptive capacity on the part of governance structures beyond the state. In other words, the more people that are forced to move because of environmental disruption, the greater the extent to which the adaptive capacity of governance systems – the ability to provide proprietary security for migrants and the displaced – becomes a variable in the design of property law. Robert Ellickson proposes that property law is optimal when it produces the lowest aggregate sum of resource access costs for property participants (Ellickson 1991). Without altering the utilitarian frame, the formulation may be revised to accommodate the adaptive capacity of decentralised non-state governance mechanisms for property in a climate-affected future.

There are a range of mechanisms in property law to ensure flexibility in the face of social-ecological complexity. These measures include private law rules relating to equitable interests, future interests, periodic tenancies, easements, and neighbourhood covenants; and public law devices such as land use planning, environmental protections and anti-discrimination or eviction safeguards. While adaptive formulations of property law are under-developed, a key characteristic identified by this chapter is a strengthened capacity to adjust property regimes to match proprietary 'facts-on-the-ground'. This type of adaptive flexibility includes recognition of (1) property rights based on possession of land rather than title documents issued by the state, and (2) property rules formulated through community-based governance systems rather than 'command-and-control' regulation by legislatures. Although other legal mechanisms allow for adjustments to documented ownership rights, a focus on possession and community-based regulation illustrates the shifts required for adaptive perspectives on property law.

The legal recognition of possession as a source of property rights to land moves beyond simple hierarchical paradigms that limit freehold ownership to rights granted from or through a sovereign state. While space does not permit a technical description, both civil and common law systems include rules that recognise long-term possession as a source of ownership rights to land (e.g., rules of adverse possession or acquisitive prescription). However, Fitzpatrick and Compton show through a survey of global property law that the significance of possession as a source of property rights has reduced over time as a result of laws that restrict claims based on adverse possession or acquisitive prescription against public land and registered private titles (Fitzpatrick and Compton 2021). The rationale includes claims that title registration provides more prospects of *ex ante* certainty than rules favouring possession. However, possession remains a primary mechanism for poverty-affected migrants and the displaced to claim proprietary entitlements to land. Moreover, acts of possession in informal settings often have a long-term character – with some settlements in India and Latin America in place for over 50 years. In these circumstances, and with almost a billion people living in informal settlements, it is time to revitalise rules of possession in adaptive formulations of property law.

The legal recognition of community land tenure systems provides a further illustration of adaptive perspectives on property law that move beyond hierarchical sovereign state-centred paradigms. Community land tenure systems act as resilient sources of tenure security for migrants and the displaced. Typically, people who move from their homes do so through established social networks, most commonly centred around family relationships and ethno-linguistic affiliations. Informal urban settlements, in particular, act as host communities for in-migration through kinship pathways (Fitzpatrick and Monson 2021). The capacity to absorb in-migration includes mechanisms to provide access to land in a settlement. In these circumstances, utilitarian frames for legal design may more readily accommodate the adaptive capacity of community-based systems in circumstances of elevated human mobility risks. In other words, and all else being equal, the more a polycentric property system is affected by human mobility the more likely that property law should allow for adaptive community-based land tenure regimes. Such an approach builds on Elinor Ostrom's criteria for legal recognition of community rules where they provide more efficient reductions in the social costs of competitive races to appropriate resources (Ostrom 1990).

CONCLUSION

For many parts of the Global South, obtaining registered rights to land is too expensive for poor migrant, displaced or relocated groups affected by climate or disaster displacement. These circumstances highlight the importance of context for the design of property law. There is a need to move beyond generalisable models that promote a myth of hierarchy without acknowledging the prevalence and persistence of polycentricity. The starting point should be a process of comparative institutional analysis – where the capacity of governments to manage governance systems relating to land is explicitly incorporated as a variable in the design of property law. This type of comparative institutional analysis moves beyond Coasean models that assume government capacity to allocate and record rights as a basis for efficient markets in land, and allows for legal design to calibrate to weak, fragile, or conflict-affected state contexts (Enemark et al. 2014).

Re-calibrating property law for a climate-affected future may build on Ellickson's normative proposal that property law is optimal when it produces the lowest aggregate sum of resource access costs for all property participants. Without adjusting the utilitarian frame, this chapter suggests that adaptive approaches to property law should accommodate the global reality of polycentric property systems. In particular, property law may be optimal for a climate-affected future where it produces the lowest objective costs of resource access for participants that include large numbers of mobile groups living in informal settlements. As a result, adaptive property law may accommodate high mobility contexts where flexible laws that support proprietary facts-on-the-ground prove more efficient than bright-line rules based around principles of sovereign grant and title registration. This normative framing highlights the potential for policy junctures in climate-vulnerable contexts, where flexible laws that support network alignments at scale for polycentric governance systems may prove more efficient than conventional rules which focus on certainty of expectations for rights-holders recorded in government land administration systems.

REFERENCES

Adler, J. H. 2016. Dynamic environmentalism and adaptive management: legal obstacles and opportunities. PERC Reports, reprinted from *Journal of Law, Economics & Policy* (Summer 2015), 11, 133–161.

Aligica, P. D., and Tarko, V. 2012. Polycentricity: from Polanyi to Ostrom, and Beyond. *Governance* 25, 237.

Ayres, I., and Braithwaite, J. 1994. *Responsive Regulation: Transcending the Deregulation Debate.* Oxford, Oxford University Press.

Barnes, R. A. 2013. The capacity of property rights to accommodate social-ecological resilience. *Ecology & Society*, 6, 10.

Bennear, L. S., and Coglianese, C. 2013. Flexible approaches to environmental regulation. In Kamieniecki, S., and Kraft, M. E. (eds.) *The Oxford Handbook of U.S. Environmental Policy.* Oxford, Oxford University Press.

Biddle, J.C., and Baehler, K. J. 2019. Breaking bad: when does polycentricity lead to maladaptation rather than adaptation? *Environmental Policy and Governance*, 29, 344.

Bindoff, N. L., Willebrand, J., Artale, V., Cazenave, A., Gregory, J., Gulev, S., Hanawa, K., Le Quéré, C., Levitus, S., Nojiri, Y., Shum, C. K., Talley, L. D., and Unnikrishnan, A. 2007. Observations: oceanic climate change and sea level. In Solomon, S., Qin, D., Manning, M., Chen, Z., Marquis, M., Averyt, K. B., Tignor, M., and Miller, H. L., 2007. *Climate Change 2007: The Physical Science Basis. Contribution of Working Group I to the Fourth Assessment Report of the Intergovernmental Panel on Climate Change.* Cambridge, Cambridge University Press.

Black, J. 2008. Constructing and contesting legitimacy and accountability in polycentric regulatory regimes. *Regulation & Governance*, 2, 140–41.

Bordreaux, K., and Aligia, P. D., 2007. Paths to property: approaches to institutional change in international development. *The Institute of Economic Affairs*, 60–63.

Calabresi, G., and Melamed, A. D. 1972. Property rules, liability rules, and inalienability: one view of the cathedral, *Harvard Law Review*, 85, 1089.

Chaffin, B.C., Gosnell, H., and Cosens, B. A. 2014. A decade of adaptive governance scholarship: synthesis and future directions. *Ecology & Society*, 19, 3, 56.

Coldham, S. 1979. Land tenure reform in Kenya: the limits of law. *Journal of Modern African Studies*, 17, 04, 615, 618.

Cole, D. H. 2011. From global to polycentric climate governance. *Climate Law*, 2, 395.

Cooter, R., and Schaefer, H.-B. 2009. Law and the poverty of nations. Also at http://law.usc.edu/academics/assets/docs/cooter.pdf.

Cosens, B. et al. 2021. Governing complexity: integrating science, governance, and law to manage accelerating change in the globalized commons. *PNAS*, 118, 36.

Cosens, B. et al. 2020. Designing law to enable adaptive governance of modern wicked problems. *Vanderbilt Law Review*, 73, 6, 1687–1732.

Cotula, L. 2012. Land 'grabbing' in the shadow of the law: legal frameworks regulating the global land rush. Reprinted in Rayfuse, R., and Weisfelt, N. (eds.) *The Challenge of Food Security: International Policy and Regulatory Frameworks*. Cheltenham, UK and Northampton, MA, USA, Edward Elgar Publishing.

Craig, R. K., Garmestani, A. S., Allen, C. R., Arnold, C. A., Birgé, H., DeCaro, D. A., Fremier, A. K., Gosnell, H., and Schlager, E. 2017. Balancing stability and flexibility in adaptive governance: an analysis of tools available in U.S. environmental law. *Ecology & Society*, 22, 2, 3.

Craig, R., and Ruhl, J. B. 2014. Designing administrative law for adaptive management. *Vanderbilt Law Review*, 67, 1–87.

de Soto, H. 2000. *The Mystery of Capital: Why Capitalism Triumphs in the West and Fails Everywhere Else*. New York, Basic Books, 39.

Durand-Lasserve, A., and Royston, L. 2002. International trends and country contexts – from tenure regularization to tenure security. In Durand-Lasserve, A., and Royston, L. (eds.) *Holding their Ground: Secure Land Tenure for the Urban Poor in Developing Countries*, London, Earthscan Publications, 1, 25.

Ellickson, R. C. 1991. *Order Without Law: How Neighbors Settle Disputes*. Cambridge, MA, USA, Harvard University Press, 167, 283.

Enemark, S., and McLaren, R. 2017. Fit-for-purpose land administration: developing country specific strategies for implementation. In Burnod, P., Rakotomala, H., Saint-Macary, C., and Gubert, F. (eds.) *Responsible Land Governance: Towards an Evidence-based Approach*. World Bank Conference on Land and Poverty, World Bank Publications.

Enemark, S., Bell, K. C., Lemmen, C., and McLaren, R. 2014. Fit-for-purpose land administration. *World Bank and the International Federation of Surveyors FIG*, 9.

Fan, L. 2010. Scoping study on housing, land and property rights in post-earthquake Haiti. Oxfam Great Britain; GFDRR (1 July 2010) Haiti earthquake reconstruction: knowledge notes from DRM Global Expert Team for the Government of Haiti. Global Facility for Disaster Reduction and Recovery.

Fitzpatrick, D. 2016. Fragmented property systems. *University of Pennsylvania Journal of International Law*, 38, 137.

Fitzpatrick, D., and Compton, C. 2021. *Law, Property and Disasters: Adaptive Perspectives from the Global South*, Abingdon, Routledge, 1st edn.

Fitzpatrick, D., and Monson, R. 2021. Property rights and climate migration: adaptive governance in the South Pacific, *Regulation & Governance*, 15, 1.

Fitzpatrick, D. 2007. *Scoping Report: Addressing Land Issues after Natural Disasters*. Global Land Tools Network.

Fitzpatrick, D. 2006. Evolution and chaos in property rights systems: the Third World tragedy of contested access, *Yale L. J.*, 115, 996.

Foley, A., Ramankutty, N., Brauman, K., and Cassidy, E. S. 2011. Solutions for a cultivated planet. *Nature*, 478(7369), 337.

Grain. 2014. Hungry for land: small farmers feed the world with less than a quarter of all. *Farmland*, 5–6.

Gunderson, L. H., and Holling, C. S. 2002. *Panarchy: Understanding Transformations in Human and Natural Systems*. Washington US, Island Press.

Haroen, T. S., Achmad, C. B., and Rusmawar, W. 2005. Cadastral reconstruction in Aceh: a newborn concept of adjudication. International Federation of Surveyors South East Asian Survey Congress (Bandar Seri Begawan, Brunei Darussalam, 21–25 November 2005).

Harper, D. A. 2014. Property rights as a complex adaptive system: how entrepreneurship transforms intellectual property structures, *J. Evol Econ*, 24 335, 335.

Holling, C. S. 2001. Understanding the complexity of economic, ecological, and social systems. *Ecosystems*, 4, 390, 392–394.

Holling, C. S. 1973. Resilience and stability of ecological systems, *Annu. Rev. Ecol. Syst.*, 4, 1.

IAEG. 2002. Inter-Agency and Expert Group (IAEG) on MDG Indicators. Millennium Development Goals Indicators.

Jia, G., Shevliakova, E., Artaxo, P., De Noblet-Ducoudré, N., Houghton, R., House, J., Kitajima, K., Lennard, C., Popp, A., Sirin, A., Sukumar, R., and Verchot, L. (2019) Land–climate interactions. In Shukla, P. R., Skea, J., Calvo Buendia, E., Masson-Delmotte, V., Pörtner, H. O., Roberts, D. C., Zhai, P., Slade, R., Connors, S., van Diemen, R., Ferrat, M., Haughey, E., Luz, S., Neogi, S., Pathak, M., Petzold, J., Portugal Pereira, J., Vyas, P., Huntley, E., Kissick, K., Belkacemi, M., and Malley, J. (eds.) *Climate Change and Land: An IPCC Special Report on Climate Change, Desertification, Land Degradation, Sustainable Land Management, Food Security, and Greenhouse Gas Fluxes in Terrestrial Ecosystems*, 133.

Keohane, R. O., and Victor, D. 2011. The regime complex for climate change. *Perspectives on Politics*, 9, 7.

Lowder, S. K., Skoet, J., and Singh, S. 2014. What do we really know about the number and distribution of farms and family farms in the world? Background paper for The State of Food and Agriculture 2014. ESA Working Paper No 14-02, 8.

Marshall, G. R. 2009. Polycentricity, reciprocity, and farmer adoption of conservation practices under community-based governance. *Ecological Economics*, 68, 1507.

Merrill, T. W., and Smith, H. E. 2000. Optimal standardization in the law of property: the *numerus clausus* principle, *Yale L. J.*, 110, 34.

Merrill, T. W., and Smith, H. E. 2001. The property/contract interface, *Columbia Law Rev*, 101, 773.

Merrill, T. W., and Smith, H. E. 2001. What happened to property in law and economics? *Yale L.J.* 111, 357.

Merrill, T. W., and Smith, H. E. 2011. Making Coasean property more Coasean, *J Law & Econ*, 54, 77.

Morin, V. M., Ahmad, M. M., and Warnitchai, P. 2016. Vulnerability to typhoon hazards in the coastal informal settlements of Metro Manila, the Philippines. *Disasters*, 40, 693.

National Economic and Development Authority. 2013, Reconstruction assistance on Yolanda: build back better.

Nguyen, M. A. 2006. Analysing the encroachment process of informal settlements in the periurban of Ho Chi Minh City, Vietnam, 36, 42.

North, D. C., and Thomas, R. P. 1973. *The Rise of the Western World: A New Economic History*. Cambridge, Cambridge University Press.

O'Driscoll Jr., G. P., and Hoskins, W. L. 2003. Property rights: the key to economic development, *Policy Analysis*, No. 482, August 7.

Ostrom, E. 2010. Polycentric systems for coping with collective action and global environmental change. *Global Environmental Change*, 20, 550.

Ostrom, E. 1990. *Governing the Commons: The Evolution of Institutions for Collective Action*. Cambridge, Cambridge University Press.

Ostrom, V. 1999. Polycentricity. In McGinnis, M. (ed.) *Polycentricity and Local Public Economies: Readings from the Workshop in Political Theory and Policy Analysis*, Ann Arbor, University of Michigan Press, 52–74.

Philippines Ordinance. 2013. No. 2013-12- 15A: an ordinance providing for a 40-meter no build zone for residential housing within the territorial jurisdiction of the City of Tacloban.

Philippines Stat. Authority. 2007. Population and Housing Census 2007: Table 7. households by tenure status and region, https://psa.gov.ph/sites/default/files/attachments/Philippines_Table%25207.pdf.

Rabé, P., Thenekham, T., and Vongdeuane, V. 2007. Study land management and planning in Lao PDR, Land Policy Study No. 10, Vientiane.

Reerink, G. 2009. Land registration programmes for indonesia's urban poor: need, reach, and effect in the Kampongs of Bandung. In Ubink, J. M., Hoekema, A. J., and Assies, W. J. (eds.) *Legalising Land Rights: Local Practices, State Responses and Tenure Security in Africa, Asia and Latin America*. Leiden, Leiden University Press, 24–6.

Rights and Resources Initiative. 2014. What future for reform? Progress and slowdown in forest tenure reform since 2002, Washington, DC, Rights and Resources Initiative, 16–17.

Sherwood, A., Bradley, M., Rossi, L., Guiam, R., and Mellicker, B. 2015. Resolving post-disaster displacement: insights from the Philippines after Typhoon Haiyan (Yolanda). Brookings and International Organization for Migration (IOM) 53–5, https://www.brookings.edu/wp-content/

uploads/2016/06/Resolving-PostDisaster-DisplacementInsights-from-the-Philippines-after-Typhoon
-Haiyan-June-2015.pdf.

Smith, H. E. 2009. Community and property: community and custom in property. *Theoretical Inq. L.* 10, 5.

Smith, H. E. 2003. The language of property: form, context, and audience, *Stan. L. Rev.* 55, 1105.

Struyk, R.J., Hoffman, M. L., and Katsura, H. M. 2000. *The Market for Shelter in Indonesian Cities.* Washington, DC, Urban Institute Press, 93–95.

Thomas, A. R. 2015. Resettlement in the wake of Typhoon Haiyan in the Philippines: a strategy to mitigate risk or a risky strategy? Brookings-LSE: Project on Internal Displacement, 6–19, https://www.brookings.edu/wp-content/uploads/2016/06/Brookings-Planned-Relocations-Case-StudyAlice-Thomas-Philippines-case-study-June-2015.pdf.

Tilman, D., Balzer, C., Hill, J., and Befort, B. L. 2011. Global food demand and the sustainable intensification of agriculture. *Proceedings of the National Academy of Sciences*, 108, 50, 20260.

UN-Habitat. 2013. State of the world's cities 2012/2013: prosperity of cities. World Urban Forum.

UN-Habitat. 2010. Land and natural disasters: guidance for practitioners, 82–4.

UN-Habitat. 2003. The challenge of slums: global report on human settlements.

UN Secretary-General. 2001. Road map towards the implementation of the United Nations Millennium Declaration, Rep. of the Secretary-General, UN Doc. A/56/326 (Sept. 6, 2001).

Valentini, R. 2019. Framing and context. In Shukla, P.R., Skea, J., Calvo Buendia, E., Masson-Delmotte, V., Pörtner, H. O., Roberts, D. C., Zhai, P., Slade, R., Connors, S., van Diemen, R., Ferrat, M., Haughey, E., Luz, S., Neogi, S., Pathak, M., Petzold, J., Portugal Pereira, J., Vyas, P., Huntley, E., Kissick, K., Belkacemi, M., and Malley, J. (eds.), *Climate Change and Land: An IPCC Special Report on Climate Change, Desertification, Land Degradation, Sustainable Land Management, Food Security, and Greenhouse Gas Fluxes in Terrestrial Ecosystems*. Intergovernmental Panel on Climate Change (IPCC). Cambridge, Cambridge University Press, 88.

Von Benda-Beckmann, F. 1995. Anthropological approaches to property law and economics. *European Journal of Law and Economics*, 2, 309.

Wiener, J. B. 2017. Risk regulation and future learning. *European Journal of Risk Regulation*, 8, 4–9.

World Bank. 2005. Project appraisal document: proposed multi donor trust fund for Aceh and North Sumatra grant in the amount of US$28.50 million to the Republic of Indonesia for the reconstruction of Aceh Land Administration System Project. http://documents.worldbank.org/curated/en/471081468050634900/text/32716.txt.

Yonetani, M. 2014. The evolving picture of in the wake of Typhoon Haiyan: an evidence-based overview. Available at https://www.iom.int/files/live/sites/iom/files/Country/docs/The-Evolving-Picture-of-Displacement-in-the-Wake-of-Typhoon-Haiyan.pdf (accessed 16 March 2018).

15. Adaptive governance for disaster risk reduction

R. Patrick Bixler, Sandeep Paul, Debasmita Bhakta,
Tamar Farchy, Jessica Olson, Matthew Preisser and Paola
Passalacqua

INTRODUCTION

The importance of disaster risk reduction (DRR) as a policy issue has grown significantly in recent decades. The increased frequency and intensity of natural disaster events across the globe have granted the problem significant policy attention. There has been a substantial escalation in the scale of the affected population, the number of lives lost, and economic losses in recent years (CRED, 2021; CRED and UNDRR, 2020). In the year 2020 alone, the Emergency Events Database (EM-DAT) reported 389 natural disasters globally which affected 98.4 million people, costing US $171.3 billion and the death of 15,080 people (CRED, 2021). Between 2000–2019, the world lost an estimated 1.23 million lives to natural disasters with an estimated economic loss of $2.97 trillion USD (CRED and UNDRR, 2020). In these 20 years, 7,348 natural disasters were reported compared to 4,212 in the previous 20 years, with much of this coming from the substantial rise in the number of climate-related disasters (CRED and UNDRR, 2020). These trends are only expected to continue along with the emergence of climate related risks.

Along with the growth in the threat posed by natural disasters, there has also been a significant change in both understanding about disaster risk and the governance approaches towards it. Disaster risk is no longer solely equated with the effects of a single hazard but more with multiple risks posed by multiple hazards and their interactions. This emanates from a broader conceptualisation of disaster risk as a function of multiple drivers of vulnerability such as hazard exposure, sensitivity, and adaptive capacity (Bixler, Yang, et al., 2021; DasGupta and Shaw, 2017; World Bank, 2012; UNISDR, 2015; Adger, 2006). The emerging risk at any point is a result of complex interlinkages and interactions between social, economic, political, ecological, and built environment variables operating at multiple scales through multiple actors. Policy needs to be anticipatory and can no longer solely focus on response and recovery. This is in tandem with current disaster risk reduction (DRR) practices, dissociating itself from the technocratic paradigm of disaster management and moving more towards systemic risk and system-based approaches (DasGupta and Shaw, 2017; UNDRR, 2019). Policy needs to enhance inherent resilience and reduce inherent vulnerabilities of the social-ecological-technical system (SETs) in consideration (Chang et al., 2021; Balch et al., 2020). This governance transition accounts for all phases of the hazard cycle: preparedness, response, and recovery (see Figure 15.1).

The guiding belief now is that disaster risk practices have to be "multi-hazard and multisectoral, inclusive and accessible in order to be efficient and effective" (UNISDR, 2015). DRR practices are increasingly converging with development goals and climate change actions given the synergies between international policy agendas like the Sendai Framework

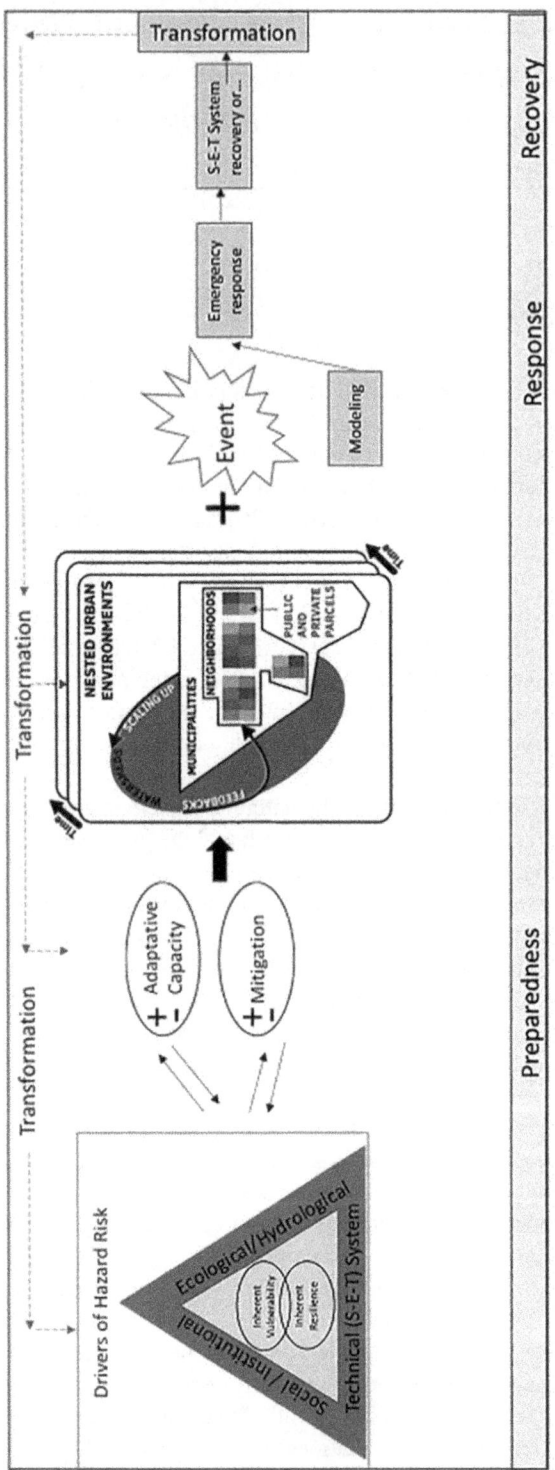

Figure 15.1   Phases of the hazard cycle from drivers to transformation

for Disaster Risk Reduction (SFDRR), Sustainable Development Goals (SDGs), and the UNFCCC Paris Agreement. Short-term and long-term objectives and actions in these agreements are heavily interdependent, creating a layer of complexity and uncertainty to specific DRR policies and linking previously unconnected actors in new ways. This is similar story to what has been empirically observed in other multi-lateral institutions (Kim, 2013). Traditional governance arrangements are too rigid, fragmented, siloed, and lack collaboration across multiple scales. There is a need for an alternative frame of governance – namely adaptive governance – that can effectively respond to the complexities and uncertainties associated with reducing risk from climate-related socio-natural disasters.

The concept of adaptive governance (AG) was born to deal with the increased uncertainty and complexity in social-ecological systems (SESs) (Chaffin et al., 2014; Folke et al., 2005; Olsson et al., 2004; Dietz et al., 2003). Throughout this chapter, we extend the application of adaptive governance to social-ecological-technical systems (SETs) as an alternative approach to governance that fails to deal with multiple pressures at diverse scales and multiple interactions. The challenge is explicitly evident in issues like climate change where the problem may have global origins but require governance responses at all multiple levels (Colloff et al., 2021; Newig and Fritsch, 2009; Dietz et al., 2003). Resilience to disasters is thus a product of multiple stakeholders interacting and blending different types of adaptive capacities (Bixler, Paul, et al., 2021; Parsons et al., 2016; Norris et al., 2008) and mitigation capacities (Fournier et al., 2016) across multiple spatial and temporal scales across all phases and across multiple hazards. Hurlbert (2018) defines adaptive governance as: "A range of political, social, economic, and administrative systems that develop, manage and distribute a resource in a manner that promotes resilience through collaborative, flexible, and learning-based issue management across different scales". AG can be also understood as a "pattern of practices" (Brunner et al., 2005) or as a set of conditions for managing social-ecological systems (Djalante et al., 2011; Folke et al., 2005).

In both approaches, the end goal is that of achieving the desired state of social-ecological systems (Chaffin et al., 2014). The concept was a meeting point for a diverse set of theories like adaptive management (Gunderson and Holling, 2002; Holling, 1978), adaptive co-management (Carlsson and Berkes, 2005; Olsson et al., 2004), collaborative governance (Bodin, 2017; Emerson and Nabatchi, 2015; Ansell and Gash, 2008; Sabatier et al., 2005) and their outgrowths (Chaffin et al., 2014; Djalante et al., 2011). Though specific differences persist, all theories converge at questioning the traditional top-down environmental policy and management of natural resources and by advocating for a more flexible, participatory, and decentralised decision-making process. Core adaptive governance principles include: polycentric and multi-layered institutions, adaptive issue management based on social learning and continuous knowledge generation, self-organisation and networks, participation and collaboration in governance, etc. to deal with uncertainty and complexity in SETs (Hurlbert, 2018; Berardo and Lubell, 2016; Bixler, 2014; Chaffin et al., 2014; Djalante et al., 2011; Berkes, 2009; Pahl-Wostl et al., 2007; Folke et al., 2005).

In this chapter, we identify and elaborate on the connection points between disaster risk reduction and adaptive governance. We elaborate on four characteristics of adaptive governance – polycentricity, collaboration, self-organisation, and learning – and discuss the relevance for disaster risk reduction. We then explore the examples from the literature and present a case study of Houston, Texas post-Hurricane Harvey. We conclude with the challenges, opportunities, and a toolkit for advancing adaptive natural hazard governance.

ADAPTIVE GOVERNANCE AND DISASTER RISK REDUCTION

The most crucial connecting link between AG and DRR is the concept of resilience. For disaster risk reduction, resilience is the end goal that it strives to achieve (Brunetta et al., 2019; Frantzeskaki et al., 2016; UNISDR, 2015; Djalante et al., 2011; Manyena, 2006). All risk reduction efforts should build and strengthen the resilience of community, urban, regional, and global systems. Resilience can be considered a set of capacities (Pfefferbaum et al., 2013), a set of common interests (Brunner et al., 2005) or the common goal that policy aims to achieve (Woodruff et al., 2021). The connection between resilience, adaptive governance, and disaster risk reduction is implicit through many major policy frameworks, if not already explicit.

Munene et al. (2018) have pointed out that there is considerable evidence for the presence of AG characteristics in the Sendai Framework. The Sendai Framework adopted in 2015 is unarguably the most influential policy agenda in the domain of disaster risk reduction and reflects the latest and most acceptable paradigm determining DRR policy action across the globe. The DRR principles put forth by the Sendai Framework align well with the core AG characteristics and the high frequency of AG phrases in the text of the agreement also points towards the compatibility of the concept with the philosophy of the Sendai framework (Munene et al., 2018). According to Djalante et al. (2011, p. 1), "there are four characteristics of AG that are important to help increase resilience to natural hazards. These are namely polycentric and multilayered institutions, participation and collaboration, self-organisation and networks, and learning and innovation". These are interlinked and support each other to promote resilience.

Multilayered and Polycentric Institutions

Polycentric systems are characterised by multiple centres of power and authority that produce coordinated decisions. The units are independent but interdependent and exist at different scales of government. McGinnis (2016) provides a three-part definition of what can constitute a polycentric governance system. According to this:

> A polycentric system of governance consists of (1) multiple centres of decision-making authority with overlapping jurisdictions (2) which interact through a process of mutual adjustment during which they frequently establish new formal collaborations or informal commitments, and (3), their interactions generate a regularised pattern of overarching social order which captures efficiencies of scale at all levels of aggregation, including providing a secure foundation for democratic self-governance. (McGinnis, 2016)

Such a system can be of very high utility to DRR efforts to promote resilience. Risk reduction of climate impacts is no longer restricted to the policy domain of a single actor, isolated community, or a single state. It is now an active arena of various types of state and non-state actors. Often it is the non-state actors that have more capacity and resources than state actors. Events like the Indian Ocean tsunami and earthquake of 2004, 2010 Haiti earthquake, Tohoku earthquake and tsunami, and Fukushima nuclear disaster of 2011 have established beyond doubt that collaboration and coordination across institutions and national or local boundaries is required. Although polycentric systems can appear complex with multiple centres of power operating at different scales, the application of the concept to disaster governance has often yielded positive results across the globe (Aoki, 2016; Djalante et al., 2011; Fournier et al., 2016; Walch, 2019).

Participation and Collaboration

AG has been widely discussed by experts as a potential alternative in varying socio-ecological contexts where current governance limitations are resulting in sub-optimal outcomes (Lei et al., 2015; Varma et al., 2014) or as a response to newly emerging issues (Bronen and Chapin, 2013). Participation and collaboration are suggested mechanisms to improve outcomes. Though the form of participatory governance differs depending on the location this allows bringing together formal and informal knowledge and promotes accountability, a sense of ownership, and transparency (Djalante et al., 2011; Huitema et al., 2009; Munene et al., 2018). This could complement and improve the scientific management of risk that may be already present. Relying solely on scientific management for risk reduction can be problematic as any management approach that disregards politics and local knowledge can lead to policy gridlocks (Brunner et al., 2005) in turn exacerbating the vulnerability of the social-ecological-technical system.

One major advantage of AG is that the approach is highly flexible and can be tweaked to factor in the idiosyncrasies of the locale of application. This is one of the major reasons behind the popularity of the concept in both developed and developing worlds. For example, Lei et al. (2015) while advocating for AG in the Chinese context point out that pathways of community participation might be different in their study area. Community participation may not organically occur due to the unwillingness of Chinese people to get involved in governance (Lei et al., 2015) or segregation of the public in policy making (J. Li et al., 2020). In such situations, for AG to operationalise, leadership needs to come from within the management organisations. This points towards the flexibility of AG models that ensures the applicability of the concept to varying contexts. Even though AG and its allied models have participatory governance as its core element, the operationalisation need not be the same everywhere. The flexibility also arises from the fact that AG in itself is not the end and is only an instrument to attain the desired state of SETs.

The collaborative decision-making process can not only improve the quality of policy but also improve implementation and reduce vulnerability in the event of a disaster. Learning and innovation are related features of AG with positive implications for DRR. AG allows for continuous integration of diverse types of knowledge and provision of feedback into the system to allow flexible adaptive management (Folke et al., 2005; Hurlbert, 2018). Effective and sustainable risk reduction and adaptation strategies can emanate from local knowledge and indigenous practices too. Learning from such practices and how they fare when faced with disasters can prove to be extremely useful. One such example would be the utility of Mangroves to protect from coastal flooding and tsunami (Menéndez et al., 2020; Pearson et al., 2020; Unnikrishnan et al., 2012). Understanding how the local communities use and value mangroves can greatly aid the management of these ecosystem services (Pearson et al., 2020). They not only supplement scientific knowledge but also are cost-effective.

Self-organisation and Networks

The ability to self-organise and the presence of networks is another characteristic of AG that can promote resilience in DRR efforts (Djalante et al., 2011). These networks often form an important characteristic of a multi-level, multi-actor AG governance structure. For successful disaster risk reduction, it is essential that the governance system should have active involvement of actors beyond the state including the global scientific community, international and national donor agencies, non-governmental organisations, etc. Risk reduction of disaster is no longer restricted to the policy domain of nations but is an active arena of various types of non-state actors who have more capacity and resources than national actors. Nevertheless, collaborations between state and non-state actors across various levels are often limited to times of crisis. It is at this juncture networks present an opportunity for sustained interactions and collaborations. Intentionally building networks prior to an event can lead to resilience related mitigation implementation (Bixler et al., 2020).

Djalante (2012) points out that networks like multi-stakeholder platforms can be avenues to practicalise AG as they create spaces for collaboration and learning promoting more coordinated and integrated actions in DRR. Being part of networks can help the governments to address their limitations like lack of financial resources or technical capacity to implement risk reduction efforts. This can also be an avenue of learning and innovation from other members of the networks. The transnational municipal networks that facilitate climate and disaster resilience in cities are an example of such networks. Some prominent examples of such network initiatives are Cities for Climate protection by International Council for Local Environmental Initiatives (ICLEI), C40, 100 Resilient Cities, Asian Cities Climate Change Resilience Network (ACCCRN). (Djalante et al., 2011). These network initiatives have greatly aided the DRR efforts in global cities through the diffusion of best practices, aggregation of resources, and creating avenues for collaboration of multiple stakeholders (Fisher, 2014; Keck et al., 1998). Informal networks, led by policy entrepreneurs can perform the crucial function of setting the agenda and bringing together policy alternatives. These networks can identify knowledge gaps, support information flow, and create nodes of expertise that create a knowledge system (Folke et al., 2005).

Innovation and Social Learning

Innovation and experimentation are also equally important when applying the AG framework to DRR strategies. People's perceptions about disasters and their response need not be static. It has been shown that risk perception, disaster preparedness, and mitigatory behaviour are affected by past experiences (Bixler, Paul, et al., 2021; Grothmann and Reusswig, 2006; Lindell and Hwang, 2008; Weinstein, 1989). Any DRR strategy should factor in these past experiences and learnings from them to ensure a better response to the vulnerabilities. The learning can be social, institutional, or organisational and can support flexible institutions in the governance system paving the way towards innovation and in turn increased resilience (Djalante et al., 2011; Fournier et al., 2016).

It has been argued that integrating AG dimensions to governance models can fix the deadlocks created by current prescriptive hierarchical approaches. For example, Varma et al. (2014) argue that the adaptive governance approach can address the existing ambiguity and incoherence about the convergence of disaster risk reduction and climate change adaptation in

India. In India, the policy design at both the national and subnational level follow a top-down expert-driven approach. The proclivity is for command-and-control governance resulting in limited institutional capacity for learning and flexibility in the region (Sud et al., 2015; Varma et al., 2014). Through a case study of two flood-affected locations, one urban and one rural, the authors identify the challenges posed by the current governance model and opportunities presented by AG approaches (Varma et al., 2014). Through the iterative group modelling process in the study areas, the authors demonstrate that forums of social learning can lead to innovative solutions that can better integrate DRR and climate policy (Varma et al., 2014).

Similarly, Lei et al. (2015) examined the DRR approach in Guangdong province of China to mitigate the risk posed by typhoons. Through a causal analysis of typhoon disasters, the authors question the disaster management regime that prefers structural mitigation measures over other strategies. It is argued that disaster management based on the creation of structural projects has not only fully served its intended purpose but also often increases the existing vulnerability through secondary hazards like dam failures, landslides, storm surges, debris flows, etc. (Lei et al., 2015). Additionally, structural projects in the region are also suffering from challenges like high maintenance costs and limited scope for cost-effective sustainable expansion. Lei et al. (2015) presents the AG approach as a more feasible and realistic solution to the limitations of disaster management of typhoons and offers an alternative conceptual model stressing AG characteristics multi-stakeholder participation and multi-scale coordination. De Abreu and de Andrade (2019) point out that lessons from adaptive governance can be applied to non-natural disaster scenarios like industrial disasters also. According to the authors, the AG approach can tackle industrial disasters which turn into "wicked problems" (de Abreu and de Andrade, 2019; Rittel and Webber, 1973). Using the empirical evidence from "Fundão tailings dam breach in Brazil" caused by a private mining company, authors suggest an analytical framework for dealing with industrial disasters in which the government fails to play the role of key actor and coordinate other actors involved (de Abreu and de Andrade, 2019). The framework puts forth an adaptive governance structure based on a triple-loop social learning system for relief and resilience. It is stressed that integrated cooperation, adaptive structures, joint knowledge production, and informal learning processes are essential for coping and transformation (de Abreu and de Andrade, 2019).

AG has also been put forth as a way forward in newly emerging problems like climate change-induced migrations (Bronen and Chapin, 2013). Bronen and Chapin (2013) outline an AG framework that can inform the strategies for governing the climate-induced community relocations in Alaska. Biophysical changes induced by climate change are forcing some communities in Alaska to relocate but the process was constrained by governance limitations (Bronen and Chapin, 2013; Huntington et al., 2012; Marino and Lazrus, 2015). Alternative attempts to respond to the situation through boundary organisations have also met with delays owing to statutory and institutional barriers (Bronen and Chapin, 2013). According to Bronen and Chapin (2013) a "dynamic and locally informed institutional response" is required in these communities. The relevance of the AG approach for such situations majorly arises from the fact that it does not restrict itself to technocratic knowledge but also provides room for integrating other types of knowledge into the governance strategy. Such situations warrant novel institutional responses that have more open and flexible decision-making structures.

INTEGRATING ADAPTIVE GOVERNANCE TO DISASTER RISK REDUCTION EFFORTS: EXAMPLES FROM THE LITERATURE

There has been an increased application of adaptive governance to specific disaster risk reduction efforts as AG has emerged as a more prominent model of environmental governance.

Flood Risk Governance

Flood management is one such DRR domain that has witnessed concentrated efforts to integrate adaptive governance approaches. Sustainable water management was an early area of focus for adaptive governance (Chaffin et al., 2016; Cosens and Williams, 2012), perhaps making the transition to the context of flooding easier. The concept has gained much popularity in socio-ecological contexts of European countries where flood governance was witnessing a gradual shift towards a risk-oriented paradigm (Fournier et al., 2016; Molenveld and van Buuren, 2019; Priest et al., 2016). With the increased awareness of the complexity of the systems, the proclivity is for more integrated and participatory management approaches in place of traditional static flood management approaches (Pahl-Wostl et al., 2007). The multi-layered safety (MLS) strategy introduced to the Dutch water policy is an example of such shifts. The MLS strategy represented a punctuation to the traditional approach that relied solely on flood defence structures and introduced a more polycentric and adaptive approach (Molenveld and van Buuren, 2019; van Buuren et al., 2016). This envisioned the involvement of a larger set of actors including municipalities, regional river authorities, local governments, and private stakeholders in the long-term policy development along with traditional actors. The conscious effort to maintain a balance between bottom-up and top-down decisions through multilevel governance is also visible in other mitigation efforts like the famed room for river program (Fournier et al., 2016).

England is another country that has invoked AG principles considerably into flood mitigation strategy. Fournier et al. (2016) argue that the current form of flood governance in England is quite close to the aspired forms of adaptive governance. The flood mitigation governance in England has a well-structured multilevel governance system where each institution's duties and functions are clearly defined. Most responsibilities are carried out by Lead Local Flood Authorities (LLFAs) while the strategic overview of risk management is performed by the Environmental Agency (Fournier et al., 2016; Priest et al., 2016). The other major actors include Internal Drainage Boards, highway agencies, and water companies. There is also a strong multi-actor approach based on active citizen participation. Citizen engagement is not limited to policy formulation but extends to project implementation. The partnership approach is followed in project funding which allows new actors to have financial stakes in the project and source funds at the local level through local authorities, the private sector, or civil society (Fournier et al., 2016).

The extent to which AG was implemented to flood governance often varies considerably. Fournier et al. (2016) provide a comparative analysis of AG application to flood mitigation in six European countries – Belgium, England, France, Netherlands, Poland, and Sweden – and report considerable variation among them. It was reported that AG is a work in progress in all the case study countries and is at different stages of implementation. For example, the AG approach is more mainstream and better developed in flood governance in England, the Netherlands, and Belgium (Fournier et al., 2016). In the case of France, Sweden, and Poland, at the time of comparison, the approach lagged in terms of the degree of institutionalisation as most of the efforts were localised (Fournier et al., 2016).

Earthquakes and Tsunamis

Successful integration of AG principles has been reported also from non-European contexts such as Japan. One such example is provided by Aoki (2016) who studied the case of the 2011 Great East Japan earthquake and tsunami. Japan, which used to follow a semi-decentralised disaster governance system, experienced an unprecedented manpower crisis in the aftermath of the 2011 disaster (Aoki, 2016). The disaster resulted in a severe manpower shortage in municipal governments. The ex-ante arrangements could not supply enough manpower, especially for recovery and reconstruction. The response to the issue took the form of a polycentric governance arrangement that could successfully source manpower from various groups like other municipalities, business corporations, non-profit organisations, and the private sector (Aoki, 2016). The response did not take the form of a singular model but followed a collaborative approach that was continuously adapted depending on the context and need. The resultant situation was that of an institutional change that substantially increased Japan's disaster governance capability (Aoki, 2016).

Cyclones and Hurricanes

A similar but more elaborate institutional change that integrated AG principles was also reported from the state of Odisha in India (Walch, 2019). Walch (2019) presents Odisha as one of the few successful cases of integration of AG principles to DRR in the developing country context. The state of Odisha is highly susceptible to tropical cyclones and used to suffer regularly from heavy loss and damages. The biggest calamity was the cyclones in the year 1999 which killed more than 10,000 people. In response to the event, the state underwent a massive institutional change by actively adopting the key AG characteristics. Authors argue that the state was able to substantially reduce its risk via these strategies as evident by the performance of the state in 2013 cyclone Phailin which affected 11 million people but resulted in the death of only 23 people (Walch, 2019). The primary argument put forth here is that the critical event in 1999 acted as a window of opportunity. This along with the presence of a committed political leadership enabled a successful transformation of DRR and the adoption of AG principles (Walch, 2019).

Wildfire

Although less likely to be labelled disaster risk reduction, the intersection of wildfire management and adaptive governance is prevalent in forest management literature (Abrams et al., 2015; Hamilton et al., 2019). Increasingly large and intense fires are a pressing challenge for many countries across the globe (Duane et al., 2021). Community fire resilience is inherently complex, multi-scalar, networked, and polycentric (Abrams, 2019; Bixler et al., 2018). Because fire transmits across jurisdictions or land ownership, it requires multi-organisational cooperation across a landscape and consists of local to national stakeholders (Fischer, 2018; Goldstein and Butler, 2009). And although different actors strive to coordinate mitigation and response activities, persistent limitations exist to sharing resources and responsibilities and thus, rather than being adaptive, wildfire management is in a continued state of "parallel play" (Davis et al., 2021).

A CASE STUDY IN HOUSTON, TEXAS

Houston, Texas, USA, is one of the most disaster-prone regions in the United States. Houston's lack of land use regulations and general lax urban planning practices have created the conditions for a perfect storm of repeated catastrophic disasters, namely resulting from hurricanes and flooding events. Prior to Hurricane Harvey, the Greater Houston area was inundated by major floods annually in 2015 and 2016. The May 2016 Flood, known as the "Tax Day Flood," motivated both city officials and non-governmental organisations to take a more serious approach to collaboration in the context of disaster preparedness and response.

Hurricane Harvey was a category 4 hurricane that made landfall in Texas on August 27th, 2017. Over the course of two weeks, Hurricane Harvey dumped over 60 inches of rain in some locations with a storm surge contributing to over 10 feet of flooding. By the end of the storm, there was over $125 billion in damages with over 300,000 structures damaged or destroyed, making Hurricane Harvey the costliest natural disaster in US history – tying with Hurricane Katrina that struck New Orleans in 2015 (Blake and Zelinsky, 2017). Over 30,000 people were displaced because of the storm, and some 17,000 rescues occurred. The numbers of Hurricane Harvey have no analogue, although unprecedented events like Harvey could become the norm as the world's climate continues to change (Rusca et al., 2021).

Houston is known for its laissez-faire politics built on planning deregulation, free entre-preneurism, low taxes, and public disinvestment (Malecha et al., 2021; Harper, 2004). This has historically benefitted elite social classes while simultaneously exacerbating disparities through environmental deregulation and the inequitable distribution of flood risks (Harper, 2004). What is often referred to by residents as a complete lack of urban planning in the met-ropolitan area has led to decades of low-density development forcing residents and businesses to continually expand cities outwards. The expansion of impervious surfaces because of this urban sprawl has led to extensive wetland degradation, thus reducing rainfall infiltration, subsequently increasing residents' exposure to flood risks (Blessing et al., 2017). Because of Hurricane Harvey's unprecedented precipitation levels, coupled with decades of urban poli-cies promoting growth in a region that is dominated by low-lying flatlands, floodwaters were able to expand far outside of the Federal Emergency Management Agency (FEMA) flood-plains. In fact, the majority of flooding occurred outside of designated floodplains, meaning the majority of homes that were flooded during Hurricane Harvey were not required to have flood insurance and were therefore not covered by storm damages (Smiley, 2020).

Response and Recovery

Hurricane Harvey's staggering and historic impacts served as a catalyst for actors in the public, private, and civil sectors to dedicate heightened efforts to disaster mitigation and recovery planning. In practice, disaster management is commonly split into four successive stages: mitigation, preparedness, response, and recovery. In Houston, collaborative groups have historically formed to tackle each of these stages separately but have primarily been focused on mitigation and recovery. The recovery process itself has multiple timelines: immediate and short-term recovery lasts anywhere from six months to one-year post-disaster, while long-term recovery can last up to five years post-disaster. In cases of catastrophic disasters, which are significantly more severe than other disasters such as Hurricanes Katrina and Harvey, long-term recovery poses an especially significant challenge.

Collaboration and inter-organisational dependence and information sharing were vital during Hurricane Harvey and the recovery process. Non-governmental organisations and city and county officials alike relied on shared resources to manage the rapidly unfolding crisis to assist residents in need of recovery. The magnitude of Hurricane Harvey's catastrophic impacts inspired many previously unengaged non-profit organisations to expand their scope to include disaster recovery. Numerous foundations developed grants to these organisational shifts and federal and state emergency funding enabled local agencies to contract non-profits to assist in recovery efforts. Non-profits focused on "unmet needs". These needs were most often additional financial assistance, the rebuilding of homes and businesses, and physical and mental health concerns that are not addressed by federal insurance claims and loans.

Long-term recovery was also able to leverage existing networks, such as the Harris County Long-Term Recovery Committee (HCLTRC) that was formed in 2016 after the Tax Day Floods. This LTRG is co-led by the United Way of Greater Houston and Ready Harris – the Harris County Department of Emergency Management. The Houston chapter of United Way plays a highly central role in the community and operates a community resource centre that is extensively utilised by local non-profits to host events. Further, United Way independently steers a network of affiliated agencies and grantees, many of whom are also members of the HCLTRC. This centrality uniquely positioned United Way to serve as a network weaver and facilitator in post-Harvey collaborations as they emerged (Q. Li et al., 2020).

Mitigation and Adaptive Capacity

Disaster mitigation has long been a research focus of the Gulf Coast, but the magnitude of Hurricane Harvey's devastation led to a surge in research dedicated to understanding the impact, risk factors, and causes of the storm. Like the previously examined cases with governmental and non-governmental entities, researchers developed collaborative networks for resiliency, mitigation, and recovery research. Collaborative partnerships between researchers and on-the-ground disaster response organisations are particularly useful during data collection post-disaster to avoid duplication of efforts and to ensure even sampling coverage of areas affected (Horney et al., 2019). To this end, the work of the National Institutes of Health Disaster Research Response Program (DR2) was utilised extensively by research communities to share resources and best practices surrounding research on the public health implications of Harvey. The building blocks for DR2s efforts in Houston were set up in 2015 when the National Institute for Environmental Health Sciences convened workshops with research, public health, emergency management, and community stakeholders (Horney et al, 2019). Collaborations involving these actors developed in a two-year period prior to Hurricane Harvey's landfall, to support Houston's repeated and ongoing disaster incidents. These prior collaborations – and subsequent trust-building – enabled these organisations to swiftly respond to the health and environmental impacts of Harvey.

The Greater Houston Flood Mitigation Consortium (GHFMC) was founded during Harvey's immediate aftermath to foster collaboration between the major academic institutions of the Gulf Coast Area. While DR2 emphasises collaboration among practical disaster response and academia, the Greater Houston Flood Mitigation Consortium focuses more acutely on adaptation research. Since Harvey, GHFMC has produced numerous reports outlining the risk of flooding to affordable family housing, drainage and development regulations, and flood mitigation projects by watershed. Further, the academic collaboration has developed neighbourhood-specific resiliency plans in areas surrounding vulnerable watersheds. This collaborative effort has focused on bringing together many different academic areas of expertise, including hydrology, coastal resiliency, urban planning, and community development.

However important, these efforts at mitigation often overlook the importance of reducing sensitivity and growing adaptive capacity of households. Black and Latinx residents experienced disproportionate housing damage from Harvey because of a mix of open ditch stormwater infrastructure, spatial distribution of physical exposure, and the location of low-income housing in floodplains (Lieberknecht et al., 2021). Planning and policy should not only consider mitigation efforts – flood proofing, green and grey infrastructure, wetland restorations, urban design, and voluntary buyouts and resettlement – but should consider the existing inequalities in flood exposure and impacts and consider how to reduce sensitivity to impacts and increase adaptive capacity.

Transformation

Despite the empirical evidence of the characteristics of adaptive governance in Houston's disaster risk reduction, what is really needed is active adaptation and transformation of the social-ecological-technical system where mitigation, adaptive capacity, exposure, response and recover occur. There is important research exploring the interdependence of organisations, infrastructure networks, and communities during Hurricane Harvey including studies that emphasise resiliency planning and management (Dong et al., 2020; Farahmand et al., 2020; Q. Li et al., 2020), inter-organisational communication (Rajput et al., 2020) and planning networks (Hannibal et al., 2021).

A key take-away from Hurricane Harvey specific studies is the importance of pre-existing networks (Hemmer and Elliff, 2020) and consistency (Ybarra, 2019) at all stages of disaster planning. While there is agreement that responsibility-sharing is necessary across different levels of government, evidence suggests that governmental actors have a more influential role in coordination (Hannibal et al., 2021; Li, Hannibal, et al., 2020). During Hurricane Harvey, government organisations primarily generated information, while non-government organisations mainly disseminated information (Rajput et al., 2020). Transformation may require a fundamental shift in how information is generated, whose knowledge is valued, and how information is disseminated across different phases of adaptive hazard governance. The "interconnections" between natural, built, and social systems illuminate the point that adaptive hazard governance must include non-traditional disaster risk reduction actors to transform these systems to be more adaptive.

THE FUTURE FOR ADAPTIVE HAZARD GOVERNANCE: CHALLENGES AND OPPORTUNITIES

The growth in adaptive governance scholarship in recent decades represents the growing acknowledgment of the shortcomings and incompatibility of traditional disaster risk reduction goals and traditional approaches to governance. In the above discussion, we have outlined how the concept of adaptive governance can aid disaster risk reduction efforts. The utility arises from the inherent convergence of conceptual frameworks and objectives: increasing resilience of social-ecological-technical systems. The AG characteristics like polycentric governance, participatory approach, adaptive and flexible governance, learning and innovation, self-organisation, and networks are already being applied to natural hazard governance in many countries and contexts. However, the application of concepts in actual practice varies considerably. This could not only lead to suboptimal outcomes but also negatively impact the resilience of SETS under consideration. The situation also points towards the need for more scholarship on outcomes and implications of integrating AG and DRR from diverse contexts.

Challenges of Adaptive Hazard Governance

Adaptive governance is being stressed as an essential alternative that could manage the intrinsic complexity and uncertainty of disaster risk and ensure the resilience of SETs. However, operationalising AG remains an uphill task. Often excessive attention is provided to any one of the AG characteristics rather than others. The growing popularity of polycentric governance is an example of this tendency (Djalante et al., 2011). Such tendencies ignore the fact that these characteristics are highly interrelated and support one another.

Even in scenarios where there was a conscious effort to implement AG was faced with multiple challenges and considerable differences reported in the degree of adoption of individual AG features like multilevel governance, flexibility in governance arrangement, multi-actor networks, opportunities for experimentation, or social and institutional learning (Fournier et al., 2016). It has been argued that even in the successful cases, the result was substantially different from the envisioned. Molenveld and van Buuren (2019) points out the flood governance approach that was implemented in the Netherlands is less adaptive than the originally formulated approaches.

In practice, the implementation is heavily influenced by the current institutions and elements of path dependency (Molenveld and van Buuren, 2019; van Buuren et al., 2016). The changes like devolution of power and authority, presence of new stakeholders, diversification of strategies, new legal frameworks, etc. can meet with resistance from traditional institutions and actors. In places like the Netherlands, the impact of path dependency can be stronger given a long history of disaster response and the presence of highly evolved institutions. The mechanisms of path dependency limited the degree of change in Dutch scenarios included power asymmetries, intrinsic opaqueness, and complexity of politics and social perceptions about protection and safety (van Buuren et al., 2016). Path dependencies need not be solely institutional but can also be technological and infrastructural. The high cost associated with changing the existing disaster prevention structures or disposition of them for certain technological fixes could hamper the implementation of AG initiatives. Such a situation can limit the policy learning leading, in turn, limiting the potential of transformation.

The implementation may differ substantially from theory leading to unplanned outcomes. For example, polycentric governance arrangements in practice can suffer from multiple limitations like more complex decision making, potential loss of economies of scale, high transaction costs, duplication of efforts, reduced democratic accountability, etc. (Djalante et al., 2011; Huitema et al., 2009; Pahl-Wostl et al., 2007). According to McGinnis (2016), six potential traps that polycentric arrangements can face include "structural inequities, incremental bias, high levels of complexity, structural fissures, coordination failures, and, ultimately, a lack of normative clarity". Not all normative preferences are usually attainable in practice. The collective action across multiple levels and scales need not be always smooth and can render the decision-making process complex if there is a lack of coordination or intrinsic biases. The ability to self-organise could be affected by social asymmetries, the nature of democratic practices, etc. The institutional legacies can potentially limit the independence and authority of actors at lower scales. The good news is that "negative implications of the limitations inherent in one dimension can often be compensated by the effective operation of other dimensions of this concept" (McGinnis, 2016, p. 15). For example, formalising the role and responsibility of organisations involved through legal structures may counter structural fissures in the political system. Fortunately, in our scenario, it is reasonable to expect that most of these challenges will be limited given the increased integration of climate change action with the disaster risk reduction paradigm.

Another important question that arises with respect to the transition to AG approach is how well it will perform in contexts with limited opportunities for participatory forms of governance. Limited participation or reduced interest from certain groups can limit legitimacy, reduce social learning and exchange of knowledge, lead to a limited sense of ownership or belonging, etc. (Djalante et al., 2011). The availability of democratic freedoms to effectively participate vary substantially across the countries. How can an AG approach be implemented in such situations is a question that merits more inquiry? Sharing of power or producing joint DRR solutions with other stakeholders can potentially challenge the hegemony of dominant actors (Munene et al., 2018). It is to be noted that even in conventional democratic societies, a participatory approach can be both time-consuming and resource consuming (Djalante et al., 2011).

Opportunities of Adaptive Hazard Governance

The latent potential to institutionalise and formalise disaster risk reduction as adaptive hazard governance is tremendous. While disasters and catastrophic events themselves act as the necessary window of opportunity, the success of transformation depends on the presence of supportive governance arrangements, informal networks, level of trust in co-actors, level of social and economic inequalities, legal and financial resources, and presence of incentives for actors to participate and collaborate (Djalante et al., 2011; Folke et al., 2005). The efforts to integrate adaptive governance to risk reduction should actively factor in these idiosyncrasies and their interlinkages in the target locations while planning the transition. This can also aid the conceptual development of both adaptive governance and disaster risk reduction scholarship. Advancing scholarship and practice relies on better acknowledgement, and implementation, of adaptive hazard governance frameworks and special considerations that for different phases of hazards.

Additionally, some general guidelines and tools can be utilised to facilitate the necessary structures and processes of this approach. These include recognising and distributing power, valuing diverse knowledges, building trust, generating collective stories, and knowing how to talk about disasters and climate change to diverse audiences. To further elaborate on these points, we have developed a toolkit that can be accessed here: https://sites.utexas.edu/rpbixler/files/2022/01/Adaptive-Hazard-Governance-Toolkit.pdf.

REFERENCES

Abrams, J. 2019. The emergence of network governance in U.S. National Forest Administration: Causal factors and propositions for future research. *Forest Policy and Economics*, 106, 101977. https://doi.org/10.1016/j.forpol.2019.101977.

Abrams, J. B., Knapp, M., Paveglio, T. B., Ellison, A., Moseley, C., Nielsen-Pincus, M., and Carroll, M. S. 2015. Re-envisioning community-wildfire relations in the U.S. West as adaptive governance. *Ecology and Society*, 20, 3, art 34. https://doi.org/10.5751/ES-07848-200334.

Adger, W. N. 2006. Vulnerability. *Global Environmental Change*, 16, 3, 268–281. https://doi.org/10.1016/j.gloenvcha.2006.02.006.

Ansell, C., and Gash, A. 2008. Collaborative governance in theory and practice. *Journal of Public Administration Research & Theory*, 18,4, 543–571.

Aoki, N. 2016. Adaptive governance for resilience in the wake of the 2011 Great East Japan Earthquake and Tsunami. *Habitat International*, 52, 20–25. https://doi.org/10.1016/j.habitatint.2015.08.025.

Balch, J. K., Iglesias, V., Braswell, A. E., Rossi, M. W., Joseph, M. B., Mahood, A. L., Shrum, T. R., White, C. T., Scholl, V. M., McGuire, B., Karban, C., Buckland, M., and Travis, W. R. 2020. Social-environmental extremes: Rethinking extraordinary events as outcomes of interacting biophysical and social systems. *Earth's Future*, 8, 7, e2019EF001319. https://doi.org/10.1029/2019EF001319.

Berardo, R., and Lubell, M. 2016. Understanding what shapes a polycentric governance system. *Public Administration Review*, 76, 5, 738–751. https://doi.org/10.1111/puar.12532.

Berkes, F. 2009. Evolution of co-management: Role of knowledge generation, bridging organizations and social learning. *Journal of Environmental Management*, 90, 5, 1692–1702. https://doi.org/10.1016/j.jenvman.2008.12.001.

Bixler, R. P. 2014. From community forest management to polycentric governance: Assessing evidence from the bottom up. *Society & Natural Resources*, 27, 2, 155–169. https://doi.org/10.1080/08941920.2013.840021.

Bixler, R. P., Jedd, T., and Wyborn, C. 2018. Polycentric governance and forest landscape restoration. In *Forest Landscape Restoration*, Vol. 1, pp. 176–197. London, Routledge.

Bixler, R. P., Lieberknecht, K., Atshan, S., Zutz, C. P., Richter, S. M., and Belaire, J. A. 2020. Reframing urban governance for resilience implementation: The role of network closure and other insights from a network approach. *Cities*, 103, 102726. https://doi.org/10.1016/j.cities.2020.102726.

Bixler, R. P., Paul, S., Jones, J., Preisser, M., and Passalacqua, P, 2021. Unpacking adaptive capacity to flooding in urban environments: Social capital, social vulnerability, and risk perception. *Frontiers in Water*, 3, 101. https://doi.org/10.3389/frwa.2021.728730.

Bixler, R. P., Yang, E., Richter, S. M., and Coudert, M. 2021. Boundary crossing for urban community resilience: A social vulnerability and multi-hazard approach in Austin, Texas, USA. *International Journal of Disaster Risk Reduction*, 66, 102613. https://doi.org/10.1016/j.ijdrr.2021.102613.

Blake, E. S., and Zelinsky, D. A. 2017. National Hurricane Center Tropical Cyclone Report: Hurricane Harvey (Issue 5). https://www.nhc.noaa.gov/data/tcr/AL092017_Harvey.pdf.

Blessing, R., Sebastian, A., and Brody, S. D. 2017. Flood risk delineation in the United States: How much loss are we capturing? *Natural Hazards Review*, 18, 3, 04017002. https://doi.org/10.1061/(ASCE)NH.1527-6996.0000242.

Bodin, Ö. 2017. Collaborative environmental governance: Achieving collective action in social-ecological systems. *Science*, 357(6352), eaan1114. https://doi.org/10.1126/science.aan1114.

Bronen, R., and Chapin, F. S. 2013. Adaptive governance and institutional strategies for climate-induced community relocations in Alaska. *Proceedings of the National Academy of Sciences*, 110. 23, 9320–9325. https://doi.org/10.1073/pnas.1210508110.

Brunetta, G., Caldarice, O., Tollin, N., Rosas-Casals, M., and Morató, J. (Eds.). 2019. *Urban Resilience for Risk and Adaptation Governance: Theory and Practice*. Berlin, Springer.

Brunner, R., Steelman, T. A., Coe-Juell, L., Cromley, C. M., Edwards, C. M., and Tucker, D. W. (2005). *Adaptive Governance: Integrating Science, Policy, and Decision Making* (p. 368 Pages). New York, Columbia University Press.

Carlsson, L., and Berkes, F. 2005. Co-management: Concepts and methodological implications. *Journal of Environmental Management*, 75(1), 65–76. https://doi.org/10.1016/j.jenvman.2004.11.008.

Chaffin, B. C., Garmestani, A. S., Gosnell, H., and Craig, R. K. 2016. Institutional networks and adaptive water governance in the Klamath River Basin, USA. *Environmental Science & Policy*, 57, 112–121. https://doi.org/10.1016/j.envsci.2015.11.008.

Chaffin, B. C., Gosnell, H., and Cosens, B. A. 2014. A decade of adaptive governance scholarship: Synthesis and future directions. *Ecology and Society*, 19(3). https://www.jstor.org/stable/26269646.

Chang, H., Pallathadka, A., Sauer, J., Grimm, N. B., Zimmerman, R., Cheng, C., Iwaniec, D. M., Kim, Y., Lloyd, R., McPhearson, T., Rosenzweig, B., Troxler, T., Welty, C., Brenner, R., and Herreros-Cantis, P. 2021. Assessment of urban flood vulnerability using the social-ecological-technological systems framework in six US cities. *Sustainable Cities and Society*, 68, 102786. https://doi.org/10.1016/j.scs .2021.102786.

Colloff, M. J., Gorddard, R., Abel, N., Locatelli, B., Wyborn, C., Butler, J. R. A., Lavorel, S., van Kerkhoff, L., Meharg, S., Múnera-Roldán, C., Bruley, E., Fedele, G., Wise, R. M., and Dunlop, M. 2021. Adapting transformation and transforming adaptation to climate change using a pathways approach. *Environmental Science & Policy*, 124, 163–174. https://doi.org/10.1016/j.envsci.2021.06 .014.

Cosens, B., and Williams, M. 2012. Resilience and water governance: Adaptive governance in the Columbia River Basin. *Ecology and Society*, 17, 4. https://doi.org/10.5751/ES-04986-170403.

CRED. 2021. Disaster year in review 2020 global trends and perspectives -Cred Crunch (Issue No 62; Cred Crunch). The Centre for Research on the Epidemiology of Disasters. https://emdat.be/sites/ default/files/adsr_2020.pdf.

CRED and UNDRR. 2020. The human cost of disasters: An overview of the last 20 years (2000-2019). The Centre for Research on the Epidemiology of Disasters and UN office Disaster Risk reduction. https://www.undrr.org/publication/human-cost-disasters-overview-last-20-years-2000-2019.

DasGupta, R., and Shaw, R. 2017. Disaster risk reduction: A critical approach. In Ilan Kelman, Jessica Mercer, and JC Gaillard (Eds.), *The Routledge Handbook of Disaster Risk Reduction Including Climate Change Adaptation*, Abingdon, Routledge (p. 560).

Davis, E. J., Huber-Stearns, H., Cheng, A. S., and Jacobson, M. 2021. Transcending parallel play: Boundary spanning for collective action in wildfire management. *Fire*, 4, 3, 41. https://doi.org/10 .3390/fire4030041.

de Abreu, M. C. S., and de Andrade, R. de J. C. 2019. Dealing with wicked problems in socio-ecological systems affected by industrial disasters: A framework for collaborative and adaptive governance. *Science of the Total Environment*, 694, 133700. https://doi.org/10.1016/j.scitotenv.2019.133700.

Dietz, T., Ostrom, E., and Stern, P. C. 2003. The struggle to govern the commons. *Science*, 302, 5652, 1907–1912.

Djalante, R. 2012. Adaptive governance and resilience: The role of multi-stakeholder platforms in disaster risk reduction. *Natural Hazards and Earth System Sciences*, 12, 9, 2923–2942. https://doi.org/10 .5194/nhess-12-2923-2012.

Djalante, R., Holley, C., and Thomalla, F. 2011. Adaptive governance and managing resilience to natural hazards. *International Journal of Disaster Risk Science*, 2, 4, 1–14. https://doi.org/10.1007/s13753 -011-0015-6.

Dong, S., Li, Q., Farahmand, H., Mostafavi, A., Berke, P. R., and Vedlitz, A. 2020. Institutional connectedness in resilience planning and management of interdependent infrastructure systems. *Journal of Management in Engineering*, 36, 6, 12.

Duane, A., Castellnou, M., and Brotons, L. 2021. Towards a comprehensive look at global drivers of novel extreme wildfire events. *Climatic Change*, 165, 3, 43. https://doi.org/10.1007/s10584-021 -03066-4.

Emerson, K., and Nabatchi, T. 2015. *Collaborative Governance Regimes*. Georgetown, Georgetown University Press.

Farahmand, H., Dong, S., Mostafavi, A., Berke, P. R., Woodruff, S. C., Hannibal, B., and Vedlitz, A. 2020. Institutional congruence for resilience management in interdependent infrastructure systems. *International Journal of Disaster Risk Reduction*, 46, 101515. https://doi.org/10.1016/j.ijdrr.2020 .101515.

Fischer, A. P. 2018. Forest landscapes as social-ecological systems and implications for management. *Landscape and Urban Planning*, 177, 138–147. https://doi.org/10.1016/j.landurbplan.2018.05.001.

Fisher, S. 2014. Exploring nascent climate policies in Indian cities: A role for policy mobilities? *International Journal of Urban Sustainable Development*, 6. https://doi.org/10.1080/19463138.2014.892006.

Folke, C., Hahn, T., Olsson, P., and Norberg, J. 2005. Adaptive governance of social-ecological systems. *Annual Review of Environment and Resources*, 30, 1, 441–473. https://doi.org/10.1146/annurev.energy.30.050504.144511.

Fournier, M., Larrue, C., Alexander, M., Hegger, D., Bakker, M., Pettersson, M., Crabbé, A., Mees, H., and Chorynski, A. 2016. Flood risk mitigation in Europe: How far away are we from the aspired forms of adaptive governance? *Ecology and Society*, 21, 4. https://www.jstor.org/stable/26270027.

Frantzeskaki, N., Kabisch, N., and McPhearson, T. 2016. Advancing urban environmental governance: Understanding theories, practices and processes shaping urban sustainability and resilience. *Environmental Science & Policy*, 62, 1–6. https://doi.org/10.1016/j.envsci.2016.05.008.

Goldstein, B. E., and Butler, W. H. 2009. The network imaginary: Coherence and creativity within a multiscalar collaborative effort to reform US fire management. *Journal of Environmental Planning & Management*, 52, 8, 1013–1033. https://doi.org/10.1080/09640560903327443.

Grothmann, T., and Reusswig, F. 2006. People at risk of flooding: Why some residents take precautionary action while others do not. *Natural Hazards*, 38, 1–2, 101–120. https://doi.org/10.1007/s11069-005-8604-6.

Gunderson, L. H., and Holling, C. S. 2002. *Panarchy: Understanding Transformations in Human and Natural Systems*. Island Press.

Hamilton, M., Fischer, A. P., and Ager, A. 2019. A social-ecological network approach for understanding wildfire risk governance. *Global Environmental Change*, 54, 113–123. https://doi.org/10.1016/j.gloenvcha.2018.11.007.

Hannibal, B., Woodruff, S., and Malecha, M. 2021. The overlap of collaboration and planning networks: A Post-Harvey Study. *Journal of Planning Education and Research*, 0739456X2199589. https://doi.org/10.1177/0739456X21995899.

Harper, J. 2004. Breathless in Houston: A political ecology of health approach to understanding environmental health concerns. *Medical Anthropology*, 23, 4, 295–326.

Hemmer, L., and Elliff, D. S. 2020. Leaders in action: The experiences of seven Texas superintendents before, during, and after Hurricane Harvey. *Educational Management Administration & Leadership*, 48, 6, 964–985. https://doi.org/10.1177/1741143219873073.

Holling, C. S. 1978. *Adaptive Environmental Assessment and Management*. John Wiley & Sons. http://pure.iiasa.ac.at/id/eprint/823/.

Horney, J. A., Rios, J., Cantu, A., Ramsey, S., Montemayor, L., Raun, L., and Miller, A. 2019. Improving Hurricane Harvey disaster research response through academic–practice partnerships. *American Journal of Public Health*, 109, 9, 1198–1201. https://doi.org/10.2105/AJPH.2019.305166.

Huitema, D., Mostert, E., Egas, W., Moellenkamp, S., Pahl-Wostl, C., and Yalcin, R. 2009. Adaptive water governance: Assessing the institutional prescriptions of adaptive (co-)management from a governance perspective and defining a research agenda. *Ecology and Society*, 14, 1. https://doi.org/10.5751/ES-02827-140126.

Huntington, H. P., Goodstein, E., and Euskirchen, E. 2012. Towards a tipping point in responding to change: Rising costs, fewer options for Arctic and global societies. *AMBIO*, 41,1, 66–74. https://doi.org/10.1007/s13280-011-0226-5.

Hurlbert, M. A. 2018. Adaptive Governance of disaster drought and flood in rural areas. Berlin, Springer International Publishing. https://doi.org/10.1007/978-3-319-57801-9_2.

Keck, M. E., Keck, P. of P. S. M. E., and Sikkink, K. 1998. *Activists Beyond Borders: Advocacy Networks in International Politics*. Ithaca, NY, Cornell University Press.

Kim, R. E. 2013. The emergent network structure of the multilateral environmental agreement system. *Global Environmental Change*, 23, 5, 980–991. https://doi.org/10.1016/j.gloenvcha.2013.07.006.

Lei, Y., Liu, C., Zhang, L., Wan, J., Li, D., Yue, Q., and Guo, Y. (2015). Adaptive governance to typhoon disasters for coastal sustainability: A case study in Guangdong, China. *Environmental Science & Policy*, 54, 281–286. https://doi.org/10.1016/j.envsci.2015.07.016.

Li, J., Lei, X., Qiao, Y., Kang, A., and Yan, P. 2020. The water status in China and an adaptive governance frame for water management. *International Journal of Environmental Research and Public Health*, 17,6, 2085. https://doi.org/10.3390/ijerph17062085.

Li, Q., Hannibal, B., Mostafavi, A., Berke, P., Woodruff, S., and Vedlitz, A. 2020. Examining of the actor collaboration networks around hazard mitigation: A hurricane Harvey study. *Natural Hazards*, 103, 3, 3541–3562. https://doi.org/10.1007/s11069-020-04142-1.

Lieberknecht, K., Zoll, D., Jiao, J., and Castles, K. 2021. Hurricane Harvey: Equal opportunity storm or disparate disaster? *Local Environment*, 26, 2, 216–238. https://doi.org/10.1080/13549839.2021 .1886063.

Lindell, M. K., and Hwang, S. N. 2008. Households' perceived personal risk and responses in a multihazard environment. *Risk Analysis*, 28, 2, 539–556. https://doi.org/10.1111/j.1539-6924.2008.01032.x.

Malecha, M. L., Woodruff, S. C., and Berke, P. R. 2021. Planning to exacerbate flooding: Evaluating a Houston, Texas, network of plans in place during Hurricane Harvey using a plan integration for resilience scorecard. *Natural Hazards Review*, 22, 4, 04021030. https://doi.org/10.1061/(ASCE)NH .1527-6996.0000470.

Manyena, S. B. (2006). The concept of resilience revisited. *Disasters*, 30, 4, 434–450. https://doi.org/10 .1111/j.0361-3666.2006.00331.x.

Marino, E., and Lazrus, H. 2015. Migration or forced displacement? The complex choices of climate change and disaster migrants in Shishmaref, Alaska and Nanumea, Tuvalu. *Human Organization*, 74, 4, 341–350. https://doi.org/10.17730/0018-7259-74.4.341.

McGinnis, M. D. 2016. Polycentric governance in theory and practice: Dimensions of aspiration and practical limitations. *SSRN Electronic Journal*. https://doi.org/10.2139/ssrn.3812455.

Menéndez, P., Losada, I. J., Torres-Ortega, S., Narayan, S., and Beck, M. W. 2020. The global flood protection benefits of mangroves. *Scientific Reports*, 10, 1, 4404. https://doi.org/10.1038/s41598-020 -61136-6.

Molenveld, A., and van Buuren, A. 2019. Flood risk and resilience in the Netherlands: In search of an adaptive governance approach. *Water*, 11, 12, 2563. https://doi.org/10.3390/w11122563.

Munene, M. B., Swartling, Å. G., and Thomalla, F. 2018. Adaptive governance as a catalyst for transforming the relationship between development and disaster risk through the Sendai Framework? *International Journal of Disaster Risk Reduction*, 28, 653–663. https://doi.org/10.1016/j.ijdrr.2018 .01.021.

Newig, J., and Fritsch, O. 2009. Environmental governance: Participatory, multi-level – and effective? *Environmental Policy and Governance*, 19, 3, 197–214. https://doi.org/10.1002/eet.509.

Norris, F. H., Stevens, S. P., Pfefferbaum, B., Wyche, K. F., and Pfefferbaum, R. L. 2008. Community resilience as a metaphor, theory, set of capacities, and strategy for disaster readiness. *American Journal of Community Psychology*, 41,1, 127–150. https://doi.org/10.1007/s10464-007-9156-6.

Olsson, P., Folke, C., and Berkes, F. 2004. Adaptive comanagement for building resilience in social–ecological systems. *Environmental Management*, 34, 1, 75–90. https://doi.org/10.1007/s00267-003 -0101-7.

Pahl-Wostl, C., Sendzimir, J., Jeffrey, P., Aerts, J., Berkamp, G., and Cross, K. 2007. Managing change toward adaptive water management through social learning. *Ecology and Society*, 12, 2. https://doi .org/10.5751/ES-02147-120230.

Parsons, M., Glavac, S., Hastings, P., Marshall, G., McGregor, J., McNeill, J., Morley, P., Reeve, I., and Stayner, R. 2016. Top-down assessment of disaster resilience: A conceptual framework using coping and adaptive capacities. *International Journal of Disaster Risk Reduction*, 19, 1–11. https://doi.org/ 10.1016/j.ijdrr.2016.07.005.

Pearson, J., McNamara, K. E., and Nunn, P. D. 2020. ITaukei ways of knowing and managing mangroves for ecosystem-based adaptation. In W. Leal Filho (Ed.), *Managing Climate Change Adaptation in the Pacific Region* (pp. 105–127). Berlin, Springer International Publishing. https://doi.org/10.1007/978 -3-030-40552-6_6.

Pfefferbaum, R. L., Pfefferbaum, B., Van Horn, R. L., Klomp, R. W., Norris, F. H., and Reissman, D. B. 2013. The Communities advancing resilience toolkit (CART): An intervention to build community resilience to disasters. *Journal of Public Health Management and Practice*, 19, 3, 250–258. https://doi .org/10.1097/PHH.0b013e318268aed8.

Priest, S. J., Suykens, C., Van Rijswick, H. F. M. W., Schellenberger, T., Goytia, S., Kundzewicz, Z. W., van Doorn-Hoekveld, W. J., Beyers, J.-C., and Homewood, S. 2016. The European Union approach to flood risk management and improving societal resilience: Lessons from the implementation of the

Floods Directive in six European countries. *Ecology and Society*, 21, 4. https://www.jstor.org/stable/26270028.

Rajput, A. A., Li, Q., Zhang, C., and Mostafavi, A. 2020. Temporal network analysis of inter-organizational communications on social media during disasters: A study of Hurricane Harvey in Houston. *International Journal of Disaster Risk Reduction*, 46, 101622. https://doi.org/10.1016/j.ijdrr.2020.101622.

Rittel, H. W. J., and Webber, M. M. 1973. Dilemmas in a general theory of planning. *Policy Sciences*, 4, 2, 155–169. https://doi.org/10.1007/BF01405730.

Rusca, M., Messori, G., and Di Baldassarre, G. 2021. Scenarios of human responses to unprecedented social-environmental extreme events. *Earth's Future*, 9, 4, e2020EF001911. https://doi.org/10.1029/2020EF001911.

Sabatier, P. A., Focht, W., Lubell, M., Trachtenberg, Z., Vedlitz, A., and Matlock, M. (Eds.). 2005. *Swimming Upstream: Collaborative Approaches to Watershed Management*. Cambridge, Mass., MIT Press.

Smiley, K. T. 2020. Social inequalities in flooding inside and outside of floodplains during Hurricane Harvey. *Environmental Research Letters*, 15, 9, 0940b3. https://doi.org/10.1088/1748-9326/aba0fe.

Sud, R., Mishra, A., Varma, N., and Bhadwal, S. 2015. Adaptation policy and practice in densely populated glacier-fed river basins of South Asia: A systematic review. *Regional Environmental Change*, 15, 5, 825–836. https://doi.org/10.1007/s10113-014-0711-z.

The World Bank. 2012. The Sendai Report- Managing disaster risks for a resilient future. The World Bank. https://openknowledge.worldbank.org/bitstream/handle/10986/23745/80608.pdf?sequence=2&isAllowed=y.

UNDRR. 2019. Global Assesment Report on Disaster Risk Reduction 2019 (p. 425). United Nations Office for Disaster Risk Reduction. https://www.undrr.org/publication/global-assessment-report-disaster-risk-reduction-2019.

UNISDR. 2015. Sendai Framework for disaster risk reduction 2015-2030 (p. 32). United Nations Office for Disaster Risk Reduction. https://www.preventionweb.net/files/43291_sendaiframeworkfordrren.pdf

Unnikrishnan, S., Singh, A., and Kharat, M. G. 2012. The role of mangroves in disaster mitigation: A review. *International Journal of Environment and Sustainable Development*, 11, 2, 164–179. https://doi.org/10.1504/IJESD.2012.049180.

van Buuren, A., Ellen, G. J., and Warner, J. F. 2016. Path-dependency and policy learning in the Dutch delta: Toward more resilient flood risk management in the Netherlands? *Ecology and Society*, 21, 4. https://www.jstor.org/stable/26270023.

Varma, N., Kelkar, U., Bhardwaj, S., Singh, P., and Mishra, A. 2014. Climate change, disasters and development: Testing the waters for adaptive governance in India. *Vision*, 18, 4, 327–338. https://doi.org/10.1177/0972262914551664.

Walch, C. 2019. Adaptive governance in the developing world: Disaster risk reduction in the State of Odisha, India. *Climate and Development*, 11, 3, 238–252. https://doi.org/10.1080/17565529.2018.1442794.

Weinstein, N. D. 1989. Effects of personal experience on self-protective behavior. *Psychological Bulletin*, 105, 1, 31–50.

Woodruff, S., Bowman, A. O., Hannibal, B., Sansom, G., and Portney, K. 2021. Urban resilience: Analyzing the policies of U.S. cities. *Cities*, 115, 103239. https://doi.org/10.1016/j.cities.2021.103239.

Ybarra, N. 2019. Hurricane Harvey: One hospital's journey toward organizational resilience. *The Journal of Perinatal & Neonatal Nursing*, 33, 3, 246–252. https://doi.org/10.1097/JPN.0000000000000424.

16. The next decade of adaptive governance research: concluding remarks

Sirkku Juhola

OPENING REMARKS

The need to identify, develop, test, and evaluate new approaches to governance is clear as the multiple, coupled socio-ecological change drivers make it increasingly necessary to deal with uncertainty and unsustainability. Strengthening calls for transformations away from current fossil fuel-based systems towards sustainable practices, which also account for just and equal distribution of decision-making and benefits, need to be met with rigorous theorisation and application of concepts and methods across thematic areas of governance to identify ways to facilitate and achieve these goals. The increasingly uncertain global co-operation, conflict and polarisation may further create and exacerbate these challenges, putting further pressure on an already time-constrained situation.

In terms of governance theory, adaptive governance is a relatively new theoretical approach, with this volume being published roughly two decades since the term was first introduced. At the heart of the early contributions was the recognition of the urgency at which societal decision-making structures and processes also needed to change, as the global environment was changing. Furthermore, there was an acknowledgement that unless new ways of self-organisation of communities were considered in parallel or in collaboration with formal institutions and decision-making, it was likely that the necessary changes would not be achieved.

This *Handbook* brings together the current state-of-the-art research on adaptive governance by illustrating its theoretical advances, methodological developments, and empirical investigations of thematic and sectoral fields of adaptive governance practices. The questions that need to be asked to conclude this volume relate to the contribution of adaptive governance to the theoretical approaches of governing complex, socio-ecological systems, and the insights that adaptive governance bring to the wider field of societal decision-making. More specifically, how has the theory of adaptive governance advanced and has the concept itself matured through empirical validation during these two decades? In addition, what are the emerging research questions based on the current contributions to the field?

SUMMARY OF THE CONTRIBUTIONS OF THIS VOLUME

Part I: Theoretical and Conceptual Developments

The first part of this volume addresses the theoretical developments of adaptive governance with a specific focus on exploring the relationship between the existing formal institutions, and emerging, more flexible arrangements described in adaptive governance theory. In Chapter 2,

Cosens and colleagues examine the issues of legitimacy of adaptive governance in relation to the role of the state and present an interdisciplinary research agenda with research methods to support these questions. The authors argue that, as expected, traditional forms of regulation remain the most important mechanisms through which the state steers society and actors in it. However, the pressing need to move towards more adaptive modes of governance is clear and the development of new legal models to facilitate and enable self-organisation is necessary.

This concern for new legal models is also raised by Soininen et al. in Chapter 3, who see the potential for existing laws and regulations to facilitate adaptive governance. The authors perceive the role of law to have the potential to steer adaptive governance through rules that assure legitimacy and build capacity. As such, law can be an accelerant to adaptive governance, if these features are integrated into management practices and they allow for flexibility. Similarly, law can also act as a hindrance to adaptive governance, for example, through rules that lock in the monitoring of environmental impacts or participation in certain stages of environmental management, thus preventing the principles of adaptive governance to be fulfilled. The authors call for further research that incorporates additional fields of law in empirical research to further complement this conceptualisation.

The theorisation of the use of knowledge, within both formal and informal decision-making structures, is central in adaptive governance, given it is the main driving force in decision-making, i.e., the rules and practices of governance need to continuously change based on knowledge of the system governed. In Chapter 4, Wyborn and colleagues conceptualise this science–policy–practice interface and further illustrate its social, cultural, and political embeddedness. This means that there is a need to identify and critically examine who sets the agenda for the science–policy–practice interface, how relationships between actors are maintained and how the practices within it and its outcomes are justified. In essence, the authors call for the interface itself to be adaptive and flexible in order for adaptive governance to flourish.

Part II: Latest Trends in Methods

Methodological approaches in adaptive governance research have a dual purpose. They can either be used as methods to collect empirical evidence of adaptive governance taking place, or they can be used as active tools through participation and engagement to facilitate adaptive governance to take place. The chapters in this part highlight the importance of scale and the need to pay attention to issues of power and social context when designing stakeholder interaction. In Chapter 5, Alexandra and colleagues use futures-thinking and associated methods to consider how adaptive governance can contribute to transformations. Central to this is that futures-oriented methods can support capacities to engage with uncertainty, develop and integrate necessary knowledge, envision the transformation, foster reflexivity, and address contestation. The authors further call for engagement with futures-thinking and methods in relation to adaptative governance to enable the consideration of plural and long-term perspectives, and the integration of knowledge across scales and political realities.

In Chapter 6, Nikkanen and Räsänen address the second crucial scale in adaptive governance research. The spatial mismatch between the governed resources and the governing entity has been at the core of adaptive governance dilemmas, as confirmed by Nikkanen and Räsänen. This can lead to governance failures, lack of collaboration and conflicting objectives of governance of different entities. Most interestingly, the authors find that despite this central focus, the actual use of spatial data and methods in adaptive governance literature is sparse, illustrating a pressing need to develop methods. To spark this off, the authors propose several ways to use risk maps, and discuss how different types of participatory and participatory and crowdsourced information can aid in this.

This issue of political realities and complexities of governance is discussed in detail in Chapter 7 by exploring a method that makes that reality abstract to allow stakeholders to experiment with different types of governance strategies. Edwards, using an example case of a serious game, shows their potential in bringing together stakeholders to discuss complex real life governance challenges. Two key insights can be drawn. First, serious games, to account for the complexity of the situation portrayed, take a long time to develop. The process can be lengthy and requires multiple iterations with a clear purpose and objectives defined early in the process. Second, facilitation pre- and post-game takes time, and it is important to consider what types of resources are required. This is especially true in cases where there are research-related elements in the game that require data to be collected. A post-game debriefing may also help participants to distil lessons from the session into their everyday life.

Part III: Governance Contexts and Case Studies

This third part of this *Handbook* portrays the diversity of thematic governance areas within which adaptive governance are applied and advanced. The first two chapters in this part focus on a specific local resource-use governance dilemma, review the progress to date and consider the ways in which adaptive governance principles have become realised. The following chapters then discuss how adaptive governance can be used to examine new fields and in terms of interpreting the national governance context. The remainder of the chapters illustrate cases where the common change driver is global, most often climate change which presents challenges for several governance fields. Overall, the chapters highlight the continued dominance of natural resource, environment, and sustainability-related fields in the adaptive governance scholarship, while new governance fields are testing and adopting its theory and concepts.

In Chapter 8, Abrams and Elbakidze consider that adaptive governance within the forestry sector has become an actionable paradigm to challenge the conventional forest governance models that prioritise optimisation of use over broader sustainability concerns. Within this paradigm, new networks and partnerships are used to experiment and test forest management measures, illustrating how the approach can contribute to sustainable use of forests. However, the authors raise a concern of how far this experimentation can flourish in an institutional context where the formal structures of decision-making do not change, or at least to a sufficient degree to allow for these new forms to gain ground. Thus, while benefits can be seen in the emergence of adaptive forest governance, its durability over time needs to be further investigated.

Similar questions are raised in Chapter 9 by Quimby, who examines adaptive governance in the context of marine governance. Marine environments have always been a particular focus of adaptive governance scholars and Quimby notes that there are encouraging examples of the application of adaptive governance approaches on regional and local scales around the globe. However, the author also stresses that despite these positive examples, there are also challenges that can be identified. These include fostering institutional variety, similar to forest governance, as well as inclusion of stakeholders with procedural equity and politics in mind.

In addition to these more traditional fields of natural resource governance, there are also entirely new fields that are testing the explanatory power of adaptive governance. One of these new fields is data governance and open data ecosystems, which are discussed in detail in Chapter 10. In a case from Shanghai, Wang illustrates how community-driven governance practices can be an effective way to identify distributed resources for building data infrastructure and test new governance practices that support the open data ecosystem. In reflecting the usefulness of considering this research approach, Wang points out the duality of IT in adaptive governance, namely governance via knowledge sharing technology and data governance itself. To further explore and expand this new area of governance, the author calls for further research on the data logics and the sociotechnical learning arrangements. Furthermore, Wang argues that a focus on IT-related issues is also relevant outside of the field of data ecosystems, as the datafication of ecosystems governance itself is rapidly expanding. This means understanding how IT can be used in this and what implications it has for adaptive governance approaches.

In addition to examining single governance fields, adaptive governance has also been applied to interpret broader, national governance contexts. In Chapter 11, Huang and Westman show how adaptive approaches can co-exist in an often-assumed command-and-control political system in China. Viewing ecological civilisation through the lens of adaptive governance, the authors raise three important lessons of pragmatism, incrementalism, and verticality. The first of these stresses the need to account for local conditions, the second the adoption of the principles through non-disruption, and the last the importance of national-local interactions between actors. All in all, the chapter demonstrates the need to direct the attention of adaptive governance scholars towards empirical national cases that go beyond single local cases to examine how adaptive governance features are becoming institutionalised and what implications this may have.

The following chapters in this part discuss the ways in which adaptive governance approaches can address global change drivers, the impacts of which are uncertain over temporal and spatial scales. In Chapter 12, Hovelsrud and Westskog shed light on two cases to illustrate adaptive governance of climate change taking place. The authors show how societal responses to climate change continue to be weak due to lack of identification of responsibilities, the degree of required changes in social systems remains unclear, and, finally, the central role of land use as a cause of climate change drives conflict with other levels of governance. Adaptive governance approaches have the potential to alleviate these issues and they may enable a more rapid response although the authors caution against this, as it may have the potential to circumvent democracy, which remains the necessary cornerstone of society.

The complexity of adapting cities for climate change through adaptive governance further requires flexibility of institutions and adequate mechanisms for mainstreaming, as adaptation is not a sector-specific activity. Jurgilevich, in Chapter 13, stresses the need to widen the definition of urban climate change adaptation towards a broader one of sustainable development to address the root causes of vulnerability, which render some parts of the population more vulnerable to climate change impacts than others. Adaptive governance as an approach can help with this, particularly in terms of its focus on dealing with uncertainty and harnessing future-oriented planning.

Climate change as a global change driver can also spark a reconsideration of specific steering mechanisms as demonstrated by Fitzpatrick in Chapter 14. As displacement of people due to climate change is likely to increase, particularly in the Global South, securing rights to land through property law becomes even more challenging. Thus, Fitzpatrick calls for an institutional reconceptualisation of how existing polycentric systems may be harnessed, as well as what changes this may imply to existing paradigms. A normative formulation of adaptive property law would allow for flexible laws that support existing realities on the ground and result in the lowest objective costs of resource access for participants that include large numbers of mobile groups living in informal settlements due to disasters, for example.

Chapter 15 focuses on the role of adaptive governance in disaster risk reduction. Bixler and colleagues review experiences so far and note that adaptive governance approaches have been applied in many countries with varying approaches and successes. While adaptive governance holds promise as a governance approach to help reduce and manage responses to disasters, the implemented outcomes are rarely exactly what is deemed theoretically optimal. New ways of organisation, for example, through networks that involve new actors and devolve power, can lead to resistance and be impossible to carry out due to institutional path dependency. Nevertheless, there is potential to pursue arrangements that support adaptive governance by facilitating informal networks, enhance levels of trust between co-actors and harmonise levels of social and economic inequalities in the immediate aftermath of a disaster. Guidelines on how to practically do this have recently been developed, as also demonstrated by the authors.

THE NEXT DECADE OF ADAPTIVE GOVERNANCE RESEARCH: EMERGING QUESTIONS

It is clear that adaptive governance as a theoretical approach has advanced in the last decade, evidenced by the proliferation of literature, as well as the chapters in this book. In their review of the state of the art nearly a decade ago, Chaffin et al. (2014, p. 1) defined adaptive governance as 'a range of interactions between actors, networks, organisations, and institutions emerging in pursuit of a desired state for social-ecological systems', a definition which has not seriously been challenged in the decade past. While there have been calls for further problematisation of the social in the conceptualisation of the socio-ecological system, also in this *Handbook*, the basic premise of adaptive governance has remained largely unchallenged.

Overall, the key features of adaptive governance of polycentricity, networks, acknowledgement of scale and diversity of actors have remained at the heart of theorisation. Critical voices in the field have expressed concern over the simplification of the social in the socio-ecological system (see Chapter 1, Introduction), and this has been perhaps the most important development in the field. It has been visible in contributions that have explicitly discussed the role of power in complex governing contexts with diverse sets of actors, as well as the use of specific instruments which have adverse consequences for some groups and how these could be reconceptualised. These issues are also raised in the chapters of this *Handbook*, illustrating how the work continues across multiple governance fields.

To further summarise the contribution of this volume to the state-of-the-art discussion on adaptive governance, it appears to be pertinent to reflect the chapters in light of the last stocktake of adaptive governance by Chaffin et al. (2014). Their review examined the field after the first decade, concluding that while there is momentum in the field, open questions remain. Now, after another decade has passed, allowing for further reflection, it appears that these points raised by Chaffin et al. are not too dissimilar to questions posed in this volume.

To conclude their assessment of the first decade, Chaffin et al. (2014) point towards three research areas with corresponding questions that scholars should engage with. First, Chaffin et al. (2014) question the relationship between the principles of adaptive governance and of good governance in general. They question what extent the principles of good governance, legitimacy, equity, and justice ought to be incorporated to adaptive governance theory or whether the desired state of the ecosystem is an overriding goal? And whether the desired state could or should be achieved at the expense of the principles of good governance? Here one could reasonably expect then the field to have broadened out the definition of adaptive governance, particularly from the social and governance side.

At the heart of this is the dilemma of whether adaptive governance is essentially value neutral, i.e., does it primarily view governance structures and processes and assess their functionality without attaching value to their outcomes, i.e., the desired state? This desired state can, for example, be to stay within the planetary boundaries or ensure that desired outcomes are achieved while principles of good governance are followed.

The chapters in this *Handbook*, as other contributions (see Chapter 1 Introduction), illustrate that while there is a recognition of urgency to act, adaptive governance must not be pursued at the expense of principles associated with good governance. In fact, as shown in those chapters which explore law in particular (Chapter 3 and 14 in this *Handbook*), there are ways to consider introducing adaptive features to existing governance arrangements without compromising on the democratic process and its legitimacy. Furthermore, as shown by the example of ecological civilisation in China (Chapter 13), there is a gap of viewing existing governance arrangements beyond ecosystem boundaries through an adaptive governance lens, which may yield interesting insights to the extent to which it can be seen to exist. Similarly interesting is the adoption of adaptive governance as an approach outside of the usual fields, as demonstrated by IT ecosystem management (Chapter 8).

This leads us to consider to what extent there is evidence of adaptive governance actually functioning and working as it should. Many of the chapters in this *Handbook*, as well as previous contributions (Sharma-Wallace et al. 2018), have shown that adaptive governance arrangements have emerged in isolated cases, but long-term evaluations of their impact are missing. The thematic chapters in Part III show in their reviews that while adaptive governance can contribute to advantageous governance outcomes, it is not entirely clear whether this change is temporary or sustained, and to what extent the changes are incremental rather than transformative.

The call for transformations, in terms of understanding them and/or practical facilitation of them taking place, has become of intense interest lately, and also a focus of many adaptive governance scholars. This is certainly a new avenue for adaptive governance research to discuss whether adaptive governance is part of that transformation of institutions of governance in order to achieve sustainability. Or whether adaptive governance can facilitate a transformation in society and under what conditions these may take place or not. These questions reflect the above discussion on the role of the desired state or outcome of adaptive governance.

The second issue that Chaffin et al. (2014) raise relates to the emergence and taking advantage of opportunities to transform the state of the system. This means identifying when and where such windows of opportunity may open and examining whether there needs to be legal frameworks and policy instruments in place to exploit that window. As governance is inherently multi-level, this means having the necessary networks in place to connect levels and use social and other types of capital at the right time. Here the focus ought to be on identifying the types of governance contexts, processes and capacities that support and enable adaptive governance to emerge and whether they lead to an improved, desired state.

The identification of opportunities for adaptive governance is an issue that is raised in multiple chapters in this *Handbook* (Chapters 9, 10, 11, 15). To identify these moments requires further theoretical understanding, as illustrated in Chapter 4 which presents an approach that acknowledges the political dimensions of governance and views the interactions between science and governance. This acknowledgement of the political nature can open the potential for more just and equitable modes of governance, and further facilitate the emergence of a window of opportunity with an orientation towards the future (Chapters 5 and 13).

The role of different types of methods in adaptive governance research is highlighted in this *Handbook* (Chapters 5, 6 and 7). This also raises the question whether research methods can be used as a way to help to create or exploit the window of opportunity during a participatory research project or exercise. This may, for example, be conducted through the development of a serious game (Chapter 7) which allows for a moment of consequence-free decision-making to explore different options. In addition, it is crucial to understand the role of temporal and spatial scales (Chapters 5 and 6) in incorporating additional stakeholders, which may otherwise have been ignored, as scalar understanding of the problem at hand expands.

To push the field forward, research questions could also focus on cases where adaptive governance is not emerging, rather than predominantly paying attention to 'positive' cases. Examinations of windows being missed or ignored are equally valuable and plentiful, and may help to further develop the theory of adaptive governance. Research methodologies and methods have not been at the centre of adaptive governance theorisation, and there are numerous questions related to the positionality of the researcher to the governance dilemma at hand, to the extent the research itself influences the studied case. Additionally, there is a need to innovate new methods to capture the adaptive feature of both formal and informal institutions and ensuring equality in the use of participatory methods.

The third focus area for study identified by Chaffin et al. (2014) is the question of what happens once adaptive governance has emerged and is becoming institutionalised. What happens then and who is involved, what types of reforms are required in existing formal and informal institutions? This requires turning a critical eye on the ability of the formal institutional structure to co-exist and adopt features of adaptive governance in its operation and whether this has indeed been successful in cases which have been documented.

The persistence and tenacity of adaptive governance approaches and practices is a question that requires longer term monitoring and evaluation of implementation, which is often costly and time consuming and not prioritised by researchers. The chapters in this *Handbook* provide theoretical and empirical insights into sustaining adaptive governance over time. The necessity to maintain adaptive features of institutions and legal instruments (Chapters 2, 3 and 14), as well as the science–policy interface (Chapter 4), is stressed, given that governance outcomes take a long time to become realised. Therefore, the adaptiveness and dynamic nature of the adaptive governance networks and instrument and how they place itself is necessary.

However, the chapters also highlight challenges that adaptive governance may face in solving complex issues, particularly as it will always be couched in existing, formal institutional structures, which still dominate decision-making and are likely to continue to do so. This results in power imbalances that affect collaboration across the levels (Chapter 12), which may hinder the flexibility for decision-making. Also, the allocation of resources for continued adaptive governance can be seen as a challenge, as it often requires more different types of capacities that are readily available to local or regional governments.

Emerging research questions ought to focus on developing longer term monitoring of not only the object of governance, i.e., ecosystem, but also the governance system itself and find novel ways to connect them to understand their dynamics. It is not only necessary to capture the performance of adaptive governance approaches over longer time periods past implementation but also assess to what extent they influence the existing governance structures and the resources or problem being governed.

The challenges currently facing global society are considerable. However, the authors in these chapters, while examining adaptive governance critically, have also demonstrated the continued interest and promise in this approach in facilitating change towards more sustainable and equitable ways of governing. As advocated by adaptive governance theory itself, the focus of the field should be on plurality of voices, polycentricity of research networks and flexibility and context specificity in the use of research methods when collecting data. Given the advances made so far, it is likely that the next decade of adaptive governance research will be as fruitful as this one.

REFERENCES

Chaffin, B. C., Gosnell, H., and Cosens, B. A. 2014. A decade of adaptive governance scholarship: synthesis and future directions. *Ecology & Society*, 19, 3.

Sharma-Wallace, L., Velarde, S. J., and Wreford, A. 2018. Adaptive governance good practice: show me the evidence! *Journal of Environmental Management*, 222, 174–184.

Index

Abrams, J. 135
absorptive thresholds 220
active sensing data 109
access to resources and knowledge 202
Adams, W. M. 58
adaptation 77–9
adaptive capacity 26, 28, 29, 152, 153, 177
    disaster risk reduction 243–4
adaptive co-management 2, 3–4, 19, 146, 193,
    194
adaptive governance 2, 3–7, 100
    criteria for robust adaptive governance
        17–18, 37–8, 43–9, 177
    critique of 5–7
    definitions 3, 194, 235
    elements of 115, 116
        in serious games 118–22
    interdisciplinary research framework 17–19,
        21–2, 23–4
    key features and contributions 3–4
    literature review 177–8
adaptive law 218, 219–20
    property law design 227–8
agenda setting 62, 63–4
agile governance 213
agonistic approaches 68
Aguilera, S. E. 148
Allan, C. 91–2
Anderson, B. 79
Anthropocene, the 35
anticipation
    in futures literacy 80
    link with adaptation and transformation 77–9
anticipatory governance 2, 78–9
    urban climate change adaptation 207, 212–13
        addressing uncertainty 209–11
Aoki, N. 241
Århus Convention 44
asset view of data ownership 159–60, 162–3,
    168–9, 172
Australia 91

backcasting 81–2, 86
Baggio, J. A. 104, 109
Barclay, K. 147
Basque tuna fisheries 149
Belgium 240

Bengston, D. N. 81
Bennett, E. M. 83
Berkes, F. 55
Biermann, F. 63
big data 159–60, 162
biodiversity
    conservation adaptation 86–7
    loss 1
Black, J. 224
Bolivia 133
bonding social capital 120
boundary objects 64–5
boundary organisations 65
boundary spanners 64
boundary work 64–5
bridging social capital 120
Bronen, R. 239

California Bay Delta Program 65
Canada 131
capacity
    adaptive 26, 28, 29, 152, 153, 177, 243–4
    capacities to use futures-thinking and
        methods in adaptive governance
        82–8
    development 115, 116
        serious games 120–21
    participatory 26, 28, 29–30
Carlisle, K. M. 150
Cash, D. W. 100
Catchment 2030 game 118–22
central–local interactions 180, 188, 189
certification of forest sustainability 132–4, 137
Chaffin, B. C. 3, 4, 5, 19, 178, 256–7, 258
Chambers, J. M. 60, 63–4
champions 137
change, preparedness for 38, 48–9, 177
Chapin, F. S. 239
Cheng, A. S. 135
China 239
    Bureau for Comprehensive Planning and
        Experimental Points 179
    policy experimentation in the construction
        of ecological civilisation 10, 176–91,
        255
    characteristics of policy experimentation
        187–8

socio-economic circumstances behind
    different stages 184–7
Shanghai open data ecosystem 158, 163–71
tradition of adaptive governance 179–80,
    188
Chourou, L. 119
civic epistemologies 67–8
Clarvis, M. H. 104
Cleaver, F. 5, 178
climate change 1, 79
    Conservation Futures project in Colombia
        86–7
    engaging communities in the Western US
        87–8
    migration related to 225–6, 228, 229, 239
    property law and 225–8
        design for a climate-affected future
            227–8, 229
    urban adaptation to, *see* urban climate
        change adaptation
climate change mitigation and adaptation 10,
    23–4, 192–206, 255
    adaptation 23–4, 36, 196–8
    mitigation 23–4, 36, 198–200
    opportunities and weaknesses of adaptive
        governance 200–202
    theoretical approach 193–5
Coase, R. 218
collaboration 19, 115, 116
    climate change mitigation and adaptation
        194–5, 196–7, 199, 200–201
    disaster risk reduction 237, 243–4
    serious games 118–19
collaborative governance 2, 19
    forest management in the US 134–6, 137
    marine environments 145–6
Colombia 86–7
command and control regulation 22–3
Commission for the Conservation of Antarctic
    Marine Living Resources (CCAMLR) 151
common pool resources (CPRs) 17–18, 19
commons view of data ownership 160, 162–3,
    168–9, 172
communicative learning 115
Communist Party of China (CPC) 179, 187
community-based land governance systems 221,
    224–5, 227–8
community building 165–7
community-driven governance approach 158,
    170, 173
community empowerment 115, 116, 120
Community Fisheries Action Roundtable 149
complexity 117
    forest management 127–9
    law as a complex system 49–51

sociotechnical and open data ecosystems
    171–3
urban climate change adaptation 207
Comprehensive Everglades Restoration Plan
    (CERP) 40
Compton, C. 224–5, 228
conflict, dealing with 37, 45–6, 177
conflicting priorities 102
Conservation Futures project 86–7
contestation, addressing 82, 84, 86
context sensitivity 194–5, 198, 200, 201
control-oriented governance approach 158, 161
coordination 115, 116, 201–2
    lacking 102
    serious games 119
co-production SPPI model 57, 59–60, 62, 63, 64,
    65, 66
Cork, S. 80–81
corporate IT governance approach 160
Cosens, B. 25, 26–7, 28
COVID-19 pandemic 1, 31, 151
credibility 62, 65–6
CRELE criteria 62, 65–6
crises 78
    forestry 129–31
    marine environments 151–2
criteria for robust adaptive governance 17–18,
    37–8, 43–9, 177
crowdsourced data 106–8
culture 195
Cumming, G. S. 100
cyclones 241

Dannevig, H. G. K. 195
data ownership 159–69, 162–3, 167–8, 168–9,
    172
data-related stakeholders 172
database development 21–2
Dalian, China 187
De Abreu, M. C. S. 239
De Andrade, R. de J. C. 239
De Soto, H. 220
decentralised disaster governance 101–2
decision lifetimes 89
decision-making
    linking with knowledge 115, 116, 121
    shared and climate change mitigation and
        adaptation 194–5, 196–7, 199, 200,
        201
demonstration/pilot zones 180–84, 185, 187
Deng Xiaoping 179
descriptive legal perspectives 39–41
dialogue 67–8
Dietz, T. 17–18, 19, 24, 25, 37–8, 54, 144, 177
digital learning mechanisms 172–3

digitised governance subject 172
Ding, X. 104
disaster governance 99, 100–101, 105–9
    possible spatial data sources 105–8
    stages of disaster management 242–3
    types of mismatches 101–2
disaster mitigation 243–4
disaster risk mapping 105–6
disaster risk reduction (DRR) 10–11, 233–51, 256
    adaptive governance and 236–9
    future for adaptive hazard governance 244–6
        challenges 245–6
        opportunities 246
    Houston and Hurricane Harvey 242–4
    integrating adaptive governance 240–42
disaster vulnerability 223–5
diversity 4
divide and dissent approach 170, 173
Djalante, R. 236, 238, 246
document analysis 28
Dolin, E. 119
Donovan, L. 121
Dorf, M. C. 30
Dunn, C. J. 104
Dunn, G. 57
dynamic adaptive policy pathways (DAPP) 210–11
dynamic risk and vulnerability assessments 211–12

earthquakes 223–4, 241
East African coastal waters 147
ecological civilisation 10, 176–91, 255
ecological pilot/demonstration zones 180–84, 185, 187
economic development 179, 184–5
Ecoparks 136, 137
Ellickson, R. C. 227, 229
Emergency Events Database (EM-DAT) 233
emergent governance 15
    multi-disciplinary web of scholarship 17–21
    research agenda for interdisciplinary learning 7, 15, 16–25, 253
    understanding through interdisciplinary dialogue 21–5
    when its facilitation is appropriate 22–5
empathy 119–20
Enemark, S. 222
England 240
environmental disruption 223–4
Environmental Impact Assessments (EIAs) 44
Environmental Impact Statements (EISs) 44
environmental law 39
envisioning transformation, capacity for 82, 84–5
Eriksson, H. 151–2

Ernston, H. 103
Eshuis, J. 7
Esty, D. C. 30
European Union (EU) 37
    Environmental Information Directive 44
    Environmental Liability Directive 46
    interactions between law and adaptive governance 44, 45, 46, 47, 48
    Marine Strategy Framework Directive (MSFD) 44, 45, 48
    Maritime Spatial Planning Directive (MSPD) 44, 47
    Regional Advisory Councils (RACs) 149
    Water Framework Directive (WFD) 40, 44, 45, 46, 48
    water law 40
Evans, L. S. 150
Everglades 40
evidence-based policy 58
Exclusive Economic Zones (EEZs) 145
experimental units 180–84, 185, 187
experimental zones 179–80
experimentation venue 172–3
experts
    advice and opinions 58–9
    role in SPPI processes 63–4
explorative forecasting 81
external critique of adaptive governance 5

Fabinyi, M. 147
facilitation of emergent governance 22–5
Ferguson, B. C. 85
Finland 24, 35, 37, 40, 42, 102
fisheries 143–4, 145, 146–52, 153
    adaptive governance and response to crises 151–2
    implementing adaptive governance 146–50
    management in the Solomon Islands 68, 69–70
Fitzpatrick, D. 224–5, 228
flexibility 194–5, 197–8, 199–200, 201
flood risk governance 240–41, 242
Folke, C. 3, 18–19, 151, 177
food insecurity 1
forcible displacement 1
forecasting 80–81, 209, 210
foresight 209–10
forest management 9, 127–42, 254
    complexity and simplification 127–9
    crises and governance responses 129–31
    cross-cutting themes 137
    global initiatives 131–4
    national initiatives 134–6
    wildfire 101, 134, 241–2
Forest Stewardship Council (FSC) 132–3

forward-looking perspectives 88–9
Fournier, M. 240–41
framing problems 61, 62
France 240–41
freedom of the seas 144
'from point to area' 179, 187–8
Fuller, B. W. 65
future-oriented risk assessments 106
futures bricolage 90
futures knowledge generation and translation 82, 83–4
futures literacy 79, 80
futures-thinking 8, 76–98, 253
    capacities to use futures-thinking and methods in adaptive governance 82–8
    link between adaptation, transformation and anticipation 77–9
    and methods 79–82
    situating adaptive governance into futures 88–92

genie expert role 63
geographic information systems (GIS) 103, 105
Gerrits, L. 7
Global South 219, 222–9
goal alignment 202
good governance 160, 256–7
governance 2–3
    definition 15
    dilemmas in open data ecosystems 168–9
    embedding futures-thinking in governance structures 91–2
    knowledge and 55
    and management 194
governance opportunities 115, 116, 121–2, 246, 257–8
government 24–5
    process 27, 28, 30
    role of 15, 17, 25–31
    structure of 26, 28–9
Greater Houston Flood Mitigation Consortium (GHFMC) 243–4
Grêt-Regamey, A. 109
Gruby, R. L. 150
Gunderson, L. H. 5

Haasnoot, M. 210–11
Habitat Conservation Plan 47
Haiti 223–4
Harris County Long-Term Recovery Committee (HCLTRC) 243
hazard cycle 233, 234
hazard maps 105–6
Heilmann, S. 176, 179, 180

hero expert role 63
Holling, C. J. 219–20
Horigue, V. 150
horizon scanning 81, 82
horizontal mainstreaming 208–9
host expert role 63–4
Houston, Texas 242–4
Hsu, D. 104
human mobility 225–6, 228, 229, 239
Humanitarian OpenStreetMap (HOT-OSM) 107
Hurlbert, M. A. 235
hurricanes 241
    Hurricane Harvey 242–4
Huxley, T. H. 143

Idaho, USA 47, 49
imagination 85
Inayatullah, S. 86
incrementalism 187–8, 189
India 238–9, 241
Indian Ocean tsunami 225
indigenous and local knowledge (ILK) 55, 67, 237
Indonesia 225
industrial disasters 239
informal networks 158
informal property systems 219, 222–9
information provision 37, 43–4, 177
information supply for urban adaptation 211–12
infrastructure provision 38, 47, 177
innovation 238–9
institutional bricolage 162–3
institutional law 42, 43
institutions 17–18, 25, 258
    current and adaptive hazard governance 245–6
    institutional dynamics and current urban adaptation context 208–9
    institutional variety and marine fisheries 146–8, 153
    legal system 49–50
    multi-layered 236–7
    nested 147, 150, 178, 202
instrumental learning 115
instruments of law 50
intact forest landscapes (IFLs) 129
interactions
    of actors facilitated by SPPIs 62, 64–5
    central–local 180, 188, 189
    spatial and mismatches 100–102
interdisciplinary research agenda 7, 15, 16–25, 253
Intergovernmental Panel on Climate Change (IPCC) 1, 59, 69, 225–6

Intergovernmental Science-Policy Platform on
     Biodiversity and Ecosystem Services
     (IPBES) 59, 68, 69, 71
internal critique of adaptive governance 5
International Model Forest Network 131–2

Japan 102
     Great East Japan earthquake and tsunami 241
Jia, G. 225–6
judicial review 30

Karkkainen, B. C. 16
Kenya 150
Kim, R. E. 29
Kireyeu, V. 103–4
knowledge
     access to relevant knowledge 202
     generation and translation of futures
          knowledge 82, 83–4
     and governance 55
     linking with decision-making 115, 116, 121
     local 55, 67, 237
     open data systems and knowledge needs 172
     usable and SPPIs 62, 65–6
knowledge sharing technology 170–71
Komi Model Forest 131

land rights, *see* property law
land tenure regimes 226
law 7–8, 35–53, 253
     complexity 49–51
     descriptive and normative perspectives
          39–41
     institutional 42, 43
     interactions between adaptive governance
          and 43–9
     procedural 42, 43
     property, *see* property law
     role in adaptive governance 25–31
     role in society 38–9
     substantive 41–2, 43
Law of the Sea 144–5
Lawrence, J. 210–11
leadership 115, 116, 121–2
learning
     open data ecosystems 170–71, 172–3
     relational 211
     serious games and 120–21
     social 115, 135, 149, 152, 161, 238–9
learning networks 152
legal mapping 28, 29
legal models 28, 30
legitimacy 62, 65–6
Lei, Y. 239
Lempert, R. 192

Lenfest Ocean Programme 65
local–central interactions 180, 188, 189
'local condition, treatment in accordance with'
     187
local knowledge 55, 67, 237
long-term perspectives 88–9
Long Term Social-Ecological-Technological
     Systems (LT-SETS) 31
Loorbach, D. 20–21
Lorenzen, M. 104
Luc Hoffmann Institute 65

mainstreaming 208–9
management, governance and 194
Mangnus, A. C. 80
Mao Zedong 179
marine environments 9, 143–57, 254
     adaptive marine governance and response to
          crisis 151–2
     fisheries, *see* fisheries
     history of marine governance 144–6
     implementing adaptive governance 146–50
marine protected areas (MPAs) 145–6
McGinnis, M. D. 236, 245–6
Merrill, T. W. 221, 222
migration 225–6, 228, 229, 239
Miller, C. A. 55
Miller, R. 79, 80
Ministerial Conference on Protection of Forests in
     Europe (MCPFE) 130
mismatches 8, 99–114, 253–4
     possible spatial data sources for adaptive
          governance research 105–8
     spatial interactions and 100–102
     use of spatial data and methods for adaptive
          governance 103–4
mobility, human 225–6, 228, 229, 239
Model Forests 131–2, 137
monitoring 213, 258–9
monocentric governance 100
Montréal Process 130
Moore, M. L. 85
Morardet, S. 117
Mudanjiang, China 187
Müller, D. 104, 109
multi-layered institutions 236–7
multi-layered safety (MLS) strategy 240
multi-level governance 4, 100, 160
     climate change mitigation and adaptation
          194, 196–203
     opportunities and weaknesses of
          adaptive governance 200–202
multi-scale futures methods 87–8, 90
Munene, M. B. 236
Munroe, D. K. 104, 109

Murphy, D. 87–8

Native American water rights 45–6
nested institutions 147, 150, 178, 202
Netherlands, the 240, 245
network governance 160–61
    forest management in the US 134–6, 137
network modelling 28, 29
networks
    disaster risk reduction 238, 244
    informal 158
    learning 152
new governance 16, 18, 19–20, 21–2, 25
new public management approach 160
New Zealand 210–11
Nordic countries 102
normalwald model 128
normative forecasting 81
normative legal perspectives 39–41
Norström, A. 59–60
North, D. C. 220
Norway 193, 195–200
    climate change adaptation 196–8
    climate change mitigation 198–200
Nykvist, B. 78

Olsson, P. 178
open data ecosystems 9–10, 158–75, 255
    adaptive governance as institutional
        bricolage 162–3
    emergence of adaptive governance 170
    governance challenges 159–61
    governance dilemmas 168–9
    Shanghai 158, 163–71
    sociotechnical complexity 171–3
    understanding adaptive governance as
        sociotechnical arrangements 170–71
open source 159–60, 162
operationalising adaptive governance 7, 15–34
    interdisciplinary research agenda 7, 15,
        16–25, 253
    role of government 15, 17, 25–31
opportunities for adaptive governance 115, 116,
    121–2, 246, 257–8
Österblom, H. 151
Ostrom, E. 17–18, 37–8, 228

Pacific Island nations 145
Pahl-Wostl, C. 115
Palau 150
Paris Agreement 235
Partelow, S. 152
participant agency 85
participation
    disaster risk reduction 237, 246

    stakeholder participation in marine fisheries
        management 147, 148–50, 153
participatory capacity 26, 28, 29–30
participatory futures-thinking methods 81, 83,
    86, 90
participatory GIS (PGIS) 106–7, 108
partnerships 134–5
passive sensing data 109
path dependency 245–6
Pedroza-Gutiérrez, C. 151
Pereira, L. 86, 92
Perry, E. J. 179
Philippines, the 224–5
Pilbeam, V. 67
pilot/demonstration zones 180–84, 185, 187
Pinchot, G. 128
Poland 240–41
policy experimentation 10, 176–91, 255
policy-pull model 57, 58–9, 60, 62, 63, 64, 65, 66
politics
    futures-thinking and addressing 90–91
    of SPPIs 61–70, 71
        towards a politically aware SPPI for
            adaptive governance 66–70
polycentricity 4, 54, 100
    disaster risk reduction and 236–7
        challenges of adaptive hazard
            governance 245–6
    fisheries management 148, 150
    property systems 218–19, 222–9
possession 227–8
power 5, 195
    asymmetries and futures-thinking 86
    imbalances in serious games 117
power sharing 147, 150, 152
pragmatism 179, 187, 189
predict and plan governance 209
predictive forecasting 80–81
preparedness for change 38, 48–9, 177
private governance 19–20
private law 38–9, 41–2
    adaptive 220, 227–8
problem framing 61, 62
procedural equity 149–50
procedural law 42, 43
process of government 27, 28, 30
Programme for the Endorsement of Forest
    Certification Schemes (PEFC) 132–3
projects 91–2
property law 10, 218–32, 255–6
    climate change-related mobility 225–6, 228,
        229
    conventional hierarchies of 220–21
    design of for a climate-affected future 227–8,
        229

and disasters 224–5
land rights and environmental disruption
    223–4
polycentricity of property systems 218–19,
    222–9
public law 38–9, 41–2
public transport 198–200
Putnam, R. D. 120

Rajabu, K. R. M. 121
Raudsepp-Hearne, C. 85
reasonable use doctrine 48–9
redundancy 4
reflexive governance 2
regional marine governance 145
regulated markets 22–3
regulation 7–8, 35–53, 253
relational learning 211
relevance 62, 65–6
remote sensing 105
representation 63
research agenda, interdisciplinary 7, 15, 16–25,
    253
research questions, emerging 256–9
resilience 18–19, 177, 220, 236
resilience assessment 28, 29
resources, access to 202
Rijke, J. 116
Rio Earth Summit 1992 132
risk assessments 211–12, 213
risk maps 105–6, 197–8
river basins 40
Robinson, J. B. 81–2
role-playing games 118, 119, 120, 123
Rotterdam 7
Rubio, I. 149
rule compliance 37–8, 46–7, 177
rule of law 50
Russia 129, 131–2

Sabel, C. F. 30
Sandbrook, C. 58
Sarewitz, D. 68
Sayles, J. S. 104, 109
scale 4, 24
scale mismatches 100–102
scenarios 81, 83–4, 85, 90
    engaging communities with climate change
        futures in the Western US 87–8
science–policy interface 5, 31
science–policy–practice interfaces (SPPIs) 8,
    54–74, 253
    case examples 68–70
    justification of SPPI processes and outcomes
        62, 65–6

models 57–60
political dynamics 61–6
towards a politically aware SPPI 66–70
who is included in SPPIs 62, 63
science-push model 57, 58, 60, 62, 63, 64, 65, 66
Science, Technology and Innovation Foresight
    programmes 78
science and technology studies (STS) 55
scientists 31
Scott, D. 68
secure property rights 220
self-organisation 17–18, 19, 22–3, 35–6
    disaster risk reduction 238
    marine fisheries 149
    property systems 219, 220
Sendai Framework for Disaster Risk Reduction
    (SFDRR) 233–5, 236
serious games 9, 115–25, 210–11, 254
    creating 118–22
    elements of adaptive governance in 118–22
    limitations and strengths of for adaptive
        governance 122–3
Shanghai, China
    Master Plan for Flexible Adaptation 210
    open data contest 164, 165–8
    open data ecosystem 158, 163–71
        evolving development and governance
            arrangements 165–8
shared decision-making 194–5, 196–7, 199, 200,
    201
Sharma-Wallace, L. 6, 115, 116
Shenzhen, China 179–80
Shkaruba, A. 103–4
simplification 127–9
Smith, H. E. 221
social capital 6, 115, 116
    serious games 119–20
social-ecological systems (SES) 19, 20, 177
    transformations 77–8
social-ecological-technological systems (SETS)
    16, 19, 20, 35–6, 50, 235
social learning 115, 135, 161
    disaster risk reduction 238–9
    marine environments 149, 152
social media data 107–8
social science research 28, 29–30
social systems 5
sociotechnical complexity 171–3
sociotechnical systems 161–2
Solomon Islands
    fisheries 68, 69–70
    National Fisheries Management Act (FMA)
        70
Southern Ocean 151
spatial data and methods 8–9, 99–114, 253–4

possible spatial data sources for adaptive
governance research 105–8
spatial interactions and mismatches 100–102
use for adaptive governance 103–4
Stafford Smith, M. 89
stakeholders
open data ecosystems 172
participation in marine fisheries management
147, 148–50, 153
standardised property regimes 220–21, 222
stationarity 89
Stern, P. C. 17–18, 37–8
structure of government 26, 28–9
substantive law 41–2, 43
sufficient information 37, 43–4, 177
surprise, engaging with 82, 83, 84
Susskind, L. 119
sustainability 6
third-party forest sustainability certification
132–4, 137
Sustainable Development Goals 145, 176, 212,
235
sustainable forest management (SFM) 130
sustained yield forestry 128–9, 130
Sveaskog 136
Sweden 240–41
forest management 128–9, 131–2
Ecoparks 136, 137
systematic land titling programmes 222
systems reflexivity 82, 84, 85–6, 89

Tacloban City, the Philippines 224–5
Termeer, C. J. 100
Thailand 101
third-party forest sustainability certification
132–4, 137
Thomas, R. P. 220
Three Horizons framework 82, 86
time 201
toll roads 200
transdisciplinary science 31
transformation 6–7, 178, 257
disaster risk reduction 244
ecological in China 186–7
fostering capacity to envision 82, 84–5
link with adaptation and anticipation 77–9
transformative governance 18, 20, 21–2, 25
transition governance 18, 20–21, 21–2, 23–4, 25
transition management 20–21
transport planning 198–200
'treatment in accordance with local condition'
187
Triple-A governance (AAA) 213
Trondheim, Norway 199–200
trust 6, 117

tsunamis 225, 241
Tuda, A. O. 147
typhoons 239
Typhoon Haiyan 224–5

UN-Habitat 222
uncertainty 54, 68, 117
engaging with future uncertainty 82, 83, 84
urban climate change adaptation 207, 209
adaptive and anticipatory governance in
addressing uncertainty 209–11
United Nations (UN) 143
Sustainable Development Goals 145, 176,
212, 235
United Nations Convention on the Law of the Sea
(UNCLOS) 144–5
United Nations Development Programme
(UNDP) 1
Triple-A governance 213
United Nations Educational, Scientific and
Cultural Organization (UNESCO) 80
United States (US) 24, 35, 36–7, 102
California Bay Delta Program 65
Endangered Species Act 46–7
engaging communities with climate change
futures in the Western US 87–8
Everglades restoration 40
Forest Service 128, 134, 135
forest management 128
collaborative and network governance
134–6, 137
Houston's response to Hurricane Harvey
242–4
interactions between law and adaptive
governance 44, 45–6, 46–7, 48–9
marine environments 145
fisheries management 148, 149
National Climate Assessment 64
National Environmental Policy Act (NEPA)
44
National Institutes of Health Disaster
Research Response Program (DR2)
243–4
United Way 243
urban climate change adaptation 10, 207–17, 255
adaptive and anticipatory governance
212–13
addressing uncertainty 209–11
information supply for 211–12
institutional dynamics 208–9
urban growth agreements 198–200
usable knowledge 62, 65–6

Van Assche, K. 5
Van Buuren, A. 195

Van den Hove, S. 55
Van Kerkhoff, L. 67
Vanuatu 151–2
Varma, N. 238–9
verticality 188, 189
Vestfold County, Norway 196–8
Vilhelmina Model Forest 131
visioning 81, 82
voluntary geographic information (VGI) 107
vulnerability assessments 211–12, 213
vulnerability development 212–13
vulnerability mapping 105

Walch, C. 241
Walker, B. 177
water law and regulation 36–7, 40, 44, 45–6, 47, 48–9
Wayfinder 29

WeChat chat groups 165–7
Weser-judgment 40
Westskog, H. 3, 194, 195
Whaley, L. 5, 178
wicked problems 192–3, 196, 202–3
wildfire management 101, 134, 241–2
windmill parks 193
Winters v. United States 45–6
woodpecker expert role 63–4
World Bank 222
Wyborn, C. 5, 6

Yucatan Peninsula 151
Young, O. R. 208
Yung, L. 89

Zhang, W. 176
zoning of forests 129